Scottish Politics

Scottish Politics

An Introduction

Neil McGarvey
and
Paul Cairney

First published 2008 by
PALGRAVE MACMILLAN
Palgrave Macmillan in the UK is an imprint of Macmillan Publishers Limited,
registered in England, company number 785998, of Houndmills, Basingstoke,
Hampshire RG21 6XS.

Palgrave Macmillan in the US is a division of St. Martin's Press LLC,
175 Fifth Avenue, New York, NY 10010.

Palgrave Macmillan is the global academic imprint of the above companies
and has companies and representatives throughout the world.

Palgrave® and Macmillan® are registered trademarks in the United States,
the United Kingdom, Europe and other countries.
ISBN-13: 978–1–4039–4328–6 hardback
ISBN-10: 1–4039–4328–1   hardback
ISBN-13: 978–1–4039–4329–3 paperback
ISBN-10: 1–4039–4329–X   paperback

This book is printed on paper suitable for recycling and made from fully
managed and sustained forest sources. Logging, pulping and manufacturing
processes are expected to conform to the environmental regulations of the
country of origin.

A catalogue record for this book is available from the British Library.

A catalog record for this book is available from the Library of Congress.

Printed and bound in Great Britain by
CPI Antony Rowe, Chippenham and Eastbourne

For Sean Michael, Linda, Evie, Alfie and Frankie

Contents

List of Boxes, Figures and Tables

Boxes

Figures

Tables

Preface and Acknowledgements

The renaming of the Scottish Executive as the Scottish Government in the early days of the Scottish National Party (SNP) administration elected in 2007 was a highly symbolic moment in the evolution of Scottish political autonomy. It summed up well the shift from the administrative devolution of the past, to the tentative steps towards autonomy in the near past, culminating in a much greater sense of Scottish direction free from the shadow of the old United Kingdom. However, it also marked a bad day for academics writing about the past, seeking consistency, and trying not to confuse students too much about what the collective name for Scottish ministers (and in some cases the civil service) is. Therefore, as much as possible we refer to the Scottish Government, if only for the sake of consistency and the need to avoid confusion. In some cases, we make clear that this refers to Scottish ministers only, but in the most part the term tends to be used as a collection of people and organizations within the government. In other cases, when it is clear that the discussion refers to the Labour/Liberal Democrat coalition of 1999–2007 we use the term Scottish Executive. As avid readers of newspaper and government reports will know, after eight years Scottish Executive is a term that is still difficult to shake off, with some people more willing to do so than others. In our case, the terms are not used to present a particular ideological position towards the amount of autonomy Scotland does and should enjoy.

This book is designed to give a comprehensive and up-to-date introduction to the study of Scottish politics for students taking courses, as well as general readers with an interest in the subject. It was conceived some time ago and has taken several years to come to fruition. On reflection this may be no bad thing as it has allowed us to assess two full post-devolution terms as well as the election of Scotland's first minority, as well as nationalist, administration. Scottish politics has undoubtedly become a whole lot more interesting after devolution. We hope this text reflects that.

As many before us have suggested, writing a textbook is more difficult than it looks. It is often more difficult than writing a monograph or a scholarly article, since with that type of work the onus is on the reader to gain the knowledge necessary to understand the author's argument. With a textbook, the onus is on the author to explain and make clear what s/he would normally take for granted. The process therefore requires a fine balance between seeking comments from academic colleagues with a specialist knowledge and a demand for detail and clarity, and editors with more of an eye for the level the book is written for and the expectations that we can assume for the reader. In the former category, we would like to thank colleagues who graciously agreed to comment on a draft of the full manuscript – Michael Keating, Allan McConnell, Alex Wright and two anonymous referees – and colleagues who (no less graciously) agreed to give comments on particular chapters or sections – David Arter, Lynn Bennie, David Heald, Grant Jordan, Nicola McEwan, Arthur Midwinter, Richard Parry and Bobby Pyper. We have also benefited from numerous conversations and interactions with students from the Universities of Aberdeen, Glasgow and Strathclyde. At different times, both of us have contributed towards University College London Constitution Unit's devolution monitoring programme (funded by the ESRC, Department for Constitutional Affairs, Scottish Government, Scotland Office and Wales Office) which has given us the discipline to remain abreast of ongoing developments in Scottish politics.

In a broader sense, we would like to thank people who have helped us in the lead up to the book. For Paul, this includes Brian Hogwood, Mark Shephard, Michael Keating, Grant Jordan and Steve Bruce who kept him in the profession long enough to become established. For Neil, this includes Arthur Midwinter, Brian Hogwood, David Judge and James Mitchell. He would like to thank his team-mates at Kerrydale Celtic Football Club who have, on occasion, provided some rather unique political insights during post-match discussions – as well as consistently ask the question are you *still* writing that book! As institutionalists, we would also like to thank the Universities of Aberdeen and Strathclyde for their support during some difficult times.

The book draws on research both authors have conducted. This includes research into changing regulatory arrangements in Scotland under the ESRC Devolution and Institutional Change programme, as well as research into the Scottish Parliament, Government and interest groups funded by the University of Aberdeen, Nuffield Foundation as well as the ESRC Devolution and Constitutional Change Programme.

Finally, we would like to thank Steven Kennedy, who not only suggested that we co-author the book, but also challenged us to complete it quickly, as well as better on more than one occasion. He has, at appropriate times, given us the encouragement, editorial suggestion as well as 'kick up the backside' required to get the job done. Of course, the final responsibility for any remaining errors rests with us.

Throughout the text readers will find words and key terms in bold – succinct definitions of these can be found on the page on which they first appear. We have also utilized boxes to give more in-depth accounts of key points, themes, background information and the like. Reference is usually made to relevant boxes in the text. There is a guide to further reading at the end of each chapter – students of Scottish politics should always bear in mind they are reading Neil McGarvey and Paul Cairney's account of Scottish politics in this book. There are many others. These guides are designed to give readers a flavour of the most relevant literature that students are encouraged to pursue. The constraints of space in a textbook means not everything can be covered in great depth; by following up these references students will be able to explore subjects in more detail.

Scottish Politics **on the web**

Additional material relating to this text including chapter summaries, self-test questions and web links, can be found at the associated website at www.palgrave.com/politics/mcgarvey. Update material will also be posted periodically on this site to keep readers up to date with major developments in Scottish politics.

NEIL MCGARVEY
PAUL CAIRNEY

List of Abbreviations

ADES	Association of Directors of Education in Scotland
AME	Annual Managed Expenditure
AMS	Additional Member System
ASBO	Anti-Social Behaviour Order
BBC	British Broadcasting Corporation
BMA	British Medical Association
BV	Best Value
BVTF	Best Value Task Force
CAP	Common Agricultural Policy
CBI	Confederation of British Industry
CCT	compulsory competitive tendering
CON	Conservative
COSLA	Convention of Scottish Local Authorities
CREST	Centre for Research into Elections and Social Trends
CSG	Consultative Steering Group
CSR	Comprehensive Spending Review
DEL	Departmental Expenditure Limit
DFM	Deputy First Minister
EIS	Educational Institute for Scotland
ESRC	Economic and Social Research Council
EU	European Union
FM	First Minister
FMQ	First Minister's Questions
FOE	Friends of the Earth
G8	Group of Eight
GERS	Government Expenditure and Revenue in Scotland
GP	general practitioner
HBOS	Halifax Bank of Scotland
HE	higher education
HMIe	HM Inspectorate of Education
IBM	International Business Machines
ICT	information and communication technologies
IGR	inter-governmental relations
IMF	International Monetary Fund
IND	Independent
IT	information technology
ITV	Independent Television
JMC	Joint Ministerial Committee

LAB	Labour
LD	Liberal Democrat
LEC	Local Enterprise Company
LSVT	large-scale voluntary transfer
MEP	Member of the European Parliament
MI5	Military Intelligence, section five
min	minority
MLG	multi-level governance
MMP	Mixed Member Proportional
MP	Member of Parliament (Westminster)
MPA	Ministerial Parliamentary Aide
MSP	Member of the Scottish Parliament
MWC	Mental Welfare Commission
NATO	North Atlantic Treaty Organization
NDPB	non-departmental public body
NEBU	Non-Government Bills Unit
neds	non-educated delinquents
NFUS	National Farmers' Union (Scotland)
NHS	National Health Service
NPM	new public management
OFSTED	Office for Standards in Education
PFI	private finance initiative
PLP	Parliamentary Labour Party
PPC	Public Petitions Committee
PPP	public-private partnership
PR	proportional representation
quangos	quasi-autonomous non-governmental organizations
RAE	Research Assessment Exercise
RBS	Royal Bank of Scotland
RCN	Royal College of Nursing
RSL	registered social landlord
SCC	Scottish Constitutional Convention
SCF	Scottish Civic Forum
SCVO	Scottish Council for Voluntary Organizations
SDA	Scottish Development Agency
SDP	Social Democratic Party
SHEFC	Scottish Higher Education Funding Council
SIP	Social Inclusion Partnership
SLD	Scottish Liberal Democrat Party
SMG	Senior Management Group
SML	Scottish Militant Labour
SNP	Scottish National Party
SPICE	Scottish Parliament Information Centre
SSCUP	Scottish Senior Citizen's Unity Party

SSP	Scottish Socialist Party
STUC	Scottish Trade Union Congress
STV	Scottish Television; single transferable vote
TUC	Trade Union Congress
UK	United Kingdom
UN	United Nations
USA	United States of America
VAT	value-added tax
WTD	Working Time Directive (EU)
WTO	World Trade Organization

Chapter 1

What is Scottish Politics?

What is 'politics'?

This book is about Scottish politics, and as a starting point it is useful to clarify what this means. The common-sense view of politics defines it by reference to institutions, calling to attention a particular arena in which politics takes place. The answer therefore appears self-evident – Scottish politics is about what goes on in the Scottish Government and Scottish Parliament. The focus is on the formal machinery and operation of government and the capacity of governing institutions to shape the behaviour of their population. This approach to studying politics is often criticized as too limiting and state-centric. It is referred to as an institutional approach. It is often criticized as offering a distinctly narrow view of 'the political', failing to acknowledge the broader societal context in which politics can take place, for example within the family, relationships, school, community and workplace.

Authority: The power to make and enforce laws or decisions.

Yet, as this book shows, using an institutional focus as a starting point to introduce a political system is useful. Why? The executive, bureaucratic and legislative branches of government are usually the arenas where political control, influence and **authority** are located in any political system. The modern state derives this power from the elected status of its decision-makers. This sense of democratic **legitimacy** gives it a source of authority – the public generally accepts the right of elected politicians to use their political authority and make laws. However, while politicians and institutions may have the legal authority to make laws, their authority may not always appear to be legitimate. For example, in the 1980s and 1990s Scottish home-rule campaigners questioned the legitimacy of the Conservative-led UK Government to govern Scotland, because of the Conservative Party's weak representation in Scotland.

Legitimacy means that a political institution is generally recognized to have the right to exert authority.

Nation: People identified by the sense of a common collective identity based on culture, ethnic origin, religion or geographic birthplace.

The institutional picture is complicated in Scotland by the existence of separate branches of government at both Scottish and UK levels. Scotland is a **nation, but not a state**. The Scotland Act 1998 sets out a clear list of reserved powers which UK State institutions in Westminster and Whitehall retain, with the rest falling

1

State: The sum total of governmental institutions and its personnel – including the intelligence services, the central bank, the police, state broadcasting, courts and armed forces – which has a monopoly of political authority.

Devolution: The transfer of political power from UK to Scottish political institutions.

under the jurisdiction of the Scottish Parliament and Government. There do, however, remain a number of policy areas where it is not possible to draw clear lines of demarcation between Scotland and the UK or Europe (see Box 1.1). The 1999 **devolution** settlement involved the transfer of powers to Scotland's governing institutions: the Scottish Government and Scottish Parliament. Without a basic knowledge of the institutional environment of Scottish politics it is difficult for any student of it to make sense of what is going on.

This book will set out in detail the context within which Scottish politics operates. In an introductory text historical and descriptive detail is important as it forms the bedrock of information from which more ambitious and theoretical work on Scottish politics can take place. An understanding of political institutions is important as they tend to set the 'rules of engagement' and the agenda of Scottish politics. Institutions are also the public face of politics. The Scottish Government, Parliament and political parties therein are the arenas in which the public perceive Scottish politics to take place. However, as a number of chapters in this book show, the Scottish Government and Parliament are not the only sources of power.

Box 1.1   Reserved and devolved policy areas

Policy areas reserved   international relations, defence, national security, fiscal and monetary policy, immigration and nationality, drugs and firearms, regulation of elections, employment, company law, consumer protection, social security, regulation of professions, energy, nuclear safety, air transport, road safety, gambling, equality, human reproductive rights, broadcasting, copyright.

Policy areas devolved   health, education and training, economic development, local government, law and home affairs, police and prisons, fire and ambulance services, social work, housing and planning, transport, environment, agriculture, fisheries, forestry, sport, the arts, devolved research, statistics

Blurred boundaries, UK/Scotland   industrial policy, higher education, fuel poverty, child poverty, dawn raids, smoking ban, Malawi, NHS compensation, new nuclear plants, effect of Scottish policies on social security, cross-cutting themes: New Deal, SureStart, 2007 election review.

Blurred boundaries, Scotland/Europe   Common Agricultural Policy, Common Fisheries Policy, EU Environment Directives, medical contracts

Source: Adapted from Keating (2005: 22); Cairney (2006a).

Governance highlights informal relationships and the blurring of boundaries between public/private action and levels of governmental sovereignty. Decision-making authority is dispersed and policy outcomes are determined by a complex series of negotiations between various levels of government and interest groups.

Discussions of institutional power can be supplemented by a range of other definitions of politics which draw attention to the wider policy process. For example, *managerial definitions* focus on the 'production' part of politics – politics exists because people want to 'do things'. This emphasis is often found in the rhetoric of modern Scottish politics and was made famous by the aim of Jack McConnell, Scotland's third First Minister, 'to do less, better'.

A major focus of debate in recent political science has been the extent to which government has been displaced or challenged by a broader process of **governance**; *governance definitions* of politics highlight the reliance of governments on a wide range of other actors. These include public bodies such as local government and 'quangos', but also private actors such as major businesses or interest groups. Therefore, a focus on policies made by institutions such as the Scottish Government alone may ignore its reliance on others to carry them out. **Interdependent relationships** between political institutions and actors are the norm in politics.

Interdependent relationships: Where political actor/institutions are reliant upon one another to achieve their goals.

To this we can add *democratic definitions* of politics which focus not only on how collective interests are aggregated, but also how these processes can be improved. The **home-rule** campaigners pre-devolution had in mind a 'more democratic' Scotland when they campaigned for a change in constitutional arrangements. This tends to be equated with two things: a high level of transparency when issues are debated and decisions are made, and a strong sense of collective participation in decision-making which produce greater levels of accountability and widespread 'ownership' of decisions. The emphasis is on deliberation, exchange and compromise and therefore the absence of secrecy, self-interest and violence in the resolution of conflict.

Home-rule: Although the term suggests independence, it is often used to refer to the self-government of a nation within a wider state.

Socio-economic definitions of politics turn our attention to the significance of gender, race and class, with politics defined in terms of social relations and extending to areas – for example, in the family, workplace and community – relatively removed from the institutions of government. Politics often occurs at a 'micro' level in these environments, but as a whole they represent the wider society and economy in which governments operate and must recognize. The most obvious manifestation of this external environment is the role of voting behaviour or public opinion (which varies by social background). The social background of decision-makers within these institutions has also risen significantly on the postwar agenda, with the pursuit of gender equality among MSPs a particular focus of the architects of devolution.

Definitions of politics are numerous; however, possibly the most relevant in any setting are those which emphasize power. Politics is about conflict between social forces, political **ideologies** and interests. Any individual or institution which engages in Scottish politics has the aim to promote their own particular interests (see Box 1.2). Within Scotland, this can include very broad forms of influence through education or culture, systematic influence through political parties or the media, or power exerted in particular areas by interest groups. Free from Scotland, the UK state, the EU or other global institutions may try to shape the agenda of Scottish politics.

Ideologies: Bodies of ideas which tend to underlie political action, e.g. nationalism, liberalism, conservatism, unionism, socialism, fascism, communism.

The most succinct *power definition* and description of politics is Lasswell's (1936) classic assertion that, 'politics is about who gets what, when and how'. This broad definition leaves open almost any avenue of enquiry for the political researcher since almost any human activity and exchange tends to involve some degree of power. It also allows analysis to extend beyond formal institutions. As Marsh and Rhodes note:

> Politics is about more than what governments choose to do or not to do; it is about the uneven distribution of power in society, how the struggle over

---

Box 1.2   Power and agenda-setting

Agenda-setting refers to the types of issues which capture the attention of decision-makers, and then the range of policy solutions which are considered. Since there is an almost infinite range of issues and solutions which *could* be considered, the choice of a small proportion represents the power of organizations and individuals to 'set the agenda'. Power is exercised not only when an issue is raised to the top of the agenda, but also when a decision is made to marginalize or ignore an issue completely (Bachrach and Baratz, 1962). Political power may also be difficult to observe if it is directed towards the shaping of preferences or a common 'taken-for-granted' understanding of what is important in political life (Lukes, 1974). A key concern of political science is the extent to which the exercise of power is diffused across the population, or restricted to a small number of elites. In modern liberal democracies such as Scotland we can point to a trend towards pluralism in the control of knowledge, to checks and balances in new organizations associated with 'new politics', and to a diffusion of power associated with governance and the interdependent nature of politics. The Scottish Government (or any other political institution) is unlikely to achieve its aims unless it forms coalitions, alliances, networks or some other arrangement with other political bodies in Scotland. Yet, this may exaggerate the power of non-state actors, or ignore the systematic forms of power (based on race, gender and class) *within* organizations.

power is conducted, and its impact on the creation and distribution of resources, life chances and well-being. (1992a: 9)

Indeed, any attempt at a narrow definition of the appropriate subject matter of politics could itself be interpreted as an exercise in power. For example, when a Scottish business(wo)man declares politicians should not be 'meddling in the commercial world', he or she is trying to narrow the scope and agenda of politics (see Box 1.2), presenting it as distinct from commercial operations. However, it could be that his or her workers have a less demarcated view of the public/private divide. As Hay argues:

> The political should be defined in such a way as to encompass the entire sphere of the social . . . All events, processes and practices which occur within the social sphere have the potential to be political. (2002: 3)

What is 'Scottish'?

If defining politics is not straightforward, then surely some comfort can be drawn from the fact that the 'Scottish' element of it is self-evident. Scottish politics is politics that takes place in Scotland . . . or is it? If only it were that simple. The broad definitions outlined above suggest that Scottish politics can take place anywhere and everywhere.

Scotland, unlike many other countries in the world, is not a nation-state – there is not a correspondence between the geographic boundaries of Scotland, the nation, and the (UK) state. Scotland, however, is not alone – 'nations' such as Catalonia, the Basque Country and Palestine also lack state structures. Some national populations such as Albanians, Serbs and Kurds are spread throughout more than one state. The position of Scotland as a stateless nation, whilst unusual in the comparative context, is not unique.

Within Scotland there are various interests with opposing views. For example, the interests of the populations of Highland and Lowland may not coincide. The urban, suburban and rural populations may offer different perspectives on issues such as transport and the environment. Religious groups and their leaders (e.g. Protestant, Catholic, Jewish, Muslim, Atheist etc.) may offer differing views on education and moral issues. Different economic interests (e.g. the unemployed, trade unions, employers, pensioners) may differ in their assessment of tax and public expenditure priorities. Scottish politics is about how these differences are mediated and resolved.

Externally, the governance of Scotland requires the cooperation of many different types of agencies and

NATO: North Atlantic Treaty Organization. A military alliance initially created in 1949 to defend Western Europe against a possible Soviet invasion. Its membership grew to 24 in 2004 and its mission changed to intervention and peace-keeping.

European Union: The union of 27 states and 490 million people designed to foster closer cooperation and economic and political ties between countries in Europe.

levels of 'government' (e.g. UK, EU, **NATO**, UN). Scottish politics thus takes place at many different levels and not necessarily within the formal machinery of government. These decisions could be taken at community, local, regional, Scottish, UK, EU or global level. We live in an era of multi-level governance (see Table 1.1) and political decisions that impact on Scotland can be taken in many arenas, some of which extend far beyond the borders of Scotland. Numerous external institutions can impinge, constrain or even dictate the agenda of Scottish politics, for example the UK Government, the **European Union** (EU) and the North Atlantic Treaty Organization (NATO). Intergovernmental bodies are creating denser connections between countries.

There are obvious political arenas – the Scottish Parliament, the Scottish Government, local councils in Scotland, the House of Commons at Westminster, the UK-based civil service in Whitehall, the UK Cabinet, the UK Prime Minister's office, the European Commission in Brussels. There are other not so obvious arenas – international trade negotiations such as the **G8 summit**, and the **World Trade Organization** (WTO); supranational bodies such as the United Nations (UN) and North Atlantic Treaty Organization (NATO); and major pressure groups such as Amnesty and Greenpeace. Other possibilities are the headquarters of multinationals with significant interests in Scotland such as IBM, Motorola, RBS and HBOS. Therefore, decisions that impact on Scottish politics may be taken in London, Brussels, Washington, Beijing, Strasbourg or almost any other major city in the world or any institution, public or private, with interests in Scotland.

G8 Summit: A gathering of the 'most economically advanced' countries – Canada, France, Germany, Italy, Japan, Russia, the United Kingdom, and the United States – to discuss global policy issues.

World Trade Organization (WTO): An organization sponsored by the United Nations to facilitate international trade.

Centre and periphery: Terms used in the study of territorial politics. Centre usually refers to the part of government in which power is concentrated; periphery refers to local, regional or territorial governments.

The state in Scotland manifests itself at many levels, and most of the key institutions of the state (MI5, Bank of England, Armed Forces, BBC) fall within the realm of reserved powers. Therefore, in territorial politics a distinction tends to be made between the **centre and periphery** of a political system. The traditions of the British State could be described as elitist and hierarchical; democracy has come from above not below. Ministers still represent 'The Crown'. Indeed one could argue that the Scottish Parliament is an arena of **low politics** (social policy, transport, local government and the like), since issues of **high politics** (economy, foreign and defence policy, border control) remain

Table 1.1 *Levels of governance in Scotland*

Level of governance	Institutional examples
International	United Nations, World Trade Organization, World Bank, International Monetary Fund, multinational corporations, international interest groups
European	European Union, EU institutions, European interest groups
UK State	UK Parliament, UK Ministries (e.g. Dept of Constitutional Affairs), UK interest groups
Scotland (State)	Scottish Parliament, Scottish Government
Scotland	Scottish Agencies, Non-Departmental Public Bodies, UK state agencies (e.g. Inland Revenue, Passport Agency), Scottish interest groups (e.g. Scottish Council for Voluntary Organizations)
Regional	Strathclyde Passenger Transport Executive, Highlands and Islands Enterprise, Health Boards
Local	32 local councils, local enterprise companies
Local community	Community councils, tenants organizations, school boards

Low politics: Policy matters deemed peripheral to the centre and devolved to territorial and local governments.

High politics: All matters that are vital to the survival of the state such as defence, foreign affairs, security and economic concerns.

located at British state level (cf. Bulpitt, 1983). Therefore, a cynic may argue that devolution is the British State's response to an internal challenge from Scottish nationalist forces – it is an accommodation to those interests, but one that leaves the essential fundamentals of the UK State intact. Sovereignty and control of issues such as defence, public finance, the economy and foreign policy lie at UK level.

This focus of territorial politics which emphasizes both Scotland's place within the UK and the decentralization and devolution of power to a stateless nation is also found in a range of Western democratic states (see for example Keating, 1998; Bogdanor, 1999; Bradbury, 2006). 'Territories' like Quebec in Canada, Flanders in Belgium and Catalonia in Spain have all enjoyed increased levels of political autonomy in recent decades. The UK itself is based in three territorial unions: England and Wales (1536); Scotland (1707); and Britain and Ireland (1800), replaced with the six counties of Northern Ireland (1921) after the 26 counties of Ireland negotiated their exit from the union.

Territorial politics, like many other branches of political science, has a predominant focus on institutions and their relationships with each other. If we

Unionism: Attachment to the principle of a unity of the United Kingdom. A 'hard line' suggests no sympathy to home-rule sentiments, while the unionism expressed by parties in the Scottish Parliament refers to devolution within the UK as an alternative to independence.

shift our attention to wider issues such as political participation and identity then we may come to different conclusions about the distinctiveness of Scottish politics. In recent decades, perceptions of Scottishness have been growing at the same time as 'Britishness' has been diminishing. **Unionism** has been the glue that binds Scotland with the rest of the UK. In the days of the British empire and the dominance of British economic interests around the world it was easy to see why the concept of the union and Britain was appealing. With the end of that Empire and Britain's relative economic decline, that appeal is no longer as readily apparent and British identity as a source of collective participation may not have the appeal or resonance it once had (Nairn, 2001).

The Scottish politics of difference

Scottish politics has in recent years developed its own agenda, separate from that of British politics. Its defining feature has been the issue of constitutional change, but there are also issues (e.g. education, local government, land reform) that have always had a uniquely Scottish angle. The party system has diverged from the UK norm, in part as a reflection of the left-of-centre focus of political debate in Scotland. A social democratic consensus around key issues is more apparent; radical politics in the form of the Greens and the Socialists is more visible. The **neo-liberal 'laissez-faire'** politics of Thatcherism in the 1980s were perceived as alien by the vast majority of Scots. Scottish political attitudes are also different. However, whilst opinion polls have tended to demonstrate a more 'progressive' attitude to issues such as income redistribution (Paterson *et al.*, 2001), they also highlight few differences in moral views (Park, 2002).

Neo-liberal 'laissez-faire': A broad strategy to 'roll back the state' or reduce public provision in favour of the private sector and the market.

Political differences in Scotland have been magnified by new post-devolution political arrangements. For example, the first-past-the-post electoral system creates majority party governments in Westminster with working parliamentary majorities of a scale that will never be achieved in the Scottish Parliament. Indeed, the Scottish Parliament has working methods and practices that deliberately eschew those of Westminster. Scottish difference also extends to the role of the state. The public-sector presence in Scotland – if measured in terms of key indicators such as expenditure, employment and housing – is more significant and the impact of commercialism on the provision of services such as education and health is less well-developed than south of the border. Fewer state activities have tended to be outsourced to the

[handwritten note: proportional representation]

[handwritten note: bigger public sector and reliance on their jobs]

Similarity to EU democracies (handwritten annotation)

market. Therefore, as a whole, devolution has allowed Scottish politics to further diverge from UK politics.

Placed in a broader comparative context Scotland does not appear so exceptional – indeed it is the UK, rather than Scotland, which appears unusual. Scottish politics is actually quite a bit like that of other small European democracies. For example, the dynamics of executive coalition politics, minority government, the more proportional voting systems used, the multi-party system, the Parliament's working procedures, the **asymmetrical constitutional settlement**, the interdependencies and intergovernmental relations between Scotland and the UK all have parallels in continental Europe. Further, the continuing question of devolution's long-term impact on the UK provides interest for scholars of territorial politics throughout the world.

> **Asymmetrical constitutional settlement**: The uneven nature of the UK devolution settlement, with no English regional devolution and different arrangements in Scotland, Wales and Northern Ireland.

Similar arrangements exist in areas such as Quebec, Catalonia and Flanders – all of these 'territories' exist within the context of claims for more governing autonomy from their respective states. Whilst being a book primarily about Scottish politics, we do at various points seek to place Scottish politics within the broader comparative context.

Of course most answers to the multitude of questions that Scottish devolution has raised will be provisional. It has been suggested that a full analysis of policy change may take 'a decade or more' (Jenkins-Smith and Sabattier, 1993; see also Pressman and Wildavsky, 1973) and yet we have had only two full parliamentary terms. As the former Welsh Secretary Ron Davies famously argued, devolution should be viewed as a 'process rather than an event'. The

BOX 1.3   Infamous quotes about Scottish politics

'Devolution, the settled will of the Scottish people', John Smith, former UK Labour Party Leader.

'A wee pretendy Parliament', Billy Connolly commenting on Scotland's new Parliament.

'Unreconstructed wankers', Alistair Campbell's blunt assessment of the Scottish media.

'Devolution is not just for Christmas', Michael Forsyth, Former Conservative Secretary of State for Scotland.

'Devolution will be like a motorway to independence with no exits', Tam Dalyell, Labour MP.

'Devolution is a process rather than an event', Ron Davies, former Secretary of State for Wales.

question of Scotland's constitutional status and the current devolution settlement remain high on the Scottish political agenda.

A Scottish political system?

Before devolution, one of the liveliest debates in the literature on Scottish
politics was about whether or not Scotland had a 'political system' (see Kellas,
1989; Midwinter *et al.*, 1991; Moore and Booth, 1989). In this book we
suggest that Scottish politics today does exhibit far more features of a political
system today than it did when Kellas first advanced the argument in 1973.
However, Scotland also has far more inextricable links
with other levels of government and states, and has
been affected by **globalization**.

Globalization: The
intensification of
worldwide economic,
social and political
convergence made
possible by
technological advance
in communication and
transport.

Easton (1953; 1957; 1965) emphasized a political
system as an entity which could be studied on its own. He
defined it as, 'a set of interactions, abstracted from the
totality of social behaviour, through which values are
authoritatively allocated for society' (1965: 57). A political system is that part of society where the ultimate
collective decisions are made. The boundary between the
political system and the rest of society need not be as clear cut as the idea of
'government and the governed'. In democratic political systems although most
people do not actively participate most of the time in a political system, they
remain part of it. Various activities such as engagement with public authorities,
the use of public goods, paying taxes and the like, mean that the relevance of politics in individual lives is always real. Participation may be as minimal as voting
in periodic elections or may expand further to interest articulation through interest groups. The important point is that the public are engaged in some way – they
are inputing demands and support to the political system. Almond and Coleman
(1960) outline three categories of input into a political system:

- *Political socialization and recruitment.* The processes whereby citizen
  attitudes to the political system are shaped and formed and the structures
  which exist to co-opt citizens into administrative and political structures.
- *Interest articulation.* The processes through which citizens express their
  demands as well as support for the political system e.g. voting, campaigning, lobbying, demonstrating.
- *Interest aggregation.* The process of linking disparate demands and interests into a coherent idea on which action may be taken. Political parties and
  interests groups are two of the key institutions fulfilling this role.

The political system itself is where power lies. In the words of Easton (1965),
'politics is the authoritative allocation of values' – a defining feature of states is

their authority to enforce collective decisions, by force if necessary. The political system makes binding decisions on a population. It has the power and authority to make decisions. Therefore, the key question is whether or not *Scottish* political institutions (rather than those in the UK, EU or beyond) 'allocate these values' with a degree of authority not witnessed before devolution.

Sovereignty: The supreme, ultimate source of authority in society. In the UK this is symbolized by The Crown in Parliament. Scottish home rule campaigners have argued Scottish sovereignty rests with its people.

Scotland remains a sub-system of the UK. Ultimate legal **sovereignty** remains in Westminster, and Scotland remains part of the broader UK political system. However, it does have devolved authority over primary legislation. This has been added to pre-existing powers safeguarded by the 1707 Act of Union over the legal, education and local government systems in Scotland. Scotland also has distinct political parties, interest groups and structures of governance. However, the UK political system has survived by displaying its capacity to respond to the stresses caused by Scottish demands for home rule. The UK political system continues to evolve and its adaptability has probably been the key to its durability.

New politics

As Chapter 2 discusses, Scottish Politics did not begin in 1999, and a wide variety of texts from the pre-devolution years still have relevance today. Yet, the main theme of much academic work immediately post-devolution was the notion of '**new politics**' (for example Brown, 2000; see Mitchell, 2000, for a critical outline). The phrase was also resurrected after the 2007 election with the election of a minority SNP administration compelling it to seek coalitions and informal cooperation with other parties. Yet there is often a lack of certainty regarding what 'new politics' actually means.

New politics: A phrase associated with supplementing the aim of devolution with a wider democratization of Scottish politics (see Chapter 11).

What we can say with most certainty is that new politics became associated with the chance devolution gave to improve the political process. It is a phrase borne out of Scottish **civic society**'s participation in the campaign for home rule and the desire that devolution be accompanied by a wider democratization of Scottish politics. A new Scottish Parliament would not only address the democratic deficit in territorial representation, but also mark a departure from the type of politics associated with 'old Westminster'. This is outlined at length by the **Scottish Constitutional Convention** (SCC) final report in 1995 and summed up in its argument that:

Civic society: An active collection of voluntary and social organizations who share the same broad interests or principles.

Scotlands New Politics (handwritten)

Scottish Constitutional Convention (SCC): An organization of political parties, interest groups, civic and religious leaders formed in 1989 to promote the principle (and detailed workings of) of devolved government.

Consultative Steering Group (CSG): The cross-party group established by the Scottish Office pre-devolution to report on the operational requirements and draft rules for the Scottish Parliament.

The coming of a Scottish Parliament will usher in a way of politics that is radically different from the rituals of Westminster: more participative, more creative, less needlessly confrontational.

Such language is closely associated with the campaigns for the Parliament, the experience of three of Scotland's major parties – Labour, SNP and Liberal Democrats – working together during the devolution referendum campaign and the four main parties working together on the **Consultative Steering Group** (CSG). Henry McLeish, former First Minister for Scotland, summed up this line of thinking when accepting the CSG Report on behalf of the Scottish Executive:

findings (handwritten margin note)

> The establishment of the Scottish Parliament offers the opportunity to put in place a new sort of democracy in Scotland, closer to the people and more in tune with Scottish needs. We envisage an open accessible Parliament: a Parliament where power is shared with the people; where people are encouraged to participate in the policy-making process which affects all our lives; an accountable visible Parliament; and a Parliament which promotes equal opportunities for all. (Cited in Brown, 2000: 550)

Westminster Errors (handwritten margin note)

These hopes for the new parliament were based on a widespread critique of the existing procedures in the UK:

- Electoral system – the first-past-the-post system exaggerates majorities and excludes small parties. It tends to result in a majority which, combined with a strong party system, ensures that one party dominates proceedings.
- Executive dominance – this 'top-down' system, in which power is concentrated within government, is not appropriate for a Scottish system with a tradition of civic democracy and the diffusion of power. In Westminster, the centre not only has the ability for force legislation through (and ignore wider demands), but also to dominate the resources devoted to policy. Parliament does not possess the resources to hold the executive to account.
- Adversarial style – most discussions in Westminster take place in plenary sessions (the whole House sits together) with a charged partisan atmosphere. There is insufficient scope for detailed and specialist scrutiny in an atmosphere conducive to consensual working practices.
- This extends to committees – the partisan nature of politics undermines real scrutiny and there are limited resources to investigate or monitor

elements of bias in report to be considered (handwritten note at bottom)

departments. Given the distinction between select and standing committees, there may be a problem of coordination and a lack of potential for long-term consensual styles to emerge.

Interest groups:
Groups of people working for a particular cause (e.g. environmental policy), profession (e.g. doctors) or segment of society (e.g. to support black and ethnic minority representation).

- Too much power is vested in the House of Lords – an unelected and unrepresentative second chamber.
- Although the government may consult with **interest groups**, this tends to be with the 'usual suspects'. This reliance on the most powerful and well-resourced groups (such as big business) reinforces the concentration of power in a ruling class.
- Since power is concentrated at the centre there are limited links between state and civic society. Outside of the voting process, there are limited means for 'the people' to influence government.

Microcosmic representation: The idea of parliament as a microcosm of the society it is designed to represent, in terms of factors such as gender, ethnic minority, age, education and disability.

- Parliamentary overload – Parliament is too focused on scrutinizing government legislation. This leaves MPs with too little time to devote to their constituencies.
- Parliament as a whole does not reflect the people that elect it in terms of **microcosmic representation**. There is a particular lack of women in Parliament as well as a tendency for MPs to be drawn from a ruling class.

These deficiencies would therefore be addressed with a number of aims:

- A proportional electoral system with a strong likelihood of coalition and bargaining between parties.
- A consensual style of politics with a reduced role for party conflict.
- Power-sharing rather than executive dominance.
- A strong role for committees to initiate legislation, scrutinize the activity of the executive and conduct inquiries
- Fostering closer links between state and civic society through parliament (e.g. with a focus on the right to petition parliament and the committee role in obliging the executive to consult widely)
- Ensuring that MSPs have enough time for constituency work by restricting business in the Scottish Parliament to three days per week.
- Fostering equality in the selection of candidates and making the Scottish Parliament equally attractive to men and women. *Core beliefs*

The literature suggests two main reasons for this exposition of new politics. The first relates to a narrative of the 'Scottish political tradition', which involves consensus or at least the pursuit of negotiated settlements rather than the imposition of policy. This would be undermined by an electoral system

consensus, disenchantment with Westminster politics

which exaggerates a majority, centralizes power, encourages adversarial politics and excludes the wider population. Rather, new political institutions would be required to foster power-sharing. A new electoral system would foster power-sharing between political parties, a new Scottish Parliament would share power with a Scottish Executive, a new set of rules of engagement would prove conducive to consensus seeking, and new channels of communication would allow a greater role for 'the people'. The second relates to the political climate in the run up to devolution. A perception of popular disenchantment with politics and politicians suggested that a new Scottish Parliament should not replicate a political system discredited in the public eye. While the situation of a Parliament in Edinburgh addresses the issue of territorial remoteness, it does not solve the problem of remoteness between the government and the governed. For politics to be participative and inclusive, its Parliament would have to play down party conflicts, assert its right to initiate as well as scrutinize legislation and prove to be a focal point for participation outwith the electoral cycle.

Since new politics became such a rallying call for the architects of devolution, this gives us a reference point with which to assess the success of devolution. Therefore, a key focus of this book is an assessment of the 'new politics in practice'. To this end, it is useful to highlight some preliminary observations from the literature:

Westminster as a caricature

bias in devolution report

The final report of the SCC should be seen as a manifesto rather than a blueprint for action. As such, its focus is on the benefits of the new and the limitations of the old. The consequence is that it tends to create a caricature of the UK political process: a UK government takes a position and attempts to impose it without consultation with Parliament, interest groups or the wider public. In contrast, the Scottish Parliament will listen, propose, consult and be more responsive to wider interests. It is not difficult to find instances which depart from this picture. For example, in many cases the Blair and Major governments have been portrayed as *too responsive* (Mitchell, 2000: 616), while the group-government process is much more open than generally assumed. We can also question the likelihood that a proportional electoral system necessarily encourages more responsive governments, since first-past-the-post systems tend to exaggerate vote swings and make the ruling party more sensitive to electoral opinion than coalitions under PR.

The maintenance of Westminster-style powers, procedures and culture

Although new politics refers to a rejection of old-Westminster, its architects have chosen to retain a number of Westminster features. This includes an assumption that the Scottish Government will govern while the Scottish Parliament performs a scrutiny role. Imported procedures can be found in the format of First Minister's Questions, the Scottish Ministerial Code and the rules governing the paid, external interests of MPs. Since many MSPs were drawn from Westminster, we may also expect 'old politics' to be a culture that is difficult to shake off.

The continued role for party politics

The Scottish Constitutional Convention (SCC) does not recognize the positive role that parties play in providing choice, encouraging debate and fostering accountability and government responsiveness. It also seems to underestimate the likelihood of partisanship to ensure that key votes are won in the Scottish Parliament (using the party whip) and establish a distance between parties for electoral advantage. There is little prospect for consensus when the two main parties disagree over fundamentals such as constitutional change and no longer have the 'common enemy' of a Conservative UK Government.

Terms such as 'consensus' and 'civic society' may be misleading

Taking consensus-seeking to its extreme may suggest an assumption that there is a rational or technical solution to policy problems. This may stifle legitimate debate and undermine policy innovation, particularly within a political system which is dominated by centre-left parties. Similar problems may exist in the assumption of a special legitimacy for 'civic society' when in fact we may be referring to small groups with vested interests.

Not all of the aims of new politics will be compatible

Devolving decisions to civic forums may increase participation but reduce accountability. Finding greater time for constituency work, combined with family-friendly business hours may undermine the ability of the Scottish Parliament to scrutinize the Scottish Government and for committees to inquire and set their own agenda. The use of a party list to select regional candidates may reinforce the power of parties to control the conduct of individual MSPs.

Consensus and bargaining

Consensus and bargaining between the Scottish Parliament and Scottish Executive was undermined as soon as Labour and the Liberal Democrats formed a governing coalition. New politics is arguably more likely to flourish if no stable coalitions are formed. A minority government may be obliged to negotiate with a number of parties to secure a majority vote on successive issues. This may allow other parties to become more involved in relationships between the executive and the civil service (since the Government would wish to ensure parliamentary cooperation at the earliest opportunity). While the formation of a coalition suggests greater cooperation between more than one party, there is also the potential for a working majority which mimics the exaggerated majority found in Westminster.

In sum, the literature suggests that the architects of new politics had unrealistic expectations about the level of consensus in Scotland and the ability to

Westminster and Whitehall: The areas in which the institutions of the UK Parliament and Government respectively are located. This phrase is often used as a short-hand term to refer to each.

maintain consensus through political institutions. Indeed, it could be that the talking up of the capabilities of the Parliament is directly linked to the largely negative media and public assessment of its initial performance post-devolution (see Mitchell, 2001; McGarvey, 2001a). However, if we view the final report of the SCC as a manifesto then there is an implicit recognition of wider political constraints. In this sense, new politics refers to an aspiration for difference at the margins – *less* partisanship, *more* public involvement, a *greater* pursuit of consensus. The notion of new politics is an aspiration; a hope that the Westminster legacy and the inheritance of pre-devolution institutions does not impinge too much on future political decisions. Yet, there is still an overarching political culture in the UK which informs the behaviour of politicians, civil servants, the media and even the public. Too many individuals involved in Scottish politics were schooled in the traditions and rituals of **Westminster and Whitehall** practice for devolution to represent a sharp break from the past.

Key themes

There are several themes which inform this book. First, we emphasize that Scottish politics today takes place within a context shaped by history, the

Assumptive worlds: Ingrained implicit beliefs and ways of thinking which could close off alternative ways of thinking.

legacy of which is embodied in both formal institutions such as the Scottish Government, the Parliament, political parties, quangos and local councils. There are also informal institutions such as constitutional conventions (e.g. collective cabinet responsibility), the 'standard operating procedures' of formal institutions and the **assumptive worlds** of political actors which structure the environment within political actors make decisions. Linked to this is the emphasis on the idea that political exchange in Scotland is constrained by the **inherited commitments** of previous decisions. Scottish politicians, when they make policy decisions, are making incremental adjustments to the historical legacy. Bureaucratic culture, interest-group pressure and wider political pressures often mean the scope for policy change is restricted.

Inherited commitments: All politicians inherit before they choose – policy programmes, government infrastructure, contracts, salaries and other commitments mean that the scope for policy change is often marginal.

Second, we recognize that Scottish politics *has* undoubtedly changed. Both formal and informal institutions have changed in significant ways since 1999. The democratic and legitimacy deficit associated with the Conservative years in office (1979–97) has been

Year zero: The treatment of 1999 as the starting point for devolution analysis.

resolved by the creation of the new democratic processes, not least the Parliament itself. Whilst 1999 did not mark **year zero** it has resulted in changes within all of Scotland's key political institutions. These changes were fuelled by expectations that a type of consensual politics engendered by party and civic society cooperation in the 1980s and 1990s would continue after devolution. However, the reality of post-devolution political and policy processes suggests that these hopes were unrealistic as soon as the 'common enemy' (the Conservative Government in the UK) was removed.

Third, we explore the extent to which devolution has satisfied nationalist demands. The UK state has successfully accommodated the demands for increased levels of autonomy from the Celtic fringe with Scotland, Wales and Northern Ireland all gaining different forms of devolution since 1999. The British political system remains intact. Devolution, however, did not mark the end of the constitutional debate in Scotland. Indeed, if anything, it has added fuel to the fire. The election of the first SNP administration in 2007 could represent a significant turning point in this respect. The constitutional issue continues to simmer not far from the agenda of Scottish politics and it appears when fiscal, representational and inter-governmental issues are discussed. Demands emanating from Scotland are likely to place the British political system under increasing strain – more accommodation of Scottish distinctiveness and difference may be required.

Fourth, we place emphasis on the broader dynamics of policy-making. In Scottish public policy-making most attention tends to be focused on the policy formulation and output stages. However, an examination of the agenda-setting and implementation stages can also be revealing. The subject of finance, although often considered boring and technical, should not be neglected by any student of Scottish politics. An understanding of Scottish politics today should involve the scope of analysis extending further than Scotland's formal governing institutions. Understanding new electoral and democratic processes, voter behaviour, the different forms of policy delivery as well as the broader financial and governing context is necessary so that a more rounded account of Scottish politics can be given.

These themes are outlined in greater depth in subsequent chapters. Chapter 2 outlines the historical and cultural context of Scottish politics. Students of Scottish politics should take history seriously. As Bulpitt once argued, 'history is too important to be left just to historians' (1983: 54). Recent political history in Scotland is a story of how various political institutions, galvanized by Scottish public opinion, placed demands on British government forcing it to accommodate Scottish differentiation whilst retaining the integrity of the British political system (see Midwinter *et al.*, 1991: 196–9). This chapter provides a brief **narrative** of Scotland's recent political history and then focuses on the role of the media in Scottish politics. This allows us not only to

Narrative: An account and story of events. In politics narratives of the same events can often vary with different perspectives evident.

explain the idiosyncrasies of modern Scottish politics, but also to gauge the media's attitude to it (particularly since expectations associated with new politics were so high).

Chapter 3 outlines details of Scotland's major political parties and the impact of devolution on their role and structure. It outlines a brief review of the history of each party including details of both UK and Scottish election results. It then considers broad developments in the Scottish party system since 1999. It reviews and assesses the role and functions of political parties as well as trends in party organization and how they are impacting on the parties in Scotland.

Chapter 4 focuses on electoral processes in Scotland. Scotland today has four separate electoral systems for elections to local councils, the Scottish Parliament, the House of Commons and the European Parliament. Each voting system has parallels in the wider world and owes more to European than British democratic tradition. The chapter then outlines details of Scottish local election results, and also examines recent Scottish social attitudes drawing on both pre-and post-devolution Scottish election studies. Political campaigning in an age of multi-level elections is also discussed and the impact of devolution on both UK and Scottish campaigning assessed.

Chapter 5 discusses the Scottish Parliament and places it within the wider context of Scottish politics, highlighting its symbolic significance and suggesting that it cannot be viewed as a 'stand-alone' institution divorced from other key political institutions and pressures in Scottish politics. The chapter also contrasts the legislative processes of the **Holyrood** Parliament with those of Westminster. It then examines the role of parliamentary committees, and assesses the significance of Parliament's influence when passing legislation.

Holyrood: The area of Edinburgh where the Scottish Parliament is located – it is often used as a short-hand term for it.

Chapter 6 examines the political leadership and civil service within the Scottish Government. It outlines and assesses the role of the Scottish Cabinet and the First Minister, and it also acknowledges the differing environments within which the Scottish Government has operated – the Labour–Liberal Democrat coalition (1999–2007) and SNP minority administration (2007–). It then describes the basic structures of Scotland's civil service, the social background of civil servants and assesses the impact that the civil service has had on post-devolution policy processes.

Chapter 7 examines the governmental institutions beyond Holyrood, including local government and public bodies that do not fit neatly into the conventional central/local government classification (e.g. CommunitiesScotland, Scottish Enterprise, Local Enterprise Companies). It also examines policy initiatives such as public–private partnerships and social inclusion. The chapter

Reserved and devolved powers: The Scotland Act 1998 listed the reserved powers (e.g. defence, social security, foreign affairs. fiscal, economic and monetary policy, immigration) to be retained by the Westminster Parliament. By default, those not listed, became the responsibility of the Scottish Parliament.

Europeanized: Refers to the process whereby the policy competence of the European Union has expanded into an ever-increasing range of areas such as fisheries, agriculture and environmental policy.

then assesses the relevance of 'governance' to discussions of Scottish politics, examining the changing manner of public service delivery, 'hollowing out of the state' and the movement towards a 'regulatory state'.

Chapter 8 extends the theme of multi-level governance to the influence of the UK and EU on Scottish politics. It explores the blurred boundaries between **reserved and devolved powers** as well as the means used by both governments to solve disputes. In most cases this involves the use of 'Sewel motions' passed by the Scottish Parliament to give permission for Westminster to legislate. However, in a small number of areas, the uncertainty can be exploited to allow Scotland to go its own way. The chapter then discusses one of the more curious developments since 1999: as a range of issues have been devolved, so too have they been **Europeanized**. Paradoxically, this causes a level of UK involvement in Scottish politics that may not have been apparent in the past.

Chapter 9 explores the history, development and durability of the 'Barnett formula' as a means of allocating territorial public expenditure in the United Kingdom. The chapter also seeks to confirm a wide range of themes from preceding chapters such as the Scottish political system argument, the constitutional question, the role of finance as a constraint on policy change and multi-level governance. Discussion of the politics of Scottish public finance is particularly important as it may have significant bearing on the evolution of the constitutional settlement.

Chapter 10 looks at the broader question of public policy-making in Scotland. It examines the reasons for policy convergence and divergence, and then explores the extent to which there have been 'Scottish solutions to Scottish problems'. It focuses particular attention on 'flagship' policies such as free personal care, student fees, local government elections and the smoking ban and assesses the scale of policy change from formulation to implementation.

Chapter 11 assesses developments in representative, deliberative, participatory and pluralist democracy in Scotland as a means to address the 'democratic deficit'. It investigates the importance of 'microcosmic' representation and profiles the social background of Scotland's elected representatives, assessing how closely they resemble the Scottish population that they represent. It then reviews the wide range of new forms of democratic practice in Scotland, including innovations such as the new electoral system, new arrangements for consultation and a new Public Petitions Committee.

The final chapter explores the impact of devolution on Scottish politics. Devolution is undoubtedly a *necessary* condition for a higher degree of political and policy autonomy in Scotland, but it is not necessarily *sufficient*. This chapter also examines developments as regards the constitutional issue in Scottish politics.

Throughout the book, three axes of comparison can be detected. First, we at various junctures place Scotland in a comparative context. Scottish politics has evolved in the shadow of Westminster governing arrangements. It therefore represents an obvious point of comparison for voting systems, legislation, bureaucracies and broader governance issues. However, in recognition that the UK political system is quite exceptional we also seek to draw comparison with the wider world. Second, we compare contemporary Scottish politics with the aspirations that preceded the establishment of the Scottish Parliament. The story involves the role of idealism in political change. We place the aspirations of 'new politics' against the reality of contemporary Scottish political practice. Third, we assess the relevance of some concepts and theories developed in the political science literature against the actual practice of Scottish politics.

In summary this book is about Scottish politics. Despite our acknowledgement of its place within the wider UK political system we view it as a legitimate unit of political analysis. Scotland should be viewed as a very interesting subsystem of UK politics. We contend that what is going on in Scottish politics should of course be of interest in itself to students of politics. In an introductory book there is little advantage in seeking to overwhelm students with comparative data and theories. Describing *what* is happening in Scottish politics is a precondition of explaining *why* it is occurring. However, where appropriate we do try to place Scottish politics within its wider comparative context and introduce some relevant theories to both inform and develop our description and analysis.

Further reading

For general discussions on the nature of politics and power see Crick (1993), Dahl (1961), Laswell (1936), Lukes (1974), Leftwich (1984). On conceptualizations of Scottish politics pre-devolution see Brown *et al.* (1998), Kellas (1989), McCrone (2001), Midwinter *et al.* (1991), Paterson (1994). On territorial politics see Bulpitt (1983), Mitchell (1996b), Bogdanor (1999) and Bradbury (2006). For post-devolution books on Scottish politics see Keating (2005a), Lynch (2001), Wright (2000), Hassan and Warhurst (2002). On 'new politics' see Arter (2004), Brown (2000), Keating (2005a), McGarvey (2001a), Mitchell (2000), Miller (2000), Scottish Constitutional Convention (1995), Shephard *et al.* (2001).

Online sources

For Scottish politics online see:

Scottish Parliament   http://www.scottish.parliament.uk/
Scottish Constitutional Convention Report   http://www.cybersurf.co.uk/scotparl/
   briefing/Scc_prop.html
Report of the Consultative Steering Group   http://www.scotland.gov.uk/library/
   documents-w5/rcsg-00.htm
The Economic and Social Research Council 'Devolution and Constitutional Change'
   research programme   http://www.devolution.ac.uk
University of London's Constitution Unit's devolution monitoring online
   http://www.ucl.ac.uk/constitution-unit/leverh/monitors.htm
Scottish politics online site   http://www.alba.org.uk
UK Politics page   http://www.ukpol.co.uk

Chapter 2

Devolution: Historical and Social Context

Scottish politics today is not taking place within a vacuum – important legacies from previous developments continue to shape and structure Scottish
political institutions and behaviour. Therefore, any examination of Scottish
politics should look well beyond the establishment of
the modern parliament in 1999. In this chapter we seek
to outline a brief historical narrative of Scotland's
contemporary political history. Our discussion focuses
on the postwar period, and particularly from the 1960s
when **constitutional issues** came to the forefront of
Scottish politics. It highlights:

**Constitutional
issues:** Those relating
to the structure and
fundamental political
rules of a nation or
state.

- the development of **administrative devolution** in
  Scotland and the legacy of the Scottish Office's
  roles and responsibilities;
- the links between such devolution and the rise of
  the home-rule movement;
- a comparison of the referendum campaigns in 1979
  and 1997; and
- the work of the Scottish Constitutional Convention
  as one of the main architects of new politics.

**Administrative
devolution:** The
partial devolution of
administration and
policy responsibilities
to the Scottish
Office before
legislative devolution
in 1999.

The main problem for students of Scottish politics is that its main developments have tended to be subsumed within the wider story of UK politics.
This is compounded by the fact that narratives of UK
politics tend to have a very centralist slant. Yet, as
Rokkan and Urwin (1983) note, the UK's **union-state**
is unique in comparative terms. Therefore, to understand UK politics it is necessary to look beyond the
narrow confines of governing institutions in
Westminster and Whitehall (Rhodes, 1988; 1997).
While the dominant framework for the study of UK
politics has been the Westminster Model (see Box
2.1), scholars of Scottish politics (Kellas, 1989;
Midwinter *et al.*, 1991; Brown *et al.*, 1998) have
presented an alternative story.

Union state: The Act
of Union 1707
ensured that certain
aspects of the
Scottish polity would
remain intact.
Therefore, while the
UK resembles a
unitary state, the
centre's ability to alter
sub-governmental
units in Scotland is
uncertain.

Box 2.1   The Westminster model of UK politics

The Westminster model refers to 'the concepts, questions and historical story used to capture the essential features of British government which, through sheer longevity, form the conventional or mainstream view' (Bevir and Rhodes, 1999: 216). It was the dominant narrative of UK politics emphasizing the importance of institutions such as prime minister, cabinet, political parties, the civil service and parliament. The Westminster model contains prescriptive and descriptive elements, which are not always easy to disentangle. While there is no single accepted definition of the Westminster model we can identify a number of its characteristics:

- *Majority party control of the Executive*. The single-member plurality system (or first past the post) exaggerates the majority of the biggest party.
- *Two party system based on single-member constituencies*. The electoral system also exaggerates the swing of votes to produce two-party dominance.
- *Institutionalized Opposition Party*. This creates a party of government and an officially recognized party of opposition in Parliament
- *The importance of constitutional conventions*. For example collective cabinet responsibility.
- *Doctrine of parliamentary sovereignty and the unitary state*. The UK Parliament has the power or make or un-make any laws
- *Accountability through elections, and Ministerial responsibility*. The government receives a mandate to govern and is held to account at the ballot box. Ministers are responsible for the Departments of State which they are in charge of.
- *Personalized view of power – it belongs to particular actor or institution*. Like the media projection of politics, power is assumed to be held by individuals or institutions. It is a very simplistic view of power summed up in the old Prime Minister versus Cabinet 'Power' debate which used to appear in UK politics textbooks.
- *Focus on institutions*. Institutions such as prime minister, cabinet, political parties, the civil service and parliament are deemed to be where power lies; that is, political power is assumed to be where it is supposed to be in a democratic sense.
- *Inductive legal-historical methodology*. The way to understand UK politics is through an understanding and appreciation of its legal basis and history.

The Westminster model suggests strong central control. Power resides within central government or the 'core executive', and this is furthered by the following factors:

- The reliance on representative democracy and parliamentary rather than popular supremacy except during elections.
- The first-past-the-post electoral system allows an exaggerated majority and hence governing party control over Parliament.
- The power of the prime minister to control cabinet and hence ministers.
- A politically-neutral civil service which operates under the convention of individual ministerial responsibility (IMR). That is, civil service decisions are made on the basis of, or anticipation of, ministerial wishes.

So power is centralized and elitist and governing is top-down or 'one way traffic from those governing (the Government) to those being governed (society)' (Richards and Smith, 2002: 3; see also Marsh *et al.*, 2001; Rhodes, 1997; Bevir and Rhodes, 1999; Bache and Flinders, 2004). There is therefore little room for discussion of power in the periphery, or organizations such as local government or the Scottish Office/Executive/Government.

Unitary state: A state in which all constitutional power (legal, executive and parliamentary) resides in the centre. Sub-governmental units may exist but are subject to change from the top.

Viewed from Scotland and the rest of the 'periphery', the UK was never a **unitary state** but a state of unions (Mitchell, 2006). Scotland was part of the UK and the 'centre' was dominant in terms of political power, but Scotland had retained some distinct features of nationhood. As Paterson (2000b: 2) notes, the union with England was partial with the major institutions in civic life retaining a separate Scottish identity. Paterson (2000b) argues the incorporation of Scotland into Britain was always incomplete because Scotland's elites negotiated to retain control over religion, law, education and local government. McCrone argues that,

> Scotland's professional classes – lawyers, doctors, teachers, churchmen – while socially conservative, embody the institutional survival of distinctive Scottish 'civil society', and can be considered as keepers of native institutions. (1992: 143)

In recent decades distinct Scottish institutions and endeavours in the fields of sport and culture could be added. Overall, distinctively Scottish institutions such as education bodies (e.g. Universities Scotland), professional associations (e.g. Law Society, Educational Institute for Scotland), and sporting institutions (e.g. SportScotland, Scottish Football Association) have contributed to a picture of Scottish distinctiveness within the UK. These differences have been reinforced and reproduced through the Scottish media which has diverged (to some degree) from a UK or London-centric focus. This involves not only the choice to cover different stories, but also to deal with the same stories differently. Yet, one of the first decisions of the SNP government in 2007 was to establish a commission to consider the future direction of the broadcast media and to highlight a lack of indigenous programming. Therefore, the role and independence of a Scottish media is open to considerable debate. The second section of this chapter seeks to assess the role the media plays in contemporary Scottish politics. We pay particular attention to the relationship between the media and the new Scottish political institutions, since the former played a key role in the heightening of expectations for new politics during the campaign for home rule.

Administrative devolution and the 'Scottish political system'

Devine (2006: 1) cites the oft-quoted former Canadian Prime Minister, Pierre Trudeau's remark during a speech to an American audience in 1969:

living next to you is in some ways like sleeping with an elephant: no matter how friendly and even tempered the beast, one is affected by every twitch and grunt.

In many ways this simile could equally be applied to the relationship between Scotland and England. Scotland has always been the junior partner in the union – it has less than 10 per cent of England's population (in 1707 it was closer to 20%). Yet, as the British state, economy and empire expanded its scope and influence, Scotland appeared to accept its position within it enthusiastically. The political identity that flourished was one of unionist nationalism which has two elements: the belief that Scotland had to remain in the union to realize its potential as a nation, and the belief that in the absence of Scottish nationalism, the Union could have degenerated into an English takeover of Scotland (Brown *et al.*, 1996: 11). If the union was ever questioned by campaigners it was not to seek its repeal, but to make minor adjustments. The first politically significant home-rule movement in Scotland in the late nineteenth century sought modest devolution of responsibilities from London rather than outright separation. This is not unusual even in the contemporary context – often national minorities resolve that their self-determination can be adequately exercised as part of a larger state.

In part, calls for political devolution were muted because the British state addressed them with a form of administrative devolution. There are two notable aspects to this process. First, the **Scottish Office** created in 1885 was relatively small, taking over responsibility for little more than a number of small existing governmental bodies. The post of Secretary of State for Scotland, created some decades later, was also fairly low status – a symbolic gesture to address nationalistic grievances over the way the union was handled in London, rather than one which marked a shift in power. Second, however, these moves created a precedent – that when Scotland's policy circumstances are different, Scotland's policy response and hence administrative arrangements should be different. This became important in the early twentieth century and then the postwar period, as the Scottish Office began to grow in tandem with the growth of the state (see Mitchell, 2003a). The Secretary of State also became a figurehead for the articulation of Scottish interests in Cabinet.

Scottish Office: The territorial department of the UK Government which existed from 1885–1999.

These developments provide the context for the most significant debate on the distinctiveness of Scottish politics before devolution. This centred on James Kellas' *The Scottish Political System* which ran to four editions from 1973–89. His arguments represented a reaction to the 'homogeneity thesis' which suggested that the UK was a unitary state with no significant territorial dimension. Rather, Scotland entered into a union with England and negotiated the retention of a number of distinct Scottish arrangements in law, education, religion and local government. For Kellas, there were two pre-conditions for a

Scottish political system (which were both met). First, the majority of the population would see their national identity as primarily Scottish rather than British. This was furthered by the retention of Scottish culture and education, as well as the commonly held idea of Scotland as a 'stateless nation'. Second, Scots could appeal to Scottish institutions as a means of, 'articulating and aggregating their interests' (Kellas, 1989: 211). These existed in the form of Scottish MPs, interest groups, media, the Scottish Office as a focus for demands, and a Scottish public service and legal system to execute decisions and adjudicate disputes (see also Paterson, 1994).

Much intellectual energy was then spent debating the levels of political autonomy vested in Scotland institutions. The anti-case rested on the argument that sovereignty resided elsewhere. In other words, the final decision on policy in Scotland was made in the UK Cabinet, not the Scottish Office (Moore and Booth, 1989; Rose, 1982). The basis for a credible counter-argument was best articulated by Bulpitt, whose *Territory and Power in the United Kingdom* (1983) still informs contemporary debates on devolution. Bulpitt suggests that for long periods the 'periphery' (organizations such as local or territorial government) benefited from a form of autonomy caused by a lack of attention to local matters by the 'centre' (which we can take to mean central government). Central actors looking for a quiet life will inevitably focus their attention on 'high politics' (which used to refer to the Empire and foreign affairs) and leave the 'low politics', or relatively unimportant aspects of territorial affairs, to peripheral institutions. Therefore, while the UK government may have the ability to intervene in Scottish politics, 'it is a mistake to equate potential power with actual power' (1983: 29–30). We can see evidence of this autonomy through neglect in the development of the Scottish Office's responsibilities. The Scottish Office also had significant discretion in implementing policy, while the 'Barnett formula' gave it a similar ability to direct spending priorities.

Yet, this autonomy was limited to certain policy areas (such as education) left relatively untouched by the union, and to issues which received minimal central government attention. The Scottish Office was never a particularly innovative political institution and its scope for policy leadership and autonomy was limited (Midwinter *et al.*, 1991: 78). Further, Midwinter *et al.*, describe the Scottish Secretary as

> a relatively junior British Cabinet Minister with limited powers of innovation . . . If Ministerial power is measured by the extent to which a Minister can initiate and implement a policy, then the Scottish Office works within tight constraints. It was never intended to be an innovatory department and performs best in articulating and defending Scotland's interests. (1991: 57)

On the few occasions when the Scottish Office initiated policies it was within strict parameters or due to exceptional circumstances (1991: 57). For Midwinter *et al.*, the phrase 'administrative devolution' was something of a misnomer as it conveyed the idea that the Scottish Office represented a form of self-government:

> In reality the Scottish Office is neither an example of devolution, which would involve a capacity to take authoritative decisions and responsibility to a Scottish constituency, nor merely a form of field administration for UK departments. Rather, it is an example of territorial division of administrative responsibilities, existing alongside the more familiar functional ones. (1991: 61)

The autonomy argument was particularly undermined by the experience of the Thatcher government and the apparent willingness of Conservative ministers to ride roughshod over policies and institutions previously seen as insulated within Scotland. In these circumstances, a more convincing picture of the Scottish Office was as the UK's largest pressure group – that is, a focal point to ensure that Scottish interests presented a united front in negotiations with Whitehall departments. The Scottish Office had a wide range of responsibilities, but was not powerful within Whitehall. It rarely led UK policy and was set up to influence and then implement the policies of other departments (Midwinter *et al.*, 1991; Keating, 2005a; Cairney, 2002).

The modern-day relevance of this story is two-fold. First, changes to Scottish public administration have been piecemeal and incremental over the course of the twentieth century. The important point to note is that there is a significant legacy from the development of the Scottish Office's roles and responsibilities. The recent introduction of a Scottish Parliament in 1999 builds on this established legacy by inheriting rather than choosing its policy responsibilities (such as health, education and social work). Second, the gradual process of public administration reform taken cumulatively did amount to a change in the landscape and terrain of Scottish politics, and this change has been accelerated by political devolution.

The rise of the home-rule agenda + *Political History*

The successful campaign for home rule in Scotland also built on many previous efforts. Indeed, various organizations – such as the Scottish Home Rule Association – have campaigned for Scottish home rule over the course of the past 120 years (Mitchell, 1996a). Although none were successful, they highlight that the campaign for Scottish home rule is not a uniquely modern phenomena. It was also not the sole preserve of the Scottish National Party (SNP) which was formed in 1934 – well after various political interests had been campaigning for home rule.

Mitchell (1996a) identifies four routes to home rule – all of which can be identified in Scotland:

- *The creation of home-rule pressure groups.* In Scotland these included the Scottish Home Rule Association, the Scottish Covenant Association and the Campaign for a Scottish Assembly. After the 1992 Conservative General Election victory Scotland United was established.
- *The establishment of constitutional conventions.* The Scottish Constitutional Convention met between 1989 and 1995 (see Box 2.4). After the 2007 Scottish parliamentary election, the three unionist opposition parties established a Constitutional Commission exploring the potential for more political power for the Scottish Parliament.
- *The use of petitions and referenda.* The Scottish Covenant in 1949 which advocated a Scottish Parliament within the Union had nearly 2 million signatures. The 1979 and 1997 referendums were important landmarks in contemporary Scottish politics.
- *The creation of a political party to campaign for constitutional change.* The SNP is the most obvious party, but perhaps the biggest turning point in contemporary Scottish politics was when the Labour Party fully committed itself to devolution in the 1980s.

When a political consensus amongst three of Scotland's four main political parties, as well as important institutions in Scottish civic society, coalesced around the constitutional convention, Scottish constitutional change became almost inevitable. Indeed, home-rule pressure groups became almost unnecessary as a large majority of Scotland's trade unions, professional associations, local councils, religious organizations all became part of a political movement in favour of devolution.

Yet, this was not always the case. The SNP was until the 1970s Scotland's only political party consistently campaigning for constitutional change. Up until its major breakthrough (in the Hamilton by-election victory in 1967) it campaigned largely unsuccessfully (with the exception of its first seat won in 1945). Until the 1970s Scottish party politics largely mirrored two party British politics. The two main parties – Labour and Conservative (the Scottish Unionist Party until 1965) – dominated elections, between them taking nine out of ten votes (see Chapter 3). The differences between party support north and south of the border were negligible and the push for devolution was not always strong. In part, we can explain this with reference to the welfare state. In the immediate aftermath of the Second World War, the creation of the Welfare State 'had forged a new and significant meaning of Britishness' (McCrone, 2001: 21).

This was also supplemented by the accommodation of Scottish interest within the Union. Although the immediate postwar decade can be viewed as unionism's heyday in Scotland, a key part of unionism as an ideology has been an accommodation of Scottish distinctiveness and difference. In the 1950s the Conservatives (in office at UK level 1951–64) doubled the number of Scottish Office junior ministers from two to four and established the Balfour

Commission to inquire into the workings of government and the management of the Scottish economy. The Commission recognized a 'general deterioration' in the relationship between Scotland and England (Harvie and Jones, 2000: 65). The Labour Party had flirted with the idea of home rule – in 1947 the Scottish Council of the Labour Party endorsed it, in 1958 it rejected it. A recognition of Scottish distinctiveness and difference was therefore already part of the political landscape in the 1950s. *Home rule and Empire Decline*

However, it was in the 1960s that the issue of home rule came to feature more prominently in the Scottish political agenda with the SNP expanding its membership rapidly. The British Empire and economy had been in relative decline in the postwar period (although in absolute terms the economy had continued to grow). The benefits of the union with England were beginning to be more seriously questioned with the British economy faltering relative to its competitors. **Harold Wilson**'s 'white heat of technology' speech in 1963 foreshadowed his 1964–70 administration's emphasis on UK re-modernization. *Build up of pressure*

Harold Wilson: The Labour UK Prime Minister 1964–70 and 1974–76.

Yet, in Scotland the re-modernization agenda fitted quite neatly around the political agenda of constitutional change. The SNP's breakthrough in 1967 marked it as a serious electoral force in Scottish politics and the party made further gains at the 1970 and both 1974 UK General Elections (see Table 3.1). As the SNP were making spectacular electoral gains the two major parties were responding to the perceived demand for constitutional change. In government at the UK level the Labour Party established the Kilbrandon Commission in the late 1960s to look into the constitutional question. Ted Heath, then leader of the Conservative and Unionist Party, announced – in what he called his Declaration of Perth (1968) – a commitment to the establishment of a Scottish Assembly with legislative, deliberative and inquisitorial powers. However, whilst in office between 1970 and 1974 nothing was done as the UK Government awaited the outcome of the Kilbrandon Commission set up by the previous Labour Government.

Secretary of State for Scotland: Prior to devolution, this post carried with it full UK Cabinet status and the individual occupying it was the minister responsible for running the Scottish Office. Post-devolution this minister is responsible for the Scotland Office (located in the UK Department of Constitutional Affairs) with this responsibility shared with another ministerial portfolio.

The Kilbrandon Commission's Report was published in 1973, recommending the establishment of a Scottish Assembly with legislative powers covering the main areas of social policy dealt with by the Scottish Office. However, other policy areas such as law and order and economic development were to remain under the **Secretary of State for Scotland**, who would remain elected through the Westminster Parliament. Moreover, the Secretary of State for Scotland would retain veto powers over Assembly legislation. The Assembly would enjoy no taxation powers and was to be directly elected but through the Westminster first-past-the-post electoral system.

The 1979 referendum   *What was the question?*
Devolution?

In the year after the Commission's report was published there were two General Elections held at UK level. These were the high watermark for the Scottish National Party (see Table 3.1) – at the October 1974 election the party gained over 30 per cent of the vote. SNP success also extended to the 1977 local elections (see Table 4.2) and came in tandem with the breakaway of some Labour MPs (led by Jim Sillars) to form the Scottish Labour Party (the UK Labour Party in Scotland did not change its name to this until the 1990s). The prospect of being defeated by the SNP in Scotland was very real, and therefore the Labour Party which returned to office in 1974 was well-aware of the significance of the home-rule agenda. Further, since it established the Kilbrandon Commission, and the party was compelled to follow through on its recommendations. Yet, there is slim evidence of widespread enthusiastic support at UK cabinet level, its UK National Executive Committee, Scottish Labour Executive or on the backbenches.

A Scotland Bill was introduced into the House of Commons in 1978. Since Scottish backbench support was not particularly enthusiastic (and the original bill had been unsuccessful) the government agreed to retain the full Scottish complement of 71 MPs to secure backbench support and ensure electorate approval of the scheme via a referendum. As the Bill passed through the legislature an amendment was made by Scottish Labour MP George Cunninghame (who was an MP for a London seat) requiring that the proposals be approved by not only a majority of the Scottish voters via a referendum but also 40 per cent of the registered Scottish electorate. In other words, those staying at home would be counted as 'No' voters.

Opinion polls prior to the referendum appeared to suggest that the 'Yes' vote would win comfortably. However, the 'Yes' campaign was divided, with a lack of co-operation amongst the parties in favour. The SNP support was lukewarm, with the party fearing that unqualified support may be seen as a sell-out by the **fundamentalists** within the party (Finlay, 2004: 338). The Scottish Labour Party was divided on the issue, with Labour MPs such as Robin Cook and Tam Dalyell combining with Conservatives in the 'No' campaign. Many constituency Labour Party offices did not actively campaign in favour of a 'Yes' vote. Moreover, the Labour Government was increasingly unpopular. In 1976 the UK Labour Government had been forced to accept a crisis loan of £2,300 million from the International Monetary Fund (IMF) and had implemented drastic cuts in public expenditure

Fundamentalists: Those within the SNP who believe in the 'big bang' approach to independence and are sceptical of devolution as a stepping stone.

Winter of Discontent: The 1978/9 winter period when there was widespread industrial unrest in Britain.

and public-sector wages as a condition of the loan. Therefore, the campaign and referendum took place during the immediate aftermath of widespread strike action and the **Winter of Discontent** which led to the downfall of Prime Minister James Callaghan. It was therefore not a good time to introduce a Labour-led policy whose main effect would be to, 'entrench Labour domination in Scotland through an assembly elected by the first-past-the-post system' (Dardanelli, 2005a: 321).

West Lothian question: Refers to the inability of English MPs to vote on devolved Scottish issues while Scottish MPs can still vote on the equivalent English issues (e.g. health, education, local government).

During the campaign, Tam Dalyell's infamous **West Lothian question** highlighted a series of unresolved constitutional questions of concern to those urging a 'No' vote. They were backed in terms of funding and support by Scotland's largely unionist business community. Overall the 'No' campaign appeared better organized and more coherent as those urging a negative response coalesced under one clear message. The 'Yes' campaign in contrast appeared divided and incoherent, with two separate campaigns run by, and excluding, the SNP.

How does that work for 2014?

The referendum was held on 1 March 1979 with a slim majority voting in favour – see Table 2.1. However, when the result was 'modified' to take into account the Cunninghame amendment, the 40 per cent figure was not achieved – the proportion of the registered electorate in favour was only 32.9 per cent. Despite the SNP launching a 'Scotland said Yes' campaign (which the Labour Party did not support) the agenda of Scottish politics had moved on and devolution slipped off the policy agenda. As Finlay notes,

? how did they get away with this?

> Paradoxically the policy of devolution – which came into existence primarily to stop the SNP – ended up becoming most closely associated with the nationalist party. (2004: 340)

It took the SNP almost a decade to recover. Almost immediately after the referendum campaign the SNP backed a Conservative motion of no confidence in

Table 2.1 *The 1979 devolution referendum result*

	% of votes	*% of electorate*
Yes	51.6	32.8
No	48.4	30.8
Turnout 63.6%		

the Labour Government. This vote was successful and forced a general election. According to the then Prime Minister, James Callaghan, it was like turkeys voting for Christmas. The SNP lost nine of their eleven MPs at the subsequent election, and home rule disappeared off the Scottish political agenda.

The Conservative years, 1979–97

On 3 May 1979, the election of a Thatcher-led Conservative Party marked the beginning of 18 years of Conservative rule at Westminster. At the UK level, the party secured its biggest majority of seats over Labour since 1935. In Scotland the party's support went up from 24.7 per cent to 31.4 per cent and it elected 22 MPs in Scotland – one of only two blips in an otherwise downward trajectory since the 1950s. Even the defeated Labour Party's share of the vote increased in Scotland – from 36.3 to 41.5 per cent. This was mainly due to the SNP vote collapsing from 30.4 per cent to 17.3 per cent (see Table 3.1).

Thatcherism: The personality, governing style or ideology underpinning Margaret Thatcher's term as UK Prime Minister 1979–90.

A lot has been written about **Thatcherism** and its impact on Scottish politics in the 1980s and its enduring legacy today. As Finlay observes, 'In popular Scottish mythology, the eighties match the thirties as the Devil's decade' (2004: 341). Non-Conservative Scottish politicians are fond of citing factory/shipyard/pit closures, mass unemployment, the poll tax, industrial unrest, attacks on local government, unwanted NHS marketization, a **democratic deficit** and the like. The images conjured up of Scottish politics in the 1980s is almost uniformly negative. In a sense the case made for devolution in this decade was also negative – home rule would solve the democratic deficit and prevent a London UK government imposing its will on Scotland. Scottish devolution therefore represented 'unfinished business', and a Scottish assembly could have 'defended Scotland from Thatcherism' (McCrone and Lewis, 1999: 17).

Democratic deficit: Term used in Scottish politics in the 1980s and 1990s to refer to the fact that the governing Conservative party only achieved minority representation in Scotland.

The size of the democratic deficit in Scotland increased as the decline of the Conservative Party in Scottish politics accelerated. In 1987 the party only returned 10 MPs to Westminster and much of its demise resulted from a combination of factors:

- Economic/industrial policies that left Scotland's manufacturing and industrial base to contend with the ill-wind of market forces without any intervention.
- The collapse of the residual Protestant working-class unionist vote and the appeal of unionism as a political ideology.

- The combination of increasing identification with Scottish nationality and the growing perception of the Conservatives as an English party.
- Poor territorial management and a new 'unitarism' in unionist outlook – that is, the notion that all parts of the UK be subject to similar policies, rather than the accommodation of Scottish difference.
- A policy agenda of tax-cutting, public-sector retrenchment and marketization perceived as alien and out of sync with the Scottish electorate's more **egalitarian** philosophy.
- Thatcher's failure to convince the Scottish middle classes (in sufficient electoral numbers) of the utility of her government's policies, with the Conservative electoral strategy perceived as most relevant to the South of England.
- The policy-making style of the Thatcher Government was contrary to the well-established consultative approach where the Scottish Office would allow various sectional interests of civic Scotland opportunity to impress their views on government.

Egalitarian: A belief in the desirability of political, social and economic equality.

During the Thatcher era the Scottish Labour Party re-established itself as Scotland's dominant political party. Even during the 1983 General Election when Gerald Kaufman referred to the Labour Party's

---

Box 2.2   The poll tax

The poll tax is a classic case study of how *not* to make public policy and is rightly regarded as an unmitigated policy disaster (see Butler *et al.*, 1994). The poll tax (or 'community charge' as it was officially called) was introduced to replace rates (based on the notional rental value of a house) as the local taxation used to fund local government. In the early 1980s, UK central–local government relations were marked by high-profile confrontations between metropolitan left-wing local authorities and the right-wing central government. The Thatcher government was concerned with excessive local expenditure and believed that compelling local councils to set a high profile 'community charge' for local services could help control their spending. It was hoped that high tax/spending (generally Labour) councils would be punished at the ballot box, while low spending (generally Conservative) councils would be 'rewarded'. All adults would be forced to pay the same level of tax (even the unemployed/students were compelled to pay 20%) regardless of ability to pay. When it was implemented, the fees that councils charged were far in excess of original estimates and polls suggest that voters blamed central government rather than their local council for the high level of new tax. In Scotland all of this was compounded by the fact that it was implemented a year early. The poll tax was 'the ultimate symbol of the Thatcherite imposition of unpopular policies on a reluctant nation' (Finlay, 2004: 362). It played a significant part in the downfall of Thatcher as Prime Minister and was replaced with council tax by her successor John Major.

manifesto as 'the longest suicide note in history' the party was still the 'winner' in terms of votes and seats in Scotland. While at the UK level the Labour Party only achieved 25 per cent of the vote (only 2% ahead of the SDP/Liberal Alliance), in Scotland it achieved 35 per cent, making it still the largest party even though this represented its lowest share of the Scottish vote since 1922. The real turning point came after the 1987 General Election and the re-election of Thatcher, despite a further collapse of the Conservative Party's vote in Scotland. Few would disagree that this collapse was caused by the fallout from the poll tax, with the poll tax rebellions re-igniting the devolution issue in the late 1980s (see former Secretary of State for Scotland, Ian Lang's account, 2002: 172). The campaign in Scotland was dominated by accusations that Scotland was being used as a guinea pig (the poll tax was implemented one year ahead of England and Wales) – see Box 2.2.

The Scottish Constitutional Convention, 1989–95

The widely predicted 1987 election result was the 'doomsday scenario' for home rule campaigners – the Conservative Party was re-elected despite its declining vote in Scotland. Scotland returned fifty Labour MPs who pledged to prevent the worst excesses of the Thatcherite philosophy impacting on Scotland. The political reality of the Westminster system of **majoritarian democracy** was that they were pretty powerless to do anything. In light of their weakness within Parliament, home rule campaigners sought to create extra-parliamentary pressure on the Thatcher Government.

Majoritarian democracy: A democratic system which prioritizes the will of the majority. The label is often used to refer to countries using the first-past-the-post electoral system (despite the fact that it often elects leaders/governments without a majority of the votes cast).

A Scottish Constitutional Convention (SCC) was established in 1989 (see Box 2.3). It was in reality a collection of interests who sought a middle way between the Conservative Party's uncompromising unreformed unionism and the SNP's independence. The Constitutional Convention claimed Scottish sovereignty rested with the Scottish people rather than the Crown in Parliament. This was designed to challenge the traditional Westminster argument that sovereignty lay with the UK Parliament. It ran from 1989 to 1995 with the involvement of Labour, Liberal Democrats, Ecology (renamed Green) parties as well as representatives from the Scottish Trade Union Congress, Scottish Council for Voluntary Organizations, religious leaders, local authorities and a wide range of civic organizations. According to one of its key opponents at the time, the SCC came 'to form part of that congealing consensus that presaged constitutional change and eventually form(ed) part of the foundation of such change' (Lang, 2002: 174).

Box 2.3   The Scottish Constitutional Convention

The Scottish Constitutional Convention was convened between 1989 and 1995; it asserted the sovereign right of the Scottish people to determine Scotland's form of government. Membership included the Labour Party, Scottish Liberal Democrats, Scottish Democratic Left, Orkney and Shetland Movement, Scottish Green Party, Scottish Trade Union Congress, Regional, District and Island Councils, the main Scottish Churches, the Federation of Small Businesses, ethnic minority representatives and the Scottish Women's Forum. The Convention sought to reach decision by consensus. It published its final report *Scotland's Parliament: Scotland's Right* in 1995, and argued for:

- A proportional electoral system with a Scottish Parliament of 129 members.
- An electoral contract with parties aiming for an equal representation of men and women
- A parliament with different working arrangements than Westminster including fixed terms, extensive consultation, and normal business hours, with standing orders underpinned with the principles of openness; accessibility; and accountability.
- A special declaration by the Westminster Parliament that it will not remove or amend the Scottish Parliament without consulting directly the people of Scotland and the Scottish Parliament itself.

The SCC sought to popularize the idea of home rule amongst the Scottish electorate as well and engineer elite and cross-party support in favour of devolution. It published two sets of proposals *Towards Scotland's Parliament* in 1990, and *Scotland's Parliament, Scotland's Right* in 1995. The proposals were given democratic legitimacy by the fact that a wide range of organizations were involved in their drafting, and all signed up to them. The SCC and its consensual style of operation are the roots of notions of 'new politics' in post devolution Scotland.

Its first report, *Towards Scotland's Parliament*, was published prior to the 1992 election. It was widely anticipated that Labour would win the 1992 UK Election and devolution could be implemented. However, the John Major-led Conservatives won again and there was even a minor recovery of Conservative support in Scotland with 11 seats gained. The Conservatives had campaigned by extolling the benefits of the union. The SNP vote rose again but never enough for them to gain any significant breakthrough. Their campaign slogan 'Free by '93' was hopelessly unrealistic and was used by their opponents to deride them at election counts in 1992.

After the 1992 election there were calls for mass extra-parliamentary action by MPs such as John McAllion. New pressure groups (such as *Scotland United*) sprung up and held large-scale demonstrations in Scotland's cities. The Scottish Office engaged in a 'Taking Stock' exercise. However, little changed beyond public relations spin, minor tinkerings with the Westminister Scottish Committee structure and the symbolic return of the Stone of Destiny to Scotland. Instead, the Conservative government published *Scotland and the Union: A Partnership for Good* extolling the benefits Scotland received from the union.

Therefore, the 'toll' or cumulative experience of 18 years of Conservative rule must be understood and appreciated – it is possibly the most salient factor in explaining the high public support for devolution. As Finlay has argued:

> The attack on British institutions such as the Health Service, comprehensive education, the mixed economy, and nationalized industries went down like a lead balloon in Scotland . . . and it can be argued that such institutions were a major factor in shoring up a sense of British identity in the past. (2001a: 249)

The 1997 referendum

Pressure for devolution intensified after 1992; the then Labour leader John Smith famously referred to it as 'the settled will of the Scottish people'. This support continued under Tony Blair and the Labour Party in 1995 proposed a two-question referendum. This would not only defuse the Tories' 'tartan tax' 1992 General Election campaign sound-bite (a reference to the Parliament's ability to raise income tax by 3p) but also give popular legitimacy to a subsequent devolution bill in Westminster. The UK General Election in 1997 resulted in a Labour landslide victory and in Scotland the Conservative Party won no seats and only 15.6 per cent of the vote – their lowest share since 1865 (see Table 3.1, p. 48). Plans were put in place almost immediately for the two-question referendum.

The 1997 campaign was in marked contrast to that of 1979. The 'Yes, Yes' campaign was well-funded, organized and united. All of the Scottish leaders from the parties in favour of constitutional change (Donald Dewar Labour, Alex Salmond SNP and Jim Wallace Liberal Democrats) campaigned under one umbrella group – Scotland Forward. The 'Yes, Yes' campaign was also buoyed by its association with a popular Labour Government and a feeling within Labour that the SCC had addressed most of the constitutional questions which dogged the 1979 campaign. In contrast, the 'No, No' campaign was dominated by the increasingly unpopular Scottish Conservatives and led by arch-unionist Donald Findlay through the 'Think Twice' organization. In contrast to 1979 it was poorly funded and amateurish – it was symbolic of the decline of unionism as a significant ideology in Scottish politics.

The result was inevitable. Significant majorities voted 'Yes' to both questions (see Table 2.2). Significantly, all parts of Scotland voted 'Yes' overall and the vote would have been enough to pass Cunninghame's 40 per cent

Table 2.2   *The 1997 referendum result*

	%	%
Support for a Scottish Parliament	74.3	25.7
Support for taxation powers	63.3	36.4
Turnout 60.2%		

threshold had it still been in force. On the taxation question, only in Orkney and Dumfries and Galloway did the majority vote against.

The election and referendum in 1997 marked the culmination of three decades during which the constitutional issue dominated Scottish politics. It was also a period when Scottish political behaviour began to depart significantly from that in England. Although opinion polls (see Chapter 4) have tended to show little difference between English and Scottish public attitudes to many issues, electoral behaviour has departed significantly. Moreover, the Scottish political agenda increasingly evolved in a different direction – the ideological support for unionism and Britain (at least as a unitary state) evaporated. As McCrone argues, Scotland appears to have outgrown its junior partner role in the union (2001: 28). The notion of Scotland as a potential unit of political governance in Europe appeared more viable by the 1990s (see Box 2.4).

As unionism declined as an ideology (see Box 2.5), nationalism has grown and there appears to have been some re-defining in what it means to be 'Scottish'. From 1979, notions of **social democracy**, egalitarianism and being collectivist in outlook were invoked as Scottish traits which were opposite to the dominant ideology of the then Thatcher Government. As Mitchell (2005) has noted, the period from 1979 to 1997 allowed anyone or institution opposed to the Conservative Party to coalesce under one umbrella.

Social democracy: A moderate left-of-centre political ideology with an emphasis on collectivist solutions to political issues.

The Conservative Party in Government became an 'Other' which mobilized a political base around support for devolution. The 1980s and 1990s also witnessed an increasing divergence of Scottish political parties, electoral behaviour, policy agenda and institutions from the UK. Scottish political attitudes and values were deemed different from those of Thatcher and 'middle England'. As Mitchell observes,

In essence Scottish home rule came about when what was perceived to be distinctive about Scottish politics was perceived to be under threat. Ironically, much of this Scottish base was British-made. Whether in the

Box 2.4   Scotland as a case study in the European Union and beyond?

Dardanelli (2005a) rejects the idea that the 1979 referendum failed because it was associated with an unpopular Labour Government and a poor campaign. He also questions the argument that the 1997 result succeeded following the 'democratic deficit' and dissatisfaction with a UK Conservative Government. Rather, the key difference was a shift in public attitudes to Europe. In 1979 there was greater public concern about devolution as a stepping stone to independence and this led to many supporters of devolution voting 'No'. Following the shift of the SNP's strategy to 'Independence in Europe' and a more positive public perception of the EU, the 'fear of secession' largely disappeared and supporters of devolution voted 'Yes'. Dardanelli (2005b: 1) links the Scottish experience to a wider EU picture: greater levels of integration within the European Union have increased demands for 'regional self-government' within Member States. In this context, Scotland makes an 'ideal test case' since, 'the establishment of the Scottish Parliament is . . . arguably the highest-profile case of demand for self-government at regional level in Europe'.

Keating (2001) extends a similar discussion to Catalonia within the EU and Quebec within the North American Free Trade Agreement. He finds a common desire among the public for a form of regional autonomy within a wider system of government. He suggests that as the world changes, so to does the meaning of phrases such as 'nation', 'national identity' and 'nationalism'. Since people may define their identity in terms of regions (for example, Scotland), states (UK) and beyond (EU), then referendums based on campaigns which exaggerate a stark choice between independence and integration are asking the wrong question. A form of pragmatic nationalism is also apparent in regions such as Wales and Flanders. Keating (2004b) suggests that trends in globalization and growing uncertainty about the idea of a nation state as the sole source of formal authority has led many nationalists to seek a form of regional self-government stopping short of the demands for a state. This is reflected in campaigns for devolution which do not see independence as the logical next step.

Welfare state: A set of government programmes that attempt to provide economic, health and social security for the population.

form of the policy-making institutions, the **welfare state** or the ideology of welfare state and state intervention, what came to be seen as under threat had been a very British creation. Home rulers were mobilized in defence of very British institutions but saw their protection lying in distinctly Scottish terms. (Mitchell, 2005: 25)

The reality was that for all the talk of 'the democratic will of the Scottish people' and the like the motivation for devolution and the creation of a devolved Scottish Parliament was not quite as it has been dressed up by home-rule campaigners. The key to motivating support for devolution was that it was

Box 2.5   Unionism and Scottish politics

Unionism is a political ideology that was once so dominant in Scottish politics that support for the union with England in the nineteenth century was taken for granted. The heyday for unionism was the immediate postwar period – the British Empire, the Second World War and the creation of the Welfare State all gave very real meaning to what it meant to be British and unionist. However a combination of the end of the Empire, the relative economic decline of Britain, the rise of Scottish nationalist sentiment, the collapse of protestant working-class electoral support for the Conservative and Unionist Party and the UK Government's (in particular during the Thatcher era) lack of sensitivity to the needs of territorial management have seen unionism in retreat. In recent decades, defenders of Britain and the union have had to mount vigorous campaigns extolling their alleged benefits. Interestingly more of their emphasis tends to go on the alleged costs of breaking up the union than the union's benefits. In one of the strange quirks of post-devolution politics, the UK Prime Minister Gordon Brown has gone from Scottish home-rule campaigner in the 1990s to campaigning for 'renewed Britishness' and arch-unionist in 2007. The election of the SNP in 2007 has also increased the significance of a 'unionist alliance' in the Scottish Parliament as a means to undermine the prospect of a referendum bill on independence.

a way to retain the union but deflect unwanted policies a right-of-centre UK government wanted to impose (Finlay, 2004b: 368). This also ties in with a broader comparative picture on national identities linked to the welfare state. In this case, the postwar welfare state gave a sense of social and economic security to its citizens and provided an incentive to stay within the Union. Without this security (following 'welfare retrenchment') and protection from 'the risks and uncertainties of the market', the benefits of UK-wide political structures were less apparent and territorial identities more difficult to manage (McEwen, 2006: 16). Therefore, seeking the maintenance of a welfare state and territorial representation became complementary aims.

The Scottish media

Although we can debate the relative autonomy of the media in Scotland, it is clear that it played a key role in the fuelling of expectations for new politics during the campaign for home rule. This may explain why many sections of the print media are now so quick to criticize the new political institutions in Scotland. The media are of course crucial in politics not least because they are the 'space in which politics is communicated' to the wider public (Schlesinger et al., 2001: 259). In the modern era of political spin, image and communication, the **old and new media**, are of undoubted importance. The media also tend to play a crucial role in the way alleged political scandals are reported and

Old and new media: Old media are the mainstream broadcasters (e.g. BBC, STV) and newspapers (e.g. *Daily Record, Scotsman*). New Media refers to the outputs of new information and communication technologies such as online sites, podcasts and blogs.

could be said to have played a significant role in the downfall of Scotland's second First Minister, Henry McLeish (see Box 2.6).

All political leaders recognize the political power wielded by the media. The mass media, combined with the education system, are key filters of information which substantially influence the way people perceive politics. The media can set the agenda through its dictation of headline news stories. However, in recent years the proliferation of the new media with digital and satellite television and online sources has disaggregated 'the media'. In a sense the free and diverse media in Scotland enable a wide and unrestricted pluralistic expression of views which is usually seen as good for the health of Scottish democracy. The media also tend to be viewed, along with parliament, as having the potential to keep the executive branch of government in check and call it to account.

Media coverage of Scottish politics inevitably tends to simplify politics – it seeks to find and report the 'facts' of a particular event. It projects a simplified and personalized view of politics, often reporting as if one individual (for example, the First Minister) controls this plethora of organizations that is 'Scottish Government', ignoring its disaggregation and complexity (see Chapter 7). The focus tends to be on the personalities and preferences of key decision-makers. There are, of course, instances in Scottish politics when the personalities and preferences of individual politicians are crucial variables in an explanation of events, but students of Scottish politics should be aware of the simplifications associated with this journalistic narrative.

One of the most evident consequences of devolution has been the shift in the media coverage of Scottish politics; coverage is now almost exclusively

---

Box 2.6   Post-devolution alleged political scandals: Lobbygate, Officegate, Warkgate

Ever since the Watergate scandal during President Nixon's presidency in the United States, the media coverage of many alleged political scandals tends to be suffixed with 'gate'. Scotland is no exception. 'Lobbygate' was a lobbying scandal, and the first in post-devolution Scotland with lobbyists (including the son of John Reid MP) offering clients insider-access to the corridors of political power in Scotland. 'Officegate' led to the downfall of Scotland's second First Minister, Henry McLeish; it was associated with the office expenses being claimed during his time as a Westminster parliamentarian. 'Warkgate' refers to the close association Scotland's then First Minister, Jack McConnell, had with the BBC journalist Kirsty Wark and her husband.

focused on the activities of the First Minister, Scottish Government and Parliament. Edinburgh – with the Parliament, Executive, political journalists, lobby firms and interest groups now resembling a mini-Westminster – has become the focus of both political print and broadcast journalists in the Scottish media. The Scottish MPs in Westminster (beyond those with UK Cabinet status) are barely covered by the national media, despite the fact that broadcasting is a reserved function under the terms of the Scotland (1998) Act.

Television and radio broadcasters in Scotland are bound by charter to show balance and impartiality in coverage of political parties. The only exceptions are party-political and election broadcasts. Despite this Scotland's minority parties often complain of a broadcasting bias towards the four major parties. STV, Grampian and Border television are three ITV franchises which cover Scotland, while BBC Scotland's autonomy from London is limited by its scale and budget. It does 'opt-out' of the *Newsnight* programme at 11 pm for 20 minutes but there are ongoing accusations of excessive BBC centralism and metropolitan bias with events on the Scottish periphery not placed highly enough on the BBC's UK national news agenda. This issue was raised by First Minister Alex Salmond in 2007 when he described the BBC as 'hideously White City' (referring to the location of the BBC's base in London). It was also addressed by the BBC's Director General who planned to increase Scotland's proportion of BBC output from 3 per cent to 9 per cent (BBC News, 2007).

Table 2.3   *Newspaper sales in Scotland*

Daily newspapers	Average sales (April 2007)	Sunday newspapers	Average sales (April 2007)
The Sun	402,706	Sunday Mail	464,918
Daily Record	370,286	News of the World	370,286
Daily Mail	124,689	Sunday Post	295,331
Daily Star	93,346	Mail on Sunday	113,600
Daily Express	78,504	Sunday Times	72,255
The Herald	71,262	Scotland on Sunday	67,881
Scotsman	57,079	Sunday Herald	55,668
Mirror	34,928	Sunday Express	47,881
The Times (London)	27,806*	Sunday Mirror	31,775
Daily Telegraph	25,033*	Daily Star – Sunday	30,467
The Guardian	16,083*	Sunday Telegraph	24,849
* Figures based on March 2007; April figures not available		The People	24,031
		The Observer	21,031

Source: Data from http://www.allmediascotland.com

Newspapers are often vehemently partisan in their coverage of Scottish politics, evident not only in editorial and comment columns but in the actual news content and how it is reported. Any student of Scottish politics should be cautious when reading 'insider accounts'. The Scottish political village is a very small one with much interpersonal linkage between politicians, policy advisers and journalists. From a political-science perspective one could argue that this detracts from the sense of perspective and detachment necessary to provide objective analysis. This is obviously what Mitchell is hinting at when he argues,

> There is a lot being written about Scottish politics today but too much of it resembles the work of Scottish sports journalists: writers are all too often fans with typewriters. (2001: 222)

At election time – and in particular on election day – the tabloids become almost comical in their bias (see Box 2.7). However, there is a chicken-and-egg problem of what comes first? It is difficult to disentangle cause and effect – it could be that readers select a paper to fit their politics and papers follow an editorial bias to attract particular types of reader (see Newton and Brynin, 2001). In any case tabloid sales, although high in comparison to other Western European countries, are falling. Moreover, their political coverage is being trimmed and it could be that in the age of the new media their influence (and many voters may only detect this subliminally) is waning.

The Scottish print media has had a notorious unionist bias. Save for a very brief period in the early 1990s when the *Scottish Sun* supported independence, no major Scottish newspaper has supported the SNP. However, by the 1990s the Scottish press were almost unanimously in favour of the establishment of a parliament in Edinburgh. During the first Scottish Parliamentary election campaign in 1999 the SNP were so frustrated with the negative coverage that they launched their own free newspaper during the campaign. The SNP have often complained about the London metropolitan bias in news reporting, with the main news bulletins still coming from London.

Media bias may of course not be simply about party politics; feminists, for example, often complain that the portrayal of female politicians can be sexist. It may also reflect a class bias with the coverage of political issues dominated by élite opinion, issues and agendas to the neglect of the issues which concern the socially and politically excluded.

Newspaper sales in Scotland depart significantly from those in England. Around 90 per cent of the newspapers read in Scotland are produced in Scotland (Finlay, 2004: 378). The best-selling tabloid is the same but the *Scottish Sun* is a different newspaper than its counterpart south of the border – and its sales have been inflated with subsidized low cover prices. Scottish newspapers (*Sunday Mail, Daily Record, The Herald, Scotsman, Scotland on Sunday, Sunday Herald*) which sell negligible numbers of copies in England are very prominent in the Scottish sales charts. In the past couple of decades, virtually all of the

---

Box 2.7   The tabloid media in Scotland

Bias at the 2007 Scottish Election

The Sun, 3 May 2007
Front page:
Headline: 'VOTE SNP TODAY AND YOU PUT SCOTLAND'S HEAD IN THE NOOSE'
Sub-Headings: HIGHER TAXES, JOBS ON THE LINE, DEATH OF THE UNION, DEFENCE IN CHAOS
Page 4–5 had '10 Reasons to be Fearful' with the editorial on page 6 declaring 'Only Labour can save us from a living nightmare!'

Daily Record, 3 May 2007
Front page:
Headline: Today's election is *not* about war in Iraq. It is *not* about Tony Blair. It *is* about who will run Scotland. It *is* about schools, hospitals and law and order. Do *not* sleepwalk into independence. Do *not* let a protest vote break up Britain. THINK ABOUT IT.
Pages 6, 7, 8 and 9 referred to 'COCKY Alex Salmond', had a map of 'ESTIMATED JOBS LOST/AT RISK (OVER 200,000!), an editorial urging readers 'Do note vote for Alex Salmond today' and a page urging readers to vote tactically in 10 seats (including a recommendation to Vote Tory in two of them).

The unionist tabloid media bias was not so apparent in 1992 when the *Scottish Sun* re-launched itself under the banner headline (with a Scottish Saltire in the background) RISE AND BE A NATION AGAIN – the paper announcing its (short-lived) conversion to the cause of Scottish independence. Both the *Daily Record* and the *Scottish Sun* have regularly sought to proclaim their Scottishness with advertising slogans such as '*Real* Scots Read The *Record*' and 'Standing Up for Scotland'. The *Scottish Sun* had a thistle on its mast-head for a number of years.

British newspapers tend to produce Scottish supplements or print editions. This has meant the non-Scottish editions either ignore Scottish issues or criticize the subsidies that English taxpayers effectively give to Scotland (Daily Mail, 2007). Either way, this accentuates the division between the 'UK' and 'Scottish' media.

Conclusion

In summary, this chapter has sought to provide an outline of the context of contemporary Scottish politics by highlighting both the historical legacy as well as the manner in which it is portrayed in the media. The development of administrative devolution in the form of the Scottish Office helps us understand from where the current division of reserved and non-reserved responsibilities emerged (see Chapter 8). As Mitchell (2003a: 2) argues, the Scottish Office is important not only to discussions of Scottish public administration, but also to explanations of Scottish nationalism. It encouraged a conception of Scotland as a political as well as a cultural entity. Scotland's unique political arrangements also gave rise to the pre-devolution debate about whether Scotland could be considered a political system.

The chapter has also highlighted the landmarks of the constitutional referendums in 1979 and 1997, highlighting the very different contexts in which both were played out. There is no doubt that the experience of the Conservative administrations in the 1980s and 1990s left an indelible mark on contemporary Scottish politics. Home rule became popular not solely because the population wished to express its Scottish political identity – it was also a convenient way of ensuring that unpopular policies which did not appeal to the Scottish electorate could no longer be imposed from London. The agenda of Scottish politics has increasingly diverged from that of Westminister and this increased desire for autonomy has parallels in other areas such as Catalonia in Spain and Quebec in Canada.

These developments have all been tracked by a media in Scotland which is becoming more distinctive and more likely to focus on the new institutions of Scotland. Yet, perhaps worryingly, the attitude of the media towards devolution has been negative. A key focus within the remainder of this book is to find out why. Does this negativity reflect a degree of failure of new political institutions and processes to live up to the ideal of new politics? And, if so, is this because a wide range of supporters of devolution (including the media) fuelled these expectations to a level that could never be met in practice?

Further reading

For general accounts of Scottish political history see Kemp (1993), Mitchell (1996c), Hutchison (2000), McCrone (2001), Fry (1987), Finlay (1997; 2001; 2004) and Paterson (1994). For accounts of the contemporary period see Marr (1992), Brown *et al.* (1997), Kellas (1988), Midwinter *et al.* (1991) and Bennie *et al.* (1995). For the 1979 and 1997 Referendums see Balsom and McAllister (1979), Bochel and Denver (1981), Denver *et al.* (2000) and Surridge and McCrone (1999). For analysis which places Scotland in a wider comparative context see Dardanelli (2005a; 2005b) and Keating (2001; 2004a; 2004b). For the Scottish media see Schlesinger (2000; 2004) Schlesinger *et al.* (2001), Garside (2002) and Smith (1994),

Online sources

Broadcasters:
http://www.smg.plc.uk
http://www.allmediascotland.com
http://www.bbc.co.uk/scotland/

Print media:
The Herald   http://www.theherald.co.uk/
The Scotsman   http://www.scotsman.com
Holyrood Magazine   http://www.holyroodmag.com/
BBC Scotland   http://www.bbc.co.uk/scotland/
Guardian devolved politics key links   http://politics.guardian.co.uk/
    devolvedpolitics/page/0,9136,442584,00.html
Daily Record   http://www.dailyrecord.co.uk/
Scotland on Sunday   http://www.scotlandonsunday.com/
Sunday Herald   http://www.sundayherald.com
The Press and Journal   http://www.thisisnorthscotland.co.uk
Dundee Courier   http://www.dcthomson/courier

Chapter 3

Scotland's Political Parties

The architects of new politics were critical of one-party dominance and the adversarial role that political parties played in Westminster. Yet, parties are key institutions which perform vital functions in Scottish politics, such as educating the public, providing choice and establishing a democratic link between the government and the governed (see Box 3.1). Political parties

---

Box 3.1   Key roles of political parties in Scotland

Interest aggregation. Parties serve as cohesive disciplined organizations with a card-carrying membership base. They tend to be broad coalitions – the glue that holds them together tends to be a broad commitment to a shared ideology. Their attachment to the wider electorate is, however, far looser and electoral loyalty has become weaker.

Electoral machines. They make electoral democracy work by publishing manifestos and inviting the electorate to make choices based on them. They input into the machinery of government the wishes of the Scottish electorate (although if recent electoral turnout figures are an indicator the parties are performing poorly).

Democratic linkage. Parties link Scotland's citizens to their governmental institutions, facilitating accountability and legitimacy in the Scottish Government, Parliament and local councils. They select, recruit, train and socialize the individuals who 'staff' these organizations. It has often been stated that the Parliament has been crucial in re-establishing the legitimacy of the outputs of government in Scotland.

Education. Parties inform the electorate of key political issues through policy announcements, debate in the chamber, press releases, media appearances and online sites.

Participation. Parties allow people to engage with democracy by becoming party members. As party members they can play roles in candidate selection, party policy and campaigning. However, the major political parties in Scotland have had declining memberships in recent years, with the number of activists falling significantly.

Policy-making. Once elected, Scotland's political parties (if they gain office) are keys to determining the legislative and policy outputs of the Scottish Parliament and Government. Parties in general tend to promote and establish coherence and stability in political systems by staffing the governmental and policy-making institutions.

Elite recruitment and socialization. Parties prepare candidates for elected office – they are the avenues through which ambitious politicians must travel to hold positions of influence in UK or Scottish Government.

---

were the mobilizing device of politics in the twentieth century, drawing millions of people into national policy processes (Hague and Harrop, 2001: 167).

The party system in Scotland has been significantly different from the UK for some time. As Brown *et al.* argue,

> Party labels (north and south of the border) may be similar but their histories and agendas are quite different, and increasingly so . . . the political parties in Scotland cannot be taken as British parties writ small. (Brown *et al.*, 1997: 117)

Devolution has accelerated these differences and the Scottish party system today is fundamentally different from the UK level. This has a number of aspects. First, the Scottish arms of major UK parties (Labour, Conservative, Liberal Democrat) have developed their own decision-making processes. Second, Scotland has a multi-party system which differs significantly from the two-party system we see in the UK. Third, most parties in the Scottish Parliament appear to be left-of-centre parties, in contrast to Westminster which has a significant right-of-centre Conservative presence. This chapter seeks to explain these developments by outlining a contemporary history of Scotland's six major political parties. It then explores Scotland's changing party system before examining contemporary trends in party organization and outlook.

Scottish Political Parties

Scottish National Party

The SNP achieved governmental status for the first time in May 2007; its '*raison d'être*' is a territorial demand for Scottish independence. The SNP is a relatively young political party formed in 1934 (see Mitchell, 1990b, 1996a; and Lynch, 2002b on the history of the SNP). For the first few decades of its existence it was little more than an unsuccessful minority political movement. After over 30 years of struggle (which saw only one Motherwell by-election win in 1945) its first glimpse of potential occurred in the 1960s. In the 1960s the SNP as a party had expanded rapidly – between 1962 and 1968 party membership increased from 2000 to 120,000 and the number of SNP branches rose from 40 in 1962 to near 500 in 1968, comfortably exceeding Labour (Hutchison, 2001: 119).

However, its major breakthrough came in the 1967 Hamilton by-election when it gained a Westminster parliamentary seat. Like many by-election victories in UK politics it proved a one-off – the seat was regained by Labour at the 1970 General Election. However, it was at that General

Election that SNP gains elsewhere signalled its status as a genuine electoral force in Scottish politics. At a time of worldwide economic slowdown and the end of the 'Golden Age' of postwar economic expansion in Western Europe, the discovery of North Sea oil was used by the nationalists to appeal the Scottish electorate. In the 1970s the SNP used the slogan 'It's Scotland's Oil' to argue that if the Scottish electorate voted for an independent Scotland the new oil revenue streams could be utilized to reinvigorate the Scottish economy, contribute to improved public services and secure Scotland's future.

At the first three General Elections of the 1970s the party added around 10 percentage points to its vote at each one, peaking at 30.4 per cent in October 1974 (see Table 3.1). For a brief period in the mid-1970s it looked as if it would usurp the Labour Party in Scotland. However, this breakthrough was never reflected in the number of seats won – its share of the vote translated into only 11 seats due to the perversities of the first-past-the-post electoral system. This was followed by a huge loss of votes and the loss of nine seats in the 1979 General Election (see Chapter 2). The fall-out from this defeat was a period of in fighting, retrenchment and stagnation for the SNP (see Box 3.2). As McEwan observes, 'The Thatcher years were dominated, first by a period of bitter internal division and disillusionment, and later by a period of consolidation and recovery' (2002: 50).

Table 3.1   *General election results: number of seats (% votes) won in Scotland, 1945–2005*

Elections	Labour		Cons		LibDem		SNP	
	seats	(%)	seats	(%)	seats	(%)	seats	(%)
1945	37	47.6	27	41.1	0	5.0	0	1.2
1950	37	46.2	32	44.8	2	6.6	0	0.4
1951	35	47.9	35	48.6	1	2.7	0	0.3
1955	34	46.7	36	50.1	1	1.9	0	0.5
1959	38	46.7	31	47.2	1	4.1	0	0.8
1964	43	48.7	24	40.6	4	7.6	0	2.4
1966	46	49.9	20	37.7	5	6.8	0	5.0
1970	44	44.5	23	38.0	3	5.5	0	11.4
1974 (Feb)	41	36.6	21	32.9	3	7.9	7	21.9
1974 (Oct)	41	36.3	16	24.7	3	8.3	11	30.4
1979	44	41.5	22	31.4	3	9.0	2	17.3
1983	41	35.1	21	28.4	8	24.5	2	11.8
1987	50	42.4	10	24.0	9	19.4	3	11.0
1992	49	39.0	11	25.6	9	13.1	3	21.5
1997	56	45.6	0	17.5	10	13.0	6	22.1
2001	55	43.2	1	15.6	10	16.4	5	20.1
2005	41	39.5	1	15.8	11	22.6	6	17.7

The 79 group: A group within the SNP set up in 1979 committed to moving the SNP leftward in ideological profile, in an effort to make serious inroads in the heartlands of the Labour Party in Scotland – the heavily populated and industrialized central belt.

In the late 1970s, the dis-bandment of the short-lived Scottish Labour Party (not to be confused with the present Scottish Labour Party) led by Jim Sillars led to an influx of left-wingers into the SNP and the creation of **The 79 group** within it (whose members were expelled from the party for a brief period). During this period, the party was an eclectic mix of right-of-centre traditionalists and left-of-centre social democrats and thus difficult to pin down on the **ideological spectrum**. In the late 1980s the party was part of the 'Can Pay, Won't Pay' anti-poll tax campaign (see Box 2.4). The poll tax issue dominated Scottish politics in the late 1980s and it was during this period that the party's electoral fortunes appeared to take an upswing. However, Jim Sillars' Govan by-election victory in 1988 proved to be yet another false dawn and the SNP failed to make any significant breakthrough at the 1992 UK General Election.

Ideological spectrum: A broad (and often vague) continuum used to classify political opinions. Although opinions vary across time and country, left-wing may refer to a greater belief in state intervention, the welfare state, redistribution as a form of equal outcome, workers' rights and social determinants of crime; right wing may refer to a small state, equality of opportunity rather than outcome and individual responsibility for crime.

It was only once Alex Salmond became leader (or National Convener) in 1990 that the SNP's status as a social democratic party became clearer. McEwan (2002) credits Salmond with giving the SNP a clear ideological profile that it had previously lacked. It has rooted itself on the centre-left of the ideological spectrum, with its social democratic policy platform providing the coherency necessary to reinforce its, 'credibility as an alternative to Labour in Scotland' (McEwan, 2002: 54).

The SNP's fundamental aim has always been the creation of an independent, sovereign Scottish state. However, despite a shared commitment to that aim, the party's members, activists and parliamentarians have often disagreed about the means by which to achieve it. Indeed historically the most important cleavage in the party was the one between independence fundamentalists and **gradualist** home-rulers (Mitchell, 1990b). As McEwan (2002) notes, this is a recurring tension in SNP strategy. In the 1970s and 1980s the funda-

Gradualist: Pragmatists within the SNP who believe in the strategy of pursuing an incrementalist route to independence. This strategy is dominant in SNP thinking today.

mentalist minority wing emphasized independence as the over-riding aim of the SNP. It tended to be suspicious of 'halfway house' measures and campaign against policies that would result in the dilution of the fundamental aim of independence. The success of each strategy has varied over time. For example, during the late 1980s the party sought to counter charges of separatism by redefining its constitutional goal as

Box 3.2   Factionalism in Scotland's political parties

All political parties are loose collections of individuals with varying degrees of attachment to ideologies associated with their party; all parties tend to accommodate political and ideological tensions. Political parties may be institutional structures which do not accommodate political mavericks and their discipline has inevitable consequences for individual freedom of thought and action. However, it is possible to identify factions and tendencies in all of Scotland's parties. The Scottish Labour Party is a loose collection of socialists and social democrats with varying degrees of commitment to notions of 'collectivism'. The SNP has had the historic division between gradualists and fundamentalists and once expelled a group of left-leaning activists known as the '79 Group. The Scottish Liberal Democrats were formed after a merger with the old Scottish Liberal Party and the Social Democratic Party in the late 1980s. As a party it tends to be more tolerant of division and dissent than the other parties. Numerous strands could be identified in the Scottish Conservative and Unionist Party. In recent years the division between neo-liberal free-marketeers and the more socially aware 'Wet' Tory strand could be identified. The Greens and Socialists are loose collections of movements that have traditionally eschewed political parties in favour of alternative forms of political action.

gradualists vs radicals

'Independence in Europe' – it wanted Scotland to be separate from the UK but more embedded into the European Community (now Union). This perhaps contrasts with the fundamentalists 'high-point' in 1989 when the SNP walked out of the cross-party Scottish Constitutional Convention. Yet, the gradualists have been on the rise ever since. The leadership of the SNP today is dominated by those who emphasize pragmatism and an incrementalist strategy that embraces devolution and self-government as a stepping-stone to independence. Devolution would increase the visibility and profile of the SNP, giving it a much more visible platform on which to campaign for independence. It is this wing of the SNP that has been in the ascendancy in recent years. The election of John Swinney rather than Alex Neil as the convenor following Alex Salmond's resignation in 2000 showed that the gradualists are now dominant (see Box 3.2).

Alex Salmond continued to serve as a Westminster MP for Banff and Buchan and returned as party convenor in 2004 after the party's poor showing in the 2003 Scottish Parliamentary election (see Table 3.2). His status and experience were utilized as a useful campaigning tool during the 2001 and 2005 UK General Election campaigns when the SNP were in danger of being marginalized in a UK focused campaign. Voting for the SNP to ensure that Scotland's interests at Westminster were protected has become a key theme at UK elections. The SNP also focused on the idea of increased fiscal freedom/autonomy for the Scottish Parliament as a stepping-stone towards self-government. However, some within the party criticized this issue as too complex to attract

Table 3.2　*Scottish election results: number of seats and % vote*

	1st vote (% seats)		2nd vote (% seats)		Total
Labour					
1999	38.8	53	33.6	3	56
2003	34.6	46	29.6	4	50
2007	32.2	37	29.2	9	46
SNP					
1999	28.7	7	27.3	28	35
2003	23.8	9	21.6	18	27
2007	32.9	21	31.0	26	47
Cons					
1999	15.6	0	15.4	18	18
2003	16.6	3	15.5	15	18
2007	16.6	4	13.9	13	17
Lib Dems					
1999	14.2	12	12.4	5	17
2003	15.4	13	11.6	4	17
2007	16.2	11	13.9	5	16
Greens					
1999	0	0	3.6	1	1
2003	0	0	6.5	7	7
2007	0.2	0	4.0	2	2
SSP					
1999	1.0	0	2.0	1	1
2003	6.2	0	6.5	6	6
2007	0.0	0	0.6	0	0
Other					
1999	1.7	1	5.7	0	1
2003	3.4	2	8.7	2	4
2007	3.1	0	7.4	1	1

significant electoral attention; they emphasized the need to establish the SNP's credentials as a party capable of governing Scotland – to prevent it from being viewed as a perennial campaigning party.

At the second Scottish parliamentary elections in 2003 the party suffered from the rise in support for the minor parties, losing eight seats overall despite gaining two constituency seats (see Table 3.2). Its loss of seats to minority parties diluted its status as the Scottish Labour–Liberal Democrat administration's main opposition. However, after the re-election of Salmond as party leader the party stretched ahead of the Scottish Labour Party in opinion polls leading up to the 2007 election. It was at this election that the SNP finally made its electoral breakthrough, achieving its highest ever share of the

Scottish vote (32.7%) and defeating the Scottish Labour Party in terms of both votes won and seats gained. In May 2007 the SNP became Scotland's largest party and also the party of Government when Alex Salmond was elected as First Minister leading a minority SNP administration.

Overall, it appears that devolution has brought with it significantly increased opportunities for the SNP. First, it has allowed the party to grow and mature into a more credible force, following reforms to its management, organization and communication. Second, the SNP receives more votes in Scottish Parliament elections than it does for Westminster. Third, the new electoral system ensures that Scottish Labour's vote is not exaggerated (for example, in 2007, Scottish Labour's 32.2% of the first vote earned it 51% of constituency seats; the SNP's 32.9% translated to 29%). As Figure 3.1 shows, the higher share of the vote combined with a proportional electoral system, has a dramatic effect on the SNP's electoral fortunes. Fourth, the introduction of **single transferable vote** (STV) and the party's successful campaign led to spectacular gains at the 2007 local government elections where it emerged as the party with most councillors (see Tables 4.1 and 4.2). As a result, the party spectacularly emerged from the 2007 Scottish Parliamentary election as Scotland's largest party (albeit by only one MSP), in what may well prove to be a defining election in Scottish political history.

Single transferable vote (STV): Proportional electoral system in which the voter is asked to rank his/her candidate preferences. If the first choice is elected or rejected, their vote transfers to the next candidate on the list.

The Scottish Labour Party

The Scottish Labour Party (as the Labour Party in Scotland re-named itself in 1994) was Scotland's largest party at all UK General and Scottish parliamentary elections from 1964 to 2003. Numerous analysts have noted Labour's dominant position in Scottish politics. Donnachie *et al.* refer to, 'Labour's hegemony nationally and locally in much of urban-industrial Scotland during the past fifty years' (1989: 1). Hassan refers to the Scottish Labour Party as

> one of the most important and defining institutions in the last 100 years plus of Scotland . . . an institutionalized party – blurring the boundaries between party and state. (2004: 1–4)

Irvine similarly refers to it as, 'Scotland's establishment party' (2004: 225), as do Saren and McCormick (2004: 100). In 2002 MacWhirter argued 'The Scottish political classes . . . remain . . . Labour dominated and shaped by the Labour state' (2002: 35).

Even at the low-point of the UK party – the 1983 General Election – the Labour Party was still the largest political party in Scotland. It has enjoyed the support of Scotland's best-selling tabloid newspaper in the 1980s and 1990s, the *Daily Record*, and up until its defeat at the 2007 election it was the largest party in local government in terms of votes, councillors and council control. The Scottish Labour Party's status until 2007, was attributable to the fact that as Scotland moved towards multi-party politics it retained its vote share while the opposition was split.

However, Labour was not dominant in the sense that the majority of the Scottish population voted for it. Indeed, it has consistently failed to secure 50 per cent of the popular vote (the last party to achieve this was the Conservative and Unionist Party in 1955). Rather, its dominance stems from maintaining around 40 per cent of the vote under a plurality system which exaggerates its support. At the Blair landslide 1997 UK General Election it secured 45.6 per cent share of the votes (its highest since 1966) (Table 3.1). However, ten years later in the Scottish Parliament elections its share fell to 32.2 per cent of the constituency vote and only 29.2 per cent of the regional vote. The Labour Party's share of the vote has moved downward at each successive Scottish election. In 1999 it had the largest Scottish Parliamentary group of MSPs (56), but this fell to 50 in 2003 and 46 in 2007 (Table 3.2).

This picture of Labour dominance also extended to Scottish local government up to 2007, but in actual fact Labour achieved over 50 per cent of the vote at the 2003 elections in only three out of 32 council areas (North Lanarkshire, South Lanarkshire, West Dunbartonshire). Twelve other councils elected Labour majorities with less than half of the vote, with the vote most distorted in Glasgow (74 of 79 wards). The introduction of the single transferable vote, and its falling vote share, hit the party hard at the 2007 local elections. At the first elections to the Scottish **unitary authorities** in 1995 the number of elected Labour councillors was 613; in 2007 only 348 were elected – moving the party into second place behind the SNP. The party now has majority control of only two councils – Glasgow and North Lanarkshire.

Unitary authorities:
In 1995 Scottish local government was reorganized from a two-tier region/district system (where functions were split) to a unitary system – where councils now undertake all functions.

Before devolution, the Scottish Labour Party was

> On one level . . . nationalized and incorporated into the British Labour Party – a highly centralized, formalized structure which allowed for little differentiation. However, on a more informal level, the Scottish party retained the discretion and freedom to invoke a distinctly Scottish agenda, symbols and language. (Hassan 2002b: 29–30)

The Scottish Labour Party, like all political parties in Scotland today, has increasingly adopted the language and symbols of Scottish nationalism. It tended to portray itself in the 1980s and 1990s as representing Scotland's interests in Westminster and Whitehall. This was *helped* by the rising proportion of

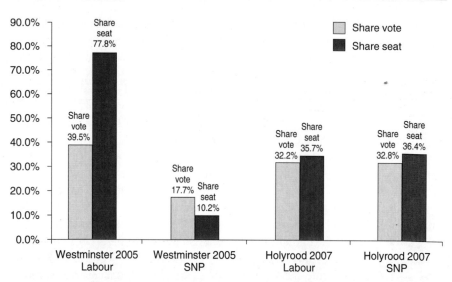

Figure 3.1   *SNP/Labour vote and seat shares at UK and Scottish elections*

Scottish Labour MPs within Westminster's Parliamentary Labour Party when the party suffered heavy defeats (allowing Scottish MPs to graduate to senior positions and culminating in Gordon Brown and Alistair Darling becoming Prime Minister and Chancellor in 2007). However, its policy stance on devolution helps it portray a level of responsiveness to Scottish public opinion and distinction from Westminster.

It is difficult to give an ideological profile of the Scottish Labour Party because it is so eclectic, and such is its scale that leaders and personalities tend to account for as much of its policy direction as underlying ideology. To the extent that one can be identified, most would accept that the Scottish party could be placed further to the left than its UK counterpart on the standard left–right ideological continuum. This reflects the dynamic of party competition – its main competitor in Scotland (the SNP) also sits on the left (see Figure 3.1), whilst at UK level the party's main challengers (the Conservatives) are a right of centre party.

Post-devolution the Scottish Labour Party has been keen to avoid an unwelcome media spotlight on Holyrood–Westminster tensions. However, such tensions undoubtedly exist, and in one notable episode the day after the 2001 General Election Henry McLeish, the then Scottish First Minister, was caught on tape denouncing John Reid, former Scottish Secretary, as a 'patronising bastard' and Brian Wilson, former Scottish Office Minister of State, as a 'liability'. The latter, along with MPs such as Tam Dalyell, reflect a part of the party that was sceptical of the need for devolution.

It is difficult to disagree with Hassan's analysis that the Scottish Labour Party, has long prided itself on its radical traditions and romantic view of itself . . . but it has increasingly become a conservative party, the political establishment. (Hassan 2002b: 43)

As an establishment party until 2007 it was a relatively conservative institution. It was almost unique amongst Western European political parties in enjoying four decades of political **hegemony** in one country. It was adept at responding to and accommodating changes in the Scottish political environment. However, the 2007 election result led to Wendy Alexander – when launching her successful bid for leadership of the Labour Party in the Scottish Parliament – suggesting that the Scottish Labour Party was at a critical juncture in its history and advocating that the party 'must take a long hard look at itself' (Schofield and Dinwoodie, 2007). By continuing to 'win' Scottish elections from the 1960s the Scottish Labour Party never had to undertake the reflective self-appraisal exercises which inevitably follow electoral defeat.

Hegemony: The ascendancy or dominance of one's political ideas within a polity.

The Labour Party in Scotland's attitude to home rule has been fluid and changeable. In the postwar period only a small minority in the Labour Party in Scotland were committed 'home-rulers' – the Scottish constitutional issue was superseded by more important socio-economic issues and the dominant focus was on the British state as a vehicle in delivering social change. Even when the party adopted its devolution policy in the 1970s it was not with much enthusiasm. It was in the 1980s that the issue of devolution began to win over the hearts and minds of party activists and parliamentarians. Devolution was seen as a way of preserving and developing the welfare state in Scotland. A campaign group within the party – Scottish Labour Action – called for more devolution of power to Scotland. The party began to accentuate its Scottish dimension. However, it should be noted that it was as late as 1994 that the Labour Party in Scotland became known as the Scottish Labour Party. The Westminster orientation of the Scottish Labour Party is reflected in the fact that only five Labour MPs stood down to become MSPs.

The Scottish Conservative and Unionist Party

The Scottish Conservative and Unionist Party's status in Scottish politics has been transformed in the past three decades. In the immediate postwar period it could claim to be Scotland's largest party and the party's performance in Scotland was similar to England (see Table 3.1). During this time the party's official title in Scotland was the Scottish Unionist Party – 'Conservative' did not form any part of the party's literature until it was reincorporated into its title in 1965, a term it had not used since before 1912 (Seawright, 2002). Unionism as an ideology has historically emphasized the sovereignty of the

Party Ideologies

Box 3.3   Ideology and Scotland's major political parties

The architects of devolution made great play of the notion of 'new politics' with the Westminster traditions of conflict, partisanship and party tribalism being replaced with a more co-operative and consensual party political system. The reality is that party labels reflect long-standing ideological traditions and rivalries that new institutional structures may only dilute.

The **Scottish Labour Party** has its roots in the trade-union movement. It has historically accommodated a wide range of left and centrist opinion. In modern ideological speak it is best classified as social democratic with an emphasis on collectivist orientated solutions to society's problems. The UK Blairite New Labour modernization between 1994 and 2007 somewhat diluted its left-of-centre outlook. Critics would suggest that its long-standing dominance of Scottish electoral politics has seen the Scottish Labour Party adopt the conservatism of an establishment party.

The **Scottish National Party**'s glue is a shared commitment to independence for Scotland. Initially the party's ideological profile was loose and difficult to detect. However, in recent years the party has adopted a social democratic stance on most issues and it operates within the same ideological terrain as the Scottish Labour Party. Indeed at recent elections the electorate have perceived the party to be further to the left than Labour. Though, like the Labour Party it has also increasingly adopted business friendly language.

The **Scottish Liberal Democrats** have an ideological profile compatible with the Scottish Labour Party and this allowed them to form a coalition from 1999–2007. In electioneering their rivals (in the main, the Scottish Conservative and Unionist Party) have been fond of labelling them 'rural Labour'. However, historically they have generally been perceived to be more 'centrist' than the SNP and Labour (although issues such as free personal care suggest a more 'left-of-centre' approach to key areas).

The **Scottish Conservative and Unionist Party** has traditionally been about continuity, eschewing any radicalism in economic and social policy, defending the union between Scotland and England and maintaining the political and constitutional status quo. Although the Thatcher years saw the party as a whole moving away from its traditional dislike of ideological inspired policymaking, the Scottish Conservatives are less likely to campaign on, for example, the benefits of the market. *— slightly more central*

The **Greens** and the **Socialists** are in reality loose collections of factions, tendencies and movements that have formed under umbrella labels. They are parties committed radical policies in areas such as equality, decentralization and sustainability. The membership and leadership of these parties are likely to be far more committed ideologues than those of the four major parties. Like the SNP, both are committed to an independent Scotland. *— extreme left*

Westminster Parliament and opposed the home-rule movement in Scotland. However, unionists have been willing to accommodate Scottish differences within fairly well defined limits.

The party's unionist stance allowed it to tap into Scotland's working-class Protestant vote for the first half of the twentieth century, allowing it to build an electoral coalition to compete with the rapidly expanding Labour Party. However, since the 1960s the party has been in almost permanent decline towards minor party status in Scotland. At the 2001 UK General Election it sunk to fourth place both in terms of votes and seats. While Thatcherism was the heyday for the popular support of the Conservatives in the UK, in Scotland this period was one of retrenchment. In Scotland the party has increasingly come to be viewed as an English party, imposing alien right-wing policies via its control of the Scottish Office. In **territorial management** terms there appeared little acknowledgement of Scottish distinctiveness, contributing to perceptions of a democratic deficit in Scotland and increasing calls for home rule throughout the 1980s and 1990s.

Territorial management: The process of managing the 'periphery' of the UK (in this case Scotland, Wales and Northern Ireland) from the 'centre' in Westminster.

At the UK level of the Conservative party, there is still some evidence of the old approach. At the 2001 General Election the UK manifesto included a commitment to stop Scottish MPs voting on exclusively English matters, and its recent UK leadership in the form of Hague, Duncan-Smith and Howard has also generally been perceived as insensitive to Scottish interests. Further, although the election of Cameron as party leader may signal a shift, the issue of how to deal with devolution and its knock-on implications for UK governance (in particular the West Lothian question) remains one that many in the party view as unresolved.

However, there are signs that, despite resisting calls for devolution throughout their 18 years in office, they have adjusted to devolution. The Scottish Conservatives have been granted more autonomy from Conservative Central Office in London. The Conservatives' 1999 Scottish election manifesto declared that 'this is a new party'. Since then the party has re-branded itself, shifting its ideological profile closer to the centre, increasing its Scottish emphasis and adopting a pragmatic approach to working within the Scottish Parliament. Seawright (2002: 80) suggests taking its re-branding a stage further and reviving its local government label of the 1960s 'the Progressives'. However, Keating (2005a) suggests that significant Conservative **re-branding** is undermined by a lack of resources (rather than central control) and at present the party remains tarnished in Scotland, associated with the perceived anti-Scottishness of Thatcherism and the 1979–97 Conservative administrations.

Re-branding: The process of re-imaging and marketing a party usually to change the electorate's perception of it. A classic instance of this in British politics is the New Labour re-branding of the 1990s.

Ironically, devolution has benefited the Scottish Conservatives. Although the party was wiped out in Scotland during the 1997 UK General Election and is still electorally weak compared to the 1950s, it was reinvigorated by the new electoral system and achieved representation of 18 MSPs via regional list seats in 1999. At the 2007 election the party gained 16.6 per cent of the first vote and 13.9 per cent of the regional vote, translating to 17 MSPs. These figures suggest that they have hit the core of their support – since 1997 its vote has stabilized in the 14–17 per cent bracket – and that re-branding may have a marginal effect.

The Scottish Liberal Democrats

The Scottish Liberal Democrats were formed in 1988 after a merger between the Liberal Party and the Social Democratic Party. The party has increasingly found itself operating on the same ideological terrain as Labour and the SNP. It is normally classified as a **centrist** party. It worked closely with Scottish Labour on the Constitutional Convention and that relationship has been solidified post-devolution with the formal coalition partnership agreements in 1999 and 2003.

Centrist: Moderate (as opposed to left or right-wing radical) political views.

In recent history the old Scottish Liberal Party has been a smaller minority – between 1945 and 1979 it never gained more than 9 per cent of the vote in Westminster elections (Lynch, 2002a: 85). Only during the Liberal/SDP Alliance period in 1983 and 1987 did the party increase its support (in 1983 to 25.4%; in 1987 to 19.4%). In the 1990s, after the merger of Liberals and Social Democrats in 1988 its support declined to around 13 per cent. However, despite this decline the Scottish Liberal Democrats actually increased its number of seats (it benefited from a geographically concentration of votes). It has concentrated support in the Scottish Borders, Highlands and Islands and North-East, and its support in recent years has been on the increase – it gained 16.2 per cent of the constituency vote in 2007.

The Scottish Liberal Democrats have always had a significant degree of autonomy from their UK counterparts. Indeed as Lynch (2002a: 84) suggests they are recognizable as a party within a party, with their own Scottish office, executive powers, policy-making capacity, staff, membership and manifestos:

the constitutional and political reality of devolution has finally caught up with the organizational reality of life within the **federal** Liberal Democrats. (Lynch 2002a: 84)

Federal: A form of organization where branches retain a degree of formally recognized autonomy from the centre.

The Liberal Democrats (as their name suggests) do not tend to operate within the same strict parameters of party discipline as the other major parties; there tends to be more of a culture of tolerance towards the political maverick and free-wheeler.

The Scottish Liberal Democrats have gained from devolution. Despite only gaining a small percentage of the popular vote they were part of the political executive in Scotland. After the 1999 election the party's parliamentary group voted 13–3 in favour of entering into coalition with Labour. As part of the partnership agreement the Liberal Democrats gained two cabinet ministers from 1999–2003 and three from 2003–07. Since then the party has grown steadily in both support and stature. At the 2001 UK General Election it held all of its seats and its level of support increased to 16.4 per cent (a 3.4% increase compared to 1997 and 2.2% compared to 1999). It was the only major party to have a rise in the actual number of votes cast for it despite the drop in turnout. For the first time ever it gained more votes than the Scottish Conservatives. Being in coalition was a useful electoral tool for the Liberal Democrats; its support crept up almost unnoticed whilst opposition fire was concentrated on the Scottish Labour Party. The party was able to claim credit for policies such as the abolishment (in reality postponement) of Scottish university tuition fees, at the same time as blaming Labour for issues such as road tolls.

At present the Liberal Democrats are largely representing middle-class rural/suburban Scotland (opposition parties have tried to exploit their association with the Scottish Labour Party by labelling them as 'rural Labour'). The introduction of Single Transferable Voting (STV) at the local government elections in 2007 has allowed it to establish a foothold in previous 'Liberal Democrat free areas'. However, contrary to expectations the party's number of councillors *reduced* from 175 to 166 in 2007, although its support overall has held up well post-devolution. At the 2007 election it gained 16.2 per cent of the first vote and 11.3 per cent of the second vote. It now has 16 MSPs.

Box 3.4 Scotland's minor parties

The *Scottish Senior Citizens' Unity Party* and the *Pensioners' Party* both stood at the 2003 election – the former in the West of Scotland Regional Lists and the latter in the East of Scotland. John Swinburne was elected as an MSP for the SSCUP on the Central Scotland list between 2003 and 2007. It gained 1.9% of the regional vote in 2007.

Solidarity was founded by Tommy Sheridan after he left the Scottish Socialist Party. It gained 1.5% of the regional vote in 2007.

The *Socialist Labour Party* is the Arthur Scargill-led party that campaigns on a UK-wide basis. It gained 0.7% of the regional vote in 2007.

The *Highlands and Islands Alliance* is a party that campaigns on the basis that the distinctive voice of this geographical area should be heard in the Parliament.

The *British National Party* is a far-right party – it stands on an anti-immigration platform. It gained 1.2% of the regional vote in 2007.

The *Scottish Christian Party* was 'Proclaiming Christ's Lordship!' during the 2007 election campaign. It gained 1.3% of the regional vote in 2007.

The Scottish Green Party

The Scottish Green Party has its roots in the Ecology Party in Scotland of the late 1970s (for a history see Bennie, 2004). It gained its independence from the UK party in 1990. Despite its media portrayal it is far from a single issue party – its policy platform includes campaigning for the Scottish Parliament to have greater control over its finances and increased powers in areas such as energy, transport, health and consumer affairs. At the 1999 Scottish election Robin Harper was the first Green MSP elected, with 6.9 per cent of the vote in the Edinburgh regional list. Its major breakthrough came in 2003 when it gained 132,000 second votes and 7 Green candidates were elected to the Scottish Parliament. The party's performance at the 2003 election (like that of the SSP) was enough to establish a formal parliamentary group that achieved recognition by the Parliamentary Bureau under its standing orders. This allowed it to submit individuals to be committee convenors and initiate parliamentary debates. The performance of the Scottish Greens brought them into line with their counterparts on continental Europe where similar parties tend to gain 5–10 per cent of the vote. The party suffered a set-back in 2007 when its vote fell to 82,584 (4%) and it was reduced to two MSPs. However, it still has the potential to influence a finely balanced Scottish Parliament and it held talks with the SNP immediately after the election to examine areas of common ground (Scottish National Party and Scottish Green Party, 2007).

The Scottish Socialist Party (SSP)

The roots of the SSP lie in the **Militant Tendency** within the Labour Party in the 1980s. It was originally called Scottish Militant Labour (SML), and led by Tommy Sheridan who had gained prominence as President of the Anti-Poll Tax Federation. In Scotland generally, the proliferation of leftist parties is both a sign of the strength of socialist ideology, as well as a reflection of its electoral failure to mobilize behind one single form (Brown *et al.*, 1997: 131). The SSP was formed in 1998 merging Militant Labour, ex-Communists and environmental activists. It brought together a loose collection of left-wing factions and tendencies. The SSP advocates a democratic, tolerant socially libertarian and modern socialism – a decentralized, high-tech and environmentally responsible independent socialist Scottish republic (Bennie, 2002: 100–1). At the 1999 Scottish election, Tommy Sheridan the party's charismatic leader was elected in the Glasgow region with 7.25 per cent of the vote. At the 2003 Election the party gained 6.7 per cent of the List vote and was rewarded with six seats. However, the fall-out from Sheridan's court case against News International in 2006 (including

> **Militant Tendency**: A far-left faction of the Labour Party which sought power within the party through gaining control of local constituency Labour Party associations. Most of its members were expelled in the late 1980s.

Sheridan forming an alternative socialist party called Solidarity) contributed to the party losing all of its seats in 2007.

Scotland's changing party system

The party system in Scotland until the late 1960s operated largely in parallel to the system in the United Kingdom. The UK national parties, the Conservatives and Labour, were electorally dominant with the Liberal Party operating at the fringes. However, the two-party system began to break down in the 1970s, with support of each of the two main parties declining at both UK and Scottish levels.

Box 3.5   Scotland's party competition since 1945

Party competition in Scotland has been in a state of transition for the past thirty years. The first-past-the-post electoral system tends to produce a two-party system (though as Colomer (2005: 1) demonstrates the number of parties can explain the choice of electoral system, rather than the other way around). However, with the decline of the Conservatives, the Scottish Labour Party gradually assumed a more dominant position in a multi-party environment. The new more proportional post-devolution electoral system has increased opportunities for smaller political parties and diluted the strength of Scotland's major traditional parties. In the postwar period Scotland's party competition has gone through four distinct phases:

1945–70: two-party duopoly   The dominance of Labour and the Conservatives in the UK was paralleled in Scotland with both parties collectively achieving around 90% of the popular vote collectively. Since 1970 the two-party share of the vote has been in decline in both the UK and Scotland.

1970–1999: Labour dominant plus three   Gradually the Labour Party in Scotland became more dominant – its previous rival, the Conservative Party, was in decline while new challengers the SNP and the Liberals/Alliance/Liberal Democrats never achieved support consistently enough for them to be considered major challengers.

1999–2007: Labour–Lib Dem coalition plus four   Post-devolution the coalition was relatively stable whilst the opposition became more fragmented. The SNP was vying with the Conservatives, Socialists and Greens for the title of opposition. The fluidity of the party system has been facilitated by the MMP electoral system and the emergence of new minor parties.

2007–: multi-party politics   The election result in 2007 which left the SNP as the largest party (by one seat) has meant that all of the elected parties in the Parliament can have influence. The SNP minority administration is reliant on the support of other parties in order to pass legislation.

In the UK the creation of the Social Democratic Party threatened to break the mould of party politics for a brief period in the 1980s. However, after their merger with the Liberal Party to form the Liberal Democrats in 1988 the mould of the Conservative–Labour duopoly has not been broken. The situation in Scotland has been far more fluid. The development of the Scottish National Party as an electoral force has seen it rise to be Scotland's largest political party in 2007. At the same time the Conservative Party has been in decline – this culminated in its electoral wipe-out at the 1997 General Election. The traditional two-party Labour versus Conservative electoral contest continues to operate at UK level while a more complicated, multi-party environment exists in Scotland. This creates a different party-political dynamic, which is best illustrated with reference to the Labour Party. At UK level it is usually labelled a centre-left party and its key opponent is a centre right party. In Scotland the environment is very different. It is a centre-left unionist party and its key opponent is a centre-left nationalist party. At UK level it faces a challenge from the right, while in Scotland it comes from the left. In terms of a simple Downsian analysis the party at UK level has an incentive to move right, while in Scotland it has more reason to move in the opposite direction (see Box 4.6).

The 'first-past-the-post' electoral system exaggerated the Labour Party's dominance. It has never gained 50 per cent of the electorate's vote in Scotland, but benefited from the divided vote share of the opposition parties. Yet, in the post-devolution period the reality of coalition and minority government, the new electoral system and the growth of new parties has diluted any impression of continued longer-term dominance and permanence. Therefore, three types of party system tend to be identified in the literature: one-party dominant, two-party and multi-party. A case could be made for describing Scotland as all three at different times. It could be described as one-party-dominant due to the electoral hegemony enjoyed by the Labour Party from the 1960s until 2007. It could also be described as two-party, as the Labour Party and SNP have been first and second (in terms of votes cast) at all elections in Scotland since 1997. It could also be described as multi-party, as post-devolution coalition or minority government will be the norm and there are now five political parties with representation in Holyrood (see Box 3.5)

It is perhaps easier to differentiate between the 'Holyrood' party system and the 'Westminster' party system. The former is far more **pluralistic** (which is only explained in part by diverging voting behaviour). Devolution and the introduction of the **Mixed Member Proportional (MMP)** system have reinvigorated the Conservatives electorally. They, along with the SNP, were the parties that suffered most from the proportional perversity of the first-past-the-post electoral system. Their vote is more evenly spread than that of Labour and the Liberal Democrats. In Westminster elections the lack of any

Pluralistic: A political system where power is diffused or where there is more than one centre of power.

Mixed Member Proportional (MMP): An electoral system which combines first-past-the-post elections with a second vote (by party) to ensure greater proportionality. Also referred to as the Additional Member System (AMS).

proportional element in the electoral system exaggerates the dominance of the UK Labour Party. Therefore, the Scottish party system has been, and still is, in the process of diverging from the Westminster party system, and under devolution it is possible that the changing Holyrood system will feed into Scottish party politics at Westminster.

The new party system in Scotland could throw up many new and interesting alliances in the future – indeed one need only look at the alliances forged in 30 of Scotland's 32 local councils to appreciate the variety of potential coalition arrangements. The Labour and Liberal Democrat parties formally cooperated between 1999 and 2007, but the future could see new alliances. For example, the SNP and the Conservatives find themselves agreeing on questions such as 'fiscal autonomy' and their respective leaders have shown great willingness since 2007 to work together in the Scottish Parliament. The SNP and the Liberal Democrats agree on the need to abolish council tax; the SNP and Greens are committed to independence; and the Scottish Conservatives, Labour and Liberal Democrats are likely to form a unionist alliance against SNP plans for an independence referendum.

Trends in party organization

All of Scotland's political parties tend to be organized around local constituency associations that operate within the borders of parliamentary constituencies. However, in recent decades party bureaucracies in the form of National (Scottish) Executives and party headquarters have drawn power away from constituency organizations; a process of democratic centralism has taken place in the major parties (the SSP and Greens remain the exceptions).

In bygone years the constituency associations were the foot-soldiers of the party and crucial to local campaigning, distributing leaflets, raising funds and recruiting new members. However, the professionalization of modern parties, new information and communication technology and the dominance of the national media has resulted in the core hierarchy of each party gaining more power. The grassroots politics of local wards, committees and constituency associations, whilst still evident, has generally diminished in importance in party policy-making terms. The parliamentary leadership and elected office-holders have tended to gain powers at the expense of party members. In some parties it was never that important in any case – membership of local parties was more about socializing with likeminded people and organizing events to raise party funds.

While it is difficult to gain precise figures for party membership in Scotland, the total membership for all parties combined is no more than

50,000 – that is, fewer than 1 in 100 of Scots are members of any party. The membership base of Scotland's major political parties reflected the civic activism of the postwar era; it could be that their declining numbers are simply a reflection of public disenchantment with mainstream politics. Recent reforms in political parties have reflected the reality of declining activism and membership; parties have striven to be more professional in electioneering and this has usually resulted in more centralized control. For example, in 2004 SNP organizational reforms included the centralization of party membership lists.

Each of the parties in Scotland holds an annual conference, and these are important gatherings in terms of electioneering and window-dressing. They are increasingly used to present as positive a picture of the party as possible to the wider electorate. In these carefully crafted, largely stage-managed affairs division, dissent and splits are carefully avoided. Conferences are increasingly moving towards being seen as a 'party rally' rather than being important policy-making forums for the major parties.

Political parties in all **liberal democracies** have tended to become more professionalized and media-focused in recent years (see Hague and Harrop, 2001: ch. 11; Calvert, 2002: 163–6). Electioneering techniques and research have become more sophisticated with parties seeking mechanisms to maintain awareness of the electorate's opinions, demands and reactions to policy issues and initiatives. As parties have matured, their internal structures have become more oligarchic with power vested in key office-holders and parliamentary leadership. There has also been a tendency towards the 'presidentialization' of party leaders; at the 2007 Scottish election the SNP campaigned for the regional vote under the slogan 'Alex Salmond for First Minister' (it was this phrase rather than the party's name that appeared on the ballot paper in some regions). The focus of the media is on the personality and skills of the leader and much emphasis is placed on the projection and image of the leadership in parties.

Liberal democracies: Countries with a system of regular and competitive elections, guaranteed levels of human rights and legal restrictions to the exertion of state power.

Electioneering post-devolution has taken an increasingly Scottish flavour. Since 1959, Labour and the Conservatives have always produced a Scottish manifesto (and Labour also produced one for the 1950 general election). Yet, these have generally followed the British manifesto with an added Scottish flavour. In post-devolution campaigns it has also become clear that the parties are making little effort to distinguish between devolved and non-devolved issues in the campaign.

Scotland's four major political parties may be referred to as what Kircheimer (1966) described as 'catch-all parties' – each has gradually diluted its ideological 'baggage' in an effort to gain more electoral success (see Box 4.6); evolved to seek to govern in the national interest (rather than represent one group); and become dominated by leaders who communicate with voters directly via television and canvass electoral support from all groups in society (to govern rather than represent).

All parties are broad churches that accommodate diverging opinions, but party leaderships tend to view division and dissent as negatives, with party unity crucial to electoral credibility. In ideological terms there is little to separate the two main parties – the SNP and Labour have tended to attract support from the same social base (see Brand *et al.*, 1994a; 1994b). Despite media portrayal the policy stances of Scotland's established political parties are notable for an absence of fundamental policy differences on most policy issues. There exists a broad social democratic consensus in Scottish politics that has been reflected in the policy agenda of the Parliament post-devolution. Much of its legislative output has been uncontroversial.

Branding, marketing and other 'modern' electioneering techniques have been utilized as each party has engaged in strategies to enhance its appeal to the wider Scottish electorate. Key to this appeal is the image as a 'Scottish Party' in the minds of the electorate. All five parties in the parliament seek to be viewed as the national party of Scotland. The socialism of the Scottish Labour Party has been diluted by policies such as public–private partnerships; the unionism and nationalism of the Tories and SNP respectively, by their acceptance of devolution and its governing structures. The Scottish Liberal Democrats were forced to compromise on key policies when working in coalition with the Scottish Labour Party.

Box 3.6   Issues for Scottish political parties today

Falling membership. All of the major political parties have experienced a long-term decline in membership – the mass participation of individuals in political parties would appear to be history.

Changing membership. The majority of members in today's political parties would appear to be 'direct-debit' members – they pay their annual subscription but show no great interest in being active in local constituency parties.

Declining party identification. The proportion of voters who strongly identify with any political party has been in decline.

Party funding. The parties in Scotland like those at UK level are increasingly reliant on donors for campaign funding.

Coalition. Due to the post-devolution change to a more proportional electoral system it is likely that all of the parties will at some point be faced with the decision of whether or not to join or cooperate with other parties in coalition. Coalition negotiations inevitably involve parties compromising their manifestos. This runs counter to the programmatic, disciplined orientation of political parties.

UK relations. All of the major parties are also represented in the Westminster parliament, thus necessitating the need for relations and parameters for the parties to be established.

The needs of the media and the requirements of organization and leadership within the parties have ensured that those at the top of each party have accrued significant powers and discretion. In the age of new information and communication technologies, parties no longer need large-scale party membership to communicate their message to the electorate. Professional and sophisticated media relations and campaigns have tended to be the defining feature of contemporary political parties, though constituency party activity is still relevant (see Denver and MacAllister, 2003; Clark, 2006).

Moreover, organizational and constitutional reforms of the major parties have facilitated more centralized control of policy. Loyalty to the party leadership is an important factor in candidate selection, places on regional party lists and promotions. As Keating observed, 'the professionalization of politics and the tight grip of the parties . . . reduced the liberating potential of devolution' (2005a: 218). Between 1999 and 2007 the SNP consistently suggested that Scottish Labour were puppets of the New Labour administration in London.

Conclusion

Political parties are very much the public face of Scottish politics – their leadership, outlook and policies dominate media coverage. The general public's perception of Scottish politics is one that is filtered to it through political parties. Parties are also very important in influencing public policy. They provide one of the key links between the state and civil society and the institutions of government and wider society (Heywood, 2002: 247). Like elsewhere in Europe, Scotland's political parties have not been immune to various trends in party structure and organization including elite centralization and professionalization, inspired in part by the need for more sophisticated media relations and electioneering. Each of the four major parties are 'catch-all' and seek to project themselves as the party concerned with Scotland's national interest.

As political institutions of mass mobilization, parties in Scotland (as elsewhere) are in decline. In post-devolution Scotland new political parties, particularly the Greens and Socialists, were successful at the 2003 Election, but suffered setbacks in 2007. Party membership in the established parties has generally been falling (though the SNP has enjoyed a post-2007 surge), voter loyalties weakening (see Chapter 4) and alternative forms of political mobilization (e.g. pressure groups, social movements, direct action) have become more important to a younger generation.

In recent years there has been a waning of the dominance of the Scottish Labour Party. It now finds itself operating in a more pluralist, multi-party political system than the one engendered by Westminster first-past-the-post elections. Scotland's political parties and its party system have diverged significantly from the Westminster arrangements; the strategy and focus is on Holyrood rather than Westminister. The 2007 Scottish election results mean that cross-party cooperation will be necessary for new legislation to be passed in the parliament.

This chapter has sought to demonstrate the fluid and changeable environment of Scotland's political parties. Scotland's political parties have formed loose alliances at various junctures (e.g. the Scottish Constitutional Convention, the 1997 Referendum Campaign, Labour–Liberal Democrat coalition government 1999–2007) although tribal loyalty and inter-party partisanship is often the norm. In 2002 Hassan (2002b: 43) suggested 'the dilution of the institutionally focused labourist culture and the development of a more open, democratic politics' will challenge Labour's dominance as a quasi-establishment party. The first post-devolution turning point came in 2003 when the 'cosy cartel' of Scotland's four major parties showed its first sign of cracking with Scotland's two minor parties moving to multi-member representation (though both suffered setbacks in 2007). The establishment of the SNP administration in 2007 is likely to signal the next post-devolution turning point for Scottish party politics.

Further reading

The collection of chapters by Hassan, McEwan. Lynch, Seawright and Bennie in Hassan and Warhurst (2002) are a useful starting point, giving useful outlines of each of Scotland's major political parties. Hutchison (2000) provides an excellent historical account of each party's development in the twentieth century.

Hassan (1999; 2002b; 2003) has published widely on the Labour Party in Scotland, and other notable works on the Labour Party in Scotland include Donnachie *et al.* (1988), Brand *et al.* (1994a), Jones and Keating (1982) and Keating and Bleiman (1979). For the SNP, Brand (1978), Brand *et al.* (1994b), Mitchell (1990b, 1996a), Gallagher (1991) and Lynch (2002b) are worth consulting. For the Conservatives in Scotland, Bulpitt (1982), Warner (1988), Mitchell (1990a), Kellas (1994), Seawright (1999), Dyer (2001) and Kendrick and McCrone (1989) represent a variety of accounts of the party's history and development.

For broader reading on political parties Garner and Kelly (1998) give a good account of the key parties in Britain today. Downs (1957) and Schumpeter (1942) represents a classic works on parties and democracy, while Mair (1990) is an edited collection by key writers on parties and party systems.

Online sources

Scottish Conservative Party   http://www.scottish.tory.org.uk/
Scottish Green Party   http://www.scottishgreens.org.uk/
Scottish Labour Party   http://www.scottishlabour.org.uk/
Scottish Liberal-Democrats   http://www.scotlibdems.org.uk/
Scottish National Party   http://www.snp.org.uk
Scottish Socialist Party   http://www.scotsocialistparty.org.uk
Highlands and Islands Alliance   http://hia.org.uk/index.htm

Chapter 4

Scottish Elections and Voting Behaviour

This chapter examines elections and voting behaviour in Scotland, focusing on the new electoral systems, the factors which influence voter choice in Scotland, and political campaigning in an age of multi-level elections. Drawing on public opinion poll research it explores the question of whether the Scottish electorate is more left-wing than its English counterpart, and the impact that devolution has had on these attitudes.

As outlined in Chapter 3, the trend in recent decades has been increasing divergence between Scottish and British electoral behaviour, as the relative fortunes of the British parties have diverged north and south of the border. The UK-based parties, although playing a key role in integrating Scotland into the British political system, have also increasingly sought to accommodate Scottish interests.

In the immediate postwar period electoral behaviour and party preferences at UK and Scottish levels were of negligible difference. Numerous factors played a role in 'uniting the kingdom' – winning the war, the continuing relevance of the British Empire, postwar economic growth and prosperity and the creation of the welfare state all gave meaning and relevance to 'Britishness'. However, as all of these factors have subsided in relevance and importance, the gap between electoral behaviour in Scotland and the rest of the UK has grown. The old stable Labour/Conservative duopoly is no more. At the 1959 UK General Election these parties gained 93.9 per cent of the vote in Scotland (see Table 3.1); at the 2007 Scottish election they did not even gain half of constituency (48.8%) or regional (43.1%) votes (see Table 3.2). The dramatic decline of the Conservatives in recent decades accounts for much of this.

The differences between elections and electoral behaviour in Scotland compared to the UK over recent decades have been significant and growing, and there are numerous stark differences:

- the existence of a **nationalist** party which means four, as opposed to three-party competition;
- the emergence of the constitutional issue on the Scottish political agenda;
- four distinct electoral systems for local, Scottish, UK and EU elections;
- a distinct and separate broadcast and print media which tends to focus on Scottish, as opposed to UK, political stories; and

- the long-term decline of the once dominant Scottish Conservative and Unionist Party.

Nationalist: An ideology which tends to emphasize the need for congruence between the geographic borders of nations and states.

The explanation for Scottish divergence is strongly linked to the emergence of a different political discourse and rhetoric in Scottish politics in recent decades, with the distinctive Scottish media, civil institutions and political parties playing their part in creating and sustaining this new process.

Electoral systems in Scotland

Until recently, all Scottish elections were conducted using the first-past-the-post electoral method. However, since 1999 the party-list method has been used for European Parliament elections, the Mixed Member Proportional (MMP) system for the Scottish Parliament and (since 2007) the Single Transferable Vote (STV) system has been used for local elections. The once dominant single-member plurality is now only used for the House of Commons. The four voting systems used to elect politicians in Scotland are outlined below:

- *House of Commons: single-member plurality*, or 'first past the post' as it is more commonly known, is a very simple straightforward electoral system. For House of Commons elections, Scotland is divided into 59 constituencies and the candidate receiving the largest share of the votes in each is elected. This majoritarian system is used for elections in the United States, Canada and India, as well as the UK. Until 2004, legislation required Scottish Parliament constituencies to have generally the same boundaries as Scottish Westminster constituencies. However, this link was broken by the Scottish Parliament (Constituencies) Act 2004 which reduced Westminster constituencies from 73 to 59 for the 2005 UK General Election. The 73 Scottish Parliament constituencies remain as they were when created in 1999. They are currently under review, with the Boundary Commission due to report prior to the 2011 Scottish Parliamentary Elections.
- *Scottish Parliament: the mixed-member proportional* (MMP) system is used for elections to the Scottish Parliament (see Shugart and Wattenberg, 2000). It combines the single-member plurality system with regional party lists. 73 MSPs are elected from constituencies using the first-past-the-post method. The 73 constituencies are based on the 1997 UK General Election 72 constituency boundaries, with Orkney and Shetland electing an MSP each instead of sharing one. The other 56 MSPs are elected from regional lists. Electors use a second vote for a political party, not directly

---

Box 4.1   The d'Hondt divisor

Party-list votes are totalled from each of the constituencies making up the region. These totals are then divided by the number of seats each party has won, *plus one*. The party with the highest resulting total elects one regional member. That party's divisor is then increased by one (because of its victory) and new figures calculated. Again, the party with the highest total wins a seat. The process is then repeated until all seven regional MSPs are elected. The aim of the system is to compensate parties which pile up votes in constituencies but fail to win many MSPs. Under the d'Hondt system, they are much more likely to gain regional members. Conversely, parties which do well in constituency elections will do less well in the top-up seats.

---

for an individual. The particular individuals selected come from lists drawn up by the political parties before the election, at a national or regional level. Scotland is divided into eight regions (for the list) with each one electing seven MSPs. The D'Hondt method (see Box 4.1) is used to calculate the MSPs the region elects. Members elected from regional geographical lists are designed to make the result more proportional.

- *Local government: single transferable vote* (STV) is the voting system used from 2007 for local elections in Scotland. Electors, instead of placing an 'X' against their preferred candidate, rate their preferences 1, 2, 3 and so on. It is designed to produce a more proportional result, minimize wasted votes and give electors more control over candidate choice – they vote for individual candidates rather than party lists. STV does this by using multi-member constituencies and by transferring votes that would otherwise be wasted. STV initially allocates an individual's vote to their first-choice preference, and then subsequently transfers unneeded or unused votes (according to the voter's stated preferences) after candidates are either elected or eliminated. It is used for elections in Ireland, Northern Ireland (except those for the House of Commons), Malta as well as local elections in New Zealand.

- *European Parliament: the party list* method of election is used to elect Scottish MEPs to the European Parliament. Scotland constitutes a single constituency with 7 MEPs elected using the d'Hondt method of selection on the basis of proportional representation.

The introduction of STV for local elections means that there are now four different voting systems for Scottish council, Parliament, Westminster and European elections. This led the Secretary of State for Scotland to establish a Commission on Boundary Differences and Voting Systems, chaired by Sir John Arbuthnott. This made a number of recommendations (Arbuthnott Commission, 2006):

An update to this since this book?

- A key recommendation (which has not yet been heeded) was an end to holding the Scottish parliamentary and local elections on the same day, in part because of the potential confusion surrounding different voting systems. The Scottish Local Government (Elections) Act 2002 introduced four-yearly terms for local councillors, identical to those of MSPs. The local elections are largely forgotten and overshadowed during the campaign with the national media spotlight almost exclusively focused on the parliamentary campaign. The May 2007 election resulted in record numbers of **spoilt ballot papers** and the existence of dual elections was cited as one of the reasons. Surprisingly, though, fewer STV ballot papers were rejected than those for constituency and regional list votes (suggesting that the design of the MMP paper may have been more at fault).

  Spoilt ballot papers: Ballot papers deemed invalid by the returning officer at election count. The Scottish Election in 2007 had record numbers of such papers.

- The MMP system should be revised to allow voters to choose between individual list candidates (and thus take the power away from parties to control the ranking of candidates on the list). If this change did not bring the anticipated benefits then the introduction of an STV method should be considered.

- The boundaries of all electoral divisions should be based on local government council areas. Therefore, in the future, so far as possible, boundaries for council areas, Scottish Parliament constituencies and Westminster constituencies should be reviewed together.

- STV should be introduced for elections to the European Parliament, so reducing the number of election systems to three.

Box 4.2   Mixed member proportional systems in comparative perspective

Advocates of MMP suggest that it offers the best of both worlds – the direct link between MP and constituent found in **plurality** systems and the sense of fairness and reduction of 'lost votes' in proportional systems. This may explain the popularity of MMP when electoral systems are being introduced or redesigned throughout the world. A form of MMP has been adopted by countries with wide and varied electoral histories such as Germany, New Zealand, Italy, Israel, Japan, Venezuela, Bolivia, Mexico, Hungary and Russia. Empirical evidence to date suggests that although MMP is more likely to produce two-party systems than other forms of PR, it is much less likely than plurality systems to marginalize minor parties.   (Shugart and Wattenberg, 2003)

advantage of mixed member proportional

- Measures should be introduced to keep voters better informed about voting systems, election results and the responsibilities of elected representatives
- A 'rapid move' towards the introduction of electronic voting and counting.

Legislation would be required in both the Westminster and Holyrood Parliaments to implement these recommendations.

Local elections in Scotland

Multi-member wards: Wards where more than one candidate is elected. Used at the local council STV elections where two, three or four councillors are elected from one ward.

The results of UK General Elections and Scottish Parliamentary Elections are given in Tables 3.1 and 3.2, while Tables 4.1 and 4.2 give details of local election results in Scotland. The introduction of a PR system for local elections was a long-running demand of the Scottish Liberal Democrats – the junior partner in the Labour-led coalition which governed Scotland between 1999 and 2007. It was introduced after the Local Governance (Scotland) Act 2004. **Multi-member wards** altered the party-political complexion of councils much more significantly than interim projections suggested (see Curtice and Herbert, 2005). Ironically the main beneficiary of the change in electoral system has been the party that was in opposition at the time – the SNP.

The SNP emerged as the largest party in Scottish local government in 2007 with 363 councillors. They were the big gainers – 'winning' the election (in terms of elected representatives) as they did at the parliamentary election. However, the party does not form a majority on any council – it is, however, the largest (or joint largest) group in Dundee, Angus, East Ayrshire, East Dunbartonshire, East Lothian, Perth and Kinross and Renfrewshire. The Labour Party was the big loser – losing over 161 councillors and control of 11 councils (compared to the post-2003 election position). Table 4.1 outlines the eclectic variety of coalition arrangements in Scotland's 32 local councils with virtually every conceivable party combination. The enhanced SNP presence in Scottish local-council chambers could be significant in 'oiling the wheels' of central–local government relations, just as the significant Labour presence did between 1997 and 2007.

As Table 4.2 highlights, it is the Scottish Labour Party who have been the big losers in the post-devolution period. This was because of a combination of decreased support and the new electoral system. Its number of councillors has almost halved since the first elections to Scotland's 32 unitary councils in 1995; the number of SNP councillors, on the other hand, has more than doubled. After the 2003 elections Labour had controlled 13 councils; after 2007 Labour controlled only two (Glasgow and North Lanarkshire). The Conservatives have also benefited from STV – increasing their level of

Table 4.1   *Local election results in Scotland, 2007*

Council	Coalition	Number of seats won					
		SNP	*Lab.*	*Other*	*LD*	*Con.*	*Total*
Aberdeen	SLD/SNP	12	10	1	15	5	43
Aberdeenshire	LD/CON	22	0	8	24	14	68
Angus	ALL-SNP	13	2	6	3	5	29
Argyll & Bute	IND/SNP	10	0	16	7	3	36
Clackmannanshire	LAB minority	7	8	1	1	1	18
Dumfries & Gall.	CON/LD	10	14	2	3	18	47
Dundee	LAB/LD	13	10	1	2	3	29
East Ayrshire	SNP minority	14	14	1		3	32
East Dunbartonshire	LAB/CON	8	6	2	3	5	24
East Lothian	SNP/LD	7	7	1	6	2	23
East Renfrewshire	LAB/SNP/IND	3	7	2	1	7	20
Edinburgh	LD/SNP	12	15	3	17	11	58
Falkirk	LAB/CON/IND	13	14	3	0	2	32
Fife	SNP/SLD	23	24	5	21	5	78
Glasgow	LAB	22	45	6	5	1	79
Highland	SNP/IND	17	7	35	21	0	80
Inverclyde	LAB minority	5	9	1	4	1	20
Midlothian	LAB minority	6	9	0	3	0	18
Moray	IND/CON	9	2	12	0	3	26
North Ayrshire	LAB min	8	12	5	2	3	30
N. Lanarkshire	LAB	23	40	5	1	1	70
Orkney	IND	0	0	21	0	0	21
Perth & Kinross	LD/SNP	18	3	0	8	12	41
Renfrewshire	SNP/LD	17	17	0	4	2	40
Scottish Borders	IND/CON/LD	6	0	7	10	11	34
Shetland	IND	0	0	22	0	0	22
South Ayrshire	CON min	8	9	1	0	12	30
S. Lanarkshire	LAB/CON	24	30	3	2	8	67
Stirling	LAB/LD	7	8	0	3	4	22
W. Dunbartonshire	SNP/IND	9	10	3	0	0	22
West Lothian	SNP/IND	13	14	4	0	1	32
Western Isles	IND	4	2	25	0	0	31
Total seats		363	348	202	166	143	1,222
Percentage of votes		30%	29%	17%	14%	12%	100%

LAB = Labour, CON=Conservative, LD = Liberal Democrat, IND = Independent, min = minority.

representation in 2007 despite a fall in their vote share to only 12 per cent. The independent councillor tradition is still very common in Scotland's more rural councils such as Highland, Argyll and Bute, Orkney and Shetland. Nearly half of all councillors (48%) were elected for the first time in 2007, which represents a significant turnover.

Table 4.2   *Local election results and party representation, 1974–2007*

Year	Labour % vote (seats)	SNP % (seats)	Con. % (seats)	Lib. Dem. % (seats)
2007 (Unitary)*	29 (348)	30 (363)	12 (143)	14 (166)
2003 (Unitary)	33 (509)	24 (181)	15 (123)	15 (175)
1999 (Unitary)	36 (551)	29 (204)	14 (109)	13 (161)
1995 (Unitary)	44 (613)	26 (181)	12 (82)	10 (121)
1992 (District)	34 (468)	24 (150)	23 (204)	10 (94)
1988 (District)	43 (553)	21 (113)	19 (162)	8 (84)
1984 (District)	46 (545)	12 (59)	21 (189)	13 (78)
1980 (District)	45 (494)	16 (54)	24 (229)	6 (40)
1977 (District)	32 (299)	24 (170)	27 (277)	4 (31)
1974 (District)	38 (428)	12 (62)	27 (241)	5 (17)

* 2007 vote-share figures relate to first-preference votes.

Scottish voting behaviour

Voting behaviour in Scottish elections has become a lot less predictable, with what were previously significant cleavages such as class and religion declining in importance. This can be said quite definitively, despite the fact that historical data prior to the 1960s on the Scottish electorate attitudes is scarce (see Budge and Urwin, 1966, for the first major study). Since then, explaining electoral choice has been one of the most vibrant branches of political science in Scotland (see Bennie *et al.*, 1997; Brown *et al.*, 1999; Paterson *et al.*, 2001; Bromley *et al.*, 2003; Curtice, 2005; Denver *et al.*, 2007).

In 1975 Pulzer stated, 'Class is the basis of British Party Politics, all else is embellishment and detail' (1975: 102). However, like much analysis of British politics at the time, it completely ignored what was going on in Scotland, since in the October 1974 UK General Election the SNP had achieved over 30 per cent of the vote in Scotland, securing votes across all social classes. Indeed one could argue Pulzer was writing just when the class basis of British political party alignment was beginning to break down. The share of the vote of the two main parties had also been in decline and for a period in the 1980s there was a lot of talk of the then **Social Democratic Party/Liberal Alliance** 'breaking the mould' of British two-party politics.

However, for much of the postwar period Pulzer's analysis was accurate at both Scottish and UK levels.

Social Democratic Party/Liberal Alliance: At the 1983 and 1987 UK General Elections the Liberal and Social Democratic Parties formed an alliance whereby they did not compete with one another in constituencies. In 1988 the parties merged to form the Liberal Democrats.

There was a high correlation between class and party alignment in Scotland (Budge and Urwin, 1966). The working class tended to identify with the Labour Party, while the middle class had a greater tendency to support the Unionist Party (as the Conservatives were called in Scotland until 1965). A class-based explanation of voter choice would suggest that Scottish voting behaviour merely reflects the socio-economic composition of Scotland – like the north-east of England it votes against the general British trend. For example, a study by McAllister and Rose (1984) found that most of the gap between Scottish and English voting behaviour could be partly explained by factors such as the socio-economic status of the electorate and the proportion of council housing in each country. Scotland has a higher social-housing occupancy rate – 30.9 per cent (Scottish Executive 2001e), and these tenants are more likely to vote Labour than owner-occupiers or those in the private rented sector (Midwinter *et al.*, 1991: 45).

One notable feature of the Scottish electorate has been subjective perception of working-class identity. The size of the working class has been falling in Scotland, by all objective indicators (see Payne, 1987). During the Thatcher era of deindustrialization the Scottish working class declined from 58 per cent to 48 per cent of the overall population (Bennie *et al.*, 1997: 100), although during that period self-perceptions of working-class identity rose from 81 per cent to 86 per cent amongst the working class and 49 per cent and 55 per cent amongst the **salatariat** (Bennie *et al.*, 1997: 102). Thus, although the class structure of Scotland and the rest of the UK is similar (McCrone, 2001: 83–4; Sweeney *et al.*, 2003: 83), subjective class identity is different.

Salatariat: Refers to the 'service classes' or 'professionals' such as teachers, managers and lawyers, but not, for example, employees of call centres or shop workers.

Class was, at least until the 1990s, an important variable in explaining the choice of Scottish voters. The 1997 UK General Election survey showed that only 6 per cent of working-class Scots voted Conservative, compared to 24 per cent of the middle class (although even the Scottish middle class do not vote for the Conservative Party in the same numbers as their counterparts in England). At British level the equivalent figure for the working class was 16 per cent (Brown *et al.*, 1999: 65). The 1999 Scottish Parliament election study also showed a clear correlation between class and party support (Denver and McAllister, 1999: 17).

Linked closely with theories of electoral choice emphasizing class are those associated with socialization. The Scottish electorate vote according to their social background and upbringing. Factors such as family, housing, community and workplace are accorded importance in shaping electoral preference (non-class based factors such as religion and gender, could also be deemed significant in such an explanation). The argument here is that such factors tend to reinforce class identity and in turn identification with the party of that class.

Psephologists:
Individuals with an interest in the study of elections and electoral behaviour.

Partisan dealignment: A shift from close ties to one party based on social factors (such as class) to more fleeting preferences.

However, a key trend identified by **psephologists** in recent decades has been **partisan de-alignment** and a decrease in the power of socialization to account for party identification (see Crewe, 1988). An individual's class background has become a less accurate predictor of voting allegiance. This is particularly the case in Scotland with the Labour Party and the SNP both campaigning as Scottish left-of-centre parties and competing for the same group of voters (see Brand *et al.*, 1993; Denver *et al.*, 2007). The link between Labour and the Scottish working class has been further diminished by their record in office after 1997 and the emergence of the Scottish Socialist and Green Parties.

Paterson *et al.* (2001: 58) report a 'dramatic' fall in the image in Scotland of the Labour Party as one that looks after working-class interests. Indeed the Scottish Labour Party is perceived as more successful at looking after middle (rather than working) class interests.

The rise of the SNP and Scottish national identity resulted in a new **cleavage** emerging in the Scottish electorate. Nationality interacted with class as a key

Cleavage: A division according to demographic characteristics (such as social class, national identity religion) used to explain political behaviour.

factor in changing electoral behaviour in Scotland in the 1980s and 1990s, and the SNP and the Labour Party have utilized both class and national identity to appeal to the electorate. In the past two decades the Labour Party has made the political aspect of its Scottish identity even more prominent, while the SNP has sought to develop a sharper and clearer progressive social democratic identity since Alex Salmond first assumed leadership. Over that period the Scottish political agenda has combined the constitutional question with 'bread and butter' class-based economic and public expenditure issues. Indeed one could argue it was the coupling together of both these issues in the shape of constitutional change as the 'solution' to the imposition of alien policies by a right-of-centre Conservative Government. In the 1980s the key cleavage in Scotland emerged as British constitutional and political conservatism against Scottish social democratic home-rulers.

The emergence of Scottish national identity as a significant cleavage in Scottish politics in the 1970s coincided with the collapse of the British Empire and the relative economic decline of Britain compared to new economic powerhouses such as the Germany and Japan in the 1960s. The politics of Scottish nationalism and identity became more evident as the appeal of being 'British' was no longer as self-evident. However, the rise of Scottish nationalism's impact on Scottish politics has been complex, wide and varied impacting on voter, party and media behaviour – therefore, it should not be automatically equated with the rise of the SNP.

Table 4.3 *Best choice for national identity, 1974–2005**

	1974	1979	1992	1997	1999	2001	2003	2005
Scottish	65	56	72	72	77	77	73	79
British	31	38	25	20	17	16	20	14

* other, 'don't know' and 'not answered' have been omitted

Sources: Data complied from Scottish Election Studies 1974–97 and Scottish Social Attitudes Surveys 1999–2006.

Table 4.3 highlights the rise in Scottish identity (and associated decrease in British identity) amongst the electorate in Scotland. The SNP has not been the sole beneficiary, with both the Labour Party and Liberal Democrats emphasizing their 'Scottishness'. Today, Scottish identity has a strong political as well as cultural dimension. Bennie *et al.*'s (1997) study highlighted how Scottish identity is intertwined with attitudes to England and anti-Conservatism. In the 1980s the Conservatives were portrayed by opposition parties as the 'class and national enemies' of the Scottish people (Bennie *et al.*, 1997: 99). This forging of class and nationality identity has been a significant part of the dynamic causing divergence in Scottish electoral behaviour. In the 1970s class and national identity were seen as conflicting cleavages, whilst in the 1980s and 1990s the association between class and national identity changed from a conflicting to a mutually reinforcing one. This was underpinned by a distinctively Scottish political agenda and discourse articulated by the opposition political parties and institutions. However, by the late 1990s such was the dominance of Scottish identity amongst the Scottish electorate that it was becoming a weaker predictor of electoral preference (see Denver *et al.*, 2000: 159–68).

Class and nationality have been two of the most significant variables in accounting for voter choice in Scotland. Another variable with some historical significance is religion. Historically in Scotland, the Conservative and Unionist Party utilized the appeal of the British Empire, religion, Ulster and a definition of Scottish nationhood derived from Presbyterian mythology to gather Protestant working class votes (see Walker, 1996). The Labour Party in Scotland has traditionally had the allegiance of the Roman Catholic community. In the early twentieth century there was a significant degree of anti-Catholic sentiment linked to the question of Irish immigration. Therefore, surveys in the west of Scotland in the 1950s and 1960s found a strong link between religion and voting, while Budge and Urwin found 75 per cent of working-class and 80 per cent of middle-class Catholics voted Labour at the 1964 election (1966: 69).

In a comparative context, the strong Catholic support for a left-leaning party is unusual – in mainland Europe it is more common for parties of the Right to secure the Catholic vote. The Scottish position probably reflects a combination of unique Scottish factors – the immigrant background of most Catholics and the large-scale unionization (and associated politicization) of the Catholic workforce. Catholics remain more pro-Labour and anti-Conservative than the population as a whole (Devine, 2000: 214).

This allegiance has proved stronger and more durable than that of the Protestant working class to the Conservatives. At the first Scottish Parliamentary elections in 1999, 60 per cent of the Catholic vote went to the Labour Party. In the 1970s and 1980s the SNP support was particularly weak amongst the 16 per cent of Catholics in Scotland. The reticence towards the SNP can be 'ascribed to the virulent strain of anti-Irish and anti-Catholic sentiment which can be found in the early history of the National Party' (Devine, 2000: 213). However, there is some evidence of the SNP beginning to make inroads into the Catholic vote in Scotland (Bennie *et al.*, 1997: 114), which may reflect the Catholic community becoming more comfortable in its Scottish identity. The proportion of Catholics describing themselves as Scottish has risen from 50 per cent in 1979 to 74 per cent in 1999. In the 2001 Scottish Social Attitudes survey, 40 per cent of Catholics considered themselves to be 'Scottish not British', compared to 35 per cent of Church of Scotland members (Bruce *et al.*, 2004: 179).

However, one should not overstate the influence of religion on political behaviour, especially when 37 per cent of Scots assert themselves to have 'no religion' which is now a higher figure than any religious denomination (Bruce *et al.*, 2004: 64) and the rate of observance is such that the Church of Scotland has placed a date on its potential demise at 2033 (Brown, 2001). Moreover, although religion's association with political identity in Scotland may be stronger than in England, it is weaker than other parts of Europe. In today's increasingly secularized Scottish society, the weakness of the direct appeal of religious-based parties was reflected in 2007 when the Christian Peoples' and Scottish Christian Party received only 2 per cent of the regional vote. In 1999 the Pro-Life Alliance received just 1 per cent of the vote in the regions where they stood, leading to Paterson's assertion that, 'There are now few Catholics who are Catholic enough to base their vote on specific Catholic issues' (2000: 227).

Religion appears to be a declining influence in Scottish electoral choice, particularly when one considers the rising number of Scots expressing non-identification with any of the established religions. The majority of Scots (60%) rarely or never attend church (Bromley *et al.*, 2003: 86–9). According to Scottish Executive (2001b) figures, just over 1.1 million Scots are active members of churches. Indeed, the most striking trend, in terms of religion in Scotland, is the increasing numbers declaring themselves to be of 'no religion'. In 1999, 37 per cent of Scots did not identify with any religion – an

Box 4.3   Section 28

The Section 28 episode highlighted how Scotland's religious leaders can influence the political process. Section 28 clause 2a of the Local Government (Scotland) Act 1986 stated that 'a local authority shall not intentionally promote homosexuality or publish material with the intention of promoting homosexuality'. In practice this meant teachers did not discuss homosexuality at all. The Labour-led Scottish Government proposed to abolish the clause in 2000, which led to a 'Keep The Clause' campaign led by a coalition of tabloid editors and church leaders, funded by millionaire Brian Souter (owner of the Stagecoach transport group). They argued that its repeal and the subsequent 'promotion of homosexuality' would threaten the traditional value of the family. The clause was, however, repealed in 2000 by a vote of 99 to 17, but concessions were given to placate religious leaders. In practice this means that while teachers are now able to discuss homosexuality, they are also required to stress the importance of a stable family life. This episode was an early indication that Scottish politics in the post-devolution era may not be quite as enlightened, liberal and inclusive as some of the home-rule campaigners had assumed.

increase by 50 per cent from 1974 (Bromley *et al.*, 2003: 87). Yet, as the experience of 'Section 28' shows, religious leaders can still exert significant political influence (Box 4.3).

There has been little work done on the impact of race and ethnicity on voting behaviour in Scotland, probably because of the low numbers in Scotland. However, parts of Scotland have significant immigrant populations; for example Glasgow has a significant Asian population (and does have both an Asian MP and MSP). Interestingly, recent survey evidence has detected this strong Scottish identity among the Scottish Asian community – 59 per cent of Asians defined themselves as Scottish Pakistani or Scottish Muslim (Kant and Kelly, 1992: 834). The UK Home Office's dispersal policy has added to the cultural mix, as has significant numbers of recent immigrants from new European Union countries such as Poland.

Another feature of electoral behaviour in Scotland worth noting is the different levels of support for the parties in different regions of Scotland. It would be wrong to suggest there is a strong rural–urban divide in Scottish politics. However, there are noticeable differences in party support in different parts of Scotland. The general decline of the Conservatives was first evident in the collapse of their support in cities such as Glasgow and Dundee in the 1980s. However, in Edinburgh and Aberdeen they remained strong – as late as 1983 the Conservatives held six of the capital's seven seats. The bedrock of support for the SNP and the Liberal Democrats has tended to be in the rural areas of Scotland.

Another suggested influence on voter choice is that of issues. Green-Pedersen (2007) charts how party competition in Western Europe is

Rational choice: An explanation of individual (or political party) political behaviour with reference to the maximisation of self-interest. In 'ideal' discussions these decisions are based on complete information and fixed preferences.

increasingly characterized by competition for the content of the party political agenda. The theory of the **rational choice** would suggest that the electorate peruses the policy manifestos of each party before making a judgement based on a calculation of the costs and benefits of each. However, the role issues play in electoral choice is debatable. There is evidence to support the claim that voters prefer the policies of parties they support (Butler and Stokes, 1974: 276–95) and the alternative – that policies determine the voters' party preferences (Sarlvik and Crewe 1983: 197–226).

Related to issue voting is the notion of **valence** voting. Stokes (1963) used the term to refer to consensual issues – like economic growth, low crime, improved healthcare – where there is broad agreement on the aims of politics. He argued that the electorate's perception of a party's capacity to deliver on such issues is highly important to party competition and electoral choice (see also Stokes, 1992). This is particularly the case during what Stokes referred to as a period of 'weak ideological focus' – parties are judged on *competence* rather than ideological differentiation. He suggested that during such periods, 'It will not do simply to exclude valence-issues from the discussion of party competition. The people's choice too often depends on them' (1963: 373). The present ideological convergence of parties in Scotland could be labelled such a period. As noted in Chapter 3 the main parties have largely converged on the same ideological/policy terrain. This makes valence

Valence: Refers to issues on which there is broad public agreement e.g. economic growth, good public services.

Box 4.4 Post-materialism and voting

Inglehart (1977) suggests that class politics was in decline with the electorate, taking material and physical well-being for granted, were entering into a stage of post-materialism. European politics was about the basic conditions of life up until the 1960s – however, now people no longer worry about material shortages and basic security. In a similar vein Dalton (1996) suggests traditional political cleavages were being replaced with new ones emphasizing such issues as the environment, minority rights and greater democratization. Modernization theories of political development in the 1960s and 1970s predicted the demise of 'pre-modern' bases of alignment such as territory, religion and ethnicity. They tend to emphasize a weakening of traditional social ties such as class, increasing secularization and a dealignment of political identification. However, beyond the emergence of the Green Party post-devolution, there is little evidence to support the thesis in Scottish politics. Indeed the rise of the SNP is an example of a party utilizing a materialist sound-bite ('It's Scotland's Oil') and a pre-modern cleavage (nationality) to develop and grow.

issues more relevant (see Clarke *et al.*, 2004). Another perspective on the decline of old tribal party loyalties is given by Inglehart (1977) – see Box 4.4.

According to Denver *et al.*, (2007), the Scottish voting behaviour literature has been dominated with a focus on 'position' – class locations, ideological stances and policy preferences – rather than 'valence' politics. Denver *et al.* (2007) suggest that valence politics have been an underappreciated factor in recent Scottish elections. Voters thus now have an increasing tendency to judge parties on such factors as performance in office, cohesion and leadership, economic competence and general image (see also Green, 2007). Indeed, this seems to have been taken to heart by the SNP, which has vowed to demonstrate its governing competence as the first step towards its pragmatic push for independence.

Party campaigning

Parties are not passive recipients of the electoral choices of voters. Downsian rational choice theory (Downs 1957) emphasizes the importance of party strategy – major parties tend to be as rational as some voters in their quest for votes (see Box 4.5).

Electioneering in campaigns has undergone significant change in recent decades. Parties have become gradually more attuned to the needs of the media and have utilized new communication and information technologies to

---

Box 4.5   Rational and tactical voting

In an early exposition of what has come to be known as rational choice theory, Anthony Downs (1957) in *An Economic Theory of Democracy* outlines a picture of democracy pervaded by rationality. Parties are conceptualized as entrepreneurs who operate in a political marketplace in which they try to attract as many voters as possible from voters (the consumers). Voters are conceived of as rational and well-informed consumers, basing their electoral choice on their scrutiny of each party's electoral platform. Parties seek to appeal to the mass of voters by offering a platform that is consistent with the median (average) voter – they offer a centrist platform in order not to alienate moderate voters who tend to form the majority of the electorate.

Downsian electoral choice theory also holds that electors are rational in who they decide to vote for. A manifestation of this is tactical voting where an elector chooses the party he/she thinks has the best chance of defeating an incumbent MP/MSP. It has been suggested (Brown *et al.*, 1999: 51) that part of the explanation for the Conservative Party's wipe-out at the 1997 UK General Election was the willingness of the Scottish electorate to vote tactically and defeat Conservative candidates. In the UK, Curtice and Steed (1997) found that of the 15 per cent who switched parties in 1997, 30 per cent did so for tactical reasons.

Box 4.6   Summary of party manifestos at the 2007 Scottish election

SNP
- Direct elections to health boards, legally-binding waiting times for patients, phase out prescription charges, individual health plans for school pupils and over 40s.
- Scrap council tax and introduce a local income tax set at 3p in the pound. Scrap Edinburgh tram scheme/rail link. Remove business rates for 120,000 small businesses.
- Smaller class sizes for P1 to P3), 50% increase in free nursery education. Abolish graduate endowment, replace student loans system, write off student debt.
- More police on the streets and new Serious Crime Task Force.
- No new nuclear power stations, more investment in developing renewable energy.
- Referendum on Scottish independence, probably in 2010.
- Double expenditure on international aid.

Labour
- £1.2 billion funding for schools and universities. Expand free pre-school education. Leaving school at 16/17 conditional on training or full-time volunteering.
- Reform council tax to reduce costs for pensioners and those in cheaper housing. No above-inflation council tax increases for four years. Double small business rates relief.
- 'Name and shame' neighbourhood troublemakers. New police powers to tackle serious and organized crime, and take advantage of new technology.
- Max. waiting times: 18 weeks outpatient treatment/16 weeks GP referral to cardiac intervention/four hours arrival-to-discharge/transfer for A&E treatment. Ban sale of cigarettes to under 18s. Increase entitlement to free school meals for an extra 100,000 children.
- At least 50% of electricity from renewable energy by 2020.
- Complete Glasgow and Edinburgh airport rail links. Re-open Waverley, Airdrie-Bathgate/ Stirling-Alloa lines. Reintroduce trams to Edinburgh.

→

---

engage with the electorate in new ways. Party image – which emphasizes such factors as an elector's *general* perception of a party, its policies or leader (Bennie *et al.*, 1997: 142) – has become more important in explaining electoral behaviour. Some voters identify with or lean towards a particular party (although these numbers are falling). Denver *et al.*'s (2007) Scottish Election study highlighted that the Scottish Labour Party still had more **identifiers** with an 'attachment' to it than the SNP despite the election result – 18.8 per cent identified with the Labour Party, while only 14.1 per cent identified with the SNP.

Identifier: Someone with a close affiliation with one party.

The image of leaders is important to how some view a party. This was highlighted at the 2007 Scottish Parliamentary election when the SNP sought to 'presidentialize' the election – on the regional list ballot paper the phrase 'Alex

Liberal Democrat
- Free playgroup places for 2-year-olds. 250 new schools and 1,000 teachers for smaller classes. Invest in further and higher education and scrap the graduate endowment.
- 100 per cent of electricity from renewables by 2050. Increase recycling rates to 70 per cent by 2020. Investment in energy efficiency, microgeneration and local power.
- 100 new local health centres; 2,000 extra nurses; and 200 extra dentists.
- Seven-year sentences for knife crimes. 1,000 extra community police officers.
- Lower business rate. Scrap council tax for local income tax.
- Faster trains between Scotland's cities and support for a high-speed link to London. Make Scotland a cycling nation. Replacement of Forth crossing and better public transport.
- A second Constitutional Convention. Voting rights at 16.

Conservative
- Review Holyrood powers, local government, cut back the size of public sector, power to directly-elected provosts. Half-price council tax for pensioners.
- Tougher sentences after three convictions. Less bail for serious offences. Youth courts for 14 and 15-year-olds. 1500 more police in neighbourhoods.
- Review to consider high-speed rail links. Remove tolls on Forth and Tay bridges.
- More power for head teachers. Boost science and technical subjects. Reinstate school boards. More flexibility on childcare. Support people onto property ladder.
- Freeze on on-shore wind farms. Grants of up to £4,000 for home-owners or businesses to install renewable energy. No block on nuclear power.
- Closed and threatened casualty and maternity wards should be preserved. Dental hygienists in schools. Improved mental health services, with waiting times measured.

Salmond for First Minister' (rather than SNP) appeared (this of course also had the bonus of ensuring the SNP appeared at the top of the ballot in alphabetical order). Scottish Labour is also assumed to have suffered by its association with the UK Labour Government's controversial foreign policy in Iraq.

As outlined in Chapter 3, in recent decades all political parties in Scotland have sought to project and emphasize their 'Scottishness'. Yet, Denver *et al.* also suggest – rather convincingly – that one of the key reasons for the SNP victory in 2007 was their positive agenda for governing Scotland, while Labour's negative campaign, and in particular their continuous reference to the risks associated with independence, was misdirected (2007: 30).

The UK General Elections in 2001 and 2005 also suggested that parties highlighted 'Scottish' or devolved issues when campaigning for representation in Westminster (see also Box 4.6). Three of the five pledges on Labour's

Scottish pledge card in 2001 referred to devolved issues! This of course is hardly surprising as issues such as health and education tend to be high on voter concerns – in 2001, 67 per cent felt these policies were crucial to deciding who they should vote for (Curtice, 2002: 11).

Yet, despite the blurred boundaries between devolved and reserved campaigning, party success is different for Holyrood and Westminster (see Tables 3.1 and 3.2 on pages 48 and 51). The SNP has noticeably achieved higher levels of support at Scottish than UK elections (which mirrors the experience of nationalist parties in other territories such as Catalonia). In the 1970s and 1980s, the SNP appeared rather opportunistic in its approach to electioneering and lacked a coherent collective image. Its *raison d'être* was independence and this was the only policy holding together a rather eclectic mix of members from across the ideological spectrum. Under the leadership of Salmond a clearer and more consistent social democratic ideological base has emerged. Post-devolution the party has sought to shake off the 'one-issue' party tag by projecting itself as a potential party of government. For example, at the first Scottish Parliamentary Elections in 1999 the SNP placed independence at the bottom of its 10-point pledge card (Jones, 1999: 3). A vote for the SNP is no longer equated automatically with a vote for Scottish independence. This strategy reached its fruition in 2007.

The Scottish Labour Party until 2007 adopted a campaign strategy largely in keeping with the UK national party; indeed, House of Commons-based MPs like Douglas Alexander and Gordon Brown have played significant roles during campaigning. The Labour Party won successive Scottish elections by strategically tailoring its message to the electorate particularly in the urban and central belt core of support. The involvement of Labour in the devolution campaign in the 1980s and 1990s was driven by their desire to maintain their hegemony in Scotland, and marked a departure from their previous beliefs in the contradictory nature of class and national political identity (Denver *et al.*, 2000: 15). Labour had to re-engage with national identity in an effort to maintain their Scottish working-class vote, as a result of the emergence of a centre–periphery cleavage in British politics.

The Scottish Liberal and Liberal Democrats have remained rooted in rural areas of Scotland – Bennie *et al.* (1997) suggest part of their strategic problem is a failure to develop a coherent collective identity – it is a party of 'local heroes'. The Liberal Democrats in 2003 successfully utilized their status as junior coalition partners in the Scottish Government to highlight their achievements.

Candidate selection

Each political party in Scotland has undergone significant transformation in its internal democratic processes post devolution, and a significant aspect of these reforms has been the new processes for the selection and election of candidates within each party. The Scottish Constitutional Convention's Electoral Agreement – signed by Labour, the Liberal Democrats and the Green Party – committed each to striving to achieve gender parity in MSPs.

The Labour Party's processes for selection at the initial 1999 Scottish Parliamentary elections were very rigorous. Candidates were asked to outline their Labour Party and life experience, commitment to the Scottish Parliament and equal opportunities, and relevant skills such as strategic thinking and action, advocacy, leadership and teamwork, communication and campaigning. The party received 600 applicants with 326 potential candidates interviewed, out of which 166 made it onto the party's approved panel of candidates. However, they faced a final hurdle – gaining a constituency party selection. This was further complicated by the fact that all of Scotland's constituency Labour parties were 'twinned' with a neighbouring constituency in order that one male and one female candidate could be selected.

The other parties also reformed their processes. The Liberal Democrats had gender balanced short-lists for constituency and list seats (though their elected candidates are predominantly male). The SNP, although not signatories to the SCC Electoral Agreement, did make efforts to achieve a gender balance. The Conservatives placed more emphasis on merit alone. What was common across all of the political parties was an increase in central party control over candidate selection (see Chapter 11 discussion on mirocosmic representation outlining how this impacted on the profile of Scotland's MSPs).

Is the Scottish electorate left-wing?

Scottish political attitudes are often characterized as being more left-wing than those in the rest of Britain (Lynch, 2001: 176). This is because election results and the parties the Scottish electorate tend to vote for are usually labelled left-of-centre. However, the evidence that the Scottish electorate have a distinct and separate more left-of-centre value system from those in England is inconclusive. Most research has tended to suggest that Scots are not as left-wing as voting behaviour would suggest (Brown *et al.*, 1998; Brown *et al.*, 1999; Paterson *et al.*, 2001).

Brown *et al.*, utilizing three scales to gauge left–right wing attitudes – socialist-*laissez faire*, liberal-authoritarian, and nationalist-cosmopolitan – do suggest that 'Scotland is different from the rest of Great Britain on all the three scales, being more socialist, more liberal and less British nationalist' (1999: 76). However, the differences are not as large as is often assumed. Paterson *et al.* (2001: 124–5) demonstrate, in many instances, just how similar the Scottish and English electorates are on key political issues. For example, 87 per cent of Scots thought 'income inequality is too high' compared to 84 per cent of the English, 78 per cent of Scots thought Government is responsible for healthcare, compared to 85 per cent of the English. An equal number (88%) in each country thought the government is responsible for maintaining the unemployed. The only issue where a sharp distinction is evident is on the question of redistribution – 61 per cent of Scots thought income and wealth should be redistributed compared to only 36 per cent of the English. Overall, a marginally higher proportion of Scots have left-wing views on most of the questions; however, there is more similarity than difference. As Paterson *et al.* note, '"redistribution" remains in the respectable political lexicon in Scotland' (2001: 126).

Conclusion

This chapter has outlined Scotland's four voting systems. The first-past-the-post electoral system is symbolic of Scotland's continued membership of the United Kingdom; the MMP system is a 'half-way house' adaptation, a compensatory proportional system (though not to the extent of some other MMP systems such as Germany and New Zealand); while the STV system for local elections has resulted in more coalition arrangements in Scotland's local councils. The introduction of both reflects an accommodation of Liberal Democrat interests by the Scottish Labour Party. The party-list system is used for European Parliament elections and reflects the European tradition of proportional electoral systems (though most European countries allow voters to have some influence over which candidates are elected through 'open' rather than 'closed' lists). The introduction of these new voting systems has resulted in increased levels of representation for all of Scotland's parties with the exception of the previously dominant, Scottish Labour Party.

The 'Scottish' dimension of elections in Scotland has been accentuated in recent decades. Since the emergence of the SNP, the constitutional issue has always been a key feature of election campaigning. Moreover, all of Scotland's parties have issued separate Scottish manifestos at UK General Elections. Each party has engaged in a strategy which seeks to project it as representing and defending Scotland's interests. 'Issues' have taken on a Scottish dimension (e.g. poll tax, water privatization, tuition fees, nuclear energy). Structural features of Scottish politics today have built Scottish political identity into Scottish political discourse (Bennie *et al.*, 1997: 160). Scotland is today a genuine multi-party democracy, with elections in all but a few safe seats, genuinely competitive.

Post-materialism: Refers to taking a basic economic security for granted and focusing instead on issues such as freedom, citizenship and the environment.

The competitiveness of elections is accounted for by the partisan de-alignment of the Scottish electorate. The trends in Scottish electoral behaviour have been related to wider themes in the electoral change literature such as **post-materialism**, rationality, partisan de-alignment and valence voting. Class, religion, housing tenure and other 'traditional' explanations of voting behaviour have all become less important in recent decades. The 2007 election of an SNP Government in Scotland could be said to be the culmination of four decades of elections where Scottish national identity has emerged as a significant new electoral cleavage. This has complicated the picture for psephologists seeking to explain why the Scottish electorate votes the way it does. The traditional anchors of voter loyalty have all receded in importance. Other factors such as general perceptions of party identity and general image, issue stances and leaders appear to have increased in importance.

Further reading

For a discussion of electoral system design see Shugart and Wattenberg (2000) and Diamond and Plattner (2006). There has been a lot of post-devolution work on Scottish political attitudes – see in particular Paterson *et al.* (2001); Curtice *et al.* (2002); Bromley *et al.* (2003) and Bromley *et al.* (2006). The key works on Scottish elections have been Budge and Urwin (1966); Brand *et al.* (1983); Bennie *et al.* (1997), Brown *et al.* (1999), Paterson *et al.* (2001) and Denver *et al.* (2007).

Online sources

Scottish Election Study 2007   http://www.scottishelectionstudy.org
Vote Scotland   http://www.votescotland.com
Electoral Commission   http://www.electoralcommission.org.uk
Fair Vote   http://www.fairvote.org
Arbuthnott Commission   http://www.arbuthnottcommission.gov.uk/
You Gov Pollsters   http://www.yougov.com
Populus Pollsters   http://www.populuslimited.com
Centre for research into elections and social trends (CREST)   http://www.crest.ox.ac.uk

Chapter 5

The Scottish Parliament: Actor, Arena and Agenda-Setter?

The Scottish Parliament has, since 1999, been the institution that has dominated media attention of Scottish politics. Most hopes for a new type of politics in Scotland were invested in the structure and operation of the Scottish Parliament. The Consultative Steering Group (CSG) – the cross-party group established to report on the operational requirements and draft rules for the Scottish Parliament – sought to enhance Parliament's ability to monitor the Scottish Government's policies and conduct, set the agenda through the inquiries process and initiate its own legislation if it identified gaps in Government policy. In other words, the Scottish Parliament had the *potential* to be an actor (as a collective body), an arena (for government legislation) and an agenda-setter (by raising issues through parliamentary questions and committee inquiries). Our task is therefore to examine the balance between these three broad roles. David Steel, the then **Presiding Officer** (see Box 5.2), argued in 2001 that the Parliament had, 'proved effective in delivering greater speed and degree of legislation for Scotland than was ever possible in the crowded agenda at Westminster' (Steel, 2001). Therefore, its effectiveness as a new arena is clear. However, an analysis of the role of the Scottish Parliament must also consider its wider influence in Scottish politics. Box 5.1 outlines the commonly cited functions of parliaments in liberal democracies.

Presiding officer: Politically impartial MSP who presides over the proceedings of the Scottish Parliament Plenary sessions, chairs the Business Committee, and gives rulings on Standing Orders.

At the heart of this new process is the role of parliamentary committees which were given more powers and a greater policy role than their Westminster counterparts. Yet, the CSG also recognized the need for the Scottish Government to 'govern' and did not equate power-sharing with the involvement of Parliament in the day-to-day decision-making process. This is an important qualification to the discussion of new politics, since the result may be a relatively powerful Parliament compared to legislatures in other countries but not compared to the Scottish Government which has far greater resources and remains a focal point for the policy process. This is particularly (but not only) the case when, as in 1999 and 2003, parties form a coalition large enough to exert majority rule on the Parliament and its committees. Therefore, the theory of parliamentary power may be qualified by the practice of parties and numerical dominance.

> ## Box 5.1 Functions of Parliament
>
> - **Law-making**. As a legislature a parliament deliberates, debates and passes new laws. The volume of new Scottish legislation vastly exceeds that of pre-devolution when it had to fit in a crowded UK Parliament timetable.
> - **Extend democratic control**. The intention of devolution was to extend the democratic control over the responsibilities previously held within the jurisdiction of the Scottish Parliament
> - **Legitimize the outputs of government**. Post-devolution the Scottish Parliament has legitimated legislation as a representative institution of the people and by providing a forum for the articulation of different interests. Parliament also provides an outlet for tensions. It gives its assent to laws originating from the executive branch of government.
> - **Socialization and training of politicians**. New parliamentarians are schooled in the 'rules' and practices of Scottish politics within the parliament.
> - **Holding the government to account**. By debating or questioning or through committees, ministers can be called to account for their actions and decisions.
> - **Providing a recruitment pool for ministers**. The Scottish Parliament provides the arena from which new ministers are recruited.
> - **Expression**. Scottish parliamentarians express the views and demands of their constituents providing a link between 'the people' and parliament.

This chapter explores these issues by examining:

- The Consultative Steering Group (CSG) proposals on parliamentary business.
- The legislative processes in Westminster and Holyrood.
- The formal structures and powers of Scottish parliamentary committees.
- The factors which qualify committee power, such as the role of parties, committee size and legislative workload.
- The significance of parliamentary 'outputs' such as committee inquiries, non-Government legislation and amendments to Scottish Government legislation.

The CSG proposals on parliamentary business

The CSG was guided by four main principles (Scottish Office, 1998a):

- The Scottish Parliament should embody and reflect the sharing of power between the people of Scotland, the legislators and the Scottish Government;
- The Scottish Executive should be accountable to the Scottish Parliament and the Parliament and Executive should be accountable to the people of Scotland;

- The Scottish Parliament should be accessible, open, responsive, and develop procedures which make possible a participative approach to the development, consideration and scrutiny of policy and legislation;
- The Scottish Parliament in its operation and its appointments should recognize the need to promote equal opportunities for all.

Its broad approach was to use Westminster as a point of departure and this is reflected in the proposals for parliamentary business. However, there are also similarities with Westminster. The most significant can be found in a description of the role of the Scottish Government:

- [The arrangements must] recognize the need for the Executive to govern, including enacting primary and subordinate legislation and obtaining approval of its expenditure proposals. (Scottish Office, 1998a: section 2.6.1)
- There appears to be little doubt that, while Members and Committees in the Scottish Parliament will have the power to initiate legislation, the majority of legislation will originate from the Executive. (Section 3.5.5)

In other areas, the broad aims would not look out of place in Westminster. The arrangements must:

- Provide Parliament with the time and opportunity to scrutinize the work of the Government.
- Allow for the debate of issues of both national and local interest.
- Enable individual Members to raise matters of concern and introduce proposals for legislation.

In other words, the CSG envisaged a traditional role for the Scottish Parliament in which the Government would propose policy and the Parliament would consider (and vote on) the principles. The difference was to come in the enhanced abilities of the Parliament to perform this scrutiny role (i.e. examining and questioning the operation of the executive branch of government) effectively, as well as the greater opportunity to introduce legislation. The former would be advanced by relatively powerful Scottish parliamentary committees which combine two separate roles found in Westminster – the **standing committee** which scrutinizes legislation proposed by the Government and the **select committee** which performs a broader monitoring role of a government department. The combination would enable members of these new committees to develop the type of specialist expertise

Standing committee: A non-permanent committee in the UK Parliament established to scrutinize Bills line-by-line.

Select committee: Committees which oversee the work of the executive branch of government (but not amendments to legislation – see standing committee).

The idea good – does it work though?

necessary to scrutinize the details of policy effectively (Section 2.13). It would also further the development of three significant roles. First, to conduct inquiries and influence the Government's future agenda. Second, to initiate legislation in areas not covered adequately by the Government. Third, to monitor the effectiveness of Scottish Government consultation with individuals and groups with an interest in policy.

The committees perform two functions. First, they ensure that the Scottish Government consults adequately before presenting legislation for parliamentary approval; and second, they consider the principles of the bill before it reaches plenary (i.e. the floor of the Parliament):

> What is desired is an earlier involvement of relevant bodies from the outset – identifying issues which need to be addressed, contributing to the policy-making process and the preparation of legislation . . . The role of the Committee would essentially be a monitoring/enforcing role to ensure the requirement is met. The Committee would always remain able to take evidence relating to the legislative proposals if it felt that the Executive's consultation process had been insufficient. (Section 3.5.4)

In a sense the CSG proposal killed two birds with one stone, since it also recognized that when Government proposals are produced in the form of a 'draft Act' presented to Parliament they are very difficult to change (Richardson and Jordan, 1979). Therefore, this 'policy-development stage':

> Would not only deliver a scrutiny stage pre-introduction, but would also allow individuals and groups to influence the policy-making process at a much earlier stage than at present. By making the system more participative, it is intended that better legislation should result. (Section 3.5.3)

This is not to say that the proposals presented to Westminster are somehow deficient because of a poor consultation process. Indeed, the main reason that 'draft Act' proposals are so difficult to change is that they are often based on painstaking consultation processes over a much longer period than it takes to process the legislation (Richardson and Jordan, 1979). Therefore, government resistance to substantive change is based on the belief that this would necessitate another round of consultation with the affected organizations. Rather, the distinctive approach in Scotland is to extend formal parliamentary involvement to the pre-legislative arena – to allow committee influence over the consultation process (to make it more 'participative') and then to consider the principles of the draft bill before it is presented to the House. While it reflects a strong commitment to widening participation, it also follows from the rejection of an equivalent to the House of Lords. With no **revising chamber**,

Revising chamber: A second legislative chamber in a bicameral system which reviews the legislative outputs of the other chamber.

there is greater emphasis on getting policy right at a much earlier stage. This is best demonstrated in a comparison of the formal legislative processes for bills in each Parliament.

However, we should bear in mind that new politics discussions often present a caricature of Westminster politics (see Chapter 1). As a result, four caveats should be borne in mind. The first is that Westminster MPs and committees may enjoy a degree of *informal* pre-legislative influence. The second is that Westminster procedures are subject to change, with a process of modernization taking place to ensure that more draft bills are produced to enable pre-legislative scrutiny and bills are referred to select committees (or committees containing members from the Commons and the Lords) (see House of Commons Information Service, 2007; Kelso, 2007; Flinders, 2007). The third is that there is a big difference between *hopes* for broad parliamentary influence and finding *evidence* of this in practice. Therefore, for example, the committee role in overseeing the pre-legislative process will not necessarily ensure meaningful involvement in the production of draft policy (Arter, 2004). Finally, it is reasonable to suggest that if 'old Westminster' is not an influential body, then the Scottish Parliament's relative strength is not that impressive.

The legislative process in Westminster and Holyrood – government bills

A comparison of the formal legislative processes demonstrates the basis for CSG changes (see Convery, 2000). In Westminster there is no formal involvement in the pre-legislative stage. The First Reading is purely formal and the bill is then printed and published. The Second Reading is the first substantive stage and this involves a plenary debate on the general principles of the bill. The principles are then approved (often without the need for a vote) and any relevant financial resolutions are passed. The bill proceeds to Standing Committee (a committee appointed by the speaker to specifically consider this bill). The committee then considers the bill and amendments to the bill on a line-by-line basis. The bill (as amended) is then 'reported' to the House of Commons and more amendments may be made at this stage. The final stage in the Commons is the Third Reading – the bill is debated but substantive amendments cannot be made. The bill then proceeds to the House of Lords, which tends to consider the bill on a whole House rather than Standing Committee basis. If the Lords does not amend, then the bill goes forward for **Royal Assent**. If it does amend, the bill goes back to the Commons for approval. If the Commons does not agree with the amendments, the bill is sent back and some negotiation takes place. If agreement is not possible, the Commons makes limited use of the Parliament Act of 1949 to overrule any Lords objection.

Royal Assent: The Sovereign formally signifies assent to Bills at both Scottish and UK level, which now becomes an Act and part of the law of the land.

[handwritten: Similar to Speaker of house of commons.]

Box 5.2 The role of the Presiding Officer

The CSG envisaged a broad range of roles and responsibilities for the chair of the Scottish Parliament:

- to be politically impartial, taking the interests of all Members equally into account;
- to preside over the proceedings of the Scottish Parliament in the Plenary session, exercising a casting vote in the event of a tie;
- to apply and give rulings on Standing Orders;
- to chair the Business Committee, which would prepare proposals for the Scottish Parliament on the agenda, organization of business etc.;
- to take decisions on the legislative competence of draft Bills; to submit Bills for Royal Assent, and other functions associated with the legislative process;
- to represent the Parliament in interactions with the Scottish Administration, the UK Parliament, and the devolved Assemblies in Northern Ireland and Wales and any inter-Parliamentary bodies associated with them;
- to represent the Scottish Parliament in interactions with other Parliaments and Assemblies furth [outside] of the United Kingdom.

Most of these roles are performed by the Speaker at Westminster and the distinctiveness of the Scottish role may be based on circumstance rather than design. For example, the role as chair of the Business Committee may only become significant under a minority administration, since from 1999–2007 the ruling coalition effectively controlled parliamentary business through its block vote. Similarly, the greater deference to the Presiding Officer in debates may result from the design of the Parliament itself, with the shape of the chamber and the use of microphones undermining adversarial confrontation. Electoral circumstances also determine the supply of candidates. In 1999 and 2003 the post was held in high esteem and the elections (through a secret ballot) of Sir David Steel (Liberal Democrat) and George Reid (SNP) were seen to an extent as rewards for previous public service. In 2007 the number of MSPs in each party was so finely balanced that the loss of one-vote (to maintain the impartiality of the role) was crucial. The election of a Presiding Officer was delayed until it became clearer which party would form a government. While Margo MacDonald, as the only 'independent', was mooted as a compromise candidate (and received 20 votes), the overwhelming choice (108) was for Conservative MSP Alex Fergusson after he (perhaps in the Westminster tradition) agreed reluctantly to stand.

In the Scottish Parliament there are differences at almost every stage. First, there is systematic involvement at the pre-legislative stage. The lead committee is given a supervisory role to ensure that the consultation process is not too short or restricted to a small number of groups. This is performed by the lead committee which is appointed after the introduction of the bill and asked by the Presiding Officer (Box 5.2) to assess the need for more consultation before the bill is considered by the Parliament in **plenary**.

[handwritten: Holyrood Method]

Plenary: The floor of the Scottish Parliament, where all MSPs are in attendance.

Second, the introduction of the bill is not a mere formality. The Presiding Officer makes a written statement that the provisions are within the competence of the Scottish Parliament, and the bill is accompanied by Scottish Government documents: a Financial Memorandum which sets out estimates of costs and explains which organizations will bear them, a brief statement of the policy (Policy Memorandum) and some Explanatory Notes. In other words, there is an expectation that the Scottish Government will justify the introduction of the bill.

Third, at stage 1 the principles of the bill are considered by the lead committee (which often takes evidence from other relevant committees). The lead committee then presents its report to Parliament, which debates and votes on the general principles of the bill. Unlike Westminster, this initial process is not a formality. The committees' deliberations are based on often extensive interviews with affected groups and the minister (accompanied by the civil service bill team), and its recommendations often translate to bill amendments at stage 2.

Fourth, at stage 2 the bill is referred back to the lead committee which considers amendments on a line-by-line basis (with the exception of 'Emergency Bills' which take stages 2 and 3 in the House on the same day). Any MSP may propose to amend the bill, but only members of the lead committee may vote on amendments. The detailed process may be preceded by a further round of interviews with ministers and affected groups.

Finally, at stage 3 the Committee of the Whole House undergoes a similar amendments process. The House considers and amends the Bill on a line-by-line basis and then debates and votes to pass or reject the bill (no Scottish Government bill has ever been rejected at this stage). The bill is then sent for Royal Assent and there is no equivalent of the legislative ping-pong between the Commons and Lords.

Therefore, the main difference is the role of the Scottish Parliament committee which oversees the pre-legislative consultation process, considers the principles of the bill before it is presented to the House, and takes evidence on the nature and effects of the bill before considering detailed amendments. The assumption is that the process enhances the role of Parliament, by removing discussion of the bill from a charged partisan atmosphere dominated by Government to a more business-like committee arena in which MSPs from all parties seek consensus. Further, since the lead committee also performs the role of a select committee, it draws on previous policy experience and regular discussions with a range of organizations (when, for example, conducting broader inquiries). This contrasts with a Standing Committee without the same level of stability and capacity to investigate.

Yet, we should not overstate the practical effects of these differences. First, there is still an assumption that Scottish committees will take a 'hands-off' pre-scrutiny role, allowing the Government as the elected government to pursue its own policies, and maximizing the use of Committee time, 'allowing Committees to focus on proposals which have already been the subject of participative involvement of interested bodies' (section 3.5.6). Second, the assumption of consensus-seeking also depends as much on the attitudes of MSPs as the institutions through which policy is processed. Finally, as the discussion of 'withinputs' below suggests, the combination of select and standing committee roles alone does not guarantee the required levels of stability and expertise.

The legislative process in Westminster and Holyrood – non-government bills

The CSG also envisaged a more significant and straightforward ability for MSPs and committees to introduce legislation. Indeed, when we compare the process with Westminster, it is difficult to see how the process could be *less* significant and straightforward!

In Westminster there is no equivalent to the committee bill, while the three main ways in which to pursue a Private Members' Bill are convoluted, with limited prospect of success (bills can also be introduced in the Lords, with no greater chance of success). To a great extent this results from party dominance in the House, with the ruling party effectively determining the amount of time allotted to the discussion of a bill. With the 'Presentation' or 'Ten-Minute Rule' options, MPs may present the title or speak for 10 minutes about the advantage of a bill.

However, since no more time for debate is given, the process is used to raise awareness and gauge parliamentary support. The greatest chance of success comes to MPs whose names appear near the top of a ballot held within two weeks of the commencement of each parliamentary session; 20 MPs' names are drawn, with those at the top receiving the most time for debate. Yet, since there is such an element of chance, MPs approach Members' Bills on the assumption that it is unlikely that they will reach the Statute. Indeed, some MPs may not decide on which bill to pursue until they are sure that they are high enough on the list. If selected, they may become a focus for interest group pressure, pursue a bill handed down by government, or use the parliamentary space in a trade with another MP. Therefore, as a whole, MP bills are most likely to be introduced as a form of pressure or agenda-setting – to highlight an issue or to encourage the government to introduce its own bill (see House of Commons Information Service, 2006).

In Scotland the process was designed to allow a more straightforward chance for MSP success (although an MSP may have similar agenda setting motives). From 1999 to 2004 the process began with an MSP registering a proposed bill with the Clerk to ensure publication in the *Business Bulletin*.

Box 5.3   Case study: the member's bill on smoking in public places

In February 2004, Stewart Maxwell MSP (SNP) introduced a bill to prohibit smoking in certain public places. This was limited in scope, applying to premises where food (largely a devolved area) is served and consumed. The process that followed the introduction of the bill demonstrates two aspects of the distinctiveness of the Scottish process. First, Maxwell was aided by the Non-Government Bills Unit (NEBU), designed to address the problem of MSP resources when drafting legislation. Second, the lack of MSP ability to consult widely with groups and affected interests is addressed by the committee process in the lead-up to its stage 1 report. At this stage the lead committee takes responsibility for the development of the bill. The Health Committee received 323 written submissions and met seven times to discuss the bill in 2004 before delivering its report. The report was supportive of the evidence on passive smoking and the principles of the bill, and critical of the voluntary arrangements between the Scottish Government and licensed premises. Although its findings were delayed until the Scottish Government consulted on introducing a more comprehensive bill, its views were well known to Scottish Ministers. Therefore, while Maxwell's bill may have still fallen at stage 1, the MSP and committee support it received added significant pressure on the Government to come forward with its own legislation. While there have been similar attempts to set the agenda in Westminster and the Lords, the process did not allow the same level of support to develop in debates and committee (Cairney, 2007b).

S/he then had one month to gather the support of at least 11 other MSPs. If this support was demonstrated, then the bill would follow the same initial procedure as Government Bills – considered and investigated at stage 1 by a lead committee before sending a report to the House. This report would inform a formal debate and vote on the bill's principles. Therefore, while it would be unrealistic to think that the process is not subject to the same type of party politics (particularly in periods of majority coalition government when bills without Scottish Government support are still unlikely to progress past stage 1), there is at least a more straightforward opportunity for MSPs to raise issues and ensure time for debate. As Box 5.3 suggests, this may encourage the Scottish Government to respond to the issue.

The CSG also proposed that committees could introduce bills within their area of competence. While the committee does not need to gather other MSP support, it is required to provide Parliament with an account of why the Bill is necessary. In effect, this usually involves a similar process of consultation between the committee and relevant groups/ experts. The bill then proceeds straight to stage 1 for full parliamentary consideration. As the CSG report suggests, this route is far less likely to be taken by committees than individual members, but the success rate is likely to be much higher.

Parliamentary Bureau: Cross-party body which proposes the programme of business in the Parliament and the establishment, remit and membership of committees.

Non-Executive Bills Unit: A clerking team within the Parliament whose role is to assist both members and committees in preparing Members' or Committee Bills and taking them through Parliament.

In both cases, we see processes which allow a degree of parliamentary consideration without reliance on Government support. However, moves since 2004 to amend the standing orders for Members' Bills demonstrate the limits to this process. From November 2004 the number of required supporters was raised to 18 and a 12-week period for public consultation was introduced. This was followed in October 2005 by the introduction of rules (to be interpreted by the **Parliamentary Bureau**) to determine which bills received the most support from the **Non-Executive Bills Unit** (NEBU). While this led to suspicion that the changes were designed to undermine the strategies of smaller parties (who could not command the MSP numbers or find alternative resources for policy development), it reflected recognition that too many complex bills could stretch the resources of the NEBU and the relevant committees. Since no equivalent changes were made to the Government bills process, we see in these most recent moves a recognition that the Government will 'govern', while non-Government bills effectively 'fill in the gaps' and compete for limited parliamentary resources.

The powers of Scottish Parliament committees

To explore the influence of the Scottish Parliament and its committees we can examine the formal powers that institutions enjoy, the factors that may undermine the exercise of those powers, and the tangible effects of these powers (Arter, 2002, labels these 'inputs, withinputs and outputs'). By combining the standing and select committee functions, the architects of the Scottish Parliament invested in Scottish committees an unusual range of powers compared to Westminster and the legislatures of most West European countries. The Scottish Parliament has permanent and specialized committees with relatively small numbers of members, a proportional (by party) number of convenors (chairs) selected by a committee, committee deliberation both before the initial and final plenary stages, the ability to initiate and redraft bills as well as invite witnesses and demand government documents (including the role of monitoring pre-legislative consultation).These are all indicators of unusually high committee strength according to Mattson and Strøm's (2004: 100–1) criteria. As Arter (2002: 99) suggests, the Scottish committee system was designed to be, 'extraordinarily deliberative, rationalistic, open and consensual':

- **Deliberative** – there is a two-stage consultation process before a bill goes to the House (first by the Scottish Government under committee supervision and second by committees themselves).

- *Rationalistic* – there is a huge information gathering exercise during consideration of issues.
- *Open* – there is good contact with groups, and the operation of the Scottish Parliament is well publicized.
- *Consensual* – there is a commitment to seeking pragmatic rather than dogmatic solutions.

However, the committee framework is also subject to practical constraints. In part, this relates to the limited resources the Scottish Parliament has in comparison with the Scottish Government. While small committees may foster a business-like attitude to politics, they may also struggle to conduct a wide range of business in a short time-period (committees were initially expected to meet once per fortnight on a Tuesday or Wednesday morning, with the Wednesday afternoon and Thursday reserved for plenary). These problems were heightened during the 1999–2003 session when committee turnover was high and the legislative timetable of the Scottish Government was very demanding (it passed 50 bills). As a result, a report by the Procedures Committee warned against the Parliament becoming a 'conveyor belt for passing legislation' to the detriment of scrutiny and influence (Procedures Committee, 2003, paragraph 1016). Yet, from 2003–07 this rate of legislation *increased*, with 53 Scottish Government bills passed (relatively time-consuming private bills also rose from one to nine).

However, by far the most significant factor is the role of parties. This was particularly the case during the coalition years (1999–2007). During this period the governing coalition had enough MSPs to ensure a voting majority on all committees and the lead member in each committee acted an informal **party whip**, with parties often agreeing a party line before the official meetings.

Party whip: A means to ensure party discipline when voting on legislation or amendments.

The parties also appoint their own convenors (although the numbers of convenors are allocated proportionately) and even decide which MSPs sit on which committees. As a result, many MSPs complained about the detrimental effects of constant party control on the 'independence' of committees (see Scottish Council Foundation, 2002). As Arter (2003: 31–2) suggests, both factors (resources and party control) came together during the committee restructuring which took place in December 2000. Those in support of the change pointed to early problems – the excessive workload of some MSPs (with some serving two or three committees) and some committees (especially the Justice and Home Affairs Committee which processed one-third of Scottish Government bills). The solution was to reduce committee membership (to seven or nine members in many cases) and create more committees where necessary (for example, a second Justice committee). This would reduce the need for some MSPs to attend multiple committees and give the overloaded committees more time to focus on work

Box 5.4 Are Scottish parliamentary committees effective?

The arguments below outline the case for each side (Arter, 2002):

Effective

1 Small size will foster an effective collective identity and hence committee autonomy.
2 The combined roles of standing and select committees will foster policy expertise.
3 Committees will foster an agenda-setting role though inquiries which are not in the control of party managers.
4 Working practices will be consensual rather than partisan.
5 The openness of proceedings will discourage adversarialism.

Ineffective

1 The committees will be too small to make scrutiny effective (especially if there are attendance problems).
2 High turnover undermines a committee ethos and the combined roles leads to overload.
3 The legislative load means that committees have no time for agenda setting through inquiry work.
4 The open process will lead to party posturing (extending to witness examination which is often ritualistic).
5 Committee specialization will fragment the House and undermine collective decision-making.
6 In effect, there is always a trade-off between broader MSP knowledge, time and turnover.

other than legislation. However, those against the change suggested that the driver was a Scottish Government wish to process its legislation more quickly and the change was forced through by the business managers of the main parties. While it is difficult to take a clear position on these arguments, we may at least say that in this case (and the discussion of Members' Bills reform) the role of parties – rather than as assumption of new politics and consensus – remained uppermost in the minds of MSPs.

In this light, a combination of Scottish parliamentary powers and constraints suggests that the *structures* of committees may not be a good predictor of the *influence* of Parliament. As Box 5.4 suggests, there is no agreement on the optimal size of committees, the optimal balance between expertise and workload, or the effect that parties will have on the operation of committees.

Therefore, to gather a more definitive picture of parliamentary influence we need to extend our analysis to 'outputs'. For example, Arter (2003) suggests that there is evidence of Scottish parliamentary influence in the healthy number of public **petitions**, the number of committee inquiries and the high number of non-Government bills. To this we can add the level of parliamentary influence on Scottish Government bills and perhaps the wider element of pressure brought to bear by oral and written questions to ministers. Yet, the tangible effect of petitions is difficult to pin down (see Chapter 11). It is therefore worth considering in detail the nature of these outputs.

Petitions: A process allowing people to bring an issue to the Scottish Parliament's attention if they can demonstrate a level of public support.

Parliamentary questions and committee inquiries

As outlined previously, Question Time, First Minister's Questions (FMQ) and the format to pursue written questions of MSPs to the Government do not differ significantly from Westminster procedures. While the Procedures Committee's recommendation to move the FMQ time slot (to noon rather than 3pm on Thursday) was agreed in 2004, this was really tinkering with a format which is essentially party-political, giving the opposition and First Minister the chance to let off steam rather than elicit serious responses. FMQs are stage-managed shows where MSPs and ministers seek to score points over their opponents and gain positive coverage in media news programmes.

To pursue constituency, factual and substantive policy points, an MSP may be better served with the written question. Interview evidence with civil servants and Government agency officials (2004) suggests that these are taken very seriously. Indeed, the usual official response (which has parallels with attitudes to freedom of information requests) is that the process takes up a disproportionate amount of limited time.

There are also occasions when parties can elicit responses to highlight perceived flaws in government policy. One notable attempt was made by Conservative Party leader Annabel Goldie MSP, who used a written question to oblige the Scottish Government to release figures on the use of Anti-Social Behaviour Orders (ASBOs). Goldie then used the information to suggest that, in comparison with England, the Government had 'gone soft' on crime. Yet, while the constituency role of MSPs is important and there are signs of agenda-setting in the process, it is difficult to see any tangible policy effects from these activities.

The same can be said for committee inquiries. For Arter (2003), inquiries represent (in part) an assertion of committee autonomy, with his interviewees suggesting that during this process the committee MSPs felt most independent from the Scottish Government. The findings may also help shape the policy agenda (examples include changes to water policy, mobile phone masts, and the push towards policy on free care for the elderly – Box 5.5).

Yet, in all cases it is difficult to find examples where the committee inquiry

Box 5.5 The Health Committee and free personal care for older people

Since a range of actors may all be involved when a policy decision is made, the influence of each is subject to interpretation and debate. This is certainly true in the case of free personal care for older people which was one of the Scottish Government's 'flagship' policies and marked significant divergence after Scotland, but not the UK, implemented the recommendations of the Sutherland report (see Chapter 9). But how influential was the Health and Community Care Committee (2000) inquiry on this policy? One way to explore this is to present two competing 'narratives' on its role within the wider political process:

A 'best case' narrative

In 1999, Westminster's Health Select Committee recommended implementing the Sutherland reports' recommendations but the government signalled its intention to target spending. In Scotland, the Scottish Government announced similar plans in October 2000. Then the Scottish Parliament's Health and Community Care report called for a full implementation of Sutherland in November 2000. This show of all-party support combined with the status of Scottish committees (and the weight of evidence gathered from interest groups during its inquiry) suggested that there would be significant opposition to a more limited policy. This contributed to a reversal of Scottish Government policy and proved more influential than pressure within the Scottish cabinet and the UK Government to follow a uniform line.

A 'worst case' narrative

Shortly after the Scottish Government decision to follow the UK line, First Minister Donald Dewar died. His successor, Henry McLeish was held in less high esteem and was keen to 'make his mark'. McLeish saw free personal care as an opportunity to address his position, and following the HCCC report which included survey evidence on public attitudes to free care, McLeish knew that free personal care would be popular and could be used as a resource. He announced his intention to pursue this policy on *Newsnight Scotland* without seeking cabinet approval. Then, when he saw the opposition in his cabinet and from the UK, he appeared to back-track. However, the costs of a media, public and parliamentary backlash soon became clear. The Liberal Democrats favoured the policy and conspired to force McLeish's hand within cabinet, since the likely alternative was a Labour defeat in the Scottish Parliament (the SNP and Conservatives both planned to vote for the policy, in part to expose Scottish Government divisions). The policy shift is therefore better explained by chance, opportunism and party politics.

does more than add to the pressure which already exists. However, this may be holding up the process to an unfair standard, since even the Scottish Government relies on a wide range of factors (such as its perception of public opinion) and events (such as crises which focus attention on issues) when pursuing policy change. What we can say with more certainty is that the first parliamentary session represented a 'honeymoon period'. The second session saw a change in committee focus towards scrutinizing Scottish Government legislation and Sewel motions (see Chapter 8). While from 1999–2003 there were 166 inquiries (Arter, 2004: 77), this fell to 99 in 2003–07 (of which 11 were short or one-day inquiries). Indeed, a common theme throughout committee 'legacy' papers (which summarise their work and suggest future business for subsequent committees) was that the scrutiny of Scottish Government business undermined independent committee investigations. For example, the Communities Committee undertook no inquiries in this period because of

> The lack of available time . . . due to the volume of legislation designated to the Committee to consider. The Committee would have preferred greater balance in the Committee's workload so that it could have had the opportunity to initiate its own work, in addition to scrutinizing legislation. (Communities Committee 2007)

A similar concern was expressed by the Enterprise and Culture Committee (2007):

> Certain subjects, such as science policy, corporate social responsibility, European structural funding, built heritage and architecture, which all fall within the remit, have barely been addressed, despite their importance. It is the considered opinion of the members of this Committee that such a wide-ranging remit is not always conducive to proper scrutiny of the subject matter and to balancing the legislative workload with own-initiative work such as inquiries.

Non-government bills

For Arter (2004: 80–1), the unusually high number of successful non-Government bills in the first session (12 out of 61) suggests that the Scottish Parliament could be considered to be a 'legislating assembly'. The importance and number of committee (3) and member bills (8) suggested that Scottish practice was, 'light years away from Westminster practice and indeed most other West European legislatures outside the Icelandic Alpingi'. Yet, the idea of a major legislating role was not envisaged by the CSG which recognized the Government's need to govern. The conclusions also do not tally with the literature on Government–parliament relations which points to an immense gulf between their relative capacities. The Government has far more resources to consult with groups and to research, initiate, draft, redraft, monitor and evaluate bills. So how do we explain the appearance of the Scottish Parliament 'punching above its weight'?

The first answer is that while these numbers are important in comparison with other legislatures, there is less reason to think that they are significant in comparison with Government bills. Non-Government bills are more restricted in their scope by the relative inability of MSPs to consult widely with interest groups and rely on a large specialist staff to research and draft the bill. They tend to address relatively limited aspects of public policy or take a long time to pass (e.g. in the first session, members passed bills to allow St Andrews University to provide post-graduate medical education, fine the owners of fouling dogs and to address issues the Government did not have time for – such as the law on leaseholds and mortgage rights).

Experience from the two most significant members' bills in the first session demonstrates this point. While the bill passed to outlaw fox hunting was significant (at least symbolically) and, at the time, marked divergence from England and Wales, it also took up an incredible amount of committee resources and took two years to pass. Similarly, while the Abolition of Poindings and Warrant Sales Bill 2001 represented a significant victory for campaigning MSP Tommy Sheridan (particularly since it spurred on the threat of a Labour backbench rebellion to ensure its passage), the bill did not provide an alternative method of debt collection. Rather, it contained a clause to give enough time for the Scottish Government to develop its own plans. In the event, the Government amended Sheridan's bill (against his wishes) to give them an extended period of review. Then, when it introduced its own bill, it resisted all attempts by Sheridan to amend its legislation.

The second answer is that the first session was the honeymoon period of new politics. In the second session, only three members' bills were passed. While one member passed a bill to outlaw the discouragement of breastfeeding in public places, the other two may have little more than symbolic importance. One introduces a bank holiday to celebrate St Andrew's Day (but not the requirement for banks to close) and one obliges large shops to close on Christmas day (which virtually all do anyway). Similarly, the second session saw committees raise their total from three to four bills (of which two related to the conduct of MSPs), in further recognition that committees legislate only as a last resort or in areas with cross-party significance.

The third answer is that the Scottish Parliament did *not* pass an unusual number of bills. While it passed 25 **non-Government bills** (19.5% of 128) from 1999–2007, 10 were private bills which: (a) for the most part progressed major private transport projects rather than a parliamentary agenda; (b) undermine MSP capacity (to the extent that the Scottish Parliament voted to replace the private bills process with parliamentary approved ministerial orders for major transport developments); and (c) have equivalent numbers in Westminster. If we remove private bills, then the 15 represents 12.7 per cent of all public bills, compared to 11.1 per cent in Westminster in the same period (House of

Non-Government bills: Bills introduced into Parliament by MSPs or Committees.

Commons Information Service, 2006: 7). Therefore, the Scottish Parliament's abilities to initiate legislation are less significant than the early numbers suggest and it is unclear just how much the Scottish Parliament's 'powers' translate to more significant policy outcomes than we see in Westminster.

Influencing Scottish Government primary legislation

Of course, with non-Government bills we may be setting too high a standard to assess the legislative role of the Scottish Parliament. Since the CSG suggests a traditional scrutiny role, then perhaps this is where we will see the added value of the committee process. This begins at stage 1, with committees assessing the principles of the bill and evaluating the stakeholder consultation process (including the option to recommend more consultation or undertake its own oral sessions).

A 'best-case' analysis of this process is that since the Scottish Government is generally good at consulting widely (see Chapter 6), the committees rarely have to invoke their powers. Further, in the rare occasions they do, this is taken seriously and acted upon. For example, in 2006 the Education Committee intervened when examining the Protection of Vulnerable Groups (Scotland) Bill. The bill followed UK legislation based on the Bichard Inquiry into the Soham murders. While Bichard made recommendations for England and Wales, the Scottish Government (2006c) took the opportunity to 'learn lessons', close possible UK loopholes and reform the often-criticized Scottish system. However, at stage 1 the committee highlighted a lack of sufficient consultation around part 3 of the bill (on disclosure and sharing information) and criticized the fact that too much was left to regulations rather than **primary legislation.** Following oral evidence with groups critical of the proposed scheme, it recommended successfully that part 3 be dropped from the bill.

> **Primary legislation:** Legislation made by the legislature – to be contrasted with secondary legislation made by the executive branch of government usually within boundaries laid down by the legislature.

Similarly, the Health Committee's relatively assertive stage 1 report on the Adult Support and Protection (Scotland) Act 2007 prompted changes when its oral evidence sessions revealed disagreement among voluntary organizations about the tone and scope of the bill. The bill was designed to 'fill gaps' left by legislation on incapacity and mental disorder in which state intervention only takes place when individuals lack the mental capacity to make their own decisions. With the new bill, such intervention would take place if the individual had capacity but was deemed to be in an excessively vulnerable position. The oral evidence highlighted that groups representing older people were in favour but charities representing people with learning disabilities objected. Following a Health Committee recommendation, the bill was amended to exclude the latter and to remove the ability of the Scottish Government to amend the bill in future without primary legislation.

At stage 2 (following parliamentary approval of the bill's principles), committees then have the ability to scrutinize and amend the bill in detail. This is followed at stage 3 by Whole House consideration of final amendments and a final vote (if necessary) to approve the bill. The convention is that the most significant amendments will be considered at stage 2 in the relatively business-like and expert committee arena, to allow the fullest possible scrutiny and to guard against the possibility of 'bounced' amendments (in which the Scottish Government amends a bill at the last moment to circumvent scrutiny). It is perhaps at stage 2 that we would expect to find the added value of Scottish Parliament committees, since the combination of standing and select committees allows for detailed consideration by MSPs specializing in the relevant policy area. But how do we demonstrate this value? Shephard and Cairney (2004, 2005) analysed all amendments to Scottish Government bills in the first parliamentary session (1999–2003), leading to four main findings:

- The Holyrood process appears to mirror the data collected by Griffith (1974) on Westminster. The Scottish Government appears to dominate the stage 2 and 3 processes since it proposes the vast majority of all successful amendments, while MSPs propose most of the failed ones.
- However, this does not necessarily undermine the process. Most of these amendments are either a mere consequence of the drafting rules or relate to the type of detail that the Scottish Parliament would expect the Government to deal with. In this sense, 'dominance' refers to a power *granted by* Parliament rather than a power *over* Parliament. Further, if we examine the most substantive amendments, then committee and parliamentary influence becomes much clearer.
- A central part of this process involves MSPs withdrawing amendments at stage 2 when assured that the Scottish Government will address the issue and bring forward an amendment at stage 3. Indeed, withdrawal explains the majority of 'failed' amendments.
- Although the Government used its majority to win almost all of the votes on amendments, very few (3%) reach this point.

A best-case analysis suggests that the process is based on trust and a good working relationship between Government and legislature. It is demonstrated by the willingness of the Scottish Government to explain and justify all of its amendments and for MSPs to accept them without the need to vote. Perhaps more significantly, it is also demonstrated by a willingness of MSPs to accept the need for the Government to address their concerns and revisit the issue on their behalf. Much of this process is based on norms or conventions in the spirit of 'new politics' which endured throughout the first full session (particularly when the minister had previous experience as a committee member).

The evidence also suggests that the Government shows a healthy respect for the centrality of committees to legislative scrutiny. Whilst the plenary stage is relatively partisan and the Government can rely on its majority, it has demonstrated a clear willingness to remove most controversial decisions from this arena and into a less partisan committee arena designed to foster power sharing between Government and parliament. At the heart of this process is the trade of withdrawn amendments for Government assurance. Indeed, this trade, combined with direct MSP influence, accounts for almost 60 per cent of substantial amendments presented at stage 3 of the process (Cairney, 2006b).

But what would a less sympathetic explanation highlight? First, we could argue that the examples of *Adult Support* and *Vulnerable Groups* are atypical since the Scottish Government rarely withdraws legislative proposals in response to parliamentary concern. Second, the examples demonstrate that MSPs are reliant on interest groups to raise issues and propose amendments. This points to the Scottish Parliament as an *arena* as much as, if not more than, an *actor* or agenda-setter in its own right. Third, we should view the amendments process in context and not overestimate its significance. As a whole, Government bills do not change significantly from introduction to Royal Assent. The bills represent 'draft Acts' and a particularly strict rule on 'wrecking amendments' means that a bill can not be amended in such a way as to undermine its original principles. Therefore, amendments may be 'substantial' in relation to other amendments but not to the bill itself. Indeed, even the most amended bill in the first session (which became the Mental Health Act 2003 after 1000 amendments were passed) resembled closely its original draft, since the bill was lengthy, complex and represented two years of negotiation with interest groups (interview, Health Committee adviser, 2006). Fourth, it is just as likely that amendments are withdrawn by MSPs, not out of a sense of cooperation, but because a series of lost votes would be dispiriting.

Finally, it is still the Government which produces and amends the majority of legislation in Scotland since it has the resources to do so. Indeed, this may be a better explanation of the low rates of voting. Since many amendments are technical in nature, MSPs (and particularly those new to committee or scrutinizing only in plenary) may not have the knowledge to recognize the effects most amendments make. This gulf in knowledge and resources is magnified greatly when we extend our analysis beyond primary legislation. Most bills contain general provisions stating that ministers may order **statutory instruments** or produce guidance in furtherance of the bill, after its completion. The **Subordinate Legislation** Committee tends to act to qualify this power by insisting (via subject committees) that statutory instruments are subject to committee scrutiny and

Statutory instruments: An order, regulation or rule made by Government, issued, or granted under a power or authority conferred by previous statute.

Subordinate legislation: A collective term for statutory rules, regulations, ordinances, by-laws and rules.

approval. However, the sheer number of instruments (4,470 in the first two parliamentary sessions) means that most are skimmed and only a small number are referred to subject committees for further analysis. Subordinate legislation therefore represents a further ability of governments to make decisions outwith the parliamentary spotlight (see Page, 2001).

The effect of minority government

Of course, the assumption behind much of this analysis is that Scotland is governed by a coalition government with a legislative majority. With a majority the Government can ensure safe passage for its legislation and operate in relative autonomy before presenting plans to Parliament. Since May 2007 there has been a minority administration without a parliamentary majority. The hopes associated with 'new politics' may be more furthered by a minority government which is obliged to negotiate with a number of parties to secure a majority vote on each successive issue.

In turn, this may suggest the Scottish Government may not present 'draft Acts' to the Scottish Parliament at all if it is not confident about the likely results. This was a feature of the SNP's initial strategy in 2007 which saw a number of '1st 100 days' commitments modified to reflect its minority governing position. Yet, we should not get too carried away with these hopes even after the results of 2007. Since there is perhaps a centre-left consensus in Scotland, it is unlikely that the SNP will present too many proposals that are opposed in principle by the other parties. This suggests that most of the conditions outlined in this chapter still apply. Small size, MSP turnover and legislative loads may still undermine the abilities of committees to scrutinize, amend and initiate legislation. The gulf in resources between Government and Parliament remains. It would therefore be ironic if the post-2007 period saw the same level of expectations for new politics that we witnessed in 1999.

Conclusion

The CSG recognized the need for the Government to govern and its plans for committee powers may be seen as an improvement on Parliament's traditional scrutiny role rather than the pursuit of an innovative or new relationship. Indeed, it is doubtful if any such plans would be fruitful without a wholesale change to the structure of government. From what we know about 'old Westminster' and beyond, there is an immense gulf between the capacities of the legislature and the Government. The Government has far more resources to consult with groups and to research, initiate, draft, redraft, monitor and evaluate bills. Therefore, while the Scottish Parliament's powers are extensive in comparison to most West European legislatures, it is much more difficult to demonstrate the effects of their powers in relation to the Government in the first two parliamentary sessions.

The results suggest that even a 'best case' analysis of Scottish parliamentary influence is heavily qualified by the role and power of the Scottish Government. In other words, the evidence suggests that the Scottish Parliament is more an arena for political parties and governmental legislation than an actor or agenda-setter in its own right. This does not necessarily suggest that the Government attempts to *subvert* the process envisaged by the architects of new politics. Indeed, in many cases we can identify business-like committees whose decisions are respected. In this sense, new politics refers not only to the institutions, but also the actions and attitudes of the participants. Rather, the logic of consultation between interest groups and government at an early stage suggests that most policy is formulated outside the legislative arena, while any legislation to be passed tends to be presented at an advanced stage.

To a large extent, this process is consistent with a traditional role of Parliament – to invite its Government to present well-thought-out proposals and to consider the principles rather than the details of legislations. In other words, the Government may be 'robbing' the Parliament of powers, or decision-making is *devolved* by Parliament to the Government, with the former providing a wider legitimacy to decisions taken by a small number of actors (Judge, 1993). This legitimizing function of the Scottish Parliament is one that deserves emphasis – it has 'solved' the perceived democratic (or more accurately legitimacy) deficit of Scottish politics. No one today questions the accountability and legitimacy of the outputs of government in Scotland, in the way that they did in the years leading up to devolution, largely because of the existence of the parliament.

In summary, any discussion of the Scottish Parliament's role in Scottish politics must be qualified by an acknowledgement of the Scottish Government – the two institutions exist in a relationship of mutual interdependency. The Government derives its legitimacy from the Parliament, while the latter relies on the former to take care of the business of government and administration. Therefore, while there are obvious differences between the Scottish and Westminster Parliaments in terms of layout, culture and convention, each institution serves the same functions. Similarly, although the Scottish Parliament enjoys more powers, it is difficult to see how this translates to superior 'outputs'. Indeed, given the current orthodoxy on the (limited) significance of Westminster, it would be difficult to get excited about the added value of the Scottish Parliament from such a low base. In the future, more systematic comparisons with continental European practice may be better comparators, particularly since the 'good bits' of new politics were largely derived from these countries (Arter, 2004).

Further reading

Many of the examples discussed in this chapter are outlined in more detail in the 'Scottish Parliament' section of the Devolution Monitor Reports 2006–08 (http://www.ucl.ac.uk/constitution-unit/research/devolution/devo-monitoring-programme.html). These reports began in 1999 and are still archived here: http://www.ucl.ac.uk/constitution-unit/publications/devolution-monitoring-reports/index.html. On the role of parliaments see Judge (1993), Norton (2005) and Rush (2005); for Scottish parliamentary committees see Arter (2002, 2003, 2004). On the story of free personal care for the elderly policy see Shaw (2003); SPICE (2000b)

Online sources

Scottish Parliament   http://www.scottish.parliament.uk/

Scottish Constitutional Convention Report   http://www.cybersurf.co.uk/scotparl/briefing/Scc_prop.html

Report of the Consultative Steering Group   http://www.scotland.gov.uk/library/documents-w5/rcsg-00.htm

House of Commons   http://www.parliament.uk/commons/

Scottish Affairs Select Committee   http://www.parliament.uk/commons/selcom/scothome.htm

National Assembly for Wales   http://www.wales.gov.uk

Northern Ireland Assembly   http://www.ni-assembly.gov.uk

Chapter 6

The Scottish Government

Despite calls for a new form of democracy and parliament, Scotland's political system has a powerful executive at the centre. This was not the case before 1999 since the Scottish Office was a **territorial department** devoted in the most part to implementing and adapting UK policies. Devolution is therefore as much about a shift in power between executives as it is about new forms of public and parliamentary participation.

Territorial department: A UK department established to oversee public administration in a particular territorys e.g. Scottish Office, Welsh Office, Northern Ireland Office.

Scotland's central government has evolved over the course of the past two centuries. The Scottish Office was established in 1885 and for a long time was a patchwork of loosely related departments. It was only in the latter half of the twentieth century that a **corporate structure** emerged. Pre-devolution, the Scottish Office lacked democratic legitimacy and was basically an example of administrative devolution (Mitchell, 2003a: 215). In many ways the shift in corporate titles from Scottish Office (1885–1999) to Scottish Executive (1999–2007) and finally to Scottish Government (2007–) captures the story of recent Scottish political history. It is a body which began as a UK territorial department, developed into a relatively autonomous executive with its own policy-making capacities under the Labour/Liberal Democrat coalition, and then began to assert its (albeit qualified) independence from the UK under the SNP.

Corporate structure: A unified organization with a centre overseeing its constituent parts.

This chapter outlines in detail what the Scottish Government is and does – first, by making the distinction between Scottish Government ministers and the civil service and, second, by outlining their respective structures and responsibilities. The current structure of Scottish Government is outlined in Box 6.1.

As in previous chapters, it is useful to start with a comparison to the UK government. Many aspects are similar – there is cabinet-style government, ministers are effectively chosen by the First Minister (FM), and ministers are in day-to-day control of their portfolios, with the FM enjoying roaming influence. However, there is less evidence of direct central influence in Scotland compared to the Prime Minister or the Treasury and more scope for collective decision-making. Further, ministerial and departmental functions often do not coincide in Scotland – this can foster **joined-up government** or lead to problems with coordination.

Box 6.1 The structure of the Scottish Government – with responsibilities (from June 2007)

Office of the First Minister. Head of the devolved Scottish government: responsible for development, implementation and presentation of Government policy, constitutional affairs, and for promoting and representing Scotland.

Finance and sustainable growth. The economy, the Scottish Budget, public service reform, de-regulation, local government, public service delivery, cities and community planning, General Register Office, Registers of Scotland, relocation, e-government, Scottish Public Pensions Agency, procurement, budgetary monitoring, business and industry including Scottish Enterprise, Highlands and Islands Enterprise, trade and inward investment, corporate social responsibility, voluntary sector and the social economy, community business and corporate development, European Structural Funds, energy, tourism, land use planning system, climate change, building standards, transport policy and delivery, public transport, road, rail services, air and ferry services, Scottish Water.

Education and lifelong learning. Further and higher education, science and lifelong learning, school education, training and skills, HM Inspectorate of Education and the Scottish Qualifications Authority, nurseries and childcare, children's services, children's hearings, social work and HM Social Work Inspectorate.

Health and wellbeing. NHS, health service reform, allied healthcare services, acute and primary services, performance, quality and improvement framework, health promotion, sport, public health, health improvement, pharmaceutical services, food safety and dentistry, community care, older people, mental health, learning disability, substance misuse, social inclusion, equalities, anti-poverty measures, housing and regeneration.

Justice. Criminal law and procedure, youth justice, criminal justice social work, police, prisons and sentencing policy, legal aid, legal profession, courts and law reform, anti-social behaviour, sectarianism, human rights, fire and rescue services, community safety, civil contingencies, drugs policy and related matters, liquor licensing, vulnerable witnesses, victim support and civil law, charity law, religious and faith organizations.

Rural affairs and the environment. Agriculture, fisheries and rural development including aquaculture and forestry, environment and natural heritage, land reform, water quality regulation and sustainable development.

Source: Information from Scottish Government (2007); accessed 15 Nov. 2007.

The biggest difference from 1999 to 2007 was the coalition government in Scotland. There is some debate over the relative influence of the coalition partners. The Liberal Democrats certainly seemed the best prepared for coalition and their position was strengthened by formal agreement. However, the evidence on policy outcomes is mixed. Since 2007 the SNP has assembled a minority government with a 'slimmed-down' cabinet and a greater commitment to collective decision-making.

Joined-up government: The ability to cross traditional departmental boundaries and address policy in a holistic manner.

Next Steps: A policy initiative established by the Conservative Government in the late 1980s to split policy formulation and implementation functions. Parts of the civil service are given agency status within government departments.

De-layering: A reduction of the distance or management 'layers' between the chief executive (or minister) and the organization's staff.

With the civil service the terms of debate are slightly different. Some comparisons can be made about the social backgrounds of civil servants in the UK and Scotland. However, there is more of a focus on the centralizing influence of a UK civil service through background, culture and socialization. This ties in with an argument, presented in the early years of devolution, that the civil service represented a stumbling block to the type of radical policy change envisaged before devolution. Yet, this picture of the civil service as a source of inertia may be based on an old 'Yes Minister' caricature which has long been undermined by initiatives in the UK such as **Next Steps**, **de-layering** and the increase in outside policy advice. It is also based on the legacy of the Scottish Office as a body viewed with suspicion by Scottish interests during the Thatcher years.

It was certainly more of an implementing rather than initiating body during this period. As a result, the *policy capacity* was not there immediately following devolution and it struggled to adapt to the need for policy innovation and increased policy coordination across departments. The civil service was a neglected area of SCC and CSG study and much MSP frustration with the civil service was based on a misunderstanding of its role. The civil service exists to serve ministers, not the Scottish Parliament, and it was initially ill-equipped to deal with the avalanche of parliamentary requests. Therefore, the effect of a common framework of assumptions and concerns within the UK civil service as a whole may be overstated as an explanation for inertia. Our final discussion is the effect that the SNP has had since 2007, with independence for the Scottish civil service high on its agenda.

Scottish Government ministers – how do they compare to the UK?

Scotland's government

Although it is tempting to credit the SNP government with the desire to 'pick fights' with the UK, there were also some notable disagreements in the past. One such instance revolved around the collective name to give Scotland's new ministers. Although the Scotland Act 1998 refers to the **Scottish Administration**, the preferred term of the UK Government (and Donald Dewar's choice after civil service advice) was the **Scottish Executive** which distinguished it from (and perhaps gave it a status below) the UK government. However, it is a confusing

Scottish Administration: The collective term used in the Scotland Act 1998 to describe Scottish ministers.

Scottish Executive:
The collective term adopted from 1999–2007 to describe Scottish ministers (but often used to describe ministers and civil servants as a whole).

Scottish Government: The collective term adopted from 2007 to describe Scottish ministers (but often used to describe ministers and civil servants as a whole).

term which seems to refer to Scottish ministers and/ or the civil service at different times. This has led to some debate over the use of the term **Scottish Government**. In particular, the use of 'government' became associated with Henry McLeish's term as First Minister in which he tried to assert Scottish political autonomy. Although the term *Welsh Assembly Government* seemed to pass without much attention (Keating, 2005a: 96), McLeish's plan, 'led to a thinly veiled rebuke from No. 10 and outpourings of derision from both within and out-with the Labour Party' (Saren and Brown, 2001: 7). Yet, the term 'Government' is now the official title after an SNP re-branding in 2007. More serious academic debate over the appropriateness of the term is linked to discussions of multi-level governance and whether or not Scotland now has a 'political system'.

Cabinet government

In Scottish Government the main difference (from the UK) is in the numbers of ministers, with a smaller ministerial team reflecting Scotland's size and scope. While the UK government has 22–3 members, Scotland's cabinet had 12 during the coalition years of 1999–2007. This was headed by the First Minister and included the Lord Advocate, who is not an MSP but is responsible for taking the lead on some legislation and advising the Cabinet on legal matters (see Box 6.2).

These 12, combined with seven deputy ministers and the Solicitor General (the Lord Advocate's deputy prosecutor) made up the Scottish Government until 2007. One of the first innovations by the SNP – when forming a minority administration in 2007 – was to 'slim down' the Scottish Cabinet to six ministers (or 'Cabinet Secretaries') and ten deputies (not

Shirley McKie: A police officer whose fingerprints were said (wrongly) to be found in a murder scene in 1997. The Scottish Executive settled out of court in February 2006, awarding McKie £750,000 for what ministers said was an 'honest mistake' by fingerprint experts at the Scottish Criminal Records Office.

including the two legal posts). The move was highlighted by the SNP as a first blow in its efficient government agenda, but would also ensure a smaller and more manageable group, particularly compared to the UK Cabinet which is often described as an arena for broad discussions rather than a decision-making body. Indeed, even a coalition Cabinet in Scotland would be more likely to produce a meaningful collective body, given its smaller size and the tradition of cooperative working inherited from the Scottish Office (Keating, 2005a; Parry, 2001).

However, we can qualify this in three main ways. First, the UK system includes far more cabinet

Box 6.2   The Lord Advocate

The Lord Advocate has two distinctive features. The first is that s/he participates in Cabinet and the Scottish Parliament without being an MSP. The second is that the Lord Advocate combines roles which are performed by two people in the UK – chief legal adviser and member of the Scottish Cabinet (the Attorney General) and Scotland's chief prosecutor (Director of Public Prosecutions). During Colin Boyd's term (1999–2006) the **Shirley McKie** case raised questions of possible conflict between the Lord Advocate's roles and whether any of Boyd's decisions were motivated by political rather than legal considerations. The background of Boyd's successor, Elish Angiolini, was also notable. Angiolini had a legal-civil service background (as a formal **fiscal** and then Solicitor General) and was not an **advocate** (the status of advocate was seen traditionally as a symbol of independence from government). When the SNP formed an administration in 2007 it announced that Angiolini would remain as chief legal adviser but (to emphasise separation and de-politicization) would no longer attend Cabinet meetings unless invited.

Fiscal: The Procurator Fiscal's office is Scotland's public prosecution authority.

Advocate: A lawyer 'called to the bar' and with a right of audience in the higher courts. Advocates give specialist legal advice without forming a contractual relationship with clients – suggesting a high degree of independence. The Faculty of Advocates is an influential pressure group in Scottish Politics.

committees than Scotland and these may function as effectively as a source of policy coordination. Second, from 1999–2007 most broad decisions on policy had already been agreed and enshrined in the coalition's partnership agreement. This relegated the importance of Cabinet meetings to ad hoc decisions or marginal changes to policy.

Third, the idea of collective cabinet responsibility was often undermined by its lack of enforcement, and early experience suggested that it was adhered to in theory but not in practice. This was highlighted in 2002 after a Scottish Government minister (Mike Watson) campaigned publicly against the closure of a hospital in his constituency (Mitchell, 2003c; Winetrobe, 2003). In the aftermath, Watson did not resign (for this reason) and was not replaced by First Minister Jack McConnell (although Lynch, 2005, suggests it is telling he did not regain office after the 2003 elections). A similar process followed Cathy Jamieson's reluctance to support McConnell during the Scottish Executive's and UK Government's dispute with fire-fighters (see *Scotsman*, 2002). In December 2006 the limits to collective action were more clearly defined when Malcolm Chisholm resigned as Communities Minister. Chisholm's position appeared to become untenable after he voted with the SNP in opposition to the UK Government's White Paper on Trident. In this case, precedent suggests that if Chisholm had merely broken ranks and spoken against UK government policy (as he did when criticizing

Cabinet government: Government through ministers selected by the First Minister, who provide collective political leadership and ratify important policy decisions.

'dawn raids' on asylum-seekers) he might have kept his job. However, the line was crossed when he voted for the SNP motion – even though the motion had no formal weight and there was no need for a Scottish Executive position on the issue (Cairney, 2007d: 17). Overall though, the Scottish Government has inherited a broadly similar form of **Cabinet government**.

Ministerial recruitment

Although the First Minister requires formal parliamentary approval for ministerial choices, s/he effectively makes the final decision when the coalition has a majority in the Scottish Parliament (as does the Prime Minister). As Keating (2005a: 96) suggests, Jack McConnell's removal of most of the cabinet following Henry McLeish's resignation suggests that, 'the FM in practice has almost complete freedom in hiring and firing'. In theory, a minority government may present more problems of approval if cross-party opposition is used as a tactic (as in the European Parliament approval of Commissioners – Judge and Earnshaw, 2002). However, there is no evidence of this to date.

A more significant constraint is the pool of recruitment, particularly when a party is in office for a long period with little MSP turnover. Labour in the UK could often choose from over 400 MPs to fill around 100 government posts. They could also increase this pool by sending people to, and recruiting from, the House of Lords (2005: 97). In contrast, the Scottish First Minister from 2003–7 had just 49 MSPs from which to choose seven senior ministers, five junior and eight **Ministerial Parliamentary Aides** (MPAs). Given that Labour was also entitled to nominate eight committee convenors, the numbers suggested that most Labour MSPs (including those removed by McConnell when he was first elected) had an excellent chance of receiving some sort of patronage (Lynch, 2005; Mitchell, 2003c).

Ministerial Parliamentary Aides (MPAs): The equivalent of Westminster Parliamentary Private Secretaries. Between 2003–07 the Scottish Executive had eight MPAs.

Given this limited room for manoeuvre, it is perhaps surprising that (Labour) Scottish ministers spent no longer in post than their UK counterparts. The average term of 18 months suggests that few have been in post long enough to master their brief or do anything more than manage crises (2005: 98). From 2007, the pool of recruitment for the SNP was even more limited, with the need to find an entire ministerial and deputy ministerial team (since there were no coalition partners) and links to parliamentary committees from 47 MSPs. In part, this was addressed by limiting the size of the cabinet to six senior ministers (and dispensing with MPAs), with the remainder of the party standing an excellent chance of selection for relatively junior posts.

The role of the First Minister in policy departments

Like the Prime Minister, the First Minister (FM) does not oversee a large government department. Rather, s/he has the ability to contribute to the policies of other departments. This intervention, and the ability to coordinate policy from the centre, should be less difficult with a smaller government and the ability of the First Minister to micromanage a smaller ministerial team.

However, the FM does not enjoy the same level of resources at the 'centre' as the PM. As with many aspects of the new government, this partly follows the legacy of the Scottish Office which had a small centre with a federal structure of departments (Keating, 2005a: 96–7; Parry, 2001). Yet, even in the UK, where the PM has more resources and a range of policy units which report straight to Number 10, this does not translate to a strong centre. This is demonstrated well by the experience of public-service agreements which were designed to set and then oversee targets related to efficiency within Whitehall departments. The targets were originally overseen by a unit within Number 10 but then transferred to the Treasury in recognition of the 'weakness of the centre' but also the strength of the Treasury which could influence departments through extensive controls of public expenditure (Richards and Smith, 2004: 188).

The Treasury became an even more powerful actor in UK domestic policy, involved in policy innovation and holding departments (but not the Scottish Government) to strict performance and expenditure targets. Lynch (2005: 434) points to some moves in this direction in Scotland, with a growing 'core Government' of FM staff, **policy advisers,** divisions for media communication and legal services, plus a growing Finance Department which oversees the work of others. The latter role was then extended even further by the SNP's introduction of a Finance and Sustainable Growth department with direct control over a wide range of functions (Box 6.4). Yet, finance departments in Scotland still do not enjoy the status or policy capacity of the Treasury, while the FM does not command the resources available to the PM. First Ministers therefore work better when cultivating relationships with departmental ministers rather than pursuing the ability to monitor and control departments directly. Much therefore depends on the personality of the FM.

Policy advisers: Civil servants or government appointed individuals recruited to advise Scottish Cabinet Secretaries and Ministers.

First Ministers since 1999

It is significant to note that in his 10 years of office, Tony Blair was the UK counterpart of four First Ministers. This brief average tenure makes it difficult to make many comparisons with the UK or conclusions about the effect that each FM had within the Scottish Government, particularly since the first two resided over the transitional phase of devolution and all four have operated either within coalition or minority government (see Lynch, 2006). However, the experience of Dewar and McLeish is also in some respects the most informative, with the evidence suggesting that Cabinet splits (which did not seem to relate to coalition government) were just as regular a feature in Scotland.

Donald Dewar, May 1999–October 2000 (Labour)

Dewar was one of a number of MSPs with a long career in Westminster (over 25 years) and he was Secretary of State for Scotland before being elected to the Scottish Parliament. In his brief tenure as FM (he became ill in May 2000 and died in October 2000) Dewar was seen as a cautious FM focused on the early development of institutions rather than the detailed workings of policy departments. Early accounts focus on his 'honeymoon period' which saw the first successful attempt to create a working relationship within a coalition government and 'genuine collective decision-making' within Cabinet (Pyper, 2000: 79). This was followed in 2000 by 'constant infighting in his Cabinet' (Mitchell *et al.*, 2001: 51) and wider public controversies such as the abolition of section 28/2a (see Box 4.4) and the expense of the Scottish Parliament (Dewar made many of the decisions on its development before the Scottish Parliament opened).

Henry McLeish, October 2000–November 2001 (Labour)

McLeish was also an MP with some UK (deputy) ministerial experience. While he was the shortest-serving Labour FM, his term was perhaps the most memorable. In contrast to Dewar (and as demonstrated by the case of free personal care for older people), McLeish was prepared to intervene in departmental decisions and face-down opposition in Whitehall, particularly when this allowed him to pursue populist policies and put a 'Scottish stamp' on policy (Keating, 2005a: 96). However, McLeish also suffered the effects of intra-party dissent and Cabinet in-fighting despite promising a more inclusive and consensual style of leadership. Indeed, his style often exacerbated the problem, with an offer to Labour MSPs of more access to the civil service widely criticized and a tendency to make policy 'on the hoof' contributing to dissent within his own party. McLeish was perhaps seen as an easy target for critical journalism and this culminated in his resignation when he dealt badly with publicity surrounding 'Officegate' (see Box 2.6; Mitchell 2003c; Shephard and Cairney, 2004).

Jack McConnell, November 2001–May 2007 (Labour)

McConnell started life as a teacher and then councillor before becoming General Secretary of the Scottish Labour Party. When he lost the leadership election to McLeish in 2000, the latter (allegedly) passed on the 'poisoned chalice' of education minister to reduce McConnell's popularity and cement his own position. Yet, McConnell emerged unscathed by offering generous terms to Scotland's main teaching union, the Educational Institute of Scotland, and appearing to solve a bitter dispute between teachers and local authorities over pay and working conditions. This allowed him to emerge as an almost unanimous choice to succeed McLeish. McConnell became the only FM with no Westminster experience and this lack of personal relationships in the UK may have contributed to his strategy of seeking close relations with New Labour in London (in contrast to McLeish who felt comfortable enough to argue with UK colleagues). McConnell's fortunes within Cabinet also contrasted with McLeish's, in part as a reflection of his willingness to dispense with most of the (Labour) Cabinet he inherited. McConnell was more likely than his predecessors to recognize the limitations of devolution, preferring to lower expectations and promising 'to do less, better' (Shephard and Cairney, 2005). He also rarely intervened in departmental decisions, preferring to pursue cross-cutting themes such as 'environmental justice' (Keating, 2005a: 97), sectarianism and public-service reform (although much of the latter was delegated to Finance Minister Tom McCabe).

Alex Salmond, May 2007– (SNP)

Salmond became the third FM to have extensive Westminster experience (but the first with civil-service experience). Indeed, his decision in 2000 to leave the Scottish Parliament to become a full-time MP was criticized frequently during Labour's 2007 election campaign (Salmond's position was that after resigning as party leader, he should not overshadow John Swinney's leadership). Salmond's relationship with the UK government became an obvious source for attention in the early months of the SNP's new administration, but Salmond's early style tended towards reasoned argument (with the exception of his comments on outgoing PM Tony Blair) rather than a much-anticipated adversarial position (although see Chapter 8). Within the Scottish Government, Salmond continued McConnell's light touch over departments and the delegation of much oversight to the increasingly significant finance department (with John Swinney as the new 'Minister for Everything'). He has had a more external focus than previous FMs, seeking to advance Scotland's interests in European and international forums.

Deputy First Ministers, 1999–2007

Jim Wallace served as party leader and Deputy First Minister (DFM) for six years (1999–2005). Unlike the FM, the DFM also took on a ministerial post. Wallace, who was formerly an advocate before being elected to Westminster, served as Justice Minister for four years and made his mark on this brief by resisting the more punitive agenda of New Labour and gaining small but significant differences to freedom of information legislation (Keating *et al.*, 2003). In 2003 Labour insisted on the Justice brief and the LD agreement to support much of its agenda on crime and anti-social behaviour, with Wallace moving onto Enterprise and Lifelong Learning. In 2005 he was replaced (as party leader, DFM and Enterprise Minister) by Nicol Stephen. Stephen soon became involved in attempts by both parties to differentiate themselves in the run up to the 2007 election.

Joined-up government?

Ministerial and departmental functions often do not coincide in Scotland. Further, given the greater scope for cabinet government and collective decision-making, we may be tempted to think that this factor could be used to the Scottish Government's advantage. Indeed, perhaps the arrangements are a consequence of the pursuit of joined-up government, or the ability to cross traditional departmental boundaries and address policy holistically.

However, there are a number of factors which undermine this picture. First, the existence of 'ministers without ministries' was not planned in the aftermath of devolution. Rather, it is yet another, 'hangover from the Scottish Office days' when there were far fewer ministers than there were departmental responsibilities (Parry and Jones, 2000: 54; Keating, 2005a: 98). Further, these pre-devolution arrangements rarely produced the type of joined-up government that we might assume took place. The pre-devolution experience of issues which required a joined-up approach – such as community care – suggests that problems with the fragmented administrative arrangements were only solved after devolution, by placing most responsibility within the health department and its ministers (Rhodes *et al.*, 2003: 95).

Second, the potential for coherence is often exaggerated since there are still clear administrative divisions between policy areas regardless of where we put them and who heads up the departments. For example, in the coalition years, higher education (and lifelong learning), transport and enterprise were combined in Scotland to support the importance of HE to business and the economy. However, distinct **policy communities** still surrounded HE on its own and as part of a UK set-up. Similarly, the department for Rural Affairs may have included the environment, but this does not on its own overcome divisions between agricultural and environmental *interest groups*, with the former dominant in terms of public expenditure (Keating, 2005a: 98). Further, Parry (2001: 40–1) points out that one of the Scottish Government's early **policy disasters** – the failure to deliver higher-level exams results in 2000 – is a good example of departmental boundary problems, with the Scottish Qualifications Authority, 'sponsored by the

Policy communities: Close, enduring and stable relationships between decision-makers and interest groups (a type of policy network).

Policy disasters: Policies that suggest government incompetence and can cause the loss of political authority within a political system and often have considerable costs for a government, including financial and electoral.

Department of Enterprise and Lifelong Learning but serving the education system'.

Third, the idea of a rational rather than political apportioning of responsibilities was undermined when Wendy Alexander appeared to be bribed by Jack McConnell into staying in office with the promise of a huge department with a wide range of responsibilities (an alternative view is that Alexander fought to keep post-16 education and McConnell outflanked her by giving her an impossible workload). Alexander was subsequently dubbed 'Minister for Everything' (see Mitchell, 2003c). More recently, the SNP appears to be guilty of the same push for a departmental fiefdom in *Finance and Sustainable Growth* for John '38 jobs' Swinney in the name of joined-up government and central coordination.

Coalition government

A proportional electoral system ensures that most Scottish governments will be minority administrations or composed of more than one party (see Box 6.5). From 1999–2007 the latter involved a coalition between Labour and the Liberal Democrats. In turn, the strength of the parties within the coalition determined the make-up of Cabinet, with the Liberal Democrats able to exploit a fall in Labour MSPs in 2003 to gain an extra place. From 1999–2003 the Liberal Democrats had two of the 12 ministers in Cabinet (17%, reflecting a 17/ 73 or 23% share of seats), rising to three of 12 (25%, reflecting a 17/67 or 25% share) from 2003. Both parties also agreed a process of internal selection by each party when supplying ministers (rather than the need to agree jointly the Cabinet personnel). However, this is where the agreement ended, and the differing cultures of the two parties were exposed when they entered into negotiations in 1999.

Interviews with senior Liberal Democrat officials (in Laffin, 2005: 4–6) suggest that while Labour was used to internal negotiations with unions and local government, the Liberal Democrats (LDs) preferred a more open system. The LDs' weaker centre made it necessary for the party's MSPs as a whole to agree policy and cooperate within the lifetime of the Parliament. Also the LDs were more prepared and presented more demands during the 1999 negotiations (a 25-page list compared to Labour's four). This surprised Donald Dewar (and the civil service), who expected the LDs to agree a set of broad principles. A big part of the different LD approach was experience of coalition in the 1970s which represented a 'lost opportunity' to 'extract significant concessions' from the UK government. The lesson was that they had to present, and get Labour to agree to, a series of detailed commitments. In contrast, Labour (and the civil service already used to supporting the 'government of the day')

Box 6.3 Majority, coalition and minority government

In Lijphart's (1999) terms, the UK is a *majoritarian democracy* with single-party government. This contrasts with a wide range of other countries, suggesting that any departure from the UK system in Scotland may mark a step *closer* to the international norm. Comparisons of single party and coalition governments raise both empirical and normative discussions. For example, a major concern of Lijphart (1999) is to demonstrate that *consensual democracies* are as conducive to effective government and economic growth as majoritarian democracies despite their more convoluted decision-making structure. **Normative arguments** reflect debates found on electoral systems. For example, PR systems may be more representative and consensual (or at least more conducive to bargaining), while single-party governments may be more accountable and responsive to electoral swings. A broad concern in PR systems is whether parties signal an intention to form a coalition or exaggerate party differences to seek a distinct electoral platform. More particular issues refer to the time taken to agree a coalition's agenda (Scotland's five days in 1999 was significantly shorter than the three week average in West Europe), the 'tightness' of the coalition agreement (the junior partner normally prefers a more detailed agreement), the status of the Cabinet as a body ratifying decisions in lower-level coalition forums, and the propensity of the national government to influence sub-national arrangements. Minority governments are most common in countries with a propensity for consensus, when parliaments allow all parties some influence outside of government and/or when the main party can rely on another party for support in the legislature (see Seyd, 2002).

expected spending and policy commitments made from 1997 to continue with some slight modifications.

Normative arguments: Normative theories are outlines of how things *should be* rather than how things *are*.

The key to LD success was therefore the partnership agreement which formally tied Labour to a series of policy measures. However, there is a degree of uncertainty about the relative levels of success of the coalition partners. The most systematic examination of this point is by Roddin (2004) who argues that the Liberal Democrats did proportionately well out of the 1999 agreement (according to the number of their manifesto commitments included in it as a proportion of their size within the coalition). Yet, this may be partly explained by the similarity in Labour and LD manifestos which ensured that many LD aims were accepted without negotiation.

Its more distinctive policies which entailed significant spending – such as free prescriptions, free dental check-ups and the abolition of higher education tuition fees – were less likely to succeed. The first two were dropped, while the third was subject to intense negotiations which spilled over into the UK arena, with pressure brought to bear by UK ministers and attempts by Dewar to influence Wallace (Box 6.6) via UK party leader Paddy Ashdown (Laffin, 2005: 6). An eventual compromise was reached in which the issue was sent to review (by a committee headed by Andrew Cubie). While the subsequent legislation ensured that fees would not be introduced in line with England, the results also represented a significantly watered-down version of LD policy, particularly since there was enough opposition support to ensure the same outcome that the LDs enjoyed with free personal care (see Chapter 8).

From 2003, the Liberal Democrats appeared to be in a stronger bargaining position following the drop of Labour seats from 56 to 50. The size of the coalition majority was also smaller (from 73 to 67 of 129) and very little parliamentary dissent could be tolerated. From the experience of 1999, this may have suggested that more concessions would have to be made to the LDs to ensure that the party as a whole could be relied upon to maintain the coalition line in Parliament. Yet, Labour was also becoming an experienced coalition partner (with some potentially rebellious backbenchers), and took great lengths to ensure that both parties signed up to complete cooperation over agreed policies (Laffin, 2005: 7; see also Scottish Labour & Scottish Liberal Democrats, 2003: 49).

As a result, the LDs enjoyed some success, with the most notable commitment the decision to introduce proportional representation (by the single transferable vote) in local government elections in the face of widespread Labour party opposition. The LDs also secured a commitment to introduce free eye tests. Yet, this came at some cost, including support for Labour's crime agenda, and significant concessions over issues such as free prescriptions. Nicol Stephen also had the unenviable task of publicly supporting policies against LD wishes – in the decision to support a major motorway bypass scheme as transport minister and then to introduce fees for English medical students studying in Scotland as enterprise minister. As in 1999, the negotiations were made easier by a broad level of agreement on issues such as class sizes, teaching, healthcare and the economy.

Minority government

Following the election results in May 2007, the Liberal Democrats declared publicly that they would not enter into coalition with Labour or negotiate with the SNP until they dropped plans for a referendum on independence. This left the door open for the SNP to attempt to form a minority government. To bolster their numbers when electing ministers, the SNP negotiated (in exchange for assurances on certain environmental policies) the support of the two Green MSPs. The operation of a minority administration in the Scottish Parliament is new and significantly different territory. However, this difference may be exaggerated given the resources available to the Scottish Government in comparison with the Scottish Parliament. Further, the effect on ministerial and Cabinet decision-making is less clear. While we may be tempted to assume a greater coherence for single-party government (particularly since the Cabinet is smaller), the experience of coalition is that tensions existed within the parties themselves. The increasing size of the Finance Department may also cause tensions over the relative status of ministers and a greater push towards power at the centre (although there has been no evidence of this so far).

The Civil Service

A government's civil service is key to its ability to research, develop, consult on, and implement policy. Given the number of ministers, their length of time in the job and the enormous pressures on their time, the civil service is the mainstay of government, providing an institutional memory, choosing and setting the agenda for consultees and preparing legislation to present to Parliament.

There are three main civil services: UK Home (which includes Scotland), Diplomatic and Northern Ireland. Scottish Government civil servants are all recruited on merit and are non-party political in the Home branch. Like the UK-based civil service they have a culture of subordination and impartiality. Civil servants are permanent and serve with equal loyalty to all elected governments. It is important to emphasize that although civil servants may appear before select committees, they serve ministers in Government *not* MSPs in the Parliament. Although civil servants are legally subordinate to ministers and responsible for implementing the decisions of their political masters, the size of the bureaucracy and the limits to ministerial input suggest that much power is invested in the civil service. The UK civil service has tended to have a **generalist** (rather than specialist) **ethos**. Few of the highest ranking civil servants come from professional backgrounds – administrative, policy analysis and advisory, communication and managerial skills tend to be deemed important.

Generalist ethos: The civil service in the UK tend to be recruited for their generalist (e.g. communication, policy analysis) as opposed to specialist (e.g. narrow professional) skills

While we acknowledge a perceived lack of policy capacity in the Scottish civil service compared to Whitehall, Box 6.4 shows that its capacity compared to the Scottish Parliament is unmistakable. The Scottish Government civil service also plays a key role within the devolution settlement. Supporters of the Union feared that the introduction of a new Scottish Parliament would mark a 'slippery slope' towards independence. Its architects were conscious of the need to introduce structures to ensure smooth relations between Scotland and the UK and to prevent the types of disputes which could cause divisions. One of these 'checks and balances' was the maintenance of a unified UK civil service which would ensure relations between the two countries could be managed without a constant reference to formal procedures which were less

Box 6.4   The Scottish Government budget and staffing

- The total size of the UK public sector workforce was 5.8 million at a cost of approximately £8.8 billion (excluding defence and the 'devolved' administration) (HM Treasury, 2007; Cabinet Office, 2007).
- The planned cost of Scottish Government administration for 2007–08 was £244 million, of which £163 million was staff costs (Scottish Government, 2005).
- In 2007 the number of civil servants working for the Scottish Government was 16,550 (headcount, including temporary staff) (Cabinet Office, 2007).
- A focus on permanent staff in 2005 showed that only 12,320 (26%) of the civil servants working in Scotland were employed by the Scottish Government. The remaining 35,810 (74%) were employed by Whitehall departments. This included 6,870 (civilians) working for the Ministry of Defence, 8,780 for the Inland Revenue and 12,750 (i.e. more than the Scottish Government total) for the Department of Work and Pensions (Cabinet Office, 2005).
- However, relatively senior staff were concentrated in the Scottish Government (210 or 75% of the 280 Senior Civil Service grades working in Scotland) (author calculations from Keating and Cairney, 2006: 56; Cabinet Office, 2003).
- The total number of staff employed by the Scottish Parliament (excluding those directly employed by MSPs) was 400 in 2007 (Scottish Parliament, 2007).

conducive to negotiation and compromise. Section 51 of the Scotland Act makes it clear that service of the Scottish Administration (the official term) shall be service in the Home Civil Service. This UK model has no parallels in other intergovernmental systems, whether British-derived (Canada, Australia) or European federalist (Germany) (Parry 2001).

Intergovernmental relations with officials have rested not on legal status but on a mutual trust and recognition of a common approach – that of a professional, non-partisan service engaging with the political priorities of their ministers (Parry, 2003). This represented an important and positive role within the UK. The role of the civil service within Scotland also showed signs of improvement, with most interest groups expressing satisfaction with their access to, and impact on, the development of policy by the Scottish Government. Yet, at least in the early years of devolution, the civil service in Scotland was more likely to be portrayed negatively, as a legacy of the past and a block to change in the future. As Ford and Casebow (2002: 46) put it, a view held widely among the media, politicians and 'independent commentators' was that the service became a break on innovation and an obstacle to reform, broadly untouched by the change in political culture engendered by the new constitutional and democratic arrangements.

Yet, the *basis* for this alleged source of inertia was less clear. There are many other contenders to explain this perception of inertia, such as a lack of attention to problems of implementation or a collective attachment to unrealistic expectations about the amount of policy change which can occur in a short time (this is common to most political systems – see Hayes, 2001). Further, even if we do lay the blame at the door of the civil service, it is still worth considering specific reasons for their role. Was it based on:

- An *unwillingness* to support change based on a cultural and political attachment to the UK state? To explore this explanation, we can examine the similarities in social backgrounds, the level of contact between the Scottish and UK civil service, and the obstructive role the UK civil service as a whole may play.
- An *inability* to support change as quickly as expected by ministers? Some former ministers argue that policy initiation was hampered by a civil service not equipped to provide information and advice, forcing them to seek assistance from party, group and think tank sources. To explore this explanation, we can examine the legacy of the structure of the Scottish Office, the attention paid by the SCC and CSG to civil service reform and the capacity of the civil service to support ministers.

The social background of civil servants

There is a long history of viewing senior civil servants as part of the 'ruling class' and sharing its social background as part of a socialization process: 'mostly men drawn from upper middle-class families and educated at private schools and **Oxbridge**' (Keating and Cairney, 2006: 53). Indeed, private schools and Oxbridge education may be seen as the key means to train elites in a similar way for powerful roles in the future. But is this still the case and does it extend to Scotland?

Oxbridge: The collective name for the universities of Oxford and Cambridge.

The short answer is that the evidence is inconclusive, particularly since direct comparisons are made difficult by the relative seniority of civil servants in the UK (Scotland has only one **Permanent Secretary** compared to 27 in Whitehall). The evidence suggests that: (a) levels of private schooling are falling among senior civil servants (from 88% of Permanent Secretaries from 1974–7 to 62% in 2004, or 42% of grades 1–3); but (b) the levels among Scottish civil servants are significantly lower still (33% of the Senior Management Group, which was until 2007 – when replaced by the Strategic Board – the senior decision-making body in the Scottish Executive).

Permanent Secretary: The most senior civil servant in the Scottish Government or UK Ministry.

Levels of Oxbridge education are also understandably lower, although 33 per cent of the SMG (compared to 48% in equivalent UK grades) is still high. There are also just as many (if not more) men in senior positions in Scotland. Taken as a whole, there are significant overlaps in social background.

Yet, the evidence also highlights differences according to levels of

Box 6.5   The civil service in a comparative perspective

Comparisons with a range of European countries reinforce the similarities between Scotland and the UK. This includes: a narrow definition of civil service (Germany includes the education profession, France the health service and Sweden local government); the lack of politicization at senior grades (which is apparent in most systems, particularly in Belgium, Austria and Italy); a high regard for civil servants (unlike in Italy and Greece); a centralized method of elite recruitment (unlike Germany and Sweden where individual agencies recruit their own staff); and a generalist rather than a specialist background in the top grades (unlike Spain and in Austria). Indeed, there are few factors – such as relatively low levels of representation of women at senior grades and a relatively high status for finance ministries – which are consistent throughout comparative studies (see Page and Wright, 1999).

'Scottishness', with most senior civil servants in the Scottish Government born, schooled and taking higher education in Scotland (2006: 54). Further, it is difficult to translate levels of shared background to tangible political effects. Perhaps a common upbringing allows contact between civil servants to be straightforward, but it is difficult to say more than this.

Socialization and the level of UK-Scottish contact

A more likely candidate for UK influence comes from a combination of this background with the encouragement of shared attitudes through training and socialization. This point is made most forcibly by Rhodes *et al.* (2003: 82):

> No matter how differentiated the UK civil service has been, the power of the centre has been sustained by transfers. Devolution did not change anything; there is a commitment in the concordat between the Cabinet Office and the Scottish administration to promote inter-administration mobility.

Yet, the evidence suggests that the actual levels of mobility were never high, with the Scottish Office, 'dominated by Scots, who tended to remain in that department, apart from short spells working in London . . . where they learned the ways of Whitehall' (Keating, 2005a: 102). This continued after devolution, with the first Senior Management Group (SMG) containing four of ten civil servants with Whitehall experience, falling to two of nine in 2004 (although in both cases this included the Permanent Secretary). Further, if we look beyond the SMG to the Heads of Group (one payband below the SMG and now termed 'Directors'), then we see that only 34 per cent have spent any time in Whitehall. This falls below 30 per cent if we exclude English civil servants transferring from Whitehall departments, to seek policy-influencing work at a relatively low payband within the Scottish Government (Keating and Cairney, 2006: 55). As Parry (2003) suggests, while some experience in Whitehall may advance careers, this is increasingly undermined (especially in young high flyers) by the 'lack of attraction in relocating'. Civil servants in the Scottish Government can advance their careers more quickly with secondments to other parts of the public or private sectors in Scotland.

This suggests that the idea of civil service unity across the UK does not derive from a Whitehall culture as such, but from a need felt by senior civil servants in Scotland to continue to contribute to a UK policy process. In other words, the limited time spent on official secondment may be supplemented by frequent spells in Whitehall as part of a Scottish Government delegation. As Parry and Jones (2000: 63) suggest:

> Fears of being excluded from the Whitehall club of policy formation were a dominant theme in office thinking, and indeed the Permanent Secretary and other staff made a point of travelling to London to occupy visibly the place that was left on offer at meetings of their Whitehall counterparts.

Yet, even this desire to contribute to UK policy has been undermined over time by significant Whitehall ignorance of political differences in Scotland (see below) and a decreasing willingness among civil servants to trade-off time spent in the UK for time lost developing policy in Scotland. This is particularly the case in departments such as health and education where policy divergence suggests that the UK and Scottish agendas are unlikely to converge (making it likely that the Scottish Government input in the UK will have marginal significance).

The civil service as a source of inertia?

Even if we accept that there is still a centralizing force within the unified civil service, can we go further to suggest that the civil service is necessarily a source of obstruction? An anecdotal story from Ian Lang's (former Conservative Secretary of State for Scotland) memoirs would suggest so:

> One day I wanted to write some notes for a speech and it suddenly struck me that, whilst oceans of printed verbiage washed daily across my desk, there was never any plain, blank paper within reach. I opened every drawer – empty. So I rang through to my private secretary: could I have some plain paper please? He rushed in. Was there some kind of problem? No, I just wanted to write something so I needed some paper. He went out and came back after a pause, holding in front of him like a dead rat, one single sheet of plain white paper, which he solemnly laid on my desk. After an apprehensive glance at me he left and I suddenly realized how civil servants

controlled their 'masters' always keep them supplied with an endless supply of neatly prepared memoranda. Never give them time to think for themselves. Above all, never give them paper with nothing on it. (Lang, 2002: 64–5)

However, the traditional *Yes Minister* version of the civil service role depended on factors – such as civil service control of the flow of information to ministers and the means to implement policy – which have been undermined over time, while the caricature comes under increasing challenge within the UK literature (see Richards and Smith, 2004). Since 1979 we have seen a variety of civil service reforms which undermine the notion of its dominance of the policy process, including:

• Attempts to reduce civil service numbers under Thatcher and Blair,
• The personalization of promotion,
• Efficiency scrutinies,
• The Next Steps process of separating policy units from implementing agencies (which was already apparent in Scotland).
• De-layering the civil service to ensure that ministers have direct contact with those developing policy at lower levels within the civil service (which may be less relevant in Scotland since directorates are headed by relatively senior civil servants).
• The greater use of advisers as an alternative source of advice (although fewer have been employed in Scotland).

Therefore, even if we could identify some widespread desire for continuity within a unified civil service, we should have less confidence about its ability to thwart change. Perhaps a more realistic expectation for the gap between (often unrealistic) expectations for rapid policy change and actual events is an *inability* rather than unwillingness to deliver ministerial and parliamentary aims in such a short time period. This resulted from the legacy of the Scottish Office's role and responsibilities and a lack of attention to how this role would have to change to serve the new political institutions.

The legacy of the Scottish Office

Mitchell (2003a: 5) outlines three main functions that the Scottish Office played in Scottish politics:

• it was the institutional expression of the union state demonstrating that Scotland would be treated distinctly but within a centralized state;
• articulating Scottish interests at the heart of government, especially in the cabinet and Whitehall; and
• administering a growing range of duties.

During the Thatcher period in office a greater emphasis was placed on the latter role with the Scottish Office implementing policy within a framework set by the UK Government. There was increasing pressure from the top to implement policies with little 'ownership' among Scottish participants. As a result, Ford and Casebow (2002: 46) suggest this produced a 'siege mentality' in which many Scottish interests were hostile to a Conservative government which had no interest in the views of outside organizations. While this may be an exaggeration (particularly given Chapter 2's discussion of the Scottish Office as the UK's largest pressure group), the civil service was not engaged in the same kind of work before devolution.

Following devolution, its role went from filtering up to Whitehall and managing implementation, to policy initiation and development which requires different skills. This involves providing support to a significantly expanded ministerial team and, 'a whole new game of dealing with interest groups, now better organized, more vocal and with an outlet in the Parliament' (Keating, 2005a: 104). This required a significant amount of 'policy capacity', or a large staff engaged in researching and consulting on policy initiatives, which took time to develop. In the meantime, the civil service relied heavily on outside interests to replace its own research capacity, consulting frequently with expert groups and local government (2005: 104). Indeed, the positive consequence is that this contributed to what might be called a 'Scottish policy style' with close contact between the Scottish Government and interest groups within a small and fairly tight-knit policy community.

Perhaps more worrying was the lack of a relationship between the Scottish Government and Scottish Parliament in the early years of devolution. The Scottish Office was not used to dealing frequently with Parliament or its MPs who spent most of their time in London rather than Edinburgh. The new relationship, which saw a huge rise in parliamentary scrutiny through new select committees and parliamentary questions, therefore required a 'change of style and pace' to reflect new parliamentary demands, which the civil service appeared unable to deliver in the first two years (Ford and Casebow, 2002: 47). A particular issue was the time and resources needed to answer parliamentary questions. As Parry and Jones (2000: 60) suggest, the 'volume of parliamentary business, such as a four times greater number of parliamentary questions . . . took everyone by surprise' (see also Leicester, 2000: 22).

The Scottish Government and new politics

As with the discussion of ministers and civil servants, the time taken for civil servants to adapt may be mistaken for opposition, particularly since many MSPs were not familiar with the traditional role of civil servants answering to ministers rather than directly to Parliament (Keating, 2005a: 104). Further, it is unwise to place this problem at the door of the civil service, since this relationship and the future role of the civil service was ignored by the CSG, media, ministers and even civil-service unions in the run-up to devolution (Pyper, 1999). Indeed, Parry and Jones (2000: 53) suggest that since the CSG had 'steered clear of the Government branch or the relationship between ministers, civil servants and MSPs', much of the detailed planning was left to the discretion of the first Permanent Secretary, Muir Russell. Then, when Dewar became interested, his interventions regarded, for example, the number of ministerial appointments (which was higher than Russell expected) rather than accountability.

Therefore, despite the new politics agenda of change in most other areas of politics, 'devolution was accompanied by the continued prevalence of UK civil service norms and Westminster modes of accountability' (2000: 53). These norms suggest that the civil service can give the Scottish Parliament and its committees information, but not answer questions on policy, since this line of accountability for the decisions made within the Scottish Government remains with ministers (Kirkpatrick and Pyper, 2001: 6). Scottish ministers did not attempt to change this relationship (which may be in their interests since it ensures that ministers are at the centre of policy) and so it took time for all concerned to adapt:

> There was a process of mutual learning and . . . most civil service departments have established a fairly stable relationship with 'their' parliamentary committee, providing policy briefings and information where requested. (Parry and Jones, 2000: 59)

The SNP and an independent civil service

At present, the civil service and its management, recruitment and equal opportunities policy is a reserved matter. Therefore, the civil service in Scotland may have a 'practical loyalty' towards their respective ministers, but an 'ultimate loyalty' to the Crown and Whitehall (Rhodes *et al.*, 2003: 97). Therefore, not surprisingly, the formation of an SNP administration has highlighted the prospect of a more independent Scottish civil service which enjoys a formal status within the Union (as in Northern Ireland). While we do not present a view on the pros and cons of this policy, this chapter at least qualifies the idea that this would represent as significant a break from the past as portrayed in the media.

Would independence affect the power to recruit? At present Scottish ministers do not have the power to 'hire and fire officials'. They are bound by codes established at the UK level, and the need for Prime Ministerial ratification of senior appointments demonstrates Whitehall's 'last word' on the issue (Parry, 2003). Yet, 'in practice the First Minister has a strong say' on senior appointments and there is no evidence that Whitehall imposes decisions (Keating, 2005a: 103; Parry, 2003).

Would independence affect mobility and training within the services? Fears about reduced mobility are based on an exaggerated idea of mobility in the past which is not borne out by the evidence in this chapter. This level of integration is, 'often more of an aspiration and official policy than a reality' (Keating and Cairney, 2006: 53). Yet, the experience of Northern Ireland suggests mobility would be affected, with permanent transfers made more difficult (Parry, in correspondence).

Would independence undermine intergovernmental relations? The evidence from Northern Ireland is that relations between the services can be fruitful (Rhodes *et al.*, 2003). Further, as with mobility, the arguments for a unified civil service may be based on hopes rather than evidence. Whitehall departments often forget about Scotland and therefore neglect to consult before making statements on UK policy without Scottish provisions (Keating, 2005a: 125; Cairney, 2007f). Further, given that this forgetfulness may turn to wilful neglect under an SNP government, a more formal relationship with systematic procedures to consult may in some cases improve the relationship. The evidence from the Scottish Government's Permanent Secretary John Elvidge suggests that the informal contacts between civil servants in Scotland and England have already diminished, with a more formal relationship following the unwillingness of separate governments to reveal sensitive aspects of policy development (particularly following a high-profile disagreement on foot-and-mouth compensation – see BBC News, 2007). Therefore, any further change would be, 'breaking quite a slender thread' (see Cairney, 2007h).

Therefore, an independent civil service in Scotland would not represent a complete break from the past. Rather, it would accelerate developments which have already been taking place since devolution. As things stand, the autonomy of the Scottish Government and its ministers is a 'mixed bag', with considerable discretion over, for example, the substance and timing of public sector pay deals, but also constraints over the number of appointed special advisors (who are also prohibited from managing civil servants – Parry, 2003).

Conclusion

The Scottish Government's ministers and civil servants stand at the centre of the Scottish policy process. Ministers are the focal point for this power in relation to Parliament and wider society, but the resources (e.g. expertise, knowledge, networks) held by civil servants are crucial for the development, legislation and implementation of policy over the long term. This makes them powerful actors in Scottish politics.

Although it may seem easier for the First Minister to coordinate and even micromanage this process, s/he does not enjoy the resources found in the UK necessary to monitor the day-to-day activities of departments. The centralizing resources of the First Minister when set against those in Whitehall (Prime Minister's department, Cabinet Office, The Treasury) are very weak. Much power therefore still resides in individual departments and their ministers (although time will tell if the moves towards a 'Scottish Treasury' will come to fruition). The same story can be told of the likelihood of joined-up government in Scotland, with examples of institutional failure, problems of coordination and the case of the 'Minister for Everything' undermining the idea that this will necessarily be easier in a small country. There is also evidence of a similar level of disagreement and power struggles within Cabinet which relate more to factions within the Labour party rather than (or despite) the role of the Liberal Democrats within coalition government. Therefore, SNP and minority administration success may depend as much on the spirit of cooperation as the size and structure of government.

The civil service plays a number of positive roles, including the support of ministers to formulate and implement policy, consultation with interest groups, and managing relations with the UK government. Yet, most early portrayals of civil servants were negative, focusing on their inability or unwillingness to support the type of policy process and policy change envisaged by the architects of devolution. The evidence from this chapter suggests that such problems were temporary. After a period of adaptation and transition, the civil service has adjusted to devolution and there is little evidence of them acting as a potential break on further devolution.

Analysis of the backgrounds of civil servants, their level of experience in Whitehall and their links to Whitehall policy discussions suggests that the ability and desire of Scottish civil servants to support the centralizing role of Whitehall is diminishing over time. Analysis of the legacy of the Scottish Office and the lack of attention to civil-service accountability before devolution suggests that what appeared to be obstruction was actually a period of adaptation to the new political institutions in Scotland. Since these issues have now been resolved, more recent evidence points to the development of open policy networks with interest groups and mature relationships with parliamentary committees.

The formation of a minority SNP government has highlighted the issue of civil-service independence in Scotland. However, the Scottish Government already enjoys a degree of political autonomy from the UK and such moves may formalize many procedures already in place.

Further reading

On discussion of developments in Scottish government and the civil service the relevant sections of Constitution Unit's monitoring reports are an invaluable resource see: http://www.ucl.ac.uk/constitution-unit/research/devolution/devo-monitoring-programme.html and http://www.ucl.ac.uk/constitution-unit/publications/devolution-monitoring-reports/index.html.

The chapter on Scotland (usually by James Mitchell) in the yearly edited books – Hazell (2000; 2003) and Trench (2001; 2003; 2005) are also very useful summaries of developments in Scottish government and politics. On coalition governments see Lijphart (1999) and Seyd (2002, 2004). On the civil service, Richard Parry's publications are the key guides to developments – see Parry and Jones (2000), Parry (1999a; 2001; 2002; 2003). For the definitive history of the Scottish Office and its role in Scottish politics read Mitchell (2003a). Pre-devolution literature on the Scottish Office and government worth exploring are Pottinger (1979), Kellas and Madgwick (1982), Gibson (1985), Parry (1987; 1993), Midwinter *et al.* (1991), Kellas (1989; 1991b) and Hutchison (1996).

Online sources

Scottish Government   http://www.scotland.gov.uk/
Scottish Government Central Research Unit   http://www.scotland.gov.uk/cru/
UK Cabinet Office   http://www.cabinet-office.gov.uk
Scottish Ministerial Code   http://www.scotland.gov.uk/About/14944/684

Chapter 7

Governance Beyond the Scottish Government

Central vs local government

Much academic debate in recent years has focused on the changing nature of *governance* (Pierre 2000; Rhodes 1997; Stoker 1999; 2000). From a central-government perspective, this 'problem' of governance may refer to a lack of central control since the government relies on a wide range of organizations to formulate and then deliver policy. From a 'democratic' perspective, the problem may be one of accountability when decisions are taken and public money spent by unelected bodies. More broadly, the idea of governance suggests a world beyond the Parliament and Government and that a focus on institutions alone will leave too many gaps in our knowledge of Scottish politics. This chapter fills in these gaps by examining the various organizations and arrangements in place beyond the formal institutions of Parliament and central government in Scotland. The Scottish Government does not 'execute' many of the public policies over which it has responsibility for. Public policies in Scotland tend to be implemented by an eclectic mix of different types of institutions, agencies and bodies.

duties of local councils

Local councils are the main mechanism for public service delivery – accounting for approximately 40 per cent of the Scottish budget (McConnell, 2004: 1) and employing over 240,000 staff (double the number of NHS employees). They deliver a broad range of public services, including education, social work, housing, police, fire, roads and transport, leisure services, planning and economic development. They also undertake a variety of regulatory activities such as environmental health, licensing and trading standards. Local councils have local expertise, control policy implementation and have some independent tax raising powers (2004: 220).

However, it is also important to emphasize the democratic, political and governmental dimension of local authorities. Many of Scotland's well-known national politicians served their 'political apprenticeships' as local councillors. Councils have an elected status the other bodies discussed in this chapter lack. They are not simply administrative bodies – local councils are also the lynchpin though which the pluralism of political, civic and social life is established. Councils act as important counter-weights to excessive centralism in the Scottish polity – vibrant, strong, well functioning sub-national units of local government are important for pluralism in Scotland. Therefore, councils should not be viewed as merely local administrative bodies delivering national public services.

Government agencies: Stem from the Thatcher Government's civil service Next Steps initiative in the late 1980s which sought to separate the policy advisory and operational management functions of the civil service. The latter being undertaken by Agencies.

Quasi-autonomous non-governmental organizations (quangos): An organization funded by government but operating at 'arms length' from ministerial control.

Private finance initiative (PFI): Policy introduced by the John Major-led UK Conservative Government in 1992 which involves the private sector designing, building, financing and operating public utilities such as the Skye Bridge.

Public–private partnerships (PPPs): PFI re-branded by the UK Blair-led Government.

Many of the other bodies responsible for public service delivery do not share this potential for 'legitimate' pluralism. They are often called 'the unelected state' in Scotland. Scotland, like most European countries, has 'an extensive layer of delegated governance which is administratively "thick"' (Denton and Flinders 2006: 65). These include local health boards, **government agencies**, and **quasi-autonomous non-governmental organizations (quangos)**. One objective of devolution was to strengthen democratic accountability and scrutiny of such bodies through closer links to the Government and Parliament (Midwinter and McGarvey 2001a). At times this agenda has linked to the idea of a 'bonfire of the quangos' in which unelected bodies would be dismantled or subsumed within central government. More recently, the SNP introduced elections to health boards. Yet, quangos also perform useful functions and many would not enjoy the same legitimacy if perceived to be too influenced by ministers. There have also been trends towards the further inclusion of the private sector in the delivery of public services, through policies such as the **private finance initiative** and **public–private partnerships** which suggests that the 'problem' of governance will increase in significance.

This chapter outlines the changing environment of Scottish governance and assesses the concept's relevance to discussions of Scottish politics, looking at questions such as the changing manner of public-service delivery, the alleged 'hollowing out' of the state and the movement towards a regulatory state. It introduces key bodies in Scottish politics that do not fit neatly into the conventional central/local government classification and highlights policy areas which best capture the changing nature of Scottish governance.

Local government

Local government in Scotland consists of 32 unitary local councils created in 1995, and Box 7.1 outlines their defining characteristics. In 1996 these councils took over the functions of the previous 53 district, nine regional and three

Box 7.1   The defining characteristics of Scottish local government

Midwinter neatly summarises the essential features of Scottish local government:

*   directly elected by popular franchise;
*   multi purpose bodies;
*   responsible for service provision within a defined geographical area;
*   may only act within the specific powers set by Parliament;
*   power to raise local taxation (council tax accounts for roughly 20% of local government expenditure); and
*   corporate bodies whose powers are vested in the whole council.

Source: Adapted from Midwinter (1995: 13).

islands councils (see Table 4.1 for a listing of the councils). The rationale for this reform put forward by the Conservative UK Government (see Scottish Office 1991, 1992, 1993b) caused much controversy at the time mainly because of the top-down unilateral nature of its imposition (see for example Midwinter, 1995; McGarvey and Midwinter, 1995; Midwinter and McGarvey, 1998). Local government is fundamental to understanding governance in Scotland – roughly 45 per cent of all public-sector jobs in Scotland are in local authorities (McConnell, 2004: 1).

Councils have an interdependent relationship with the Scottish Government. The Scottish Government requires them to efficiently deliver services in accordance with their national political and financial priorities and parameters set by them. In return councils expect the Scottish Government to provide the financial resources and legislative framework necessary to do so, without limiting the councils' degree of political autonomy to represent their local communities effectively (see McConnell, 2004: 211–12).

The role of councils is not restricted to implementation. The Scottish local councils' umbrella body, the **Convention of Scottish Local Authorities** (COSLA), local authority professional groups (such as the Association of Directors of Education or Social Work) and individual councils are all engaged regularly in policy formulation and consultation with the Scottish Government. Local government is thus a very important institution in Scottish politics. Yet, local government seldom captures the Scottish media focus or headlines. This is despite that fact that it has grown significantly in both scale and expenditure in the postwar period as a key agent of the welfare state (see Newton and Karran, 1985; McGarvey, 1998).

Convention of Scottish Local Authorities (COSLA): A national body which represents Scottish local authorities. Individual professions have their own representation – e.g. the Association of Directors of Education.

> **Box 7.2   Local governance in comparative perspective**
>
> The story of local government service delivery reform in Scotland is by no means exceptional when compared with the experience of other countries in Western Europe – although the Thatcher Government in the UK took these much further than most. The shift from a direct service delivery role to one of a number of bodies 'governing' at local level is consistent with the dominant tradition and norm of European local government working with and through other organizations. In France there are examples of private and semi-public companies in service provision. In Italy voluntary organizations, workers cooperatives and other service delivery organizations have a long tradition. In Sweden arms-length voluntary and private contractors have been involved in local public service delivery (see Batley and Stoker 1991; Denters and Rose 2005).

In the postwar period services such as education, social work and housing were significantly expanded and professionalized at a UK level, underpinned by the political consensus that grew out of the Labour Government's Welfare State programme from 1945–51. Local government was expanded on the values that underpinned the welfare state – statutory standards achieved through regulation and underpinned by a **public-sector ethos** (see Pratchett and Wingfield, 1996).

Public-sector ethos: A commitment on the part of those working in the public sector to serving the public good.

This notion of a public-sector ethos was challenged and subject to considerable pressure from the 1970s as central government, in common with governments in other countries (see Box 7.2), adopted policies designed to allow alternative delivery agencies a role, for example **compulsory competitive tendering** (CCT). The critique of direct provision came not only from academic and think-tank critiques of the public sector (see Niskanen 1971, 1973 and Dunleavy's 1980 opening chapter) but also the Conservative party which began to articulate an ideological opposition to the 'paternal' or 'nanny' role of the state. Ian Lang, former Secretary of State for Scotland, summarized this critique when he suggested that the:

Compulsory competitive tendering (CCT): A Conservative Government (1979–97) policy which compelled local councils to tender-out specified services such as refuse collection, catering and grounds maintenance.

postwar consensus – founded on support for monopolistic, one-dimensional public service delivery, with public services themselves acting as purchaser, provider and regulator – was unsustainable. It was a recipe for spiralling costs and ultimately poorer services. (1992: 3)

good summary

Postwar consensus:
Term often used to
refer to the postwar,
pre-Thatcher period in
British politics
(1945–79) when there
was alleged
agreement between
the two main parties
over such things as the
welfare state and
economic policy.

Best value: A policy
introduced by Labour
post-1997 to replace
compulsory
competitive tendering
in local authorities. It
is designed to ensure
public bodies have
arrangements in place
to secure continuous
improvement in public
services.

**Large-scale
voluntary transfers**
(LSVT): Transferring
council housing stock
to new registered
social landlords.

As a result, local government in the UK has gone
through an almost continual cycle of reform since 1979
(see Midwinter 1995 and Stoker 2004 for reviews).
New public management ideas were influential in
many of the reforms initiated during the Conservative
years. Various policy initiatives (often continued under
Labour) were a direct challenge to the traditional direct
public-service provision model of local government.
These include **best value** (BV), the right to buy council houses, **large-scale voluntary transfers** (LSVT),
and public–private partnerships (PPP) (see Box 7.3).
These were accompanied by moves to ensure that local
authorities could not overspend, with periods of rate-
capping followed by the introduction of the poll tax to
enable local voters to punish councils for presenting
excessive bills for too many services (see McConnell,
2004). According to various commentators we were
entering a new era of local governance (see Rhodes,
1997; Stoker, 1999; 2000; John, 2001; Leach and
Percy-Smith, 2001).

The Thatcher government experience suggests an
extensive ability of the centre to reorganize and control
local government in the face of opposition. This reinforces a legalistic reading of local government that
suggests councils are subordinate bodies in relation to
Parliament. All council duties and competencies can be
traced back to Acts of Parliament and no council can
act *ultra vires* (beyond its powers). The evidence also
suggests few Scottish differences during this period. The Scottish Office was
unable (since it was a subordinate territorial department) or unwilling (since it
was run by Conservative ministers sympathetic to Thatcher ideas) to seek a
different Scottish solution. Therefore, post-1979 central-local relations across
Britain as a whole deteriorated and the centre relied on regulation rather than
consensus.

Perhaps the only significant difference in Scotland was that there was
enough personal contact to foster something resembling a working relationship (McGarvey, 2002: 30). To a large extent, this is related to the difference
of scale – with only 32 councils and one representative body (COSLA),
central–local relations tend to be conducted in a less formal manner with interpersonal relations the norm. Central–local government relations in Scotland
have tended to be more cordial than England, even during the Conservative
years in office (when COSLA supported the campaign for home rule).

Following devolution in 1999, councils still remain subordinate to the
Scottish Parliament which can abolish, restructure or merge any local authority

Box 7.3   The politics of public–private partnerships

Between 1997 and 2007, PPPs became increasingly common as the financing vehicle of choice for the renewal of Scotland's public-sector infrastructure. PPPs are essentially Private Finance Initiative projects re-branded and re-labelled by the UK Labour Government. Typically PPP schemes involve a 20–35-year time period during which a commercial company or consortium undertakes to design, build, finance, operate and maintain a project (e.g. school) in return for an annual lease payment from a public-sector partner (e.g. local education authority). PFI/PPP schemes have been used in numerous projects including Skye Bridge, Bowhouse Prison in Kilmarnock, the modernization and refurbishment of many schools in Scotland, new hospitals and the 'missing link' M74 road project on the south side of Glasgow.

PPP has been widely criticized (and indeed rejected as a policy by the SNP Government). The Left see it as the latest encroachment of big business into the public sector. Other criticisms include the lack of public accountability, high transaction costs and, from a trade-union perspective, the negative impact on worker terms and conditions (see Unison 2001). Given these criticisms, why has government used PPPs? We suggest possible explanations:

- From 1997 the UK Labour Government was keen to dampen fears in the markets that it would increase spending and raise public borrowing substantially. Part of this strategy was to promote borrowing in the private sector to pay for capital investment for public projects. This also satisfies EU limits on public borrowing in member states. The Labour-led Scottish Executive between 1999 and 2007 made a 'virtue out of necessity' by publicly supporting PPP projects.
- PPP allows the government to focus on strategic priorities and policies leaving operational tasks such as facilities management to its commercial partner. This allows the government to plan and budget more effectively as long-term contracts pass significant ongoing maintenance contracts to the private sector. Risk associated with the ownership of assets is transferred to a commercial partner.
- PPP is often compared to the use of a credit card, lease agreement or overdraft rather than a mortgage. The government's case is the additional expense of a lease agreement is justified by the urgency of the spending on public infrastructure.
- One of the unintended consequences of public body budget constraints in the 1980s and 1990s was the choice of cutting services or redirecting maintenance budgets, many public authorities understandably choose the latter. However, over time lack of maintenance and investment in public infrastructure meant many buildings were no longer fit for the purpose they were designed for. In this context, the benefit of PPP is that such 'non-essential' funding becomes a fixed cost.

(it also provides the vast majority of finance for local government expenditure – around 80%). Our discussion of new politics suggests that such an impositional style would be unlikely, while the devolution White Paper (Scottish Office, 1997 para. 6.7) made it clear that the UK Government did not envisage the Parliament taking powers from local authorities. However, devolution did significantly alter the context that local government faced, particularly since many of the Scottish Government's responsibilities are actually functions for which local councils are responsible for delivering on. As the McIntosh Commission (1999: 11) on Local Government noted:

> The arrival of the Scottish Parliament represents a fundamental change in the political landscape within which Scottish councils in future will operate. Although Parliament and local government each have a democratic base, the Parliament will have the ultimate power of determining what becomes of local government.

The recommendations of this report were wide-ranging, covering relations with the Parliament and Ministers, electoral arrangements and electoral reform, the conduct of council business and the role of community councils. The Scottish Executive accepted the overwhelming majority of the recommendations. In May 2001 it signed a Partnership Framework with the Convention of Scottish Local Authorities (COSLA) outlining a symbolic written protocol emphasizing an aspirating of constructive shared working, openness, transparency and trust. This led to the creation of new bodies such as the Renewing Local Democracy Working Group (the Kerley Group – from where the STV electoral system for local elections evolved – see Chapter 4) and a Leadership Advisory Panel (the McNish Group).

The McNish Report examining local authority internal decision-making structures outlines a story of evolution rather than revolution. Unlike the position in England, Scottish local councils were not compelled to reform themselves along the lines of creating political executives (a cabinet system). The report outlines that six initially chose to do so, with the vast majority merely streamlining existing committee structures. Since the report was published, and perhaps on the basis of councils learning from each other, more councils have followed the 'executive model' route.

This ties in with a general post-devolution picture of the Scottish Government as a source of suggestion rather than imposition, setting up frameworks to encourage a certain way of working without following the English focus on top-down regulation and reform (see McGarvey, 2005). Other examples include the agenda on the 3–18 school curriculum reform and the reform of children's services, as well as a general sense in public-sector reform that the Scottish Government will leave the delivery details to local authorities if they can demonstrate improvement in 'outputs' (Cairney, 2007e). This reflects a long-standing concern of COSLA that councils should have a general statutory power to give expression to the community leadership role of councils, free them from '*ultra vires*' and allow more flexibility in their operations. However, this is not to say that COSLA was completely successful. For example, although the Local Government in Scotland Act 2003 gave councils a broad power to 'to advance well-being', this is viewed by many councils as liable to make little difference as there are various constraints imposed on the use of this power (McConnell, 2004: 221). Similarly, although the 3–18 curriculum agenda suggests greater autonomy, this may represent the exception to a general rule that

> Education authorities deliver a policy more or less given to them. Very little is decided at the local level. Authorities can theoretically have their own versions but policy is backed up by an inspection regime pulling you back into the mainstream. Local authorities have the authority but are directed by the law and money. (interview, ADES, 2006)

This perhaps suggests a Scottish 'love of fudge' – in which organizations such as local authorities demand the freedom to conform – and returns us to the idea that most Scottish differences refer to the style rather than substance of policy-making. Yet, the example of **community planning** demonstrates that style can have an effect on substance. The policy in Scotland creates a strategic structure to oversee existing partnerships with public-sector bodies and allows for the development of a shared strategic vision for an area and a statement of common purpose (Community Planning Working Group 1998 para.11). Councils work alongside police and fire services, health boards, local enterprise companies, housing associations, benefits agencies and other bodies to create a more 'joined-up' or holistic strategic framework for governing arrangements. Crucially, the community partners feel reassured enough that the Scottish Government will not reform this system – the result is that they are more likely to invest their time and resources in a stable system.

> **Community planning**: The process of involving various public agencies in developing a strategic planning framework and vision for a local area.

The key policy in terms of public service reform has been Best Value; this is different from the initiative in England which shares the same name. It derived from a Best Value Task Force (BVTF) that included the Government, COSLA and the Accounts Commission and represents one of the first post-devolution examples of 'partnership working'. The policy was given a statutory basis by the Local Government in Scotland Act 2003. Best Value in Scotland has less emphasis on competition and open tendering, perhaps reflecting the experience of CCT in Scotland where the vast majority of contracts were not contracted out. Therefore, despite widespread academic commentary about the movement towards local governance and away from **direct service provision** in England, councils in Scotland are more likely to have an 'in-house culture'. The Scottish Best Value Task Force Report noted 'there are still those (councils) who instinctively prefer or are more comfortable with direct delivery of services' (para. 47). Best Value also requires council services to follow particular approaches to management. Requirements include the

> **Direct service provision**: Provision of public services by public institutions.

publication of local performance and service plans, the use of performance indicators, bench-marking, consultative exercises and competition as a tool. However, the consequences associated with failing to meet targets are not as punitive as in England.

Overall the post-devolution experience of local government is mixed. Positive developments include the greater physical proximity and openness of government to local authorities than the Scottish Office was in the 1979–97 period. This has been reflected in numerous consultation exercises and the volume of new legislation impinging on local authorities. Indeed, if we use consultation documents as a measure then COSLA has been the most consulted body since devolution (possibly reflecting the Scottish Government's initial lack of policy capacity). Post-devolution relations surrounding issues like community planning, best value, finance and auditing suggest a greater willingness of the Scottish Government to maintain an environment conducive to joint working.

However, post-devolution research (Bennet *et al.*, 2002) has also suggested that the greater proximity between the different levels of government in Scotland may result in the 'centre' having greater influence on local authorities. Indeed, when asked if the Scottish Executive has reduced the importance of local government, more councillors agreed (47.8%) than disagreed (42.4%). It was also suggested in local authority circles that the civil service in Scotland still used a 'command model of the world' (2002: 16). The policy environment of grant dependency and policy initiatives such as public–private partnerships (see Hood and McGarvey 2002) were also pushed heavily by the Scottish Executive during the initial years of devolution.

As McConnell quite correctly notes, while there is much talk of local authority and Scottish Government 'partnerships', for COSLA this may be aspirational, and for the Scottish Government it may be good public relations (2004: 14). There remain similarities between English and Scottish local government – 'powers of well-being, Best Value, retention of business rates at the centre, ring-fencing of grants in accordance with central priorities, support for citizen participation and encouragement of various means to boost electoral turnout' (2004: 236). Although the policy labels are similar, often the implementation structures are different. Overall, the local government post-devolution picture reflects a combination of change and similarity.

Government agencies and non-departmental public bodies (quangos)

The other key public bodies responsible for the delivery of public services are *Government Agencies* and **non-departmental public bodies** (NDPBs). The landscape of Scottish Government might be characterized as being made up by a number of icebergs (ministerial departments) which are the visible

Non-departmental public bodies (NDPBs): Government bodies at arms length from government, 'sponsored' and overseen by a government department.

'democratic' elements (Flinders, 2004). These ministerial departments act as the 'parent' departments of a wide range of quangos (see Denton and Flinders, 2006: 65–8).

Scotland's 16 agencies (see Table 7.1) are clearly linked to a Scottish Government department, are staffed by civil servants and are responsible for delivering services in accordance with Government policies. They tend to carry out a discrete area of work and their relations with the Government are defined in a policy and resource framework document which defines their operational responsibilities. The theory is that the Scottish Government retains control of policy and strategy while the Agency gets on with operational responsibilities.

NDPBs tend to be more commonly referred to as 'quangos'. Quangos are numerous in both type and number (see Table 7.2). Although it is often difficult to distinguish between agencies and quangos, the main difference is that quangos may be less subject to direct ministerial (or senior civil servant) control. This was demonstrated by the re-naming of Scottish Homes to CommunitiesScotland and its changed status from NDPB to agency. The result was a greater integration into the civil-service structure, more contact with and direction from ministers, and a greater demand from MSPs in the form of parliamentary questions (interview, Communities Scotland, 2004).

Payne and Skelcher suggest that quangos, 'are subject neither to election nor to the extensive probity and transparency standards required of local and central government' (1997: 207). They also point towards a reduction in the extent to which public policy decisions taken by these bodies are open to public scrutiny and influence. A 'bonfire of the quangos' is a recurring soundbite in Scottish politics – Gordon Brown promised one from the incoming UK Labour Government in 1995, Henry McLeish as First Minister in 2000 and Alex Salmond at the SNP conference in 2007 (see MacDonnell, 2007).

However, despite a Government review in the first 1999–2003 term, very

Table 7.1 *Government agencies in Scotland*

Communities Scotland	Scottish Building Standards Agency
Fisheries Research Service	Scottish Court Services
Historic Scotland	Scottish Fisheries Protection Agency
HM Inspectorate of Education	Scottish Prison Service
Mental Health Tribunal for Scotland	Scottish Public Pensions Agency
National Archives of Scotland	Social Work Inspection Agency
Registers of Scotland	Student Awards Agency for Scotland
Scottish Agricultural Science Agency	Transport Scotland

little changed (see Scottish Executive 2001a; 2001c). There were some abolished, some re-classified and some amalgamated. However, as Denton and Flinders note, 'The specific details of the reform plans actually represent more continuity than change' (2006: 70). Little changed because, despite all the rhetoric about democracy and abolition, quangos tend to perform key (if sometimes rather mundane) tasks that, otherwise the Government would have to ask the civil service to perform.

Quangos are useful in many ways for government. They allow for the co-optation of non-political elites into Scottish governance processes. Moreover, they allow acknowledged experts in a subject to become involved and to contribute to the provision of government services (see Hogwood, 1995; Parry, 1999; SPICE, 2000c for further discussion)

Quangos are adaptable and allow central governments to set up bodies free from damaging party-political attention and without formal checks to carry out its policies which may otherwise undermine their operations (Weir and Beetham, 1998: 203–4), although appointments to quangos are subject to checks by the **Scottish Commissioner for Public Appointments**. It should also be noted that if a Scottish minister wishes to create a new quango they must notify the relevant committee in the Scottish Parliament (Denton and Flinders, 2006: 74).

> **Scottish Commissioner for Public Appointments**: Individual responsible for monitoring and establishing a code of practice to Ministerial appointments to quangos.

A certain level of independence is often necessary for a publicly-funded body to have credibility within its policy sphere. For example, the education inspectorate HMIe (now a government agency) severed traditional Scottish Office ties after the development of the 'Higher Still' policy in which it was perceived to be too close to Scottish Ministers and effectively making, running and inspecting policy. Similarly, the credibility of Audit Scotland (a Scottish Parliament-funded body set up to report to the Auditor General and the Accounts Commission) hinges on the extent to which it can function independently of Scottish ministerial influence.

However, perhaps the best example is the Mental Welfare Commission (MWC) which is officially an NHS body sponsored by the Health Department but has to be seen as virtually independent of government to fulfil its 'statutory duty to protect people who may, by reason of mental disorder, be incapable of protecting themselves or their interests adequately'. The people most relevant to the MWC will be detained on the instigation of psychiatrists (and social work mental health officers) *within the same NHS* and therefore they cannot be seen to be merely another arm of the health service.

Like the MWC, many quangos tend to have a natural 'client' group for which services are provided. Indeed, the quango may be so associated with particular policy areas that there would be significant political costs to major government-initiated reforms without their support. Quangos can therefore be

Table 7.2   *Quangos in Scotland*

2 Nationalized Industries (Highlands & Islands Airports Ltd, Caledonian MacBrayne Ltd).

1 Public Corporation (Scottish Water).

33 Executive NDPBs (e.g. Crofter's Commission, VisitScotland, Scottish Enterprise, ScottishScreen, SHEFC, Scottish Legal Aid Board, Scottish National Heritage, Scottish Qualifications Authority, Sport Scotland).

45 Advisory NDPBs (e.g. Architecture and Design Scotland, General Teaching Council for Scotland, Scottish Law Commission, Scottish Records Advisory Council, Justices of the Peace Advisory Committee (32))

45 Tribunals (e.g. Children's Panels (32 in local councils), Parole Board for Scotland, Mental Health Tribunal for Scotland).

23 NHS Bodies (e.g. 14 NHS Boards, Health Education Board for Scotland, NHS 24, NHS Quality Improvement Scotland).

significant actors in the policy process, and many operate from a base of considerable staff resources, knowledge and expertise.

Table 7.2 outlines the different types of quangos in Scotland. Government NDPBs and NHS bodies employ their own staff (not civil servants) and manage their own budgets. Post devolution, the 28 NHS Trusts and 15 Health Boards were consolidated into 15 NHS Boards. The National Health Service in Scotland contains 23 different types of bodies delivering and overseeing health services, providing management, technical or advisory services within the NHS. These bodies have a board whose members are appointed by ministers, although one of the first SNP Government bills introduced direct elections to health boards. Scotland also retains two nationalized industries, which due to a combination of population sparsity and political pressure, have survived the sell-off of public assets in recent decades – Caledonian MacBrayne Ltd and Highlands and Islands Airports Ltd. Water also remains a public asset in Scotland.

Changing governance in Scotland?

The term 'government' has been used in general to refer to the conventional institutions and processes of the public sector, while 'governance' is a broader term for providing *direction* to the public sector – or 'steering' rather than 'rowing'. Governance is a word which can refer to a new process of governing and achieving collective action, a changed condition of ordered rule, or the new method by which society is governed (Bevir and Rhodes, 2003: 4). It has been suggested that the UK's (and by implication Scotland's) mode of governance has been changing, with the ability of the state to act unilaterally diminishing (see for example Pierre, 2000; Pierre and Stoker, 2000; Rhodes, 1997, 2000; Richards and Smith, 2002; Stoker, 1999, 2000). The suggestion is that government operates in an interdependent environment where it does not have all the knowledge and information required unilaterally to solve complex dynamic and diversified public policy problems.

Rhodes (1999) sums up the concept of governance in terms of the following:

- Interdependence between organizations with the boundaries between state and civil society shifting and opaque.
- Policy network interaction with the negotiation of shared purposes and the exchange of resources between network members.
- Complex and frequent interactions between members, regulated by trust and established 'rules of the game'.
- A significant degree of autonomy from the state, resulting in a weak capacity on the part of the state to steer the direction of policy networks.

This suggests a broad transformation in the role of government. As a result, government in Scotland (as in other liberal democracies) can no longer be conceptualized as a stand-alone institution divorced from other institutions and pressures. The suggestion is that Scottish government is less involved with the direct provision of public services, and increasingly functions instead as a regulator of networks of service provision rather than direct provider. The **limited executant capacity** of the Scottish Government in a number of policy areas is reflected in a move towards a mode of governance where its primary function is to establish a series of policy and resource frameworks within which a vast number of semi-autonomous networks of public and private bodies provide services. Between 1997 and 2007, Public–Private Partnerships (PPPs) were a good example of the changed environment of policy-making and delivery for capital investment projects (see Box 7.3).

Limited executant capacity: Suggests that the Scottish Government is reliant on many other bodies to execute its policies.

Scottish public administration now involves a complex set of institutions and actors that are drawn from, but also beyond, government. Pierre and Stoker argue, 'the essence of governance is its focus on governing mechanisms which do not rest on recourse to the authority and sanctions of government' (2000: 32). Thus,

> Conventional command and control conceptualizations about governing are no longer either fully descriptive nor fully acceptable, and provide a very incomplete notion of how governments function in contemporary advanced democracies. (Peters 1997: 51)

Rhodes refers to governance as 'the defining narrative of British government at the turn of the century' (2000: 108). However, the change is not limited to the UK – Guy Peters suggests that throughout the western world it is now accepted that

> Governance is now conceived as being possible without government, with the capacity to control assumed to be exercised equally well through social organizations as through formal government institutions. (Peters 1997: 52)

Numerous strands of academic literature link in with the governance thesis, each strand based around the consensus that traditional forms of government have been challenged by new modes of governance which emphasize management, regulation, markets and networks. This consensus includes **policy-network** conceptualizations (see Marsh and Rhodes, 1992a, 1992b; Rhodes, 1997; Smith, 1993), the idea of the hollowed-out state – Box 7.5 (see Rhodes, 1994, 1997; Foster and Plowden, 1996) as well as literature which more directly addresses the themes of regulation (Hood *et al.*, 1999; Moran, 2003). On a more global scale there is the influential **'reinventing government'** idea associated primarily with Osborne and Gaebler (1992). In the UK, the reinventing government notion has primarily been associated with the concept of new public management (NPM) (Box 7.7) (see, for example, Hood, 1994).

Policy network: A systematic relationship between interests groups and decision-makers deemed important to explain political decisions.

Reinventing government: Label given to the public-sector reform movement in the 1990s which emphasized NPM (new public management) ideas in the public sector.

The broad thesis is that power has seeped away from traditional governing institutions (e.g. Scottish Office/Government) towards new networks of service provision that involve non-governmental actors (see Box 7.4). Thus the public sector today has unclear boundaries. New agencies, civic institutions, special purpose bodies and the like are becoming the new arenas of Scottish public service delivery, and the task of Scottish governance is no longer about managing a public bureaucracy but instead managing, steering and influencing these new networks. What were previously hierarchical **Weberian bureaucracies** are being replaced with new governing structures that emphasize markets and networks.

In the early 1990s Ian Lang, then Conservative Secretary of State for Scotland, emphasized that an objective of the Scottish Office had been establishing 'a genuine plurality of organizations to deliver

Weberian bureaucracies: Deriving their label from German sociologist Max Weber, such bureaucracies are characterized by a hierarchical pyramid of authority, with clear lines of accountability and governed by rational rules or policies.

Box 7.4   Is the Scottish state 'hollowing out'?

Rhodes (1994) suggested that new developments such as the privatization/commer-
cialization of public-service delivery, the loss of functions by government to alternative service delivery agencies and the loss of functions to higher levels of
government (e.g. the EU) prompted a trend towards the 'hollowing out' of the UK
state. For Rhodes (1997), these developments were eroding central government's
capacity to govern. For example, **contracting-out** the provision of services to a
wide range of bodies suggested that the centre could not control their delivery and
was forced merely to give them direction. This also undermined notions of accountability since no one was quite sure who should be held responsible for the success
and failure of delivery. Black (1999) suggested Scotland had a 'hollowed-out state'
with 85 per cent of the Scottish Block of public expenditure being spent by bodies
out-with the Scottish Government. Moreover, unlike at UK level there is not a
powerful Treasury, Prime Minister's and Cabinet Office coordinating government.
However, the 'centre' of Scottish government (i.e. the Government) does have a
range of policy instruments which it can utilize to regulate these other bodies (see
regulation section below).

Contracting out: The situation in which the public sector contracts with another organization (e.g. commercial company) for the provision of a particular service (e.g. refuse collection).

services' (1992: 1). The public sector was to longer to
be 'purchaser, provider and regulator' (1992: 3). In
possibly one of the clearest statements of the influence
of NPM philosophy on government in Scotland, Lang
emphasized that traditional mechanisms of accountability had to be supplemented by 'more specific kinds
of accountability'(1992: 4):

> Accountability is also achieved if public services are delivered closer to the
> people who rely on them. Decisions should be taken much closer to the
> customer so that the lines of accountability are clear. And there should be
> greater openness so that the customer is empowered and enabled to hold
> public services to account. (Lang 1992: 4)

Bodies delivering public services may include the commercial sector,
professional associations, voluntary organizations (see Box 7.5), government
agencies, community groups and interest groups in civic society. The suggestion is that there has been a blurring of the traditional distinction between the
public and private sectors, with state and civil society in Scotland merging
seamlessly into one within many different policy and service delivery areas
(particularly since the Scottish Government may also rely on these bodies
when *formulating* policy).

Issues for which government used to have sole responsibility, are now the
responsibility of partnership arrangements between agencies. For example, in
the past two decades the social housing policy arena has been transformed

---

Box 7.5   Scottish Council for Voluntary Organizations (SCVO)

The Scottish Council for Voluntary Organizations is the national body representing the voluntary sector. It is an umbrella body which also acts of an interest group which seeks to advance the values and shared interests of the voluntary sector. There are 45,000 voluntary organizations in Scotland involving up to 129,000 paid staff and over 1.2 million volunteers. The sector manages an income of £3.2billion. In total, voluntary organizations employ 5% of Scotland's workforce (similar in scale to the NHS in Scotland). See http://www.scvo.org.uk.

Registered social landlords (RSLs): Landlords such as housing associations who provide social (or government-backed) housing.

with new housing associations and **registered social landlords** (RSLs) taking over what was previously the role and functions of local councils.

This of course all fits neatly into the notion of a vibrant civil society in Scotland. This views one of the key roles of government as sustaining and nurturing it, as well as providing a framework for interest expression and cooperative problem-solving. An optimistic state-centric interpretation of developments would still see the Scottish Government as having a positive role in conducting, facilitating and leading the complex range and variety of organizations in Scottish civil society. Indeed an active civil society of pluralistic interests is usually viewed as a positive in any liberal democracy.

If we accept that Scottish governance is changing then it does raise a number of issues identified by Stoker (1998). Firstly there is a divorce between the complex reality of decision-making associated with governance and the normative codes to explain and justify government. Government in Scotland has traditionally drawn from the accountability linkages derived from the processes of representative democracy (i.e. the Westminster model's focus on elections and a subordinate bureaucracy). The notion that these policy networks have significant autonomy from the Scottish Government and Parliament does not sit easily with such codes. According to Rhodes, the 'institutional complexity created obscures who is accountable to whom for what' (1997: 54).

Secondly, there is the possibility that these networks can become **elitist** and institutionalize irresponsibility by operating behind closed doors. These

Elitist: Government by a select, privileged group of people.

networks of governance and the way they do business undermine democracy and accountability, transferring decision-making into interpersonal relationships and the semi-institutionalized politics of networks. Lowi (1969) was a particular critic of the trend towards such 'government by experts' in Western liberal democracies. According to Lowi, these policy networks can reinforce existing inequalities, erode political responsibility by shutting out the public, favour established conservative interests and thus corrupt democratic government by eroding the formal mechanisms of representative democracy. Policy networks are a system of private government subject only to the most tenuous forms of accountability.

Thirdly, there is a danger of blame avoidance in such disaggregated governing structures. The more actors that become involved in Scottish public-service delivery the more potential there is for these problems to develop. For example, in the new disaggregated partnership arrangements for the building of schools and hospitals through PPP (see Box 7.3 above) goods or services previously provided in publicly owned buildings are now provided in buildings owned by commercial companies or consortia leased by the public sector. This can create a situation where the public/private sector partners blame each other for service failures.

Regulating governance in Scotland

Another strand of literature on UK Government emphasizes the substantial regulatory capability, which exists within government (see Hood *et al.*, 1999).

Evaluative state: A state with elaborate mechanisms through which to judge the worth or merit of particular activities.

Audit society: A society with extensive processes of inspection, checks and examination.

Henkel (1991) refers to an **evaluative state** and Power (1997) an **audit society**. Faced with these new networks of service provision, one response of the Scottish governmental bodies has been to use regulatory tools. Governance by regulation offers a solution to the two key governance problems identified by Rhodes (1997) – control and accountability. Regulation offers the centre (i.e. Scottish Government) the capacity to steer self-organizing networks as well as institutionalize mechanisms of accountability (see McGarvey, 2001b; Midwinter and McGarvey, 2001a). The increasing use of regulatory tools can be seen as the centre's response to the loss of control it has suffered as new modes of governance have emerged. The suggestion is that, as the old interventionist state based on monolithic public bureaucracies has declined, a new regulatory state has replaced it. Much of this regulation is based on ideas associated with 'New Public Management' (see Box 7.6).

The regulatory state thesis suggests there is 'more emphasis on the use of authority, rules and standard setting, particularly displacing an earlier emphasis on public ownership, public subsidies and directly provided services' (Hood *et al.*, 1999: 3). There is a shift away from the tradition of 'high-trust' towards a 'low-trust' arm's-length relations in government (Hood, 1994: 131) with government delivering fewer public services directly to the people, 'but regulating other bodies responsible for provision' (Hood *et al.*, 1999: 93–4). Numerous types of

Box 7.6   New Public Management (NPM)

NPM ideas tend to be associated in the UK with the Conservative central government (1979–97) management inspired marketization and financial reform programme in the 1980s and 1990s. NPM ideas tend to emphasize the following as useful tools in the reform of the public sector:

- new performance accountability mechanisms;
- decentralization, disaggregation and devolution;
- private-sector styles of management;
- managerialism;
- competition.

Initially – in the 1980s – these ideas tended to be associated with an ideological preference for less government. However, in the 1990s NPM is now much looser and more associated with a learned response to the 'realities' of governing in a complex rapidly changing environment. This is most adequately encapsulated in Osborne and Gaebler's (1992) oft-cited phrase concerning the need for less rowing (or direct public provision) and more steering (*management* of provision).

regulator inside government are identified such as public auditors, professional inspectorates and ombudsmen. In Scotland this calls attention to the activities of oversight and scrutiny bodies such as the Auditor General and Audit Scotland, the Scottish Public Services Ombudsman, and the Education Inspectorate. It also suggests that as public-service delivery becomes more complex, then individual bodies may become subject to audit from a range of scrutiny bodies. This has contributed to an agenda in Scotland (and the rest of the UK) towards a rationalization of oversight and the pursuit of a common framework to address the unintended consequences of accountability (see Box 7.7).

Yet, Scotland has not followed the same mode of regulation as the UK. One of the best examples of this is in the field of healthcare. Scotland has eliminated the relatively independent hospital trusts and the **purchaser–provider split** that was the basis of a quasi-market system in the NHS (Greer, 2005a). The Scottish Government restored the 15 Health Boards to the centre of the system (one, Argyll and Clyde, was abolished in 2005),

Purchaser–provider split: The separation of the purchasing and providing of public services. Examples are CCT (compulsory competitive tendering) in local government and health authorities 'purchasing' hospital services.

and it is these boards that directly run hospitals, receive needs-based grants for overall population health and other services and contract with general practitioners. This structure whilst not formally transferring power to health professionals, does so almost by default. By eliminating the Trust structure, it reduces the power of trust chief executives who are now (at least compared to their English counterparts) subordinates of distant Health Boards. Medical professionals appear to have

---

Box 7.7   Regulatory funding bodies

Scottish Enterprise is Scotland's economic development agency. It was established in 1990 bringing together functions previously carried out by the old Scottish Development Agency (SDA) and the former Manpower Services Commission/Training Agency. It covers 93% of Scotland's population – Highland and Islands Enterprise covering the rest. It works in partnership with the public and private sectors in Scotland with the aim to develop the Scottish economy by encouraging business, promoting and encouraging exporting, attracting inward investment and developing skills. It oversees the Scottish Enterprise Network which consists of 12 Local Enterprise Companies (LECs). These bodies engage in business development and training, environment and regeneration programmes.

CommunitiesScotland regulates Registered Social Landlord housing bodies in Scotland. It takes consideration of such things as their management systems, social inclusion and homelessness policies, customer service and communication as well as wider governance and financial management issues. Each RSL is subject to performance audit every three to five years.

The Scottish Funding Council was established in 2005 to provide a strategic overview of tertiary education and distributes about £1.5 billion in funding each year for teaching and learning, research and other activities in Scotland's colleges and universities.

---

filled this power vacuum (Greer, 2005a). As discussed in Chapter 10, in England the trend is in the other direction, with a greater use of markets and the private sector, but also a relatively punitive target-based regime to ensure compliance with a set of standards.

In education there is also a different regulatory environment. At secondary education level the first education legislation to pass the Scottish parliament placed new duties on councils (rather than schools, as in England) to raise standards. The schools inspectorate in Scotland has also tended to operate in a more conciliatory style to its counterpart in England, OFSTED. The regulatory environment of education in Scotland has always been different from the rest of the UK (Paterson, 2003), with the size of the Scottish state allowing closer links and a stronger sense of hierarchy from schools to local authorities to central government. For example, while in England the head teacher is seen as a semi-autonomous figurehead in a school (answerable to a board of governors), in Scotland s/he has a direct line manager in the local authority.

Conclusion

The apparent simplicity of the old political and administrative landscape of Scotland appears to be gone forever, and the tradition of the self-sufficient government in Scotland is being directly challenged. Scotland is moving closer to the European norm in that there is now a wide variety of organizational forms in which public-service delivery takes place. The driving force of these changes is a combination of ideology, political and wider economic pressures. The disaggregated nature of public-service delivery mechanisms can in many instances be traced to the Thatcherite 'rolling-back the state' agenda of the 1980s. The new state forms in Scotland may also reflect wider economic pressures, with private-sector interests seeking new profit-making opportunities through **outsourcing**, public–private partnership and consultancy schemes. Or, in the case of the voluntary sector, they may be based on a belief that other organizations are better placed in the community to deliver local services. Regardless of explanation, the role of local government as the direct provider of public services is changing, with increasing use of new service delivery mechanisms.

Outsourcing: Inviting bids from external sources to undertake activities previously undertaken by government employees

This picture of reform may suggest that local authorities are subordinate bodies subject to the whims of central government. Yet, local councils should not be seen as simply administrative, low level public-service delivery bodies. They are key democratic and governmental institutions. This chapter has suggested that an appreciation of the legacy and traditions of how councils are organized is fundamental to understanding the politics of public-services processes in Scotland. The public-sector tradition appears to have been more durable in Scotland than England. In other words, the Scottish Government still has a distinct policy style. Greer paints a picture of Scottish policy processes as being 'deeply rooted in the history of Scottish politics and social policy' and based on

> universalistic, directly provided, undifferentiated public services that use networks rather than competition and are governed based on a high degree of trust in the professionalism of providers. (Greer, 2005a)

Therefore, the bureaucratic governing form has not been quite displaced – it is widely recognized that bureaucracy for all its failings has numerous strengths, including reliability, predictability, probity, cohesion and continuity (Rhodes, 1997: 109). Yet, many of the key policy issues facing Scottish government today such as the environment, urban and rural regeneration, social exclusion, crime and community safety do cross boundaries inside and outside of government. The Scottish Government cannot resolve these issues by working alone.

To study Scottish politics today is to study multi-layered governance and the sheer complexity of a multiplicity of actors; interdependence; shared goals; blurred boundaries; multiplying and new forms of action, intervention and control (cf. Rhodes 1997). In many instances governing institutions in

Scotland lack the policy tools to steer collective action in the direction they desire. Moreover, the partial erosion of traditional Weberian bureaucratic structures and their replacement with institutionally complex arrangements has obscured who is accountable to whom and for what (McGarvey, 2001b).

The irony of course is that as Scottish governance becomes ever more complex the normative appeal of the old codes of accountability increases. There is a normative preference in favour of the ballot box and other democratic mechanisms working effectively to ensure accountability in public administration. Traditional legalistic and constitutional notions of public accountability still retain significant appeal for Scottish politicians, public officials, the broadcast and print media and, most importantly, the public. Indeed, one could go as far as claiming that they are projected by such bodies to such a degree that they tend to be 'the picture' of Scottish politics as understood by the general public.

In summary, any informed analysis of Scottish politics must reject the idea that there has been a wholesale shift from a bureaucratic state in Scotland; hierarchical bureaucracy is alive and well in many parts of government. Scottish government has accommodated the discourses of markets, network and managerialism in their rhetoric and accountability documentation (annual reports, strategic plans etc.), but bureaucracy remains a significant organizational form at both central and local government level. Indeed many of the requirements of regulatory activity result in a return to bureaucracy via the back door.

The notion of governance is consistent with literature on Scottish policy-making (see Chapter 10) which highlights Scottish Office/Executive/ Government policy-making style as consultative, with regular interactions, accommodation, pragmatism and incremental policy change. It is also consistent with one of the themes of this book, that is the emphasis that Scottish politics today is the constructions of past policies, ideologies and institutional processes.

Discussing developments in English local government, Stoker and Wilson suggest 'the post-Second World War form of local government has "passed on"' (2004: 247). However, in Scotland this conclusion may be somewhat premature (see McGarvey, 2005). Scottish local councils, councillors and politicians appear to have retained a greater commitment to direct public provision. Traditional working practices and inherited beliefs about the utility of direct public provision appear to be more durable in Scotland than England. The impact of devolution has been mixed with both change and similarity evident.

Pre-devolution rhetoric about a 'bonfire of the quangos' in Scottish politics was hopelessly unrealistic. As noted above, quangos exist for a wide variety of reasons, and they are deeply embedded into the Scottish system of governance. Their integration within the structures of local and central government is unlikely.

Scottish politics now takes place in an environment of multi-layered governance. The governance narrative has heuristic qualities, in that it asks different questions and generates alternative insights about Scottish politics and government. It rightly challenges the notion that you can study Scottish politics as if its governing institutions were a series of stand-alone bodies. It also emphasizes that the capacity to get things done in Scotland does not rest solely on the power of the Scottish Government to command or use its authority (cf. Stoker 1998). However, the picture painted of Scottish governance in this chapter is a conservative one with incremental change the dominant emphasis picture. Grand theories of political change in Scottish governance are inappropriate – there has been evolution as opposed to revolution in the Scottish public sector beyond the Scottish Government.

Further reading

On local government the definitive text is McConnell (2004). See also Midwinter (1995) for a good review of developments during the Conservative years. On governance see Rhodes (1997, 2000; Pierre and Stoker, 2000; Stoker, 1998. For a critique see Marinetto (2003). On the 'hollowing-out' thesis see Rhodes (1994), Black (1999) and Holliday (2000). On regulation see Hood *et al.* (1999), Midwinter and McGarvey (2001a) and Moran (2001). On quangos see Denton and Flinders (2006) for the definitive guide to post-devolution developments. See also Hogwood (1995, 1999), Parry (1999b), Rosie (2002), SPICE (2000c). On public–private partnerships see SPICE (2001), Ball *et al.* (2000), Coleshill *et al.* (1998), Hood and McGarvey (2002), Hood *et al.* (2006) and Scottish Parliament (2001).

Online sources

CommunitiesScotland   http://www.communitiesscotland.co.uk
Scottish Arts Council   http://www.sac.org.uk/
Visit Scotland   http://www.visitscotland.com/
Scottish Enterprise   http://www.scotent.co.uk
Details of Scottish Public Bodies   http://www.alba.org.uk/links/scotpubservers.html
Convention of Scottish Local Authorities   http://www.cosla.gov.uk
Scotland's NHS online   http://www.show.scot.nhs.uk
Scottish Council for Voluntary Organizations   http://www.scvo.org.uk

Chapter 8

Inter-Governmental Relations and Multi-Level Governance

Since 1999 the Scottish Government and Parliament have had greater scope to dictate the direction of public policies in Scotland. However, while political devolution has now strengthened the legitimacy of the Scottish Government, the resources and ultimate constitutional legitimacy still reside in London. This power has been compounded by the increasing 'Europeanization' of devolved policies and the need to liaise with the UK as the member state. Therefore, in common with other devolved and federal systems there exists a range of *inter-governmental relations* (IGR) mechanisms to manage this combination of the devolution of policy responsibilities and the maintenance of central control in key areas.

While IGR often refers to formal relationships, the study of *multi-level governance* (MLG) shifts this focus from power in terms of *capacity* to the *exercise* of power. In other words, while the UK government may 'win' most disputes because of its superior constitutional position, the effect of devolution is for the UK to step back or disengage from most policy areas associated with the Scottish Government. This, combined with the ability of actors such as the civil service to address issues informally, may mean that such disputes rarely arise since they are dealt with out of the spotlight. The informal route offers greater scope for more subtle forms of influence, particularly when the issue may be uncontroversial, low on the UK's agenda or favourable to the UK's interests. The discussion of Europe provides a different emphasis, suggesting that a form of UK 'disengagement' is less favourable to Scottish interests. Scotland's most pressing problem is influencing EU policy before the Scottish Government is obliged to implement it.

The aim of this chapter is to explore these issues which arise from the Scottish Government's external relations. It does so by outlining:

- The ability of IGR and MLG to guide interpretations of these relationships.
- The most common areas of overlap between devolved, reserved and EU powers.
- The means used to address the areas of overlap. This includes discussion of formal measures such as concordats, **Sewel motions** and Joint Ministerial Committees (JMCs), as well as informal channels through the civil service and political parties. For Scotland in Europe there is a combination of low formal status (since Scotland is not a member state) and a variety of informal mechanisms to exert policy influence.

- This chapter also discusses the strategies of interest groups in Scotland who are faced with uncertainty surrounding the locus of power and decision-making in the era of multi-level governance.

Sewel motion:
Passed by the Scottish Parliament to give consent for Westminster to legislate on devolved matters.

What becomes clear is that the outcomes vary by policy area and policy issue. This is particularly the case in the early years of new administrations – in 1999 when the Labour-led Scottish Executive was perhaps 'learning by doing' and in 2007 when the SNP Government took a different stance on IGR. This chapter therefore draws on an extensive range of examples since 1999.

IGR and MLG

A common theme of devolution studies is the entanglement of policy issues when decision-making power is vested in more than one actor. Although most political systems outline in detail the policy domains of each level or type of government, it is inevitable that the boundaries between policy areas will become blurred in practice. As Keating discusses (2005a: 18), these issues of territorial politics are common to most modern federal systems with the dual aim of devolving decisions and maintaining central/ broad control when appropriate. Examples include the importance of education (devolved) to the economy (reserved), harmonizing criminal laws to prevent cross-border issues, business laws (e.g. grants, local taxes) to stop companies playing authorities off against each other, and welfare rights to minimize the risk of 'welfare immigrants'.

There are two relevant approaches to this area of study. The first – inter-governmental relations – highlights country-level differences according to institutional structures, power and the recourse to established authority and formal resolution (Mitchell, 2003b; Watts, 2007; Horgan, 2004; Agranoff, 2004). With this approach we can explore the structure of UK relations – is it a unitary or union state? Can it be meaningfully compared with federal, quasi-federal or other devolved unions? What is the strength of the 'centre' and what is the frequency of formal dispute resolution?

In this regard, the UK is a difficult system to characterize. It shares some characteristics with federal states: a combination of shared rule with territorial self-government, a distribution of legal, executive and fiscal powers to allow devolved territories a level of autonomy, an 'umpire' (e.g. the JMC) to rule in disputes between levels of government, and territorial representation at the national level (e.g. the Secretary of State for Scotland). However, what sets it apart is the lack of a supreme constitution which is relatively immune from unilateral change from the top. It shares a key characteristic of unitary states since devolved territories have subordinate status within the UK. However, the terms of the Union protect (to some extent) distinctly Scottish organizational arrangements. Therefore, it can usefully be described as a 'devolved union' or 'union state'. However, a form of devolution to only 16 per cent of the population (with England effectively a unitary state) has no equivalent in other countries (Watts, 2007). Since IGR is as much about politics as it is political structures, we can make useful comparisons elsewhere. For example:

- *The role of parties*. The influence of national parties varies considerably, from Canada with a devolved party structure and differentiated party competition by territory, to Germany which has integrated parties and formal links to coordinate policy (Horgan, 2004). In Scotland, coalition government hindered our ability to assess the direct influence of the national party of government. However, the most high-profile issues from 1999–2007 arose with policies most associated with the Liberal Democrats. Further, since the election of the SNP, more issues of contention are being made public. This suggests that party (or perhaps party ministerial) links were important during Labour's term.
- *The role of the executives*. The UK's reliance on IGR through executives is common to political systems with parliamentary executives (such as Canada and Australia).
- *The role of the courts*. Although addressing IGR through the civil service (and then ministers), with the use of courts as a 'last resort' is common, the scale of the lack of legal resolution in the UK is still distinctive (Watts, 2007).

The second approach – multi-level governance – highlights informal relationships and the blurring of boundaries between public/private action and levels of governmental sovereignty. Decision-making authority is dispersed and policy outcomes are determined by a complex series of negotiations between various levels of government and interest groups (see for example Bache and Flinders, 2004a, 2004b; Hooghe and Marks, 2003a, 2003b). The focus is therefore less on formal powers and the ability to 'win' disputes, and more on the on informal means to influence decisions and, in many cases, *avoid* disputes.

In sum, we have the ability to discuss: (a) examples of the overt use of power to make decisions (often in the face of opposition); and (b) agenda-setting and the exercise of power to limit the scope of those decisions. As Baumgartner and Jones (1993: 32) suggest, this often involves competition to define policy problems in a certain way to ensure that they are dealt with in a particular decision-making 'venue' (such as the Scottish rather than UK Government). The focus of analysis often moves from the capacity to make decisions, to the level of government in which the decisions are made. Therefore, the complexity of governance arrangements and subsequent competition to ensure decision-making jurisdiction makes it difficult to predict policy outcomes just from the analysis of institutional structures.

These issues related to intergovernmental relations and multi-level governance are by no means new to Scotland. As Chapter 2 discussed, the Scottish Office's scope extended far beyond the devolved sphere since, although policy was *formulated* at the UK level, the power to *implement* public policy was routinely given to Scottish ministers. This allowed ministers to tailor Scottish policy using the scope afforded by a separate Scottish legal system, administrative structure and need for more time to implement (Cairney, 2002). Yet, the pre-devolution experience suggests that the centre is by far the most powerful actor. This is particularly the case when the centre's attention to policy in the 'periphery' is high, as it was for example during the Thatcher era. The remainder of this chapter explores the difference that political devolution has made to these arrangements.

Reserved and devolved areas in Scotland

As set out in Chapter 1, The Scotland Act 1998 specifies which matters are reserved and devolved, and the boundaries appear reasonably clear. Devolved matters are those areas not specified in the Act, as well as some extra powers granted on an *ad hoc* basis (such as the Scottish rail network in 2004). However, since 1999 there have been issues which have highlighted blurred boundaries between the policy competences of the Scottish and UK Governments (see Box 1.2). Some of these examples can be explained by the novelty of the devolution settlement and initial governmental uncertainty, which occasionally caused public confusion. For example, Scotland's Deputy Minister for Justice made two press statements on 24 July 2000; the first vowed to aid central government in the development of the Register of Sex Offenders since this involved a reserved power; the second explained that the register was a devolved responsibility (Rhodes *et al.*, 2003: 97).

Early confusion over competence was also exploited for political gain. For example, the lack of a dedicated industry minister in the Scottish Government allowed the Scotland Office to intervene in industrial policy, including the highly publicized saving of the Kvaerner shipyard in Glasgow (Parry and Jones, 2000). Such teething troubles are now healing, and this is demonstrated well by the changing status of the Scotland Office in London. This was formed to act as a conduit between the Scottish Government and Whitehall, and to administer certain reserved aspects of Scottish policy. Initially it was headed by a fairly senior member of the UK government and had the power to intervene in Scottish politics (as with John Reid and Kvaerner). However, as the confidence and the legitimacy of the Scottish Government and Parliament grew, the perceived necessity (within Whitehall) of the Scotland

Department for Constitutional Affairs: UK State Department which includes the Scotland Office. It is also responsible for the justice system; human rights law; running elections and the constitution.

Office receded. In June 2003 it was subsumed within the **Department for Constitutional Affairs** and only covered on a part-time basis by a Cabinet minister.

Policy areas with boundary issues

Yet, even following this period of transition, there are still many areas with blurred boundaries between Scottish and UK powers which are often complicated by the EU dimension. In many cases we can predict areas of overlap – a typology of policy areas with boundary issues is outlined below.

First, there are policy areas more reserved than devolved. Most economic policy, such as fiscal and monetary policy and customs and excise, is reserved. However, there is some EU influence through the distribution of structural funds to Scotland. There is also devolved control of revenue through business, water and council-tax rates, and economic development through Scottish Enterprise.

Second, there are policy areas which are devolved but Europeanized. For example, devolution of environmental and agricultural policies to Scotland has come at a time when the responsibility for policy formulation is transferring to the EU. This ensures UK influence at all stages of the process. At the policy formulation stage, the UK has the formal role as the member state. At the policy implementation stage, although the Scottish Government has much more discretion, the UK retains a monitoring role to ensure standards and targets are met by EU deadlines.

Third, there are cross-cutting and multi-faceted areas. For example, law and order is one of the policy areas with most tangled responsibilities. The Scottish Government is responsible for police, prisons, and the justice system but not the classification of drugs or policy on firearms or terrorism. This, combined with a particular need to harmonize policy (to close legal loopholes), makes it necessary to produce a particularly high number of Sewel motions (see below). The EU dimension is increasingly apparent given the cross-border nature of certain crimes (such as human trafficking) and the development of a pan-EU arrest warrant.

Poverty is another multi-faceted policy area – the Scottish Government does not control all of the relevant policy instruments. With fuel poverty, it can influence levels of insulation and heating in homes, but not the price of fuel or the level of income tax and benefits. With housing poverty, the Executive does not control housing benefits, while its ability to control the stock of social rented accommodation is limited by Treasury rules on borrowing to build. With child poverty, most policy responses are second order, focusing on access to devolved public services rather than levels of income.

New Deal: UK Government employment policy designed to get individuals off 'welfare' (social security) and back into work.

Sure Start: A UK government programme designed to ensure opportunities for children which combines childcare, early education, health and family support policies.

There are also *cross-cutting issues* in UK policies such as the **New Deal** and **Sure Start** which contain reserved and devolved elements. The changes to income support and Working Families Tax Credits also had a knock-on effect on policies such as free school meal entitlement.

Fourth there are relatively devolved areas with UK and EU elements. For example, although public health is devolved, the example of tobacco control shows the influence of all three levels of government: the EU has issued directives on minimum levels of taxation, maximum levels of tar, product labelling and tobacco advertising; UK policies on these issues go beyond the EU requirements and apply to Scotland; Scotland controls NHS treatments such as smoking-cessation clinics and nicotine replacement therapy. Similar issues arise with alcohol (the Executive controls licensing law, health education and funds NHS treatment; the UK controls tax and therefore price levels) and drugs (medical treatment is devolved; the legal framework is reserved).

There are fewer cross-cutting issues in broader health policy since the NHS is devolved to Scotland and there is very little direct EU influence. However, there are important indirect effects, such as the EU Social Chapter's Working Time Directive – the effect of which is to ensure that doctors work no more than an average of 48-hours per week. The restrictions had a significant effect on clinical cover in rural areas. Further, the current Royal College thinking on the need to centralize NHS services to maximize the benefits of clinical training and standards (still a reserved matter), combined with the WTD, ensures a prominent place for UK and EU influence in Scottish NHS organization in terms of employment and training (Greer, 2005b and 2005c).

Similarly, higher education is devolved but certain aspects are still arranged on a UK basis. The UK research funding councils are reserved bodies and the lecturing profession still has a high degree of UK mobility. The Research Assessment Exercise (RAE), which informs research funding allocations to universities, is conducted on a UK basis but then used by the Scottish Higher Education Funding Council (SHEFC) to fund in a different way. There is some European (but not EU) influence in the Bologna process to harmonize levels of accreditation in HE degrees.

Policy issues arising since devolution

In other cases, the issues are less predictable and often arise only when they are high on the agenda of one or more government (although few issues have arisen directly between Scotland and the EU). We may expect most of these disputes to arise when there is no shared party of government, particularly since Alex Salmond was critical of the 'surrenders of the previous administration . . . [to avoid being] seen arguing with their big brother' (*Holyrood Magazine*, 2007). However, the era of Labour-led coalition was not without controversy. From 1999–2007 a number of these issues rose to prominence either because the Scottish Executive appeared to encroach on, or be constrained by, reserved issues:

- Ban on Smoking in Public Places – the Scottish Executive legislated to introduce a ban on smoking in public places, an area previously considered to be reserved under concordat with the UK Health and Safety Executive (Cairney, 2007b). While the Scottish legislation proceeded by treating it as a matter of public health, its regulations extend to employment policy.
- Hepatitis C – the Scottish Executive planned to compensate people who contracted Hepatitis C from contaminated blood products in the NHS. The UK Government (with a long history of resisting no-fault compensation) threatened to withhold benefits from those compensated, then challenged devolved competence (compensation for injury and illness is reserved) until it came up with a UK-wide scheme to be implemented in Scotland
- Aid for Malawi – Scotland's extensive efforts in providing aid for, and seconding staff to, Malawi seemed to infringe on the reserved area of international aid. However, executive devolution allows Scottish ministers to further UK policy in this area.
- Dawn Raids and Asylum Seeking – the murder of a Kurdish asylum-seeker in 2001 and the operation of Dungavel detention centre (including the education and healthcare of children within it) added to public pressure for Scottish ministers to become involved in an issue considered to be reserved by the UK government. At the peak of this pressure, the detainees were removed from Scotland rather than treated differently within it. Law and order also demonstrates the overlap of responsibilities when reserved policies are implemented by devolved services. For example, the Home Office directs Scottish local authorities on immigration and controls the use of 'dawn raids' by police forces when removing unsuccessful asylum-seekers (Cairney, 2006a). Attempts by the Scottish Government to secure a 'protocol' on minimum standards of welfare and police conduct during this process had uncertain success.

Further, although the SNP Government became embroiled in a number of controversies, many of these debates between Scotland and the UK began before 2007. There are numerous examples. One of the most controversial is the consequence of Scottish policies on reserved entitlements. When the Executive introduced 'free personal care' payments of £145 per person per week to older people (in 2003 – see Chapter 10), this meant they lost entitlement to Attendance Allowance (£45–65, administered by the UK Department of Work and Pensions). The pursuit of this money became a key plank of the

SNP's 2007 election campaign. A similar issue arises with the SNP plan to replace the council tax with a local income tax which will result in a loss of Scottish entitlement to council tax benefits.

Another potential issue is nuclear power – there is some confusion over the Scottish Government's ability to either block the building of new power stations in Scotland (through devolved planning law) or decide not to build them (under executive devolution). The matter was put off by the coalition between 1999 and 2007 (the Liberal Democrats had stronger objections) but revisited when the SNP highlighted its opposition in 2007. Moreover, while the renewal of the Trident nuclear missile system is a reserved matter, Scottish concerns were raised in Parliament, in part since many would be built and/or stationed in Scotland. In 2007 a symbolic motion rejecting Trident was passed in the Scottish Parliament and the SNP Government has begun to explore its options (Gray, 2007).

There are other issues in this vein. Control of firearms is a reserved matter, but concerns over airgun injuries rose on the Scottish political agenda in 2006. While Jack McConnell attempted to influence UK policy informally through Home Office ministers, the SNP has promised to lobby for Scottish control of the issue. Another recurring issue is the complaint by Scottish fishing groups that Scottish minsters were excluded from formal EU negotiations on fishing quotas (despite representing most of the UK's fleet), while UK ministers appeared willing to trade the issue for concessions elsewhere. The prospect of Scottish ministers 'taking the lead' on these issues in the future was mooted by Alex Salmond in his first month of office. Another issue which arose in those months was when Alex Salmond blamed Tony Blair for a lack of consultation over a concordat with Libya over prisoner extraditions which could affect the man jailed for the Lockerbie bombing.

Intergovernmental relations – Scotland and the UK

This confusing overlap of responsibilities between Scotland, the UK and the EU suggests that a way has to be found for each authority to cooperate in shared policy domains. Interdependence suggests the need for joint working. However, it does not necessarily suggest that such interactions are consensual or based on an equal sharing of power. Indeed, when compared to other countries, the UK's political arrangements are unusual. Devolution in the UK is asymmetrical in two senses.

First, it was extended to a relatively small share of the UK population, with Scotland (8.6%), Wales (4.9%) and Northern Ireland (2.9%) accounting for just 16.4 per cent. Since devolution was not extended to the English regions, this means that the UK has three executives dealing with a small population and one government in charge of policy for the whole English and UK populations.

Second, as a result, the balance of power is tipped towards UK policy departments dealing predominantly with the English population. The centre is faced with a small set of devolved governments which do not match the powers of federated or devolved authorities in other countries such as Germany, Spain, Belgium or Canada. Scotland is not part of a collection of powerful regions and the UK does not have a 'supreme constitution' guaranteeing a level of autonomy for devolved governments (Keating, 2005a: 120; Watts, 2007).

What the UK does have in common with most systems is the relatively low level of contact between legislatures. It has also proved difficult for Scottish Parliament committees to arrange to hear oral evidence from UK ministers. Most parliamentary contact surrounds the use of Sewel motions (below), but even this process is managed by executives. Perhaps the only issue that keeps Scotland on the agenda in Westminster is the West Lothian Question (Box 8.1).

Rather than legislatures, most contact takes place between executives, and a number of means to frame and conduct these discussions were devised (see House of Commons Library, 2005). First, the Memorandum of Understanding sets out an overarching framework to guide the conduct of executives. It outlines the operation of the **Joint Ministerial Committee** (JMC), the coordination of policy influence in the EU and wider world, the scope of devolved governments, financial assistance to industry and the harmonization of official statistics.

Joint Ministerial Committee (JMC): An over-arching body that deals with relations between the administrations at Westminster and the devolved bodies.

Second, individual **concordats** between the Government and Whitehall Departments (all of which have now been re-named or reorganized) set out agreed policy commitments and a broad outline of devolved and reserved policy issues. Examples include: the Cabinet Office establishes the reserved nature of the civil service and sets out a broad commitment to pursue the modernizing government agenda (on public-sector efficiency); Agriculture, Fisheries and Food sets out much more extensive coordination efforts, including a commitment to monthly meetings between senior civil servants in each executive and bi-monthly meetings between ministers; Trade and Industry reiterates the need for the Executive to make its representations on EU state aid through Whitehall.

Concordats: Non statutory agreements between the UK and Scottish executive branches of government setting out clearly the relationship between both to ensure that both are aware of the requirements of the other.

Third, the Joint Ministerial Committee was set up to allow ministers (and their staffs) of the four countries to formally engage on disputes or issues of policy uncertainty (including financial matters). Its remit is to consider non-devolved matters which impinge on devolved responsibilities, and devolved

Box 8.1 The West Lothian question and the role of Scottish MPs

The unintended consequence of devolution was a series of constitutional problems. The most famous issue was dubbed the 'West Lothian Question' in the late 1970s (during debates leading up to the 1979 referendum) after Tam Dalyell MP highlighted his ability as an MP for West Lothian to vote on policies affecting West Bromwich. In other words, a paradox has arisen in which:

- Scottish MPs can no longer vote on devolved issues such as health and education policy in Scotland.
- Scottish MPs can still vote on those same issues affecting England (i.e. out-with their own constituency and country).
- English MPs cannot return the favour since these issues are devolved to the Scottish Parliament.

The initial response following devolution was to reduce Scottish representation at Westminster from 72 to 59 MPs (from the 2005 election). However, this did not solve the problem as it merely means Scotland has a roughly proportionate number of MPs in terms of population (it was over-represented in the past). Further, in a series of controversial Acts passed for England – including student fees and foundation hospitals – the government majority was bolstered by Scottish and Welsh Labour MPs.

Questions also remain about the role of Scottish MPs. Westminster does continue to pass legislation and regulations impacting on Scotland – for example on average 10 Sewel motions are passed per year. Westminster legislation determines Scottish constituency boundaries and the number of MPs and MSPs. A number of Scottish MPs remain senior figures in UK Government, most notably the Prime Minister, Gordon Brown (see Box 8.2). However, Scotland's position in London is being downgraded. The Secretary of State for Scotland is a part-time position and the Scotland Office was subsumed within a Whitehall department. The Scottish Affairs Committee is 'looking for a role' and the Scottish Grand Committee appears to be defunct since there are very few dedicated Scotland Bills. There is less public recognition of Scottish MPs and they are increasingly overlooked by both their constituents and the media in favour of MSPs.

matters which impinge on non-devolved responsibilities; to consider devolved matters if it is beneficial to discuss their respective treatment in the different parts of the United Kingdom; to keep the arrangements for liaison between the UK Government and the devolved administrations under review; and to consider disputes between the administrations (UK Government *et al.*, 2001: 17). The plenary committee (to meet once per year) is chaired by the Prime Minister, while individual policy committees are chaired by the relevant Secretary of State.

Judicial Committee of the Privy Council: One of the highest courts in the UK and the one responsible for adjudicating in matters arising from devolution

Finally, the UK Government has the ability to refer issues to the courts (who may refer the issue to the **Judicial Committee of the Privy Council**) in cases where the Scottish Parliament legislates beyond its legal competence.

However, the assumption behind these arrangements during the years of Labour-led government in Scotland (1999–2007) was that they represented a safety net only to be used in exceptional circumstances. The tendency was not to use them (see Trench, 2004). The Memorandum and the Concordats are not legally binding. Rather, they represent a, 'statement of political intent . . . binding in honour only' (2001: 5). The Memorandum's main function is to promote good communication between executives, particularly when one knows that forthcoming policies will affect the other. This emphasis is furthered in the individual concordats which devote most of their discussions to reiterating the need for communication, confidentiality and forward notice (or the 'no surprises' approach). Similarly, the JMC is a consultative rather than an executive body, with issues referred to it on the rare occasions that bilateral discussions between Executives break down. Referral of issues to the Judicial Committee is regarded as a last resort (with the Labour-led Executive more likely to 'remove offending sections' than face delay) (Page, 2005). After his election to First Minister in 2007, Alex Salmond called for JMCs to be revived (only the European JMC has met since 2002) and Gordon Brown (see Box 8.2) has indicated that this may happen (see Fraser, 2007).

Box 8.2   Gordon Brown, Prime Minister

Gordon Brown has been a Scottish MP since 1983 and became Chancellor of the Exchequer in 1997. In 2007 he became Prime Minister after the resignation of Tony Blair. Therefore, despite the advent of devolution and election of a Scottish Parliament and First Minister, Brown is the most influential politician elected in Scotland. Most of this influence came as Chancellor, with the Treasury the determinant of Scotland's share of public expenditure, and influential in key decisions to restrict borrowing to build housing, collect tuition fees and determine Attendance Allowance for those receiving free personal care (Chapter 10). Upon his move to No. 10, Brown moved to put his stamp on the UK Government's style of decision-making, from 'sofa government' to 'Cabinet Government'. This included a commitment to keeping the Government more informed of major UK decisions affecting Scotland (despite Brown's reluctance during the 2007 election campaign to commit to working with an SNP government) and a suggestion that JMCs could be reconvened. Brown appointed Des Browne as Scottish (and Defence) Secretary. A meeting between Brown, Angus Robertson (SNP Westminster leader) and Alex Salmond soon followed in June 2007.

Why have formal mechanisms been so rarely used?

There are what might be called positive and negative reasons for a lack of formal dispute resolution within the UK. Positive reasons refer to those explanations which seem to suit both parties. They include the use of the Barnett system to determine Scotland's share of public expenditure automatically rather than resorting to annual negotiations (see Chapter 9), the extensive links between the civil services of Scotland and the UK (see Chapter 6) and the fact that there has been a shared party of government from 1999–2007 (Keating, 2005a: 122–3). Although in some countries parties may be integrated, with formal means to coordinate policy, in the UK the most important links were based on personal relationships between ministers (Horgan, 2004: 124). The informal use of IGR through parties reflected a desire to avoid political embarrassment and present a united front when possible (Cairney, 2006a).

In this sense, the lack of JMC meetings from 1999–2007 reflected good working arrangements. This was in part because ministers in Scotland and London also had the opportunity to meet elsewhere – as in the case of agriculture when they meet to discuss EU legislation (Trench, 2004: 514).

On the other hand, negative reasons refer to an incomplete relationship based on an asymmetry of power. The structure and frequency of IGR may be more about UK dominance than consensus. Given the size of Scotland, the fact that Scottish policy agendas are diverging and the range of responsibilities that Whitehall departments have, there has been a tendency for UK ministers to disengage from the IGR process. The lack of JMC meetings during a Labour-led Government reflected UK disinterest: 'a clear indicator that devolution is no longer a prime concern of the Prime Minister and other politicians' (Trench, 2004: 515–6). Moreover, the civil service in Scotland is slowly moving away from the UK arena, and civil servants in Whitehall often forget about Scotland and neglect to consult, then make statements on UK policy without a Scottish qualification or opt-out (Keating, 2005a: 125).

This imbalance of power is most apparent when disputes rise to the surface. In cases such as free personal care for older people and Hepatitis C compensation, the Government was reluctant to 'rock the boat' and instead accepted UK 'victories' to maintain its good relationship with Whitehall (see Trench, 2004). However, an alternative view suggests that this may be overplaying the significance of UK dominance by focusing on a very small number of visible conflicts. If Whitehall ministers have 'disentangled themselves from devolution', then scope exists for the type of day-to-day autonomy highlighted by Bulpitt (1983: 139). Further, while Scotland appears to lose the public arguments over finance, this should be seen within a wider context of spending negotiations (see Chapter 9). Part of the reason that the Government did not pursue the issue on free personal care is that this would undermine its work behind the scenes to ensure a much greater sum towards council house debts.

Intergovernmental relations and legislation: Sewel motions

These discussions of IGR and dominance extend to the issue of legislation, since Westminster still passes more legislation and regulations for Scotland than the Scottish Parliament (Cairney, 2006a). In cases where Westminster legislation may refer to issues with reserved and devolved elements, this involves the use of legislative consent motions. These were initially dubbed Sewel motions, named after Lord Sewel, the minister responsible for ensuring the progress of the Scotland Bill through the House of Lords in 1998 (Winetrobe, 2001).

The procedure was created in anticipation of a *small number of instances* in which the UK government would legislate in devolved areas. The Memorandum of Understanding makes clear that Westminster retains the authority to legislate across the UK, but the Government will follow the convention to, 'not normally legislate with regard to devolved matters except with the agreement of the devolved legislature' (UK Government *et al.*, 2001: 8). The Sewel motion is therefore passed in the Scottish Parliament to formally express this agreement. However, the motion has also been taken to refer to Westminster legislation which alters Scottish legislative or executive functions (Winetrobe, 2005). As a result, the passing of a Sewel motion can signal three things. First, that Westminster will legislate on a devolved matter. Second, that Westminster legislation will bestow new powers to the Scottish Parliament (this has yet to happen). Third, that Westminster will delegate reserved powers to Scottish Ministers. These may usefully be dubbed 'reverse-Sewel' motions since they give back rather than remove powers.

The use of Sewel motions has been followed by a degree of controversy, with political parties (SNP, SSP and Green) and some media and academic commentators opposed in principle to their use. This is compounded by the frequency of their use, with 79 passed from 1999–2007 (compared to 103 Executive bills). This opposition is based on a combination of several arguments. First, by legislating on devolved policy, Westminster is taking back the powers granted following devolution and the Scottish ministers are dodging their responsibilities. Second, passing an issue back to Westminster undermines and limits debate in the Scottish Parliament. Third, a number of motions passed (e.g. civil partnerships and the age of consent for gay sex) demonstrated political cowardice, with the Government keen to remove the issue to another venue. Fourth, formal contact on Westminster legislation affecting Scotland should be between legislatures rather than executives, or the Scottish Parliament should have much more say in the future development of the policy involved. At present, the motion is effectively a 'blank cheque' with no limits on the timing of, or future changes to, the Westminster bill. Fifth, better yet, the principle of 'Scottish solutions for Scottish problems' suggests that Scotland should legislate even if the policies would be similar

(Winetrobe, 2005; Page and Batey, 2002; Cairney and Keating, 2004). This is the broad line taken by the SNP Government.

Yet, these concerns can be qualified. First, the numbers are misleading since: the Sewel motion generally refers to a small part of a larger bill; 18 (23%) of the 79 were reverse-Sewel motions which delegated powers to Scottish Ministers; and not all motions were opposed formally by MSPs. From 1999–2003, 20 of 41 (49%) were opposed, rising to 25 of 38 (66%) from 2003–07 in reflection of the election of Green and SSP MSPs. This reflects the fact that many motions are innocuous, dealing with anomalies which merit minimal debate in Holyrood. The high numbers can therefore be attributed to a Government 'playing safe' and referring all issues to the Scottish Parliament Second, there are many instances of all-party support for these motions as there are clear examples of cowardice (for example, the Compensation Bill to make compensation claims for asbestosis was passed for expediency). Third, it could also be argued that contact between executives is more realistic given their resources, the details of legislation and the levels of existing contact. Finally, to devote committee and plenary time to many of these motions would be counterproductive, since this would leave less time for, say, inquiries and scrutiny.

While there are clearly principled and legal arguments against the Sewel process, it is also worth considering the reasons for their use. For example, motions are used to address entangled responsibilities, with law and order a regular feature: with legislation on an international criminal court, powers of arrest are devolved, but extradition is reserved; with the Proceeds of Crime Act 2002, drug trafficking, money laundering and taxation are reserved, whilst other civil and criminal matters are devolved. There are other motions relating to reserved bodies operating in devolved areas. These cases foster a UK-wide approach to maintain consistency of standards. The areas involved – such as food standards, financial services, race relations, health protection and serious organized crime – tend to be devolved but with the potential for UK bodies to act in Scotland. A further category is motions justified mainly in terms of expediency and removing the need for identical legislation in Scotland.

While there is not an explicit discussion about expediency and political uniformity when the motions are introduced by ministers, this was certainly a feature during 1999–2007. Page and Batey (2002: 513) suggest that the driver for this uniformity came from the UK government. The Government's (unpublished) guidance on Sewel 'makes clear that most proposals for Westminster legislation in the devolved areas come from UK departments rather than Scottish ministers' (2002: 516). This proposal comes after the legislative slot has been secured and gives Scotland little time to consider the issue. So while there is no public evidence of unwillingness to cooperate, Scottish ministers 'may find themselves effectively forced to agree to Westminster legislation in the devolved areas' given the uncertainty over devolved government powers and the prospect of the UK government referring the issue to the Judicial Committee of the Privy Council (Page, 2002).

> ### Box 8.3   The House of Lords Select Committee on the Constitution (2002)
>
> One of the most systematic attempts to characterize IGR was performed by the Lords. The report suggests that when the Labour Party was in office in both Scotland and the UK, most contact took place informally through ministers, parties and the civil service. Since this contact was by email, telephone or 'quick words when people meet socially' it was not recorded in the same way as formal minuted meetings. The report suggests that such informality depends on the 'fundamental goodwill of each administration toward the others'. However, if the importance of the JMC was not made clear from the start, this may store up problems when Scotland and the UK do not share the same party of government. Giving the example of the **foot-and-mouth disease** crisis in 2001, it argues that formal IGR mechanisms have not worked well so far and that informal means cannot be relied upon in the future: 'Devolved administrations may be more conscious of their distinct interests in future, or less willing to help the UK Government resolve its own problems . . . we wish to ensure that good and effective relations between governments can continue even if the present level of goodwill should decline'.

Yet, this interpretation contrasts with the Scottish Government's insistence that most Sewel initiation comes from the Scottish Government. According to the Scottish Minister for Parliamentary Business' evidence to a House of Lords Inquiry in 2002 (see Box 8.3), Sewel selection is a 'pick'n'mix' affair following informal contacts and an analysis of upcoming Westminster legislation (Scottish Minister for Parliamentary Business 2002) While the latter may exaggerate Scottish influence, it is in the interests of both governments for the process to appear seamless, allowing loopholes to be closed and reducing the likelihood of challenge in the courts (Cairney and Keating, 2004). The Sewel procedure is a convenient tool for a Government short of parliamentary time, in broad agreement with the aims of the legislation, and in some cases anxious not to be seen 'lagging behind' England (Page and Batey, 2002: 513–14). The use of Sewel motions therefore reinforces the picture of informal IGR between executives (Cairney, 2006a).

Foot-and-mouth disease: A highly contagious viral infection affecting cloven-hoofed animals such as cows. The UK outbreak in 2000–01 led to restrictions placed on UK farmers by the EU.

Creating policy space in Scotland

A final strategy for Scottish interests seeking to influence deserved/reserved boundaries is to shift them (to treat as devolved an issue previously deemed reserved). Again, the precedent was set before devolution, with autonomy furthered by minimizing central government attention. This depended on the ability of Scottish actors to frame issues as technical or humdrum while minimizing the appearance of policy divergence. For example, the much feted example of social work reform in the 1960s was originally described as a pilot study (Kellas, 1973).

The modern equivalent is the smoking ban in Scotland which at the time marked significant policy divergence in a policy area previously deemed reserved by civil servants, MSPs, concordat and by a series of Scottish Government documents. Yet the Scottish Executive legislated in 2005 (Cairney, 2006a). Some effort to reframe the issue was therefore necessary to shift the boundaries between devolved and reserved. As interviews with civil servants suggest, this was done by redefining smoking in public places as a public health issue. In this sense, smoking is the most prominent example of the use of the 'purpose test' to determine the true nature of a piece of legislation. While the legislation affected reserved areas (health and safety; employment), the primary aim of the legislation was to pursue public health measures. However, such a test presupposes a technical side to these decisions when the decision is a political one to supersede boundaries already agreed. Therefore, the bill was as much based on implicit UK support (perhaps even to test the waters for policy in England) as an imaginative solution to devolved competence in Scotland (Cairney, 2006a).

Scotland in Europe

It is ironic that, formally, Scottish Government ministers may have less of a role in the EU than their Scottish Office predecessors (see Box 8.4). This is because, as members of the UK Government, Scottish Office ministers were involved formally in UK negotiations in areas such as fishing, where they had a particular interest and large presence in proportion to the rest of the UK. Now, this formal role is less certain and subject to constraints which seem more significant after devolution: if the Scottish Government participates, then it is bound by the UK rules of collective cabinet responsibility and confidentiality. In other words, ministers may not say publicly or to the Scottish Parliament which policies they disagree with, which becomes tricky if the UK as a whole trades fishing stocks for a 'more important' EU policy.

However, the focus of multi-level governance is on the *informal* means of access and influence in international affairs that Scotland enjoys. This is apparent in its work in Malawi, while at least one Foreign Secretary has recognized the role that the Scottish Government can play in the UK's foreign affairs (see Cairney, 2006a). Similarly, in Europe, the Scottish Government supplements its limited formal rights in the EU with informal channels of contact. As a result, we can see qualified influence. Although the UK's 'centre' controls its response to European policy, the Scottish Government enjoys considerable access to its decision-making machinery. Also, although the UK government performs a monitoring role to ensure that devolved governments implement EU policy, the Scottish Government enjoys considerable discretion in the implementation of policy.

There is some debate about the practical value of this influence (see Bulmer *et al.*, 2002 and 2006; Keating, 2005a; House of Lords, 2002), and much depends on whose influence we compare that of the Scottish Government to. If, for example, we compare its role with a government region in England, then Scotland does well. It not only has a relatively well-established office in Brussels, but its staff also enjoy diplomatic status and have formal access to the EU's communications network through its full inclusion within the UK's Permanent Representative to the European Union (an office consisting of civil servants from a range of Whitehall departments).

Further, recent reforms in the **Common Agricultural Policy** (CAP) show the flexibility to adapt EU rules to local or regional circumstances. However, there may be as many examples of constraints to discretion, such as when Scotland was free of foot-and-mouth disease long before England, but could not apply to change its export status. Scotland may therefore be best-described as a 'dependent partner' with the UK. It (along with the other devolved administrations) enjoys a privileged position within Whitehall but does not have the resources, constitutional position or direct links to the EU that Whitehall enjoys (Bulmer *et al.*, 2006: 86).

> **Common Agricultural Policy** (CAP): A controversial system of EU agricultral subsidies and programmes. It represents over 40% of the EU's budget.

The main problem in researching IGR, particularly when it is conducted informally, is that the relations are kept fairly secret. Few books or articles exist in which many civil servants or politicians are quoted openly when describing Scotland's fate in the EU via the UK. Therefore, we know that since Scotland's influence is so affected by its access to the UK, much depends on the attitude of Whitehall departments to devolution. However, we often do not know what that their attitude is. This problem was solved to some extent in 2007 when a report by the Head of the Scottish Executive's European office was leaked online briefly. Although the report largely confirms the existing literature, it is still significant since it is based on widespread interviews within the Executive. The main findings are:

- The best way for the Scottish Government to influence Europe remains through Whitehall.
- Scottish Government relationships with Whitehall departments vary, with talks most constructive when EU influence is low (for example when it makes recommendations rather than introduces directives), when Scottish Government policy is more developed, or when the Scottish department makes a particular effort to keep up regular contact (e.g. in the tourism sector).

- However, this involves a disproportionate amount of work by Scottish officials, since Whitehall departments often ignore or forget to consult their Scottish counterparts.
- In some cases, Whitehall departments have deliberately excluded their Scottish counterparts from the process, while in most cases the problem is that the Executive is not consulted at a stage early enough to influence the direction of policy.
- Direct Scottish Government contact with EU institutions (the Commission, Parliament and Council of Ministers) is limited and often discouraged by Whitehall departments.
- Ministerial links also vary according to the personalities of ministers, but also the time ministers can take out from domestic commitments. There is also a feeling that, since devolution, ministers have lost some of their clout and there is now no equivalent to the single Scottish Secretary being the figurehead for Scotland and banging the drum in Cabinet. Yet links are often good in areas where constant contact is required (e.g. agriculture and fisheries).
- The concluding recommendation is a call for greater coordination across Scottish departments, to promote a Scottish-wide show of support for policy when in contact with Whitehall.

Box 8.4   EU institutions and organizations

The three main institutions in the EU are:

- *The European Commission* – while direct links between the EC and Executive are increasingly apparent, these are used to supplement rather than subvert existing UK channels.
- *The Council of Ministers* – Scottish ministers can attend if invited by the UK, and on rare cases (e.g. fishing), they could take the UK lead.
- *The European Parliament* – Scotland has seven MEPs out of 78 in the UK and 785 overall. In 2004, Labour, the SNP and Conservatives held two and the Liberal Democrats one.

There are also a number of networks and forums to exert indirect influence without going through Whitehall (see Keating, 2005: 133–5). These include:

- *The Committee of the Regions* – set up by the Maastricht Treaty to ensure that sub-national authorities such as regional and local governments were consulted about EU policies affecting their operations. However, it is an unwieldy body (over 300 members) with no decision-making capacity and no real authority.
- *Regions With Legislative Power* – established by a smaller number of regions with direct powers to adapt EU policies (rather than local authorities with an administrative role). In 2004, Jack McConnell served as President, expressing sympathy for greater regional recognition but shying away from the more 'nationalistic tone' of other members (2005: 134).

Again, much depends on who we are comparing Scotland to. While Scottish interests may feel neglected by Whitehall, the feeling in Wales and Northern Ireland (and English regions) is that Scotland is most likely to have its voice heard (Bulmer *et al.*, 2006: 87). Further, the feeling among civil servants in the Executive's EU office (at least up to 2007) is that Scotland may have more of an influence as part of the UK's network than as a small independent country with direct access and voting rights.

How do interest groups deal with multi-level governance?

Since these governmental arrangements are so complex, it is worth exploring how interest groups adapt their lobbying strategies. There are three main points. First, not surprisingly, groups are more willing to seek access to Scottish institutions when they appear to be central to, or have a significant influence on, particular policies. Second, the strategy of groups varies according to their own resources and organizational structure. In other words, small groups with few resources to lobby tend to focus their attention on the Scottish Government as a route into the UK and EU (and even local authority) arenas. Similarly, Scottish arms of UK organizations tend to filter their views up to the UK centre, with direct governmental contact often restricted to the Scottish Government as a supplement to the main event (since Scottish arms rarely develop their own positions on EU and UK policy). Third, there is significant variation by policy area (see Keating, 2005a; Keating and Stevenson, 2001). Therefore, as a whole, we see distinct policy areas with varying group strategies within them. A number of examples should demonstrate this point.

Policy areas more reserved than devolved

Since most economic policy areas are reserved, the big banks (e.g. RBS, HBOS) based in Scotland tend to focus their efforts towards the UK and wider international fields, either individually or as part of the British Bankers' Association. They are also are part of the Scottish equivalent – Scottish Financial Enterprise – which seeks to promote a positive image of the financial sector through issues such as education and training and social inclusion. The whisky trade (which may be based in Scotland but is increasingly owned elsewhere) tends to focus almost all of its efforts at the UK and EU levels, with issues of duty and general taxation at the forefront of their concerns. The Scottish arms of business groups such as the Confederation of British Industry, Institute of Directors and Federation of Small Business in Scotland lobby in the Scottish arena (business rates, tourism, training, transport) while maintaining links with their UK organizations which take the lead on UK and European issues.

The reserved nature of employment law and the minimum wage may explain why it has taken a long time for UK unions to devolve significant resources. The biggest exception is the large public-sector trade union UNISON which represents a range of NHS staff. The **Scottish Trade Union Congress** (STUC) (a separate organization from the TUC), enjoyed close links with the Scottish Labour Party and signed a concordat with the Government to make sure that access to the civil servants was similar to access to ministers following a change of party in government. It discusses devolved matters – such as economic development, public services, 'social partnership' and lifelong learning – with blurred issues such as the health and safety of public sector workers more difficult to resolve.

> **Scottish Trade Union Congress** (STUC): An umbrella body to articulate the views of trade unions in Scotland.

Policy areas which are devolved but Europeanized

Since agriculture policy is Europeanized, Scottish groups must maintain links with the UK government to access the EU formally. The National Farmers Union Scotland (NFUS) uses the Scottish Government as a first point of formal contact while maintaining day-to-day links with the NFU England (which is a separate organization) and broad European networks. CAP reform has increased the scope for territorial differences in implementation, but most (68%) of the consultation documents issued by the Scottish Government relate to EU or UK agendas (author calculations). However, in part because the Executive is often reluctant to take a distinct policy line, the NFUS supplements these links with informal EU contact through a Brussels office it shares with the NFU.

Environmental policy has since 1999 shared a government department with agriculture. Therefore, while Friends of the Earth (FOE) Scotland (a separate organization from the rest of the UK) focuses most of its efforts in Scotland, it is realistic about its relative success given the size of the agricultural budget compared to environmental spending. While there are some relevant reserved issues (such as company law) it spends the remainder of its time linking with FOE Europe. The number of Scottish Government consultation documents arising from EU or UK agendas is similarly high (65%).

Relatively devolved areas

Compulsory education policy is possibly the best example of focused group activity at a devolved level. Teaching unions such as the Educational Institute for Scotland (EIS) focus primarily on lobbying the Scottish Government and negotiating with local authorities. Although Scottish branches of UK organizations have some degree of representation, the EIS is by far the biggest. This reflects a long tradition of difference in Scottish education. In higher education, the University and College Union (Scottish Branch) has a Scottish focus, although the existence of UK-wide arrangements for research funding and the high mobility of staff necessitates a greater degree of integration with a UK body.

Health policy is one of the most devolved areas and the British Medical Association (BMA) and Royal College of Nursing (RCN) had reasonably well-established Scottish organizations before devolution. However, while both enjoy a high degree of autonomy on Scottish matters they also complain about a lack of UK understanding of devolution and a lack of organizational devolution (which affects levels of staffing and finance for devolved offices). Both tend to focus on Scottish NHS delivery (including the terms and conditions of their staff). The Royal Colleges of Surgeons and Physicians also influence the Scottish NHS, but as a body interested in standards, clinical guidelines and delivery rather than as a union. A significant UK focus is maintained by the reservation of medical standards and training. While all of these groups have an interest in Europeanization following the effects of the Working Time Directive, lobbying would take place around the implementation.

While social work policy is devolved, there are good reasons to keep a UK as well as Scottish focus. The British Association of Social Workers (UK arm in Scotland) tends to follow policy developments. If, for example, a mental health bill or social work review is being processed by the Scottish Government it will direct its focus there. If there is an asylum bill or UK consideration of adoption, it then refocuses its efforts. This contrasts to some degree with housing and homelessness policy. Housing is devolved (although there are reserved elements such as levels of housing benefit) and groups tend to direct their efforts toward the Scottish Government and Parliament (with no real contact with MPs or MEPs).

Conclusion

Devolution has allowed the Government and Parliament to determine its style of politics and the direction of a wide range of policies in Scotland. In particular, 'flagship' social policies on student fees, care for older people and smoking in public places have shown a significant degree of policy divergence (see Chapter 10). However, if we look at the details of each case, they also betray a reliance on wider political structures at the UK level and beyond. Each example demonstrates that while general policy areas may be devolved, specific pieces of legislation and their regulations infringe upon, or have consequences for, reserved policy. Similarly, in areas such as environmental and agricultural policy, the devolution of policy downwards to Scotland has occurred in tandem with the transfer of responsibilities upwards to the EU. The consequence is that even the 'most devolved' policy areas share blurred boundaries with UK and EU policy domains.

From 1999 to 2007 this boundary issue was addressed informally and between executives (with a key role for civil servants) within the UK with little resort to concordats, the courts or the JMC. The role of the Labour Party in intergovernmental relations was significant but perhaps dependent on relationships between ministers and based on minimizing policy embarrassment than ensuring policy convergence. Given the internalization of decision-making and lack of formal dispute resolution producing 'winners and losers', it is difficult to assess Scotland's autonomy and influence. A focus on disputes and the apparent imposition of Sewel motions may suggest UK dominance. This is furthered by a study of Scotland's influence in Europe which is dependent on the attitude of Whitehall departments. Or, a focus on autonomy through UK disinterest and Scottish initiative may suggest that Scotland has influence beyond its formal structures. While it may not enjoy formal status in Europe, it is able to exploit a privileged position within the UK's political machinery. Therefore, while the study of IGR mechanisms is useful in identifying key structures underpinning governmental relations, it does not limit the scope for variation in policy outcomes.

The early literature on IGR suggests that only when we have different parties of government in the UK and Scotland will we see the significance of parties in UK IGR. The election of the SNP is therefore a crucial development, with the early evidence suggesting a greatly reduced willingness to keep disputes behind closed doors. Yet, this has not translated to formal measures previously considered to be a 'last resort' and it may not always be politically advantageous to exaggerate disputes.

Further reading

There is an eclectic mix of literature dealing with issues of multi-level governance and inter-governmental relations in Scotland. On intergovernmental relations see Bulpitt (1983), Mitchell (2003a, 2003b), Agranoff (2004), Horgan (2004) and Keating (2005a) as well as the annual publications from the Constitution Unit – Hazell (2000, 2003), Trench (2001, 2004, 2005). On multi-level governance see Bache and Flinders (2004a, 2004b). On Sewel motions see Winetrobe (2001, 2005) and Cairney and Keating (2004). For a history of the regions in Europe with reference to Scotland see Mazey and Mitchell (1993), Harvie (1994), Kellas (1991a). On EU policy-making and funding see Burrows (2000), Bache and Bristow (2003), Bulmer *et al.* (2002, 2006). On the Scottish Parliament and Europe see Salmon (2000), Baker *et al.* (2002), Heggie (2003) and European and External Relations Committee (2007). On Europe's impact on the Scottish Office/Executive see Smith (2003).

Online sources

Cabinet Office   http://www.cabinet-office.gov.uk/
Scotland Office   http://www.scottishsecretary.gov.uk/
Scotland Europa   http://www.scotlandeuropa.com
Government EU Office   http://www.scotland.gov.uk/euoffice
British/Irish Council   http://www1.british-irishcouncil.org

Chapter 9

Money and Power: Public Expenditure in Scotland

In this chapter we discuss what may be the most important area of Scottish politics. Public finance is a key aspect of the political process, and the issues raised in this chapter inform most of the themes discussed in this book. Yet, despite the importance of finance to Scottish politics, the system of raising and distributing money has not changed since devolution. Post-devolution Scotland continues to receive almost all of its funding for public expenditure from the UK Treasury in the form of a block grant. The arrangements for the transfer of this money are almost identical to those which existed pre-1999 and reflect the continued use of the **Barnett formula** to alter the block grant at the margins. This formula is the main focus of the chapter since it is key to an understanding of power relations between Scotland and the UK. These relations are linked to the idea of Scotland's 'financial advantage' compared to the rest of the UK and the ability of the Scottish Government to spend, but not raise, its money.

Barnett formula: A mechanism used by the Treasury to determine the adjustment in territorial (Scottish) public expenditure following changes to expenditure in England (in certain policy areas).

The issue of finance also informs our discussion of power *within* Scotland. For example, a discussion of the scrutiny of Scotland's budget further qualifies the extent to which Scottish Parliamentary influence exceeds its Westminster counterpart. The autonomy of local government is also considered – we discuss the level of local-authority dependence on the Scottish Government for its financial settlement and extend our analysis of central–local relations to issues of finance. In summary, this chapter:

- discusses the issue of advantage and power in relation to Scottish public finance;
- outlines in detail what the Barnett formula is and why it was adopted;
- considers why the Barnett formula has endured to this day and what this tells us about power and IGR; and
- highlights trends in Scottish Government spending and how this is scrutinized.

Advantage and power in Scottish public finance

The significance of incrementalism (Box 9.1) and the continued use of Barnett is difficult to overstate because it has been 'attacked' from a wide range of commentators for being unfair (McLean and McMillan, 2003). Indeed, although the SNP Government was highly critical of its first settlement in 2007, and there are Scottish politicians lining up to denounce the Barnett formula (Settle, 2007), there is often far more vociferous (although no more reasonable) criticism of Scotland's 'advantage' from MPs, the media and political commentators in England. In some cases, this is expressed (wrongly) as a £1,500 per person advantage in Scotland over its immediate neighbour in the north-east of England (Sky News, 2007). Scotland was initially dubbed the 'land of milk and honey' because commentators argued that the financial advantage allowed Scotland to fund personal care for older people, higher levels of staffing in the NHS, better wages for teachers, better roads and the abolition of student fees (see Mooney and Poole, 2004: 458). This argument is still recycled to this day, with more recent complaints suggesting that English taxpayers also fund free prescriptions, free eye tests, and heating and transport costs for older people (an excellent example is Chapman, 2007). The continuation of a finance system which seems so controversial is therefore highly significant; its maintenance highlights both the political costs to reform and the balance of power within territorial politics. As Keating (2005a: 140) suggests, such discussions can be divided into two main issues.

The first is an issue of advantage – whether Scotland gets *more* or *less* than its fair share of resources. The former suggests that Scottish political actors

---

Box 9.1   Incrementalism and public expenditure

A key theme of this book is the pervasiveness of incrementalism and the constraints to radical policy change. In the case of Scottish finance we can apply these discussions in two main ways. The first relates to the development of Scotland's financial settlement. As we discuss with reference to Goschen and Barnett, the various ways in which Scotland has negotiated its budget with the UK Treasury can be traced back to 'temporary' formulas which have endured to this day. Further, as incrementalism suggests, decision-makers have been reluctant to revisit policy because of the likelihood of opposition to a well-established system which reflects previous negotiations (or displeases fewer people than policy change would). The second relates to changes in Scottish spending patterns. Contemporary discussions of Treasury power suggest that policy innovation in Scotland is constrained by the UK financial settlement (see Chapter 10). On the other hand, any spending changes are likely to be incremental regardless of the source of funding, since few governments are willing to shift funding allocations beyond the margins or raise taxes to fund new initiatives. This suggests that we seek significance in the *margins* of Scottish Government spending in relation to English equivalents.

exert power successfully during public expenditure negotiations and/or that they successfully defend previously generous settlements. This may be doubly significant since devolution has operated within the most sustained period of UK public expenditure growth in the postwar period (at least until 2007). The latter suggests that Scottish oil revenue is subsidizing UK expenditure and that economic policy is geared towards the south-east of England to the exclusion of the north. Further, since it costs more in Scotland to provide the same level of service as England, the Scottish Government is actually constrained by funding levels. This contributes to an inability to introduce innovative (and expensive) public policies in Scotland unless the money can be found from cuts in other budgets. Therefore, any change to the Barnett formula will find criticism from one or both of these quarters.

The second is an issue of power – the contrast between Scotland's *lack of influence* over the way in which money is raised and its *considerable discretion* over the way it is distributed. The former refers to the power of the UK Treasury which still controls the means to raise money and then distribute it to Scotland. In this chapter we examine whether it *attempts* to exercise its power in a devolved Scotland. The latter suggests that when Scotland receives its block grant it has considerable power over how to spend it (particularly compared to other territorial governments).

The two issues of advantage and power are closely related. For example, if one concludes that Scotland acts to ensure a systematic financial advantage over the rest of the UK, this informs a consideration of Scotland's power (compared to other UK regions) in relation to the Treasury. As Chapter 8 suggests, although the Scottish Government may be subordinate to, or dependent on, the UK Government, its influence may still be more significant than an equivalent English region.

The Barnett formula and the Barnett 'squeeze'

The Barnett formula was named after Joel Barnett MP, Chief Secretary to the Treasury from 1974–79. Although this began as an interim measure in the run up to political devolution in 1979, it still operates today. The settlement covers most of the Scottish Parliament budget and accounts for approximately 60 per cent of all public spending in Scotland (the remainder is spent directly by Whitehall departments). It comprises two elements: an initial block settlement based on historic spends and the Barnett formula to adjust spending in Scotland to reflect changing levels of spending in England. In other words, the formula only relates to *changes* in the level of spending.

The formula is based on an estimate of population relativities. Initially this was a 10–5–85 split for Scotland, Wales and England which suggested that Scotland would receive 10/85 of any increase in *comparable* spending for England in Whitehall departments (or lose the same amount if spending fell).

This comparability varies according to department. While some are almost fully devolved (e.g. Health, Education and Skills), others are partly devolved (e.g. Transport, Trade and Industry) and only the comparable spending will be applied to Scotland. The size of these 'Barnett consequentials' are based on three *estimates*: Scotland's share of the UK population; the change in levels of spending of Whitehall departments; and the level of comparability in specific programmes.

Barnett 'squeeze': Denotes a rise in expenditure (using the Barnett formula) according to Scotland's share of the UK population, rather than its traditionally higher share of UK public expenditure.

Further, if we make certain assumptions – that these estimates are accurate, that public expenditure in England rises and that all other things remain equal – then the formula suggests that Scotland's relatively high share of public expenditure will be eroded over time. This **Barnett 'squeeze'** occurs because the consequence of extra spending in England is extra spending in Scotland according to population share rather than the size of the initial block settlement and relative need. In other words, let us assume that:

* Scotland initially received a block settlement which represented 120 per cent per head of spending in England;
* subsequent 'consequentials' are paid at the rate of 100 percent; than
* over time, as the size of the consequentials grows in comparison to the original settlement, the formula will bring the Scottish share down.

In other words, the 'Barnett squeeze' denotes a rise in expenditure (using the Barnett formula) according to Scotland's share of the UK population rather than its traditionally higher share of UK public expenditure. Therefore, the term 'squeeze' is misleading because it is only apparent when levels of spending are *rising*. A 'squeeze' can never refer to an actual *reduction* in public expenditure in Scotland.

Agenda-setting and the politics of public spending

A discussion of the history of finance shows that the decision to adopt and maintain the Barnett formula represents an effective form of agenda-setting. A key tenet of the policy community literature is that policy issues are portrayed as dull affairs to limit public interest and participation. If an issue can be successfully presented as a 'technical' or a 'humdrum' topic for the 'anoraks', then power can be exercised behind the scenes by a small number of participants (Baumgartner and Jones, 1993; Jordan and Maloney, 1997).

With Scottish public finance we see a consistently successful attempt by decision-makers in Scotland and the UK to keep the 'big' (and potentially most contentious) questions of funding off the political agenda. As a result, decision-makers have tended to avoid reforms since a very clear sense of winning and losing would result from any deviation from the status quo. Indeed, the only time that the big questions have received consistently high levels of attention is when they have been linked to more fundamental issues – such as devolution in 1979 and independence in 2007. Even then, it is telling that during the 2007 Scottish electoral campaign, the issue of fiscal autonomy struggled to compete with the issue of local income tax (which only accounts for around 20% of Scottish local authority budgets). Perhaps more important is the level of interest in *England*, with the election of the SNP and the reaction to a Scottish Prime Minister contributing to higher levels of media interest in Scotland's 'advantage'.

Life before Barnett

The modern history of funding settlements demonstrates the incremental and almost accidental side of Scottish politics (although see McLean and McMillan, 2003: 50 for a **Machiavellian** explanation). This began in 1888 with the **Goschen formula**, named after the then Chancellor of the Exchequer. The formula is a byproduct of the attempts by Goschen to link local revenue to local spending and separate it from funding designated for Imperial finance. Although this project failed, the formula itself lasted over 70 years as a means of determining local Scottish entitlement from the UK exchequer (Mitchell and Bell, 2002). While the figure of 11/80 of England and Wales was a rough approximation of Scotland's population share at that time, the estimate was based loosely on Scotland's contribution to probate duties (taxes levied on the estate of the deceased) and was never recalculated to take Scotland's (relative) falling population into account.

Machiavellian: A term (deriving from Niccolò Machiavelli writer of *The Prince*) used to denote a person/institution's tendency to deceive and manipulate others for politicall gain.

Goschen formula: A formula introduced in 1888 (in anticipation of Irish Home Rule) to distribute public expenditure to territorial administrations.

As the size of the UK state grew, so did the size of the Scottish Office, with the Goschen formula more or less at the heart of its budget settlement. Indeed, although the formula was not used formally from 1959, the culture of accepting Scotland's existing share as a starting point and adjusting at the margins (in much the same way that other government departments negotiated their budgets) was well-established and not challenged seriously until the 1970s. Therefore, what began as a formula which initially advantaged per capita spending in England and received minimal Scottish support, eventually became a system redistributing money to Scotland as its share of the UK population fell (McLean and McMillan, 2003: 50).

Rational decision-maker: Aspires to comprehensive rationality where he/she has unlimited resources and all the information required to make a 'rational' decision which suits all parties.

The long-term use of the Goschen formula confirms the main rule of incrementalism: that the existing or default position is difficult to shift. Fundamental change is expensive and likely to undermine a well-established negotiated settlement between competing interests. While the Goschen formula is not something that would have been chosen by a **rational decision-maker** (see Lindblom, 1975) or a more open process of decision-making, as a default position it was difficult to challenge. We may then ask why this process was eventually replaced. The answer is that a 'window of opportunity' (see Kingdon, 1984) came in the 1970s with the prospect of political devolution which drew attention to Scotland's share of public expenditure.

Barnett and needs assessment

The level of UK attention to Scotland's financial status (particularly among English MPs representing constituencies with 'comparable needs') was such that it prompted governmental action. The 'window of opportunity' was opened by the prospect of a referendum on political devolution. This reframed the image of the problem – from a *technical* process to ensure Scotland's share of resources to a *political* process providing advantage to Scotland. The Treasury's response was to commission a Needs Assessment Study to establish the share that each UK territory was 'entitled' to (based on indicators of need such as schoolchildren, pensioners, population sparsity etc.). This would then be used in negotiations with the newly-formed Scottish Assembly (although Barnett disputes this motivation – see Twigger, 1998: 8). However, this process provided a classic example of the inability of decision-makers to turn salient political issues into technical issues to be decided by the experts.

In retrospect we may say that the needs-assessment exercise was doomed to failure (in that it was not officially adopted) for three reasons. First, there is no common definition or consensus on the concept of need. More money spent on one 'need' means less on another. Second, there is the question of the quality of information: even when 'objective factors' (e.g. population sparsity or age) were taken into account it was never clear if the extra spending would refer to *inputs* (e.g. doctors), *outputs* (number of operations) or *outcomes* (equality in levels of health). Third, the outcomes from a needs assessment will always require a political decision, with the report itself representing only one aspect of that process. In this case, while the Treasury report in 1979 suggested that Scotland's greater need was 16 per cent (when at that time the level of extra spending was 22%) there was no rush to close this perceived gap.

Instead, the Barnett formula was introduced on an interim basis. Then, following the negative referendum vote, the needs-assessment agenda was quietly dropped. The Treasury was not inclined to impose a system with little more benefit than the Barnett formula in the immediate aftermath of a referendum process seen by many in Scotland as an attempt by the UK Government to thwart home rule. Effectively, the end result was the replacement of the Goschen formula with a very similar Barnett formula and, although the latter began life as an interim measure, it has yet to be challenged to the extent that it will be replaced.

In large part, this is because the process has several political advantages. First, it satisfies broad coalitions in Scotland and England. In Scotland, it maintains (at least in the short term) historic levels of spending in reflection of greater need. In England, the 'Barnett squeeze' gives the impression that over time this advantage will be eroded. Second, it satisfies many governmental interests. For the Scottish Government it provides a guaranteed baseline and a chance to negotiate extra funding. It also allows Scottish control over domestic spending, with limited Treasury interference. For the Treasury, it provides an automatic mechanism to calculate territorial shares to simplify Cabinet and departmental approval for territorial funding which represents a small part of its overall budget.

The adoption of the formula therefore represented successful agenda-setting – establishing the principle in fairly secret negotiations and then revealing the details only when the annual process could be presented as a humdrum and automatic process (allocating funding at the margins) which was efficient and had support from all sides within government. Indeed, the level of implicit support for Barnett was so high that there was no serious challenge to this formula either before or after political devolution in 1999.

Funding from other sources

If anything, the value of Barnett has been reinforced since 1999 because the trend is towards determining a greater proportion of Scottish Government spend from this process. Yet, Barnett accounts for only 60 per cent of 'identifiable' public expenditure in Scotland (Keating, 2005a: 143), with the rest determined by the UK government, either in funding which merely passes through the Scottish Government budget or is spent directly by Whitehall departments. Whitehall spends approximately 30 per cent of 'identifiable' spending in Scotland directly, with 89 per cent of this devoted to 'social protection', including family benefits, income support and tax credits (HM Treasury, 2005: 114).

The 'assigned budget' from Barnett is a subset of the Departmental Expenditure Limit (DEL) which also includes a small miscellany of funds (non-assigned budget) to cover, for example, UK initiatives such as Welfare to Work which are largely administered by Whitehall departments but have devolved elements. The DEL in 2006/7 was £25.1 billion (Scottish Executive, 2007a). The DEL is a subset of Total Managed Expenditure which also includes the Annual Managed Expenditure (£4.8 billion). The AME includes non-discretionary money merely 'passing through' the Scottish Government from the UK or EU – for example payments made under the CAP (£500 million) and to NHS/ teacher pensions (£1.9 billion).

There is also provision for *ad hoc* funding. This is often referred to as 'formula bypass'. However, this is misleading because decisions out-with the formula are actually commonplace (since the DEL is calculated three years ahead). Recent examples have been the costs of addressing foot-and-mouth disease, funding the Lockerbie trial and the 'write-off' of local authority housing debt (reflecting the Treasury's policy of promoting housing stock transfer).

good example

Box 9.2   Fiscal autonomy

Territories such as Quebec enjoy a degree of fiscal autonomy (i.e. the ability to raise and then spend money) within a federal structure of government. This suggests that Scotland could enjoy fiscal autonomy without independence. But what are the pros and cons?

For
- A clearer link between spending and taxes would enhance accountability and make the Scottish Government more responsive to public responses. It would also encourage Scotland to pursue economic growth since this would raise its income.
- Greater autonomy would allow more discretion in choosing who to tax (e.g. individuals or businesses) and how to tax (e.g. the balance between taxation and charging for services).
- Local taxation allows a greater knowledge about the preferences of the population. Central processes are less flexible to adapt to changing local circumstances.
- It creates the potential to compete with other regions. If English regions respond, taxation is kept low. If competition does not materialize, lower business rates could attract more businesses.
- It would reduce hidden inequalities such as the greater benefit from tax expenditures in England.

Against
- The centralization of taxation allows economies of scale, a wider tax base to secure more redistribution and greater insurance for regions facing exceptional difficulties.
- The legacy of higher spending in Scotland suggests higher taxes and the migration of people and businesses.
- Higher welfare entitlement in Scotland may foster welfare migration and higher levels of dependency.
- The pursuit of fiscal autonomy would raise questions which could create Scottish–UK tensions. For example, how much would Scotland pay for common UK services? What share of oil revenue would Scotland be entitled to?
- Tax competition within member states is problematic in the European Union

The Scottish Government/ Scottish Parliament can also raise money directly. It has the ability to raise (or lower) income tax by three pence in the pound; collects business rates (non-domestic rates) and distributes the money to local authorities (£1.9 billion in 2005/6); and regulates and influences the collection of council tax by local authorities (£2.1 billion – see Scottish Executive, 2007b).

However, in all three cases there is limited room for manoeuvre. For most parties there is no prospect of raising income tax given the likely political costs for a measure which would raise Scotland's total budget by less than 5 per cent. Similarly, given recent SNP proposals to lower business rates and freeze then abolish council tax, there is little prospect of the Scottish Government seeking to raise significantly higher sums from these sources. Without fiscal autonomy the Scottish Government is in a relationship of financial dependency with the UK Treasury (see Box 9.2).

Is the Scottish settlement 'fair'?

In recent years the Barnett formula and the issue of higher Scottish **per capita spending** has emerged more prominently on both the Scottish and UK political agendas. In 2007 a report by Professor Gavin McCrone suggested that Scotland, 'would be in deficit without the subsidy from the UK', while then UK Chancellor Gordon Brown argued that the gains from Scottish oil revenue were outweighed by the advantage from Barnett (Gray, 2007; Devlin, 2007). In contrast, the SNP argued that not only was Scotland 'paying its way', but its funding each year was being 'squeezed' by the Barnett formula, while some academics have extrapolated a '5 per cent cut in Scotland's workforce' as a result of the 'squeeze' (SNP, 2007; McMahon, 2007). To make sense of these debates, we can identify three distinct issues:

Per capita spending: A Latin phrase meaning 'for each head'. Used to indicate the average per person

- What was the Barnett formula *designed* to do?
- What does it *actually* do?
- Is this fair?

What was the Barnett formula designed to do?
We have two plausible answers. The first suggests that the aim of the Barnett formula was to reduce per capita spending levels in Scotland to a level similar to England. Assuming that estimates on population size and comparability are correct (and that all other things remain equal) this would seem to be the long-term consequence of rises in English public expenditure (Bell, 2001). However, Midwinter (2004a; 2004b) argues that this was never a stated aim by

the UK government. A second, more likely aim was to prevent any *further* advantage to Scotland and/or bring Scotland's per capita spending closer to the figure identified in the needs assessment. While the formula was introduced before the needs assessment was completed, Joel Barnett suggests that an estimate of greater Scottish need was identified within the Treasury to account for:

> population sparsity in Scotland, transport needs, needs because of relative ill health, rural needs and education and so on and industrial needs – but above all . . . income per head. (Quoted in Twigger, 1998: 8)

What does the Barnett Formula actually do?
While a strict application of the Barnett formula suggests long-term convergence, this relies on assumptions which may not be met in practice. The first relates to the accuracy of the estimate of Scotland's population relative to England. At the inception of Barnett this was set too high – at a level of 11.8 per cent (10/85) – and the estimate was not revisited until 1992. While the Treasury now uses more accurate annual estimates, there is still a degree of uncertainty and a time-lag between spending reviews and the new figures. Although the 2011 census will address the problem of estimates, uncertainty remains about the continuous effect of immigration, particularly from the new EU accession countries, in the south-east of England (Heald, in correspondence). Therefore, since the relative population in Scotland has fallen constantly since 1978, this overestimation of the Scottish population has for the most part 'cushioned the blow' of reduced per capita spending advantages. The second assumption is that comparable public expenditure always rises significantly (which is not always the case). The third is that the relative size of the original block settlement falls. Yet, this has been increased regularly to account for inflation. A final assumption is that all other things remain equal. However, they do not. It is normal practice for there to be examples of 'formula bypass', such as Treasury-funded pay increases for public sector staff and various other arrangements to ensure additional funding (Keating, 2005a: 145). These were negotiated and used to great effect by pre-devolution Secretaries of State for Scotland who were sensitive to levels of nationalism and keen to highlight the financial benefits of remaining within the Union. As a result, the overall Barnett 'squeeze' did not appear to materialize (Midwinter, 2004b: 505–6).

A feature of post-devolution predictions is that the 'Barnett squeeze' would be more apparent *after* 1999 since the UK Government would not feel the same need to react to high levels of nationalism. This is reinforced by Bell and Christie (2001: 145) who estimated a £1 billion or 5 per cent 'squeeze' by 2003–04. Keating (2005a: 145) also suggests that the formula has 'begun to bite' in some policy areas following a combination of accurate population estimates, minimal

Union dividend: A phrase used by Labour politicians in electioneering to bring attention to the financial benefit Scotland receives as part of the union of Great Britain and Northern Ireland.

side deals, the extension of Barnett's coverage and high levels of public expenditure in England. An alternative hypothesis is this advantage continued because it was still in the interests of the Labour-led governments to stress the benefits of the **Union dividend**. This is supported by figures presented by Midwinter (2004a; 2004b) and Schmueker and Adams (2005) which highlight stable levels of *overall* per capita spending and no evidence for the squeeze.

Is the Scottish settlement fair?

The discussion of Barnett provides only a partial answer to this question, since fair distribution can also relate to the levels of funding *raised* in Scotland and the effects of wider economic policies and other UK spending. This leads to a consideration of other factors (see Keating, 2005a: 148–50):

- Barnett only refers to comparable regional spending. If we look at UK spending as a whole, there are areas of 'non-identifiable' spending (e.g. Defence/Channel Tunnel), where Scotland does not enjoy the same 'multiplier effect' of this spending (e.g. army personnel spend their money locally and this benefits local businesses).
- The level of tax expenditure may be greater in England. For example, payments for private education (a much larger sector in England) are Value Added Tax (VAT) free, since most independent schools have charitable status.
- The Treasury raises significant revenue from taxing North Sea Oil. In 1984/5 the proportion of government revenue from oil and gas peaked at 15 per cent and now it is approximately 8 per cent (or one-third of the Scottish Government spend – see BBC News, 2006).
- Economic policies favouring the south-east of England may hinder economic development in Scotland. For example, the maintenance of high interest rates to reduce inflation or stop the south-east economy 'overheating' may disproportionately affect a Scottish economy more reliant on manufacturing.

Lies, damned lies and Scottish public expenditure statistics?

The upshot is that there is a lack of consensus on what Barnett was designed to do, what it actually does and how fair the Scottish settlement is. Further, since there is no consistent data to rely on, the different use of financial measures to make different points has become a key tool for agenda-setting. We can see this most clearly in partisan debates about Scotland's contribution to the UK Exchequer. In 2007, while Labour talked of the 'Union dividend' and argued that the Treasury, 'is prepared to fund an £11 billion fiscal deficit' the SNP referred to the non-inclusion of oil-based revenue and the biased nature of government figures (see Scottish Parliament Official Report 10.1.07 cols 30847–99). Some broader points are also worth noting:

- Spending can be expressed in 'real' (i.e. adjusted for inflation) or 'volume' terms (adjusted, if possible, for public-sector inflation). Midwinter and Burnside (2004) suggest that although spending rose from 1999–2003, 'outputs' in areas such as education fell (due in part to above inflation pay awards for doctors and teachers – see Cairney, 2007c: 27). This is key to our discussion of 'advantage' since Scotland could receive more money to fund *inputs* (e.g. doctors), but still achieve fewer *outputs* (number of operations) and less favourable *outcomes* (levels of health).
- Scotland's expenditure per capita is the figure that tends to attract most political attention – in 2005/6 it was approximately 22 per cent more than England (Schmueker and Adams, 2005: 37).
- While there are distinct Scottish Government figures, these are either derived from the same Treasury figures (HM Treasury, 2006; Scottish Executive, 2006a) or are presented in a non-comparable form, referring to funding for departments (with shifting boundaries) rather than policy areas. It is difficult to include Scotland's share of 'non-identifiable' spending (e.g. defence, international) incurred on behalf of the UK (£6.2 billion in 2004/5 – see Scottish Executive, 2006a: 19).

The result is that it is difficult to come to hard-and-fast conclusions about public expenditure statistics, since levels of comparability are often limited and the presentation of figures is determined by the source of information and the way that this information is presented. This ties in with a widespread public view that most politicians in Scotland (like everywhere else) utilise public expenditure statistics for support rather than enlightenment. A less cynical view can point to two elements. First, there are valid and reliable statistics that are collected and published without political interference, such as Government Expenditure and Revenue in Scotland (GERS) (although this was often criticized by the SNP when in opposition). Second, most politicians simply *do not know* how the public sector accounts for its own budget. An understanding of the complexities of these procedures is often restricted to expert professionals, 'and there is a danger of democratic processes becoming increasingly mystified rather than more transparent' (Ezzamel *et al.*, 2005).

Where does Scotland spend its money?

Table 9.1 (based on figures from HM Treasury, 2005: 92–3; 2006: 100–11) gives a general overview of Scottish public expenditure that highlights the

Table 9.1 Identifiable expenditure (£ million) on services (current and capital)

Fiscal year	2000	2001	2002	2003	2004	2005	2006	Rise 2000–06	Real rise	% Real rise
Gen. public services	573	596	697	756	837	841	833	260	162	28%
Public order & safety	1399	1436	1628	1655	1820	1911	2021	622	382	27%
E'prise & econ. devel.	442	583	548	463	549	625	640	198	122	28%
Science & technology	68	70	87	110	161	238	309	241	229	337%
Employment	748	712	740	736	913	802	813	65	–64	–8%
Agric., fish. & forestry	564	579	655	661	733	631	679	115	18	3%
Transport	850	908	980	1150	1725	1672	2093	1243	1097	129%
Environment protect.	877	967	1141	1028	1111	782	1135	258	107	12%
Housing/community	459	624	943	834	906	1279	1462	1003	924	201%
Health	5057	5435	5744	6710	7363	7683	8497	3440	2571	51%
Recreation, culture, religion	722	718	757	821	920	931	1050	328	204	28%
Education & training	4322	4599	5090	5246	5574	5892	6378	2056	1313	30%
Social protection	11187	11587	12934	13527	14537	15271	15967	4780	2858	26%
Total	27274	28820	31944	33701	37151	38582	41902	14628	9942	36%

Notes: The real rise calculation is based on the GDP deflator (HM Treasury, 2007). For example, the *total rise* from 2000–06 was 14,628 (41,902 minus 27,274). A rise in line with inflation (or zero real rise) would have been to 31,960. The *real rise* is therefore 41,902 minus 31,960 (9,942). Data collated from various sources: HM Treasury (2005: 92–3; 2006: 100–11).

big-spending policy areas such as health, education and training (i.e. including further and higher education), transport and public order. This impression of the *size* of each spending area is crucial when we then examine rises (or falls) in expenditure. For example, real spending on Science and Technology has risen by 337 per cent from 2000 to 2006, while in social protection it rose 26 per cent. Yet, social protection is still the biggest spending area and the *cash* rise in Science is relatively small. Therefore, a focus on change alone may exaggerate the significance of small but expanding portfolios (particularly if this involves change from a low base or a long period of underinvestment).

A focus on the big-spending areas suggests an above-average rise in health (51%), while housing (201%) and transport (129%) were clear priorities in the first six years of devolution. Perhaps surprisingly, given the wage rises for Scottish teachers and the commitment to reduce student fees, the rise in education (30%) spending is lower than average (i.e. compared to the 36% rise overall) and lower than equivalent spending increases in England (Schmueker and Adams, 2005: 39).

UK Treasury power and the Scottish political system

Chapter 2 suggests that before devolution there may never have been a 'Scottish Political System' because the ultimate authority or final decision rested elsewhere. The significance for present purposes is that this authority *still* resides elsewhere – in the hands of the UK Treasury which determines the size of Scotland's budget and its method of collection. Yet, our discussion of Barnett confuses this picture by suggesting that Scotland may have been the most likely to *benefit* from this relationship. Indeed, the history of spending settlements seems to suggest that the UK Treasury has done all it can to avoid conflict rather than impose its will publicly. In other words, we should not assume that the capacity to exert power is synonymous with the exercise of that power. The idea of Treasury power is also complicated by the fact that while it can control the *size* of Scotland's budget, it does not determine how it is *spent*.

The Scottish Government is reliant on its block grant from the Treasury. This was highlighted during the **Comprehensive Spending Review** (CSR) dispute in 2007 (Box 9.3) when Alex Salmond argued that the low rise in UK spending in 2008–09 reflected Labour's general election strategy (or its plan to accentuate spending increases in the run up to a General Election in 2009 or 2010). Many Scottish newspapers also suggested that Prime Minister Gordon Brown and Chancellor Alistair Darling were trying to constrain the SNP's spending decisions in its first year of government. These assertions are difficult to demonstrate. What we can say with more certainty is that Scotland remains heavily dependent on the UK Government's attitude to taxing and

Comprehensive Spending Review: A review by the Treasury to set three-year budgets for government departments.

Box 9.3   How much did the SNP government's budget rise in 2007?

Heated debates between the SNP Government in Scotland and the Labour Government in the UK in October 2007 show how difficult it is to calculate changes in public expenditure. In part this is because the figures presented by both sides were both correct! In other words, this is really an issue of agenda-setting and the ability to draw attention to one set of figures to paint a picture of growth or stagnation. Following its Comprehensive Spending Review (to set three-year budgets for government departments), the Treasury announced that Scotland's budget (or DEL) would rise from £26.059 billion in 2007–08 to £27.244 billion in 2008–09, £29.584 billion in 2009–10 and £33.309 billion in 2009–10. This represents an average real annual rise of 1.8 per cent. On this basis, the UK Government argued that a prudent Scottish Government should be able to fulfil all of its commitments since this represents a significant rise from a budget which has doubled in cash terms since devolution. The SNP countered this claim by pointing to a shift in the 'baseline' to calculate the figures. The 2007–08 baseline figure for Scotland's budget was reduced by £340 million to take into account lower levels of actual spending in England by the Department of Health in previous years. Therefore, the *actual* annual real rise is 1.4 per cent. Further, the SNP Government pointed out that since the baseline was reduced, the increase in 2008–09 is actually £845 million (1,185 minus 340). In cash terms this represents a rise in 3.2 per cent, but in real terms this comes to 0.5 per cent. The SNP argued that this was the lowest real annual rise since devolution (at a time when Scottish oil revenues were rising) and that it undermined its ability to deliver on pre-election pledges.

spending. Treasury rules also influence how Scottish local and health authorities fund major capital projects (such as new schools and hospitals).

This particular power of the Treasury was highlighted in housing policy where it allowed borrowing to improve the local-authority housing stock only through approved corporate bodies such as Housing Associations. In return, the Treasury rewarded a successful transfer (following a ballot of council tenants) by writing-off the debt linked to the housing stock (in Glasgow alone this accounted for £1 billion in 'formula bypass'). As a general rule with borrowing and Treasury power, the Labour-led Scottish Executive decided to make a 'virtue out of necessity'. During this period it supported housing-stock transfer wholeheartedly. However, rejections by ballot in Edinburgh, Stirling and Renfrewshire means that they will either have to re-ballot in the future, or pay for repairs through the local-authority budget and higher rents. Much depends on the amount that local authorities have spent in the past to maintain their stock (see Cairney, 2007e: 76). There has been less variation in borrowing to fund new schools and hospitals, as public bodies entered into public–private partnerships to raise the capital without raising public borrowing (see Box 7.3).

Treasury power and the strange case of EU structural funds

The issue of **EU structural funds** demonstrates the reach of Treasury power in Scotland. As Keating (2005a: 151–3) discusses, there are now four types of funds – on regional development, employment training, agriculture and fisheries. They are allocated on three bases – to regions lagging behind the UK average (objective 1), areas affected by industrial decline or rurality (objective 2), or people who are socially excluded (objective 3). While such funds were in the past given without condition, since 1988 the Commission has sought to use them as a policy instrument to further EU policy objectives. As a result, the money must be *seen* to be spent in the relevant region and it must be *added* to the original budget. The regions are also obliged to match the additional money spent.

> **EU structural funds:** are funds allocated by the EU to support the poorer regions of Europe and integrate the European infrastructure through transport projects.

On paper, this looks like a good deal for the regions since it appears that they can bypass the UK government and receive extra money directly from the EU (approximately £1.1 billion from 2000–06 – Scottish Executive, 2007c). However, a more accurate picture is that the UK as the member state negotiates the funding, with sub-national authorities often peripheral to the process (Bell and Christie, 2001: 147; Sutcliffe, 2002). Further, the Treasury treats EU structural funds as UK money since it is still a net contributor to the EU (and any direct funding would circumvent its public spending plans). Therefore, while in theory the funding is routed through the Barnett system, Scotland receives no extra money (it also has to find matching funding from within its existing budget!). The unintended consequence is that it is in Scotland's interests for *England* to receive structural funds since it will enjoy the consequentials without having to be seen to spend the money in a certain area (Keating, 2005a).

Treasury power and Scottish spending

Treasury influence over the way Scotland *spends* its budget is more difficult to demonstrate. We have three main aspects to explore. The first is that Treasury control over Scotland's total budget undermines its ability to fund any new policies with a significant cost. Therefore, any changes in Scottish spending must be incremental. As one member of the Scottish Government Finance Department (interview, 2005) puts it:

> Two-thirds goes to the NHS and local authorities and then there is justice and other sectors. So there is maybe only £1 billion left over to use our discretion with.

Box 9.4   Scottish finance in comparative perspective

Scotland's ability to determine its own spending priorities is unusual in a comparative context. In countries such as Spain, Canada and Germany the system of finance and regulation is more restrictive, with more conditions on how to spend (Greer, 2003). This perhaps reflects a greater preoccupation with strong 'fiscal accountability' in other countries. However, the ability of the Treasury to determine how taxes are raised and to influence how money is spent may suggest that these differences are exaggerated (Heald, 2001).

Given such constraints, Bell and Christie (2001: 143) suggest that any solution is likely to be limited: any redistribution would be constrained by national public wage structures and legislative commitments, cut-backs in other services would have high political costs, and new revenue resulting from fiscal autonomy is not likely to be granted by the Treasury (see Box 9.2).

Second, the Scottish Government (particularly if controlled by the same party in control at the UK level) comes under pressure to make spending decisions similar to those announced in the UK Chancellor's budget (as with education) or to play catch-up and follow UK agendas (as with the example of NHS waiting-list comparisons).

Third, in some cases Treasury rules influence Scottish policy indirectly. The most high-profile example followed its decision not to refund Attendance Allowance benefits foregone by older people receiving 'free personal care' funding (see Chapter 10).

However, in each case there are convincing qualifications to Treasury power. First, funding changes would always be incremental as there will always be constraints on the ability of the Scottish Government to raise taxes (Midwinter, 2004a). Of more importance is the rise in public expenditure and from 1999–2007 this was considerable. Second, the post-devolution trend is towards greater Scottish Government discretion in allocating resources. Even when Scotland *appears* to follow England's health spending, this may be redirected to (for example) public health rather than healthcare funding, according to different priorities within Scotland. Third, these Treasury rules may have a net benefit for Scotland. For example, the loss of Attendance Allowance benefits is more than offset by the gain in council house debt removal.

Power within Scotland: the Scottish Parliament and the spending process

The expectations for new politics also extended to a reform of the budgetary process with an enhancement of parliamentary scrutiny, debate and influence.

The Scottish budgetary process is designed to ensure the Scottish Parliament had the adequate information to scrutinize the Scottish Government budget and increase parliamentary input into the budget process (see Scottish Office, 1998b; Midwinter, 2005: 15). There is some evidence of this process making a difference – it led to increased capital expenditure in 2004, justice expenditure in 2005 and additional funding for local government late in the process in 2006. Parliamentary influence is also likely to increase with minority government.

The budget round follows a three-stage process. Stage 1 occurs only in spending review years; it involves each subject committee reviewing the strategy and priorities of their respective departments and feeding their evaluations up to the Finance Committee. Stage 2 involves an examination of more detailed proposals of the draft budget, with recommendations to the Government possible. Stage 3 involves the formal approval of the Budget Bill

In practice, there are few amendments to the budget when it reaches the draft stage. The process was never intended to allow MSPs to present alternative budget choices (except where the Government does not respond to recommendations). It is designed to increase parliamentary input to priorities in the budget process, particularly in Spending Review years (see Cairney, 2007c: 26 for an example of health committee influence). The process ensures a greater degree of openness to spending decisions than in the Scottish Office days but there is little evidence that Scotland has moved beyond a focus on the margins of spending to more comprehensive 'first principles' debates (or as one civil servant in Finance put it: 'it was easy to get large numbers past them because they tend to get stuck on the small details'). A more realistic hope for the Scottish Parliament (even under minority government) is that it prompts the Scottish Government to justify its plans, and encourages it to be clear in its aims and realistic in its expectations.

Box 9.5   Accounting for Scotland's public expenditure

The Audit Committee of the Scottish Parliament considers financial audit and value-for-money reports and monitors matters of regularity and propriety in public expenditure. The Scottish Auditor General is in charge of Audit Scotland and her/his independence is enshrined in legislation. Audit Scotland was formed in 1999 after an amalgamation of the Accounts Commission for Scotland (which still exists as a corporate body) and the National Audit Office in Scotland; auditors have responsibility to certify the accounts of public bodies. Audit Scotland audits the accounts of 67 Central Government bodies (Scottish Government departments, NDPBs, commissions), 23 NHS bodies, 32 councils, 40 police, fire and other boards and 36 further education colleges and Scottish Water. In recent decades the role of public audit has expanded into efficiency, value-for-money and performance issues. Audit Scotland now also reports to Parliament on the economy, efficiency and effectiveness with which departments have used their resources.

Public expenditure and central–local relations

A notable feature of the 2007 Scottish election campaign was that a focus on the prospect of a **local income tax** received much more attention than fiscal autonomy. The SNP proposals involve freezing council tax levels before abolishing the tax altogether and utilizing increased income tax to partly fund council services. A potential irony is that this would remove the tax/spend link at local-authority level and undermine most of the benefits associated with fiscal autonomy. Yet, the financial contribution from council tax is already marginal compared to the block grants distributed to local authorities by the Scottish Government.

Local income tax: The SNP and the Liberal Democrats have policies to replace the existing local authority council tax with a local income tax.

Indeed, the Scottish Government relationship with local authorities has a number of parallels to our UK–Scotland discussion: local authorities receive approximately 80 per cent of their funding from the Scottish Government; their own source of funding is subject to Scottish Government influence; they are managing the margins of expenditure; and the trend since 1999 has seen local council budgets 'squeezed' and falling relative to those of central government (in the context of consistent public expenditure growth).

However, this relationship is not one-way, and the Scottish Government is likely to engage in detailed discussions with local government on policy delivery since the latter spends 30 per cent of the Scottish budget and accounts for 45 per cent of the public sector jobs in Scotland. Indeed, the more interpersonal nature of central–local relations in Scotland means that the Scottish Government appears less likely to impose policy on local authorities than is the case with the UK government and English councils. A good example of this difference comes from the Scottish agenda on reforming public services to ensure efficiency savings. With the recent development of the agenda on public sector reform, we see what appears to be a Scottish Government recognition of the benefits of a 'bottom-up' approach, with an emphasis on service-led improvements backed up by central government promises to support change and intervene only if insufficient progress is made from within (Scottish Executive, 2006b).

Conclusion

Although public expenditure is one of the most important aspects of public policy, the system to allocate money to territorial governments has remained untouched for a considerable time. The same basic Goschen and Barnett method – of treating the base as a given and then amending at the margins – has been used since the nineteenth century!

The longevity of such arrangements can be explained with reference to three themes running through this chapter: agenda-setting, incrementalism *politics* and power. The Barnett formula was introduced in relative secrecy as a temporary measure and only acknowledged publicly when it had enough support within Government. Then, the formula was used to keep the potentially controversial issue of territorial finance out of the spotlight. This was even achieved following political devolution in 1999. Although the election of the SNP and the prospect of independence (and perhaps the existence of a Scottish Prime Minister/Chancellor) has ensured that Barnett is more in the public eye than ever before, there has been no serious attempt by the Government to replace it. For both the Scottish and UK Governments, it provides a mechanism to simplify territorial funding and avoid the complex and angst-ridden discussions of finance that we find in the USA and a range of other countries. Therefore, it would take a lot for both parties to renounce a system that has served them so well in the past, particularly since the alternative is a needs-based system that will struggle for political consensus.

The experience of Scottish finance informs a broader discussion of power. These issues may be best described as absolute power, relative power and perspectives of power. The centrality of the Treasury to the level of taxation raised in Scotland, as well as its influence over how the money is spent (regardless of EU involvement) demonstrates its absolute power. It also qualifies the idea of a 'Scottish Political System' since the ultimate decision-making authority resides elsewhere. Yet, from 1999–2007 the Treasury oversaw a period of staggering public expenditure growth in Scotland. The ability of Scotland to go its own way and determine its own spending priorities also demonstrates a high level of power relative to similar sub-national territories (Box 9.4). Further, from an English regional perspective, the ability of Scotland to command a systematic advantage in the face of MP and media criticism demonstrates a power not available elsewhere. It is therefore difficult to maintain this image of Treasury power as a shadow or a constraint to Scottish decision-making when there are so many envious glances from commentators in England and other countries.

The issue of finance also informs discussions of power *within* Scotland. For example, although the new politics agenda extended to the key role of the Finance committee to coordinate select committee scrutiny of the executive, the experience of coalition government suggests that the Scottish Executive was central to spending plans. Therefore the value of scrutiny was to oblige the Executive to be open about its plans and be responsive to committee concerns. It does not signal a shift of power from executive to parliament. While a period of minority government may make a difference to particular projects, the Scottish Parliament and its opposition parties do not have the resources (or ideological coherence) to make a systematic difference to the process.

Perhaps a more significant shift is from local to central. The Scottish Government Treasury-like control over local authority finance would increase if the SNP adopted a local income tax, since this would remove the ability of councils to raise funds. However, the experience to date is one of negotiation, with a reform agenda predicated on the idea of the 'Scottish policy style' which seeks consensus rather than imposes decisions (see Chapter 10).

Finally, this chapter highlights the potential for confusion and agenda-setting in the use and abuse of public expenditure statistics. Heightened attention to Barnett and Scotland's 'advantage' suggests that hyperbole and media coverage of the issue may reach an all time high. Therefore students of Scottish public finance should reserve a particular degree of scepticism.

Further reading

On budgetary incrementalism see Musgrave and Peacock (1958: 16–28) and Wildavsky (1975). On Goschen and Barnett see Mitchell (2003a, 2003b), McLean and McMillan (2003), Keating (2005a), Heald and McLeod (2002), Bell and Mitchell (2001), Christie and Swales (2006), Twigger (1998), SPICE (2000a), Ferguson *et al.* (2003), Bell (2001) and Midwinter (2004a and 2004b). On the fiscal autonomy debate see *Scottish Affairs*, issue No.41, special edition on fiscal autonomy, Keating (2005a), Bell and Christie (2001). On the politics of public expenditure see Heald (1983), Heclo and Wildavsky (1974), Hogwood (1992) and Peacock and Wiseman (1967).

Online sources

Office for National Statistics   http://www.statistics.gov.uk
Scottish Executive Central Research Unit   http://www.scotland.gov.uk/cru/
Scottish Executive   http://www.scotland.gov.uk/
Audit Scotland   http://www.audit-scotland.gov.uk
UK Government and Information Services   http://www.ukonline.gov.uk/

Chapter 10

Public Policy in Scotland Since Devolution

This chapter examines the extent to which the new political arrangements in Scotland have produced new policies. Such discussions often focus on the extent of policy **divergence and difference** between Scotland and England as a key test of devolution. This follows the image before devolution of a 'backlog' of policies which built up because Westminster did not have the time for Scottish legislation. On the basis of differing social and party attitudes and the need for 'Scottish solutions to Scottish problems', there were widespread expectations of divergence as soon as the Scottish Parliament had the opportunity to legislate. To a great extent, this picture of a 'rush to policy' was confirmed in the first eight years of devolution, since the Scottish Executive alone passed over 100 pieces of legislation in two parliamentary terms. Yet, there are three main qualifications to the idea of Scotland as a source of fast-paced policy divergence.

> **Divergence and difference:**
> Divergence suggests movement away from a common point; difference suggests that a common point may not exist.

First, in the 1980s and 1990s most policy innovation came from the UK Government. Indeed, as noted in Chapter 2, part of the rationale for devolution was the defence of existing state institutions. The 'Yes, Yes' vote in 1997 was in part 'a vote to change institutions in order to stay the same' (Mitchell, 2005: 26–7). Second, there are as many good reasons to suggest that policy will converge rather than diverge. Factors such as a shared party of government, the role of the Treasury and the Europeanization of policy undermine the idea that Scotland will necessarily go its own way. Third, there is a big difference between making the decision to be different and seeing that decision through to its final outcome.

The evidence supports these qualifications. Policy divergence through legislation has been slower to develop than we might expect, and this picture is reinforced if we extend analysis to the wider policy process. In the relatively small number of cases where significant divergence has occurred in legislation, the incomplete implementation of policy has undermined divergence.

This is not to say that policy *change* has not been significant since devolution. In many cases, significant policy changes may have a greater effect on Scotland or be missed with a focus on divergence. This suggests that a focus on being different may be inappropriate, particularly since devolution is no longer in its infancy or enjoying its 'honeymoon' period. In this sense it is

Box 10.1   Tests of Scottish policy – divergence, legitimacy and ownership

Although the extent to which policies diverge is a key test of the difference that devolution has made, we can take two other factors into account. The first is the legitimacy that an elected Scottish Parliament provides. For example, James Mitchell (in correspondence) suggests that the development of enough political maturity to produce the same policies as England (when appropriate) may be a better test of devolution success. Indeed, in some cases, the legitimacy of the Scottish Parliament may be necessary to achieve convergence, since in the past a UK-wide policy may have been viewed as top-down and imposed on a Scottish population which did not vote for the UK Government. A related focus found in other countries is on 'policy ownership'. For example, McEwan (2005, 2006) draws on the experience of Quebec which negotiated an opt-out from pan-Canadian social policies in the 1960s. This allowed it to finance and develop its own policies in areas such as health, education, income security and pensions. The focus in Quebec then shifted to policies tailored to the Québécois population by its own government, rather than the resemblance to Canadian policy as a whole (although, as in Scotland, the maintenance of a welfare state was seen as a symbol of Québécois difference). In this sense, the phrase 'Scottish solutions for Scottish problems' would refer as much to the way that policy is *developed* as to its substance and comparison with UK policy. Although the SNP Government may be associated most with difference, it also has potential to harness this idea of ownership. Indeed, just as the postwar welfare state was used to foster a sense of British identity, so too could Scottish welfare policies be used to reinforce a Scottish national identity.

more important to develop *and gain support for* policies which are appropriate to Scotland regardless of the UK government position, particularly since the key aim of devolution – to address the 'democratic deficit' – has been solved (Box 10.1). Yet, the temptation to look across the border is strong and has been reinforced not only by the election of an SNP Government keen to distance itself from its UK counterpart, but also the media reaction in London which suggests that English taxpayers are subsiding policy divergence (e.g. Browne, 2007; Settle, 2007).

This chapter therefore explores:

- How we identify and measure policy change. For example, although this chapter focuses heavily on *outputs* such as legislation, it also considers *outcomes* following implementation.
- Why policies in Scotland may diverge or converge.
- The evidence for policy change in a range of policy areas, including 'flagship' policies regarding free personal care, student fees, and the smoking ban.
- The implementation of policy.

Measuring change: what is public policy?

Although the term 'public policy' may appear self-evident, there are many ways to identify it. As Table 10.1 suggests, policy can refer to what decision-makers say they will do rather than what they actually do, the decisions made rather than the outcomes of those decisions; or short-term rather than long-term policy outcomes (see Hogwood and Gunn, 1984). In other words, policy is difficult to measure and pin down.

Politicians often make speeches announcing new policy initiatives which due to a lack of willpower, institutional constraints, and/or finance never

Table 10.1 *What is Policy?*

Policy can be:	*Example:*
A label for a field of activity	Scottish transport policy.
An expression of general purpose/ desired state of affairs	'We want to curb anti-social behaviour' (Jack McConnell).
A set of specific proposals	Draft Land Reform (Scotland) Bill – Consultation Paper.
Decisions of government	Outcome of Scottish Cabinet decision-making.
Formal authorization	Scottish Government Environment and Rural Affairs Department formal authorization of Marine Fish Farms in Scottish Waters.
A Programme	Scottish social inclusion programme.
Categorized	Regulatory, distributive, redistributive.
Highly visible	'Flagship' policies such as free personal care, student fees and the smoking ban.
'Insulated' or incremental	Seed potato regulations.
Output	Local government reorganization.
Outcome	Impact of reorganization on efficiency/democracy in local government.
A theory or model	'Give more money to Scottish police forces and crime will go down'.
A process	Agenda-setting, policy-formulation, implementation, evaluation.

Source: Table based on typology from Hogwood and Gunn (1984).

actually materialize in the form envisaged. Some policy announcements can be mere 'window-dressing' that does not involve any change in policy. This was parodied well in the *Yes Prime Minister* TV series when the top civil servant discussing a plan to reduce unemployment observed that the PM, 'is only trying to look as if he is trying to reduce unemployment. This is because he is worried that it does not look as if he is trying to reduce unemployment' (see Parsons, 1995: 15). In such cases, the aim of policy announcements is to show a *desire* to tackle intractable problems without any concrete change in policy taking place. Policy-making is often more symbolic than substantive and, in the age of spin, policy statements are often re-hashed versions of old statements with 'new' monies being announced for 'new' initiatives. Further, this lack of direction from the 'top' often leads to discretion at the 'bottom', with actors at the 'front line' delivering public services reshaping policy as they implement it.

Therefore, while this chapter examines the main legislative changes, it suggests that other measures – such as the distribution of money (Chapter 9) or the implementation of policy – may be just as important to our discussion of divergence. Policies can also be categorized differently, with, for example, 'regulatory' policies more common than 'redistributive', since the Scottish Parliament is really a spending rather than taxing body, new money is limited and it is difficult to remove money from existing programmes (Mitchell, 2004). The picture also changes frequently, with policies such as fox hunting and smoking bans introduced first in Scotland (and marking divergence) only to be followed in England.

Reasons for divergence

A number of factors suggest policy divergence will occur between Scotland and England (see Keating, 2005a; Keating *et al.*, 2003). First, *different social attitudes* exist in both countries. The more direct the link between social preferences and public policy then the more Scottish policy will diverge. However, as Chapter 4 suggests, these differences in attitudes are very subtle. Scotland may be slightly more 'left wing' when asked questions about the welfare state – suggesting a preference for public services, a larger role for the state, redistribution, and comprehensive schooling – but just as 'right wing' when it comes to law and order. Crucially, political elites must also interpret and react to those attitudes differently. For example, New Labour in England sought to create a distinct niche within the public sector for the middle classes, who would otherwise defect to private provision and weaken political support for the welfare state (levels of private medicine and education are much higher in south-east England than in Scotland).

Second, there are *different parties* in government. Although from 1999 to 2007 Scotland and England shared the same party of government, in Scotland this required coalition with the Liberal Democrats. As Chapter 6 suggests, both parties shared many policy objectives. However, in key areas such as free care for the elderly, the abolition of up-front student fees and proportional representation in local elections, divergent policy was the price Labour paid for retaining office. This was followed in 2007 by the election of an SNP government which furthered divergence in areas such as student fees. It should be noted that governments in Scotland tend to face electoral competition from left-of-centre political parties. In England, the Labour party faces right-of-centre competition from the Conservatives. Therefore, parties in each jurisdiction must act differently to command the centre ground.

Third, successive First Ministers were conscious of the need *to make Scottish Government policy distinctive*, to justify the value of devolution and to cement their own positions.

Fourth, *public sector professionals may have a larger role in policy-making* in Scotland. MSPs are more likely to be drawn from these professions than their UK counterparts, and policy is negotiated with professionals more (and imposed less) in Scotland. In turn, there is some evidence to suggest that Scottish professionals are more inclined to universalist forms of provision (Greer, 2005d; Keating and Cairney, 2006; Keating, 2005a).

Fifth, there are *differing policy conditions*. There are differences in economic structures and the values of some businesses to the economy (fishing, meat, timber, whiskey, tourism). England may have distinctive problems, such as road congestion, which places charging higher on the agenda than in Scotland where rural transport may be more of an issue. Scotland may have a less healthy population in more need of public health measures.

Sixth, it is often better to think in terms of policy *difference* rather than *divergence*. Many pieces of legislation will have different starting points based on existing administrative differences (in education, social work, probation, water). In *some cases* this will act as a springboard for further differences, particularly since in these cases there may be less of a drive to ensure uniformity.

Finally, the *policy process and style in Scotland may be different*. Policy may change as legislation passes through the Scottish Parliamentary committee process. Moreover, there was hope that devolution would lead to more fruitful contact between government and interest groups. This would not only aid implementation (with personal relationships replacing regulation and targets) but also produce *better policy* (Entwhistle, 2006). Or, as Chapter 11 suggests, a lack of policy capacity to research and formulate policy independently may suggest that policy will be subject to greater influence from the professions that civil servants rely on for information and advice.

However, there are equally convincing reasons to suggest that policies will not diverge. First, public expenditure limits and rules on borrowing dictated by the Treasury may limit policy innovation. Second, there is also a complex relationship between reserved and devolved issues which often complicates

Reasons against

policy innovation, particularly when issues cross departmental boundaries or involve the tax and benefits system. EU commitments must be implemented across the EU with a degree of uniformity. Third, there is also the UK single economic market to consider. Significant policy differences would have disproportionate effects in Scotland. For example, differences in social entitlement may lead to the problem of 'welfare immigration'.

Fourth, from 1999 to 2007 *both countries shared the same party of government*. Party and ministerial links ensured a degree of common purpose and a need to avoid the political embarrassment associated with divergence in some areas. This was further facilitated by a UK-wide civil service fostering regular contact, information sharing and informal influence. In terms of policy learning, when one country innovates, another may follow.

Fifth, *each country shares professionals*, many of whom belong to UK-wide professional associations. Furthermore, many interest groups and think tanks still operate on a UK basis and maintain a consistent lobbying line in both jurisdictions.

Sixth, due to the incremental nature of policy-making, radical change over a wide range of policies is unusual since governments inherit programmes which can not be changed overnight. This is particularly the case with 'wicked problems' (such as health inequalities) which defy obvious solutions and require a level of coordination that most governments find difficult.

Finally, Scotland and England share a range of similar policy conditions and problems such as an ageing population, low birth rate, etc. – and a broadly similar attitude to solving those problems.

Therefore, to build up a picture of the extent of policy divergence, it is necessary to examine the evidence.

Primary legislation as a test of divergence

There have been few systematic attempts to chart the trajectory of Scottish policy as a whole. One exception compares the legislative outputs of Holyrood and Westminster in Scotland's first parliamentary session, 1999–2003 (Keating *et al.*, 2003; see also Keating, 2005a). This suggests that although there was an as-expected 'rush to policy' – with 61 Acts passed and an average of 15 per year much higher than the six dedicated Scottish Acts passed at Westminster – this did not produce a radical shift from the past or from the rest of the UK: 'Devolution represents an evolutionary process rather than a revolutionary break' (2003: 131). Further, although there was a small number of 'flagship' policies – such as free personal care for older people and the 'abolition' of student fees – that marked clear divergence, most legislation highlighted less significant differences.

We can see this in discussion of their three main categories of legislation. First, although the category *Holyrood legislation with no Westminster counterpart* accounted for most (61%) of the legislation under review, most instances are either innocuous 'housekeeping' bills or bills abolishing archaic policies in Scotland that Westminster had no time for (e.g. Abolition of Feudal Tenure, 2000; Abolition of Poindings and Warrant Sales, 2001). Second, although there are many instances of *legislation that deals with the same issue but with a different policy*, most display rather subtle differences. Examples include the need to discuss a stable family life when providing sex education (the Westminster Act refers to marriage), and the rejection (in Scotland only) of proposals to make businesses charge employees who park at work. The third main category is *legislation that deals with the same issue and with the same policy, but with scope for differences in application.* This category suggests that there are numerous examples of difference, but that they are subtle and may take time to fully materialize. This mirrors the pre-devolution position in which implementation differences reflected different policy conditions and distinct administrative practices.

'Flagship' policies and beyond: 1999–2003

'Flagship' refers to legislation passed by the Scottish Parliament which is perhaps not only high-profile but also a symbol of intent. The highest profile example was the decision to introduce *free personal care* for older people, since the policy had already been rejected by the UK government. The background to this policy is the UK Government-commissioned Sutherland Report (1999; see also Simeon, 2003 and Shaw, 2003). The report recommended that long-term personal care should be provided free and should not be means tested. This reflected the anomalies which existed when the long-term care for certain chronic illnesses were treated without charge within the NHS system, while the therapeutic treatment of other conditions (such as Alzheimer's) was charged for, often as part of a wider residential care package. The recommendation was to separate the therapeutic care element from accommodation and subsistence costs and for the costs of personal care to be met by the taxpayer. This was rejected by the UK Government in favour of free *nursing* care plus means-tested and targeted personal care provision. The decision in Scotland to accept the main Sutherland recommendations therefore represented significant policy divergence. As Box 5.5 suggests, there is no shortage of contenders to explain the decision, and it is likely that policy changed as a result of a combination of factors.

The second flagship policy in the first parliamentary session was contained in the Education (Graduate Endowment and Student Support) (Scotland) Act 2001 which removed up-front *student tuition fees* and provided more financial support for some students in Scotland. In this case the level of divergence was perhaps less notable because, at the time, Scotland's Act had no Westminster counterpart and the policy favoured by the Liberal Democrats (and supported publicly by the SNP and Conservatives) had been 'watered down' in coalition negotiations with Labour – the fees were deferred and effectively reduced to £500 per year (for four years) rather than abolished (see Chapter 6). Subsequently, policy diverged further when Westminster's Higher Education Act 2004 gave universities the ability to charge 'top-up fees' of £3,000 per year (effectively raising fees to over £4,000 per year for three years) and then the SNP Government in 2007 signalled its intent to abolish student fees altogether. Yet, the picture was also complicated by the Scottish Executive's decision to introduce higher fees for English medical students in 2006 and the UK decision to reintroduce grants in 2007. In other areas, policies appear to be very similar, with any fees deferred and paid back at the same time as the student loan, and a greater reliance in England on 'foundation' degrees which mirrors Scotland's reliance on further education institutions to provide some part of higher education.

A similar picture of complexity has developed in *compulsory education* and this demonstrates well the need to look beyond legislation when examining policy. Perhaps the most high-profile policy in the first term was the pay deal awarded to teachers after a review chaired by Professor Gavin McCrone. This not only ended decades of industrial unrest (the main aim of the policy), but also allowed the expansion of teacher recruitment necessary to set maximum class sizes (this policy was accelerated under the SNP). In terms of legislation, the two Education Acts with no counterpart commit Scotland to comprehensive education and the maintenance of local authority control of schools. Yet, this is largely a symbolic affirmation of policy differences which existed long before devolution. Compulsory education has always been organized differently in Scotland which has its own policy community, history, tradition and administrative systems.

Such differences were accelerated following devolution: the development of a new 3–18 curriculum further removed Scotland from the testing regime so apparent in England (but resisted in Scotland), while legislation was introduced to abolish school boards altogether in favour of wider parent–teacher forums. This marks further divergence from New Labour policy in England which has pursued an agenda of differentiation in school provision, with private, grant-maintained and new types of schools competing with comprehensives. The competition comes from key-stage testing and 'league tables' combined with inspection regimes to determine quality.

Scotland's Mental Health Act 2003 was perhaps the best example of a significant piece of legislation with no Westminster counterpart (until the latter passed a more limited Act in 2007). Mental health also demonstrates at least three of the reasons given for devolution. First, administrative devolution (accompanied by minimal public or political awareness) allowed policy to develop differently in Scotland, with (for example) slower rates of hospital closures, different attitudes to the treatment of personality disorder in hospitals (following a high-profile breakout from Carstairs state mental hospital in the 1970s), a different inquiry process for homicides by patients receiving psychiatric care, and no Scottish equivalent to the Home Office's role with offenders in secure psychiatric units (four factors which proved crucial to the development of separate legislation). Second, the Scottish Parliament provided the legislative time for bills – the Adults With Incapacity Act 2000 was a bill in the making for almost a decade. Perhaps more impressive is the progress of the Mental Health Act. While the UK government commissioned and received its (Richardson) report into compulsory treatment by 1999, it took eight years to produce an Act with relatively limited scope. In contrast, the Millan Review in Scotland began in 1999 and reported in 2001, with substantive legislation passed by 2003. Third, the process surrounding the mental health acts in Scotland and England provides one of the best examples of differences in policy styles since devolution. Both bills address the controversial area of compulsory treatment in the community and interest-group concern has been apparent in both processes. The key difference has been the way this concern was handled. In England, the driver for change was a concern for public safety, and the unwillingness of ministers to negotiate with interest groups led to years of entrenched positions with no legislative resolution. In Scotland, ministers gave a much more free reign to Bruce Millan (former Secretary of State for Scotland), whose two-year report was based on widespread consultation and achieved huge 'ownership' among stakeholders.

'Flagship' policies and beyond: 2003–07

In the second session, the policy most associated with coalition government was the introduction of the single transferable vote in local government elections (see Chapter 4). However, the most high-profile 'flagship' policy was the ban on smoking in public places in 2005 (see Box 5.3) Smoking is an important case study because it illuminates two more aspects of the policy process (see Cairney, 2007b). First, it allows us to pinpoint direct interest-group influence (which is often assumed rather than demonstrated). In this case, interest-group frustration with a lack of progress in discussions with the Scottish Government led to support for Stewart Maxwell MSP's bill, which was seen as only a partial solution but the best on offer. The turning point came in the lead up to Maxwell's press conference to announce widespread support for his bill. Faced with the embarrassing prospect of a range of public health groups criticizing a lack of government action, the Executive promised to address the matter comprehensively in exchange for the withdrawal of public support at Maxwell's conference. Public health group support for the Executive then became crucial to 'sell' this new policy at a time when public opinion was mixed.

Second, the example confirms the value of studying multi-level governance and Scottish influence beyond its formal position. At the time, this policy not only marked a significant break from UK policy, but was also done in the face of opposition from the UK's then Secretary of State John Reid (although civil servants in the UK Department of Health were more support-ive). Indeed, soon after the legislation was announced in Scotland, similar statements of intent were made in Wales and Northern Ireland. These devel-opments were then used (successfully) by public health groups in England as leverage for change and a 'free vote' in Westminster, leading to comprehen-sive legislation in line with Scotland.

This experience contrasts with overall developments in health policy, particularly since there is now significant divergence in the management of the NHS. This is demonstrated by divergence in Scottish and English Acts.

Foundation hospitals: Introduced by the Blair led Government in England, these hospitals have a significant amount of managerial and financial freedom when compared to existing hospitals. There are none in Scotland.

While the National Health Service Reform (Scotland) Act 2003 abolishes the NHS's 'internal market' which fosters competition between providers of medical services, the Health and Social Care (Community Health and Standards) Act 2003 extends it by introduc-ing '**foundation hospitals**' (which achieve relative independence when they meet NHS targets and are then expected to follow a private business model). As with compulsory education, much of the the legislation merely formalized differences which were apparent before devolution (Cairney, 2002), but which were accelerated dramatically since 1999. In England, health policy contains the same elements as education: diversity and competition mixed with a strong focus on targets and a top-down 'command and control' style. Faith is placed in managers (with less trust in the medical profession) on the basis of a long-term belief in new public manage-ment. The Blair government also enhanced the purchaser–provider split (or internal market) by subsuming GP surgeries into Primary Care Trusts which took on the commissioning responsibilities from strategic health authorities, as well as providing incentives for foundation hospitals to look 'more private' and increasing the market share of the private sector (Greer, 2004).

In Scotland, the policy focus is more on partnership working between health (and local) authorities. The Scottish Government, due to its smaller size, is more able to centralize health policy through close involvement between senior decision-makers and health boards. Further, while England has a wide pool of experienced healthcare managers, Scotland has a 'very large medical elite infrastructure' including three Royal Colleges (Greer, 2005d). A policy community was apparent before devolution: 'the legacy of the Scottish Office was a tradition of close consultation between the (rela-tively understaffed) officials there and the medical elites' (2005d: 505). Post-devolution, the effect of this relationship was the reversal of internal market reforms and a reduced role for non-clinical managers. As Greer (2003) argues:

In the short time since devolution there has been surprising policy divergence . . . There are in most issues two poles: Scotland and England, with
the former running a health service for patients and the latter running one
for consumers. England is by far the most radical . . . Scotland is the most
traditionalist, rediscovering the virtues of the pre-Thatcher NHS . . . Where
England has in spirit and in policy opted for a market based set of solutions,
Scotland is opting for dominance by the professionals who work in the
system.

Greer's discussion is also interesting because he uses comparative analysis to
suggest that the forces of convergence are relatively weak in the UK. Scottish
governments are 'free to do what they like' if they have party control of the
legislature. Unlike the USA and Germany, there are no points of veto in the
healthcare system. Unlike Spain, Canada and Germany the system of finance
and regulation is not restrictive and funding from the UK does not come with
conditions on how to spend it.

Yet, we should not get too carried away with this picture of autonomy and
divergence, since there is also considerable indirect influence from England.
This is most apparent with its agenda on targets for waiting times and waiting
lists. While the medical operations associated with these targets account for a
very small proportion of NHS spend, the Department of Health often succeeds
in equating target success with real success in healthcare efficiency. By extension, attempts by devolved governments to set their own agenda with different
proxy indicators – for example by directing resources away from acute healthcare to wider public health measures – are often undermined by a public and
media focus on targets, often fuelled by UK ministers bemoaning the lack of
'modernization' outside England. Scottish ministers and civil servants then
get 'sucked in' to debates and feel obliged to fund reductions in waiting lists
(see Cairney, 2006c: 118).

'Flagship' policies and beyond: 2007–

The SNP's first legislative programme was dubbed 'legislation lite' by opposition parties (Gray, 2007). Indeed, there are a number of reasons to suggest that
fewer bills will be introduced (see Cairney, 2007g). First, the lack of a majority
in Parliament has limited the SNP to bills likely to receive enough opposition
support. More significant bills such as the introduction of a local income tax,
abolition of prescriptions and introduction of a 'Patient's Charter' required
consultations with groups and other parties before they could be introduced.
Second, there was a general feeling among most parties that the Scottish
Parliament had faced too much legislation in the past (Chapter 5). Third, many
major policy aims – such as civil service independence (Chapter 6), rejecting
PPP as a basis for funding capital projects (Chapter 9), and funding renewable

energy projects – may not require Scottish legislation, while significant individual decisions – such as halting the closure of certain hospital services and seeking to prevent ship-to-ship oil transfers in the Firth of Forth – were made by ministers without the need for parliamentary approval. Finally, the overall aim of the SNP is to hold a referendum on independence following a successful period of office. Therefore, its incentive is to 'do less, better'.

As a result, the first programme contained only three bills that would not have been introduced by the previous coalition government: to abolish student fees, to abolish the tolls on road bridges and to introduce elections in health boards. These were accompanied by three bills unlikely to find opposition in parliament (to update public health legislation, update flood prevention and support Glasgow's Commonwealth Games bid) and four bills inherited from the previous administration (interest to debt and damages, rape and sexual offences, reform of the judiciary and reform of culture quangos). Rather, the focus on the SNP Government was to demonstrate its governing competence, invoking the phrase 'First 100 days' to suggest that it would reform Scottish government quickly, in a way that could both be measured by all and signal the trajectory of long-term policy change (Cairney, 2007g).

Limits to a focus on primary legislation

As the examples above suggest, a sole focus on primary legislation alone may not capture the main developments, since policy is also administered from the existing statute book. In some areas (and 'cross-cutting' issues in particular) almost all policy is formulated in this way:

Social inclusion. This refers to a package of measures designed (and introduced from 1999) to tackle the social disadvantages associated with poverty caused by unemployment or low pay (see Box 10.2). It includes addressing unequal access to services such as education, health and housing, with the idea that social inclusion policies draw on, 'solidaristic notions of social integration, citizenship and community' (Fawcett, 2004: 240). There is good reason to think that Scotland's policies will be distinctive in this area, since one driver for devolution was the prospect of Scottish institutions tackling particularly bad policy conditions in Scotland (Parry, 1997 in Fawcett, 2003: 441). The left-of-centre policy bent in Scotland may also ensure a greater portrayal of exclusion as the fault of social structures and institutions rather than the individual. Further, a feature of Holyrood legislation in the first session was an attempt by a range of policy departments to highlight the cross-cutting theme of inclusion within their policies. Yet, experience to date suggests that there has been little divergence in practice. Most concrete policy has been directed at economic regeneration projects in particular areas, which represents not only convergence with the UK, but also the continuation of

Box 10.2   Social inclusion and multi-institutional policy-making

Social inclusion was a key policy priority of both the Labour–Liberal Democrat Scottish Government 1999–2007 and the UK Labour Government, though implementation structures differed. Social exclusion in contemporary political discourse has become a shorthand label to refer to individuals alienated from economic, political and social processes due to circumstances such as unemployment, poor skills, low incomes, poor neighbourhoods, bad health and lack of access to childcare. Post devolution, the Scottish Government has developed a wide variety of policies to try to tackle the problem. One of the key instruments was the creation of Social Inclusion Partnerships (SIPs) designed to tackle the problems of social exclusion, poverty and disadvantage.

There were 48 Social Inclusion Partnerships (SIPs), 34 of which were area-based initiatives; the other 14 were thematic initiatives on a range of subjects including young adults and health. SIPs are broad-based partnerships in local communities that have been deemed socially excluded. They comprise the local authority and other public agencies such as local enterprise companies, local health boards and the voluntary and private sectors. In 2004/5 SIPs were integrated with Community Planning Partnerships. SIPs worked under *CommunitiesScotland* and were service-delivery vehicles designed to help deliver the Labour–Liberal Democrat Scottish Government's social justice agenda for Scotland.

good definition

policies established well before devolution (2004: 248; Keating, 2005a: 195–203). To an extent, this reflects a lack of capacity to innovate in Scotland, with most of the initiative coming from local authorities and the voluntary sector, in the absence of a substantial presence of civil servants. However, the main obstacle was the reliance of so much policy on reserved matters such as social security (including housing benefit) and employment policy. The driver for most policy therefore came from a range of the UK Government's flagship policies – welfare to work, the minimum wage and the Working Families Tax Credit.

Rural affairs. Rural policy is a rather confusing term reflecting a desire within the European Commission to broaden agricultural policy, with a new focus on the 'economic, social and environmental needs of people living in rural areas' (Keating, 2005a: 204; Jordan and Halpin, 2006). This is driven by its Common Agricultural Policy (CAP) reforms which provide money to farmers and landowners (via Member States) only if they fulfil conditions set down by the Commission. As a cross-cutting theme, it therefore has the potential to span a wide range of policy areas – rural transport issues, access to health and education, the environmental impact of farming, economic development, and so on. Although the UK and Scotland have embraced this new approach to a degree, there are various factors suggesting that policy may diverge. While agricultural revenue and employment is more significant in Scotland, the proportion of land suitable for crops is considerably lower and so it is much more dependent on CAP support. Scottish policy is generally more sympathetic to the protection of farmers, particularly since Scotland has a larger proportion of small farms compared to the large agri-businesses in England, while the UK government has been more open to environmental lobbying and the pursuit of alternative uses for the countryside (2005: 208). There has also been no equivalent to the English population boom in rural areas which has led to pressure for housing and development, with the Scottish focus more on economic development and retaining the population. Rural affairs therefore became closely linked to the social inclusion agenda, while in England the focus was more on protecting rural areas from the worst excesses of urban overspill (2005: 205).

As a whole, there are three general themes in rural affairs. First, there is an overlap of policy responsibility between Scotland, the UK and the EU which suggests broad policy convergence with some scope for differentiation. Second, the evidence to date suggests a lack of coherence to Scottish rural affairs policy. As Jordan and Halpin (2006) suggest, the agricultural policy community still remains fairly separate from the interest groups active around

---

Box 10.3   Policy divergence in comparative perspective

As Box 10.1 suggests, territories such as Quebec and Catalonia may focus more on the ownership of policy rather than its similarity to Canadian or Spanish policy as a whole. Yet, the idea of divergence is by no means a UK preoccupation (Keating, in correspondence) and the level of attention to divergence varies over time and by territory. There is also significant variation within the UK. Northern Ireland is often characterized as the least likely devolved territory to diverge following policy innovation. This followed the suspension of political devolution from 2000–07 and the reduced likelihood of issues such as healthcare receiving party political attention (Greer, 2004). In contrast, the idea of 'Scottish Solutions' has a direct parallel in the 'Welsh Way' of consultation and decision-making. The aim of policy divergence was made clear in First Minister Rhodri Morgan's 'clear red water' speech, in which he rejected the appropriateness of New Labour policies in Wales (in favour of traditional Labour values). Examples of divergence with England include the abolition of pupil testing at key stages, the rejection of top-up fees, greater reliance on local authorities to deliver services, higher standards in housing and homelessness, and the move away from an NHS internal market and towards a public health model. As in Scotland, much divergence can be explained by different policy conditions (such as a high population spread or poor public health) and a different policy style based on close contact between decision makers, interest groups and those implementing policy. However, Wales has fewer (legislative) powers to make policy and is responsible for fewer policy areas (such as crime).

the wider agenda. Further, while a broad range of services pay lip-service to rural affairs, decision making still focuses on individual policy areas such as health, education and transport. Third, particularly within agriculture, most policy is administered without the need for Scottish legislation, since the main decisions with Scottish discretion are financial.

Limits to a focus on divergence

The point of the discussion so far is that if we look at public policy as a whole, divergence may be present in a large number of areas, but the differences are often subtle. However, this is not to say that there has been no significant policy *change*, particularly since the same policy may have disproportionate effects in Scotland.

One of the best examples in the first parliamentary session is Scotland's Housing Act in 2001 which follows England's agenda on the right to buy council houses and the transfer of housing stock from local authorities to registered social landlords (in most part because Treasury rules encourage such transfers). The effect in Scotland is larger because there is a much higher social rented sector in Scotland. In 2000, 24 per cent of housing in Scotland was owned by local authorities, compared to 13.6 per cent in England and 15.1 per cent in Wales (Stirling and Smith, 2003: 147).

In the second session, the most significant development was legislation to tackle anti-social behaviour. Crime and disorder had been a potential source of divergence in the first parliamentary session, with New Labour pursuing a fairly punitive agenda compared to a Scottish Government department led by Liberal Democrat Jim Wallace. However, from 2003 Scottish Labour took on this remit and this signalled a similar move towards legislation as the main policy instrument. Both governments focused on the introduction of **anti-social behaviour orders**, to be issued by local authorities and enforced by the police. As Keating (2005a: 203) suggests, this marked a significant 'reframing' of the problem, from one of social exclusion and disadvantage, to one which highlighted social misconduct, particularly among young people.

Anti-social behaviour orders (ASBOs): Are designed to prevent behaviour including theft, intimidation, drunkenness and violence by individuals and families who make life difficult for their communities.

Jack McConnell's particular attack on 'neds' ('non-educated delinquents'), marked the same type of shift that we saw in New Labour's increasing distance from the latter half of its famous phrase, 'tough on crime, tough on the causes of crime'. In this case, crucial differences only emerged in the enforcement of the orders, with Scottish authorities much more likely to use the orders as a last resort than in England where the uptake was high.

Divergence and implementation

Yet, divergence is still a *key* test and it is one which captures political attention, since so much political energy was vested in the idea that Scotland was different and as such required different policies. We can therefore use this idea to explore the 'success' of different policies. As students of public policy know, the story does not end with the *decision* to diverge – policy must also be *implemented*. From this starting point, it would be reasonable to assume if the implementation process is incomplete, then divergence is even less significant than the focus on legislation suggests.

This line of reasoning is most associated with the 'top-down' approach which highlights factors that ensure implementation success:

1   there is an understanding of, and agreement on, clear and consistent objectives;
2   a valid/ adequate causal theory exists, in which the relationship between cause and effect is direct (i.e. that the policy will work as intended when implemented);
3   subsequent tasks are fully specified and communicated (in correct sequence) to a team of skilful and compliant officials;
4   the required time and resources (including political will) are available, and fully committed, to the relevant programme;
5   dependency relationships are minimal and support from interest groups is maintained; and
6   external, or socioeconomic, conditions do not significantly constrain, or undermine, the process (see Marsh and Rhodes, 1992a).

By extension, partial success or policy failure (which may undermine the level of divergence) can be explained according to these requirements not being met. In such cases there is an **implementation gap** (see Hill and Hupe, 2002: 2). While such problems are common to all political systems, Scotland may also suffer particular constraints based on 'external' factors such as reserved policies, UK political interference and the unintended consequences of English policy.

Implementation gap: The gap between policy expectations and perceived policy results

The implementation gap is demonstrated well by *free personal care* for older people in Scotland. A number of factors demonstrate that this divergence was much less significant than the headlines suggest. First, we see the legacy of UK ministerial attempts to set the agenda following the publication of the Sutherland Report. They not only rejected the Report's main recommendation, but also attempted to influence the Scottish decision (and then its presentation) through its First Minister (McMahon, 2002). When Scotland adopted the policy, the Executive set a specific figure for 'free' care – £145 per person per week for personal care and an additional £65 per person per week for nursing care (in England the rates for free nursing care are £40, £80 or £129 – see Bell and Bowes, 2006). As a consequence, older people who were previously entitled to Attendance Allowance (which forms part of the reserved benefits system) no longer received it. This 'saving' to the UK Treasury was not passed back to Scotland and so the new money replaced rather than supplemented existing entitlement (£41–61 regardless of income or savings).

Second, the policy was adopted following a spell of opposition politics and Liberal Democrat support (Shaw, 2003) rather than a comprehensive consultation process to ensure smooth implementation. This perhaps explains a series of teething troubles associated with a lack of clarity in objectives (updating IT procedures, staff training and estimating take-up) which delayed the implementation date from April to July 2002. Councils also reported problems in explaining what 'free' personal care meant – that is, that it would not include 'hotel' costs for people with over £19,000 invested in savings or a house (Audit Commission, 2004: 13).

Third, the centrality of local authorities to implementation undermined central control, since in practice the money is paid by the Executive to reimburse authorities for the level of care given. The money is not **ring-fenced** and service provision becomes linked to negotiations on the (in)adequacy of the local government settlement.

Ring-fenced: Funds given to other bodies which *must* be spent on a specific purpose

The consequence for residential care is incomplete implementation, in four main areas (see Cairney, 2006d: 73). First, many councils have introduced waiting lists for people who qualify for care. Second, local authorities have not implemented Executive provisions for deferring fees until the resident dies. Third, the funding shortfall leads to disputes over the coverage of the payments (for example, whether or not it pays for meal preparation). Fourth, local authorities pass on insufficient funds to private providers. The unintended consequence is that private care homes make up the shortfall by overcharging on hotel costs for those who self-fund. Further, while the main success of free personal care has been a reduction in 'hidden need' and a significant rise in care at home, the evidence is that until very recently, local authorities did not charge the full amount for home care (with many charging an amount roughly equivalent to the Attendance Allowance). Therefore, for a large but indeterminate part of the Scottish population, the new policy replicates arrangements already in place.

Housing and homelessness. Although housing benefit and housing stock transfer is effectively controlled by the UK, most other aspects of housing are devolved and post-devolution expectations were high, fuelled by the particular attention given to these issues by Scottish ministers. Policies on homelessness and housing standards were sold as a significant break from the past and an improvement on English policy. Yet, a series of top-down factors undermined implementation success. With housing quality, Scotland proposed a higher minimum standard than England, but the lack of civil service capacity led to serious delays in meeting them.

In contrast, England became more focused on enforcing a lower standard, with more central government follow up and a relatively strong system of monitoring local-authority performance. A similar picture is apparent in homelessness policy which sees Scotland introduce wider definitions of need but without 'ring-fencing' the resources to match the expansion of policy. Therefore, Scottish groups describe the 'best homelessness legislation' but worst social housing conditions in Europe and a lack of political will to implement policy. This was demonstrated by the replacement of a senior minister with a civil servant on the implementation task-force, as well as the agenda on anti-social behaviour which threatened to exacerbate homelessness (by linking behaviour to social housing entitlement). Groups also point to England which has demonstrated a greater commitment to house building as a means of reducing pressure on social housing. In short, the Scottish Executive passed legislation but showed no sense of urgency, political will or new money. Therefore, divergence in policy formulation was undermined by implementation.

The issue of implementation also extends to areas in which there was (eventually) little divergence in formulation. For example, the ban on fox-hunting demonstrates implementation problems in both England and Scotland. Both suffer from a lack of resources devoted to enforcing the ban. As the Burns report (2000) describes: 'because the police are reluctant to enforce legislation where there is a lack of public support, they would not seek to give it a high priority', particularly since a huge police presence would be required to cover vast rural areas. This demonstrates well the difference between rhetoric and reality in policy-making, even when legislation is passed. While the issue of fox-hunting seemed to be a big priority in 2000, there is now no political weight to ensure successful implementation.

In contrast, we can see early 'top-down' signs of success in tobacco policy implementation: the smoking ban has clear aims, the short-term aim (of prohibiting smoking in public places) worked as intended when implemented, compliance was achieved by placing the onus on the host of the smoker backed up by sufficient resources within enforcement teams, public health group 'ownership' of policy is still high and social attitudes are largely supportive of the measures.

Therefore, with the exception of the smoking ban, these examples show a clear implementation gap between expectations and outcomes, suggesting that policy fails (or divergence is not followed through) if not enough of the conditions of success are met.

The 'bottom-up' approach to implementation criticizes this obsession with success and failure rather than the policy outcomes themselves and their main influences. It suggests that while central government policy may be the main influence, it competes with a variety of demands (often including competing or contradictory central government policies) and competing pressures within local implementing organizations (see Hjern, 1982; Hjern and Porter, 1981). Although national governments create the overall framework of regulations and resources, the main shaping of policy takes place at regional and local levels by implementation structures in which national considerations may play a small part. A bottom-up focus allows us to explain why the Scottish Government may lose control of its policy after it has legislated and passed on the money to local authorities or other organizations. It reinforces the general theme of *unrealistic expectations associated with new politics* running through this book. In other words, if governments do not control policy after they legislate, then it would be unrealistic to expect divergence in practice to match the levels of divergence suggested by the major policy decisions.

Conclusion

Although there are a number of ways to gauge public policy 'success' since devolution, a focus on policy divergence ties in with widespread expectations associated with 'Scottish Solutions to Scottish Problems'. Factors such as different social attitudes, the role of parties, ministers trying to 'make their mark' and differences in policy conditions all point to the likelihood for divergence. Yet, there are also many good reasons to suggest that policies will converge, including the complexities of multi-level governance, government by the same party, and the intractability of **wicked policy problems**. This suggests that we need to look at the evidence in detail to gauge the level of change and divergence.

Wicked policy problems: Long-standing public policy problems (e.g. drugs, crime, social exclusion) which require multi-agency coordinated approaches to their 'solution'.

A focus on 'flagship' policies alone may exaggerate levels of divergence with the UK. When we look at a large number of the less visible – but just as significant – policy areas, we see that this focus by decision-makers on a handful of key areas means that most are relatively ignored, with far fewer resources devoted to putting a Scottish stamp on policy.

A focus on the implementation of policy changes the picture further. The example of free personal care in particular demonstrates that there is a big difference between making the decision to be different and actually ensuring that the policy is implemented. Similarly, with housing we see a series of good intentions during the honeymoon period of the first parliamentary session, only to be replaced by relative neglect in the second session. This is not to say that policy *change* has not been significant since devolution. In many cases, such as transferring housing stocks from local authorities and introducing asbos, significant policy changes may have a greater effect on Scotland or be missed with a focus on divergence. In others, such as social inclusion and rural policies, we find that a focus on legislative divergence misses the significance of day-to-day policy-making by ministers and civil servants.

Finally, this chapter reinforces Chapter 9's conclusion that Scotland is not quite the 'land of milk and honey' portrayed in a wide section of the Scottish and English media (Mooney and Poole, 2004). There is a widespread misconception about the amount of policy innovation that Scotland's financial settlement can support. Care for older people was not 'free', student fees were not abolished (at least before 2007), and teachers are not paid significantly more than their English counterparts (with doctors often paid significantly less). The fact that the Scottish Government has to redirect money from one programme to fund another still represents the main obstacle to policy change.

Further reading

Key readings on Scottish policy change post-devolution are Adams and Robinson (2002), Greer (2004), Keating *et al.* (2003), Keating (2005a, 2005b), McLean (2003), Stirling and Smith (2003), Mooney and Poole (2004), Mooney and Scott (2004), Mitchell (2004, 2006) and Cairney (2007a). See also a special issues of the *Political Quarterly* journal 74(4) in 2003 with articles on Scotland, devolution and welfare reform.

Online sources

Centre for Scottish Public Policy   http://www.cspp.org.uk
Centre for Public Policy for Regions   http://www.cppr.ac.uk
Scottish Council Foundation   http://www.scottishcouncilfoundation.org

Chapter 11

Assessing Scottish Democracy

> The coming of a Scottish Parliament will usher in a way of politics that is radically different from the rituals of Westminster: more participative, more creative, less needlessly confrontational. (Scottish Constitutional Convention (SCC), 1995)

As noted in Chapter 2 the SCC Final Report (1995), the Yes–Yes 1997 Referendum campaign and the Consultative Steering Group Report (1999) all emphasized an aspiration of a new style of democracy and politics in Scotland. 'New politics' suggests a style of politics which is not only consensual, but also involves the participation of more individuals and groups. A central feature is the inclusion of hitherto excluded sections of society. While the most prominent example of this movement was to ensure that more women were elected to the Scottish Parliament, a broader aim was to ensure greater participation among groups held to be excluded from political participation in the past. Ethnic minorities are mentioned explicitly by the SCC, but there is also an implicit suggestion that this focus extends as broadly as possible to, for example, people with disabilities, young people, and rural populations relatively distant from the capital city.

Social partnerships: An institutional arrangement designed to bring together a sense of co-operation between a wide variety of societal groups.

Consensus conferences: The bringing together of representatives of different and opposing perspectives in a forum of discussion and deliberation.

Citizen juries: A small sample of a population designed to fairly represent the perspectives of the wider community, which hears evidence on a political issue, deliberates and drafts recommendations for a governing body.

For the architects of the devolved institutions, it would not be enough that the Scottish Parliament was *open* and accessible to this wide array of disenfranchised populations. It would also become a hub for processes which *reach out* to 'civil society' in a way never seen in Westminster. A wide number of processes were mooted in the run up to (and following) devolution, including **social partnerships**, **consensus conferences**, **citizen juries**, opinion polling and internet-based forums (many of these initiatives were also mooted at UK level by Gordon Brown when he became Prime Minister in 2007). However, the three main innovations which received the most political weight are:

Civic Forum:
Established with Scottish Executive funding in 1999 to bring together civic interests in a deliberative body. Funding was withdrawn in 2006 and the forum disappeared.

- The move to extend microcosmic representation, or the representativeness of MSPs in terms of their social background. While the SCC focus is primarily on gender, we may expect representation to extend to ethnicity, age and occupation.
- The development of the Scottish **Civic Forum** and the petitions process of the Scottish Parliament as a means for direct participation, or at least an alternative means of involvement in the political process.
- A new and improved consultation process between the Scottish Government, Scottish Parliament and a wide range of representative organizations in the community, voluntary sector, professions and business. This inclusion of hitherto excluded sections of society would come at the expense of the 'usual suspects', or the larger and better resourced groups which tend to dominate consultation time with government.

The aim of this chapter is therefore to review the theory and practice of these developments. It compares the reality of post-devolution politics with the pre-1999 discourse and aspirations.

Democracy

'Democracy', is one of the most used but also most vague and least understood terms in political science. In a broad sense, democracy is designed as a solution to the problem of reaching collective decisions without resort to violence. Introductory descriptions of democracy often begin with Abraham Lincoln's famous phrase, 'Government of the people, by the people, and for the people' (Gettysburg Address, 1863). However, this does not make clear who 'the people' are, how they should rule and how far this popular rule should (and realistically could) extend. Athenian democracy is often used as a classic example of not only direct participation, but also participation to ensure the collective rather than individual good (see Heywood, 2007, chap. 4), As Dahl notes, 'In the Greek vision of democracy, politics is a natural social activity not sharply separated from the rest of life . . . Rather political life is only an extension of, and harmonious with, oneself' (1989: 18). Yet, the major drawback is exposed when we see that only the select few (male) citizens qualified as active and entitled to vote (see Heywood, 2007).

Representative democracy: 'Indirect' democracy whereby citizens decide who should represent them in an elected chamber rather than participate directly.

Scotland is a liberal democracy, which suggests that it has a system of regular and competitive elections and that the decision-making power of elected representatives is subject to the rule of law. Liberal democracy

Deliberative democracy: Decision-making through reasoned and open discussion among the citizenry as a whole.

Participatory democracy: Decision-making with a focus on the direct participation of citizens.

also suggests a certain minimum level of civil rights and the protection of the 'minority' against the majority'. However, even with this additional definition, the term is still vague and subject to debate about how best to achieve these broad aims. Therefore, not surprisingly, the SCC and CSG appear to invoke four or even five different types– **representative democracy** (including microcosmic representation), **deliberative democracy**, **participatory democracy** and pluralist democracy – when pursuing a more effective style of politics.

Representative democracy

In a modern context, direct democracy at a national level would involve too many participants with too little time to devote to politics, and insufficient knowledge to apply to the wide range of responsibilities of the modern state. The main alternative is representative or indirect democracy in which popular sovereignty is expressed through regular elections of representatives acting on their behalf. To Schumpeter, 'the democratic method is that institutional arrangement for arriving at political decisions in which individuals acquire the power to decide by means of a competitive struggle for the people's vote' (1943: 269). While these representatives may not receive a direct mandate from the populations they represent (particularly given the heterogeneity of views within such populations), they would be responsive to their wishes in anticipation of a future electoral response. The basis for the SCC's push for devolution was that the Scottish electorate had lost this control over its representatives since it did not get the government that it voted for and could not vote that government out. A Scottish Parliament would therefore address to a large extent the 'democratic deficit' in Scottish politics.

Microcosmic representation

This idea of improving representative democracy would be extended by microcosmic representation, or the ability of MSPs to represent directly the social background of Scotland's population. The assumption here is that if elected members do not resemble the populations they are there to represent, then certain under-represented populations will be further marginalized within society. In Westminster, we can identify long-standing under-representation of women, ethnic minorities and working classes which may suggest that certain issues important to these groups may struggle to reach Parliament's agenda, however well-intentioned its elected members may be.

There are two main points to note from this type of discussion. First, there are practical limits to the pursuit of 'perfect' representation, since there is an almost infinite number of ways that we can characterize social background, while the more we divide then the more divisive the process may be. Indeed, we could argue the opposite case to the ideal of microcosmic representation – that the more an elected member feels a mandate from a particular section of society (which forms a small part of his/her constituency), then the less likely a Parliament can function as a collective body. Second, in the SCC discussion we find that concrete discussions of microcosmic representation are only present in the discussions of *gender* equality, with discussions regarding ethnicity, disability and age less prominent.

Participatory democracy

In part, the limited focus on representation is based on the argument that Scottish-based elections alone would not solve the democratic deficit. Rather, Scotland has, 'consistently declared through the ballot box the wish for an approach to public policy which accords more closely with its collective and community traditions' (SCC, 1995). In other words, devolution will be accompanied by the ability of a much wider section of the population to extend its participation beyond electing representatives, to making a direct and significant contribution to public decision making. The main innovations to this end were the development of a Scottish Civic Forum, in which a self-selecting cross-section of the population would come together to set the agenda for, or evaluate, public policies, and a petitions process which would

---

Box 11.1   Referendums in a comparative perspective

To suggest that the lack of Switzerland-style referendums is a flaw of the Scottish democratic process is misleading for a number of reasons. First, as with Catalonia and Quebec, the regional-constitutional issue is an impetus to hold referendums at the nation state level. Second, devolution has increased the potential for referendums to take place (although the most likely referendum on independence will be difficult to achieve). This (combined with other measures) marks a small step towards countries such as the USA which have limited direct democracy at the federal level, but a proliferation of referendums and initiatives at the state level. Third, most European countries err towards representative government as the default position, with referendums only triggered by government, president or parliament. In only five countries can a referendum be triggered by public initiative and in most cases there is a participation threshold which limits policy change. For example, in Italy the requirement of a 50% turnout has meant that no referendum has been successful since 1995. Finally, it difficult to justify the argument that one form of democracy is superior to another. For example, in Germany referendums have 'undemocratic overtones' following their use during the Nazi era, while France's pre-1945 referendums were, 'seen as dubiously democratic, being used by authoritarian rulers to legitimize their positions (Gallagher *et al.*, 2006: 373–6).

be open to all, with a very low threshold for participation. Yet, it is interesting to note that the proposals stopped short of a more 'radical' form of direct democracy that 'collective and community traditions' may suggest. In other words, rather than advocating, for example, the widespread use of referendums which bind decision-makers, the architects of devolution opted for forums and procedures which feed into traditional forms of participation and support representative government.

Deliberative democracy

These new types of participation contribute to an aim of deliberative democracy, in which there is reasoned discussion among a wide and active population in a setting where all participants have equal status, rather than discussions behind closed doors among a small number of elite decision- makers. Thus, the focus of deliberative democracy is not only to extend policy-relevant discussions beyond a small core executive, but also to ensure that direct and indirect democracy is more than just a show of hands or popular strength. Collective outcomes are not determined merely by the **tyranny of the majority**, but by means of extensive arguments offered by and to participants affected by policy decisions. The pursuit of reasoned argument suggests that preferences can be changed instead of just aggregated, with the end result a form of consensus not achievable through traditional forms of democracy.

> **Tyranny of the majority**: A term used in discussing systems of democracy where the decisions of the majority do not respect minority rights.

However, again, there are two main points to note about this process. First, there is no reason to assume that deliberation will extend beyond a small band of elites with the knowledge, time and resources to transform the preferences of others, particularly since there will still be a requirement for gatekeepers and experts to monitor the rules of engagement and decide what is relevant to discussions. Indeed, the use of institutions as the face for this type of deliberation may *legitimize* elite forms of power and suggest that there is more engagement among the population than exists. Second, we should be wary about ascribing too much importance to this process in terms of the SCC aims. While it advocated a civic forum to further deliberation, history proved that there was little political weight placed behind other forms of deliberative democracy such as citizens' juries and deliberative polling (which are now more in vogue at the UK level). Indeed, perhaps its main hope was that this deliberative process would be fostered mainly in the committee system of the Scottish Parliament.

Pluralist democracy

One problem with representative democracy is that even if we reduce the geographical boundaries (from the UK to Scotland), we are still faced with low electoral turnouts and a voting population with often limited knowledge of the policies of parties and candidates. An effective alternative form of participation (or, more likely, indirect influence) for individuals is through interest groups (Jordan and Stevenson, 2000). Indeed, the SCC sees a role for interest groups engaging directly with the Scottish Government and Scottish Parliament. However, it rejects the idea that this consultation will take place with the 'usual suspects', or the biggest and best resourced interest groups who already have close ties. This push for broader consultation is associated with a monitoring role performed by Scottish Parliament committees who may oblige the Scottish Government to consult far and wide until they are satisfied that all groups have 'had their say'. Yet, as discussed below, this is to assume (wrongly) that the barriers to consultation are relatively high in the UK. Further, as Jordan and Stevenson (2000: 181) argue, there is something wrong with the idea that we must *privilege* the role of previously 'excluded' or disorganized groups: 'If the small groups are re-labelled as "not popular" the arguments sound less compelling.'

New politics and strawmen

A common theme throughout these discussions of new forms of democracy is a contrast with 'old Westminster'. As Chapter 1 discussed, it soon becomes clear that this view of Westminster is based on a caricature of UK politics which is adversarial, dominated by vested interests, and based on an electoral system which funnels all political power to the centre, excluding the majority of the population from the decision-making process. Yet, ironically, the discussions of the SCC and CSG have also been criticized on a similar basis, with the aims described as naïve and not paying enough attention to political realities such as the role of parties, the logic of consultation with large, organized interest groups and the logic of executive government (see Box 11.2).

Jordan and Stevenson (2000) are critical of the tone of the SCC and CSG and argue it is damaging to the image of well-established forms of democracy. In other words, if too many claims are made for participative democracy and the need for a new approach is based on critique of representative democracy, faith is inevitably lost in both. The SCC uses popular cynicism around party politics as a justification for direct participatory democracy. Yet, the real problem in Scotland was the legitimacy deficit arising from the fact that the electorate voted for one party but got another, with the result a, 'lack of a political and parliamentary majority to reflect Scottish political views' (2000: 184). This was solved by devolution itself (and a proportional electoral system), while bringing the ballot box closer to home ensures that public opinion is reflected more in the actions of the Scottish Government. Further claims of improved democracy may therefore only have raised expectations unrealistically and undermined faith in a type of democracy *improved* by the process of devolution.

Box 11.2 New politics and democracy: criticisms

Criticisms of the notion of new politics include:

- While it may have been relatively easy to reach agreement on mechanisms for governance and participation, it would be naïve to assume that 'consensus' could be reached through deliberation. Hard choices will always have to be made in the face of dissent in some quarters since there will always be winners and losers. A 'rational' approach is therefore unrealistic.
- The pre-devolution 'consensus' in Scotland was exaggerated by a common opposition to a Conservative government and a growing awareness of the democratic deficit.
- 'Consensus' may only be achieved by stifling debate and restricting discussion to vested interests conveniently dubbed 'civil society'.
- There has been no demonstration that changing political processes increases participation.
- There is no justification for misplaced loyalty towards small/ excluded groups. Indeed, there is the potential for new bias towards very small but reasonably organized groups (or even individuals) and against inactive citizens. For example, civic forum meetings may be dominated by a small, conservative and unrepresentative group of people as a result of low participation among the general public. The question then becomes: is this better than a mass electorate choosing representatives?
- Not all of the aims of new politics will be compatible and, for example, devolving decisions to a civic forum or equivalent may increase participation at the expense of traditional forms of accountability through elections.

As a whole, one is left with the impression that the architects of devolution were trying to provide all things to all people. As a result (as Chapter 1 suggests), this myriad of hopes and dreams may have included elements which are either incompatible with each other, or in which one aspect receives more priority than another. For example, in terms of microcosmic representation, this may suggest that the focus on gender will mean that broader social aspirations are pursued with less vigour. Similarly, while there may be a focus on participation and deliberation, this is within the context of a fairly traditional starting point, with the Government there to govern and the Parliament to provide scrutiny, with its role as a hub for a range of new organizations forced to compete with its 'day job'.

It may therefore be better to view the SCC aims in the same way we would view a manifesto. As such, it focuses on the positives of new developments – a *more* representative Scottish Parliament, *less* partisanship, *more* public involvement – and uses **old politics** as a form of departure, even if there is implicit acknowledgement that parties will

Old politics: Refers to the adversarial, partisan political culture at Westminster.

have a legitimate right to compete and that consultation will inevitably take place most with the biggest and most organized, active and informed groups. We should also remember the historical context and the legacy of the 'failed' referendum in 1979. A significant driver for the SCC was to address the feeling (particularly among Labour MPs) in the 1970s that too many constitutional and procedural questions had been left unanswered before the referendum. The SCC may also have had to contend with a general cynicism about politics and the need to articulate the benefits of producing more politicians.

It is in this light that we can assess the practical effects of Scotland's new democratic processes. New politics involves not only the participation of more people and groups, but also a style of politics which is more consensual and less adversarial. This will be fostered by a more open and accessible parliament, a mechanism to allow people to petition parliament, a forum for public deliberation and a statutory requirement for the Government to consult widely before legislating. This sentiment is furthered by the CSG. People find it difficult to influence legislation, with consultation ineffective and policies only becoming public following the publication of legislation. The CSG therefore recommends the greater use of draft Bills which are still open to change and a Scottish Parliament committee role in ensuring wide consultation. In this context of more limited aspirations, it may be more realistic to look for marginal (but still significant) changes caused by the initial expectations surrounding new politics and the willingness of new Scottish institutions and MSPs to uphold these values.   In this sense, the identification of partisanship, an imperfect petitions system or consultation with the 'usual suspects' does not undermine fully the appearance of 'new politics'.   The question, rather, may be: how different is Scotland's politics? Or, how much change has there been? We can explore this in the following sections:

- Microcosmic representation – is the social background of MSPs representative of the Scottish population?
- How much new participation has been fostered by the Scottish Civic Forum?
- What difference has the provision of a clear petitions system made?
- Is the consultation process for interest groups open and accessible?

Microcosmic representation

Gender, ethnicity and disability

The success of the SNP's Bashir Ahmad in 2007 marks the first ethnic minority candidate to be elected to the Scottish Parliament since devolution. The previous lack of representation *perhaps* reflects the old politics reluctance of parties to give ethnic-minority candidates winnable seats (although it will now take only one additional MSP to resemble the 1.4 per cent of ethnic minorities

Table 11.1 *Male and female elected members in Holyrood and Westminster, 1997–2007*

	Scottish Parliament			Scottish MPs			MPs rest of UK	
	1999	*2003*	*2007*	*1997*	*2001*	*2005*	*2001*	*2005*
Women	37%	40%	33%	17%	15%	15%	18%	20%
Men	63%	60%	67%	83%	85%	85%	82%	80%
Number	129	129	129	72	72	59	587	587

in the Scottish population). There have also been no instances of significant disabilities among the new crop of MSPs, despite a broad commitment to enhancing participation among these social groups. Therefore, a far better candidate for 'making a difference' following devolution is the level of representation of women. As Table 11.1 suggests, the proportion of women in the Scottish Parliament began at 37 per cent in 1999, rising to 40 per cent in 2003 but falling to 33 per cent in 2007. These proportions are consistently higher than among Scottish MPs (and the rest of the UK) in Westminster. Indeed, at its peak in 2003, the 40 per cent in Holyrood was well over double the 15 per cent Scottish female representation in Westminster.

However, there are also significant differences by party, with much of the advance since devolution explained by the high number of women among the Scottish Parliamentary Labour Group. Labour was the party which made the clearest commitment towards gender parity in candidate selection (perhaps as much in reflection of UK party policy as Labour's experience in the SCC) and it achieved this with twinned constituencies rather than with the help of proportional representation (in which gender would alternate on the regional candidate list under the Mixed Member Proportional System). As Table 11.2 shows, the initial figure of 37 per cent in the whole Parliament owed much to the number of Labour MSPs and, to a lesser extent, a higher than average proportion of women (43%) in the SNP (then the second largest party).

In the other two main parties, the number of women was (and remains) relatively low. Perhaps ironically for the Liberal Democrats so involved in the SCC, 12 per cent is lower than its 16 per cent UK average, and since from 1999 to 2007 it did not propose one female minister within the coalition, this contributed to relatively low female representation in government (around 25%). For the Conservatives (which had the only female leader before Wendy Alexander became the leader of Labour in 2007), 29 per cent is much higher than the 9 per cent of Westminster MPs in 2005 (see Keating and Cairney, 2006). In 2003, the overall proportion of 40 per cent resulted from a rise in Labour to 56 per cent, while the drop to 36 per cent among the SNP was offset by a reduction in its overall numbers. In 2007 the SNP had a much bigger

Table 11.2 Male and female elected members in Holyrood by party, 1999–2007

	Labour			SNP			Conservative			Liberal Democrat		
	1999	2003	2007	1999	2003	2007	1999	2003	2007	1999	2003	2007
Women	50%	56%	50%	43%	36%	25%	17%	22%	29%	12%	12%	12%
Men	50%	44%	50%	57%	64%	75%	83%	78%	71%	88%	88%	88%
Number	56	50	46	35	27	47	18	18	17	17	17	16

impact. While it became the largest party with 47 seats, the proportion of women in its ranks fell to 25 per cent. Therefore, while Labour maintained gender parity, its dwindling numbers meant that the overall proportion of women in Holyrood dropped to one-third, the lowest level since devolution.

Social class and occupation

As Keating and Cairney (2006) suggest, there were countervailing pressures on recruitment by class and occupation in Scotland. While there was a general commitment to broaden recruitment and create a more open political class more representative of the country as a whole, there was also a strong trend within Britain and Western Europe to narrow recruitment to the professional middle classes and those occupations that lend themselves easily to political life (for a fuller discussion of these **'politics-facilitating' professions** see Box 11.3 and Cairney, 2007a). The evidence suggests that the latter influence is more important (particularly among women), with recruitment to the Scottish Parliament accelerating postwar trends away from the working classes and towards the professional (including lawyers and teachers) and politics-facilitating (including party workers and trade-union officials) occupations. For example, Shephard *et al.* (2001: 96) report that 19 per cent of Scottish MPs in 1997 had some experience in blue-collar or industrial work, compared to less than 2 per cent of MSPs in 1999. Keating and Cairney (2006: 46) show this effect on Scottish Labour in particular, with blue and white-collar backgrounds accounting for 42 per cent of Scottish MPs from 1945–70, falling to 10 per cent in 2005 compared to 2 per cent of MSPs in 2003 (despite these occupations accounting for almost half of the Scottish population).

In the other direction, Scottish MP professional backgrounds rose from 36 per cent in 1945–70 to 46 per cent in 2005 compared to 56 per cent of MSPs

> **Politics-facilitating professions:** Professions which help a candidate secure election and/or perform the role of an MP.

Box 11.3   Politics 'facilitating' professions

The typical career path of European MPs includes securing a university degree, a prominent position within a political party, election to local or regional government and entry into a 'politics-facilitating' occupation. This refers to a job which helps a candidate secure election and/or perform the role of an MP. Traditionally this refers to 'professional' or 'brokerage' occupations such as lawyers and teachers who have communication and advocacy skills that transfer easily into the political arena. More recently, it refers to 'instrumental' occupations, such as party worker or MP assistant, which are seen as a more direct 'stepping-stone' to elected office. Criticism is often made that the recruitment of politicians from such a narrow range of occupations inhibits their capacity to truly represent (see Cairney, 2007a).

in 2003, while politics-facilitating backgrounds rose from 15 per cent to 29 per cent and 32 per cent respectively. This bias towards professional and politics-facilitating occupations is reflected in the other main parties. There are perhaps only two significant differences. The first is that a 'professional' background for Labour MSPs is much more likely to refer to public sector occupations such as social work, teaching and nursing (perhaps in reflection of devolved responsibilities) than the other parties which draw more from the private sector. The second is that Scottish Labour made a concerted effort to reduce candidate selection from local government, which is increasingly seen elsewhere in the UK and Europe as part of a career path towards higher office. Scottish Labour bucked this trend to an extent, with less than 45 per cent serving previously as councillors compared to over 60 per cent in Westminster and the Welsh Assembly (Keating and Cairney, 2006).

Education

In Westminster it was almost traditional for MPs to have received an education from an independent school followed by three years at Oxford or Cambridge University (see Keating and Cairney, 2006). This is still the case for Conservative MPs elected in 2005, with 58 per cent educated privately and 45 per cent graduates of Oxbridge. Devolution therefore makes a difference, with only one of 18 MSPs (in 2003) educated at Oxbridge and one-third educated privately. There are similarities with the Liberal Democrats, although the private school (35%) and Oxbridge (18%) contingent, while lower than the UK (45% and 37%), is higher than the rates for Scottish MPs (27% and 9%). The SNP also had unrepresentative levels of private schooling among its MSPs in 2003 (11%). For Labour MSPs, the numbers are significantly lower. For Scottish Labour MPs (10%) and the rest of the Parliamentary Labour Party (PLP) (21%), the figures for private education are much higher than the 3.5 per cent of the population in Scotland and 6 per cent in England. For Labour MSPs, the figure of 4 per cent is almost representative, while there were no Oxbridge graduates (compared to 2.5% of Scottish MPs and 21% in the rest of the PLP). Therefore, taken as a whole, MSPs are less likely than MPs to have been educated privately or at Oxbridge. Yet, only Labour MSPs come close to resembling these levels in the Scottish population. Further, all four main parties enjoy incredibly high rates of higher education overall. While the participation rate among the Scottish population (45–50%) is high compared to the rest of the UK, it cannot compete with the 80–90 per cent levels among MSPs (which is also higher than MPs in the UK).

Age

When elected in 1999, MSPs were more representative of the Scottish population than Scottish MPs (see Shephard *et al.*, 2001). For example, the figure of 30 per cent in the population aged 20–39 was almost met by MSPs (29%) but not MPs (10%). The average age of MSPs (45) was also significantly lower than MPs (50). Yet if we look at the average age when MPs *were first elected*, this falls to around 40 (2001: 89). These figures still hold in 2005, with more MPs (in Scotland and the rest of the UK) aged over 50 (64% compared to 52%) but far fewer MPs aged over 50 when first elected (13% compared to 35%). In 2007, the proportion of MSPs under 40 has fallen to 13 per cent, while MSPs in their 60s has risen to 16.3 per cent (compared to 5.5% in 1999 – see SPICE, 2007: 66). This suggests that the level of youthful representativeness in the Scottish Parliament was only a temporary result of the new Parliament

Therefore, the differences in Scotland regarding microcosmic representation relate primarily to gender. While there are more women, fewer 'usual suspects' from local government, and fewer MSPs from private schools, MSPs are more likely than MPs to be white, middle-aged, middle-class, and university-educated with a professional or 'politics-facilitating' background. The resemblance between MSPs and the Scottish population therefore depends on where we look and which party we examine. Indeed, without the social background of Scottish Labour MSPs, the difference made by devolution may have been negligible.

Quite how this relates to the conduct of MSPs and the issues they pursue in the Scottish Parliament is open to question. There are few convincing demonstrations of the links between social background and policy outcomes (although there is more on gender – see Childs, 2004).

The Scottish Civic Forum (SCF)

Of course, if Scottish citizens had concerns about their MSP representing their views indirectly, they could go along to a civic forum meeting and express them in person (see Box 11.4 for an outline of the functions of the SCF). There are two main points to note about the SCF. The first is that its practices embodied

---

Box 11.4   Functions of the Scottish Civic Forum

- provided information about Scottish Government consultations and how to respond;
- ran regular events to give people the opportunity to influence government through the forum;
- provided a range of facilities such as crèches, lip-speakers and interpreters to make sure that there were fewer obstacle to participation, and
- introduced regional coordinators in 2003 to make sure that the Scottish population as a whole could be represented.

the spirit of the original SCC aims; however, the second point is that it no longer exists!

The SCF began life in 1999 with Scottish Executive funding of approximately £100,000 per year. This was cut by 50 per cent in 2005 and then completely abolished in 2006. Following a decision by the Scottish Parliament Corporate Body not to replace the funding, the SCF closed. This is perhaps the best sign of its perceived importance among the main political institutions, but was this impression matched elsewhere? Certainly, the more established interest groups did not rate it as an avenue for influence. Most groups either suggested that the forum was a 'talking shop' or that they did not want their influence diluted as part of a wider body, since every voice was deemed to be equal within that forum. Therefore, approximately 40 per cent of the membership used the forum minimally, since they had more direct avenues of influence through organizations such as the Scottish Trade Union Congress (STUC), the **Scottish Council for Voluntary Organizations** (SCVO) and the Convention for Scottish Local Authorities (COSLA) or the ability to engage with the Scottish Government directly.

> **Scottish Council for Voluntary Organizations** (SCVO): A national umbrella body which represents the voluntary sector.

The remaining 60 per cent was made up of professions which struggle for access within their own organizations (for example, local branches of larger organizations), community groups and interested individuals (who tended to be retired from work). This is not surprising since the forum was in part set up to provide a venue for less well-established but active populations. Yet, there are also signs that participation was not particularly high among these groups. An interview with the SCF's director in 2004 confirms this picture, suggesting that even though regional coordinators were making local meetings better, it was, 'difficult to get 50 people in a room'. Indeed, to achieve around 15 in a regional meeting required a lot of effort from regional coordinators, calling likely participants to remind them of meetings and often *transporting* people to meetings. Therefore, even by taking to extreme these practical measures to reduce the barriers to participation, the SCF did not succeed in increasing public participation significantly.

A similar picture can be painted regarding the links the SCF enjoyed with the Scottish Parliament and Scottish Government. Links with Scottish Parliament were sporadic and often undermined by political party partisanship. Although list MSPs were often more likely to be involved, and some individual MSPs expressed interest in using the SCF to reach out and experiment with consultation, the numbers of MSPs attending meetings was minimal. While links with the Scottish Executive were more frequent, and the Executive commissioned specific work as part of consultation exercises, there were clear cultural differences in expectations for these exercises. The Scottish Executive wanted a relatively short feedback report with analysis, but the SCF was committed to recording *all* views, with little editing to ensure that every voice was heard (or at least recorded). As a result, the overall success of the SCF was difficult to identify. Its influence on policy was difficult to see and feedback from participants who traditionally felt politically excluded was difficult to gather.

Public petitions

Like the civic forum, the petitions process was designed to be an improvement on old Westminster practices, which were complex with no demonstrable end result: 'another example of Westminster's perceived remoteness and lack of connection to ordinary citizens' (Lynch and Birrell, 2001: 1–2). To address this, petitions were part of a wider process of 'linking the Scottish Parliament to the people'. Unlike the civic forum, the petitions process is much more likely to be judged a success. Anyone taking a tour of the Scottish Parliament with MSPs will soon hear that, 'it is the jewel in our crown'. There is also evidence of high rates of participation, with 964 petitions initiated from 1999–2006 (Carman, 2006), while the electronic submission system is admired and emulated by a number of other legislatures (Arter, 2004a: 22). However, there are four questions that we need to ask about petitions, to see if these levels of prestige and participation translate to something beyond a symbolic difference with the UK:

- Who proposes them?
- How are they dealt with?
- What are the constraints to their influence?
- Is there a tangible effect on public policy?

Who proposes them? International experience suggests that petitions are most likely to be used effectively as part of a wider lobbying strategy by established groups and business interests rather than the previously disenfranchised. To an extent we can see this from Lynch and Birrell's (2001: 8) analysis of the first two years of the Scottish Parliament, since around 40 per cent of petitions were proposed by interest groups and businesses. Yet, as they suggest, these groups (bar the odd exception such as the National Farmers' Union) seem to be less well-established and so their activities conform much more to the idea of community pressure. There is also little evidence that large business groups are lobbying this way. This picture is reinforced by Carman's (2006) analysis of the first seven years. Individuals account for 53 per cent of all petitions proposed, while community group petitions (18%) outnumber those of more established interest groups (15%) and businesses (3%). A less welcome statistic relates to the number of petitions proposed by the same individuals, with five people accounting for 11 per cent of all petitions. Further, 47 per cent of all petitions have only one signature and the median is two! This is put into perspective by a single e-petition which generated 1.5 million signatures in the UK to oppose road charging. There is also a clear bias in petition initiation towards older, male, middle-class, university-educated and politically active individuals (Carman, 2006). Therefore, while the low levels of business and pressure group activity suggests that the process is used largely by the population it was intended to reach, the analysis of individuals does not demonstrate that it is any more successful at reaching out to previously excluded groups than the civic forum.

How are they dealt with? In its first year the Public Petitions Committee (PPC) acted like an intermediary, merely collecting the petitions and sending them onto the relevant subject committees (or directly to the Scottish Executive). As Lynch and Birrell (2001: 4) suggest, this process was helped by the fact that members of the petitions committee were also members of many of the subject committees they referred the petitions to. This ensured that many were followed up in subsequent meetings, while the two-way process was reinforced by MSPs attending PPC meetings and expressing interest in particular areas (although since 2004 MSPs are no longer allowed to propose petitions). In its second year the PPC became more conscious of its options. As the Procedures Committee (2003) discusses:

> Was the PPC simply a post-box, reflexively feeding petitions where appropriate to subject committees for consideration, or was it able to take a more active initial role itself in looking critically at petitions? The PPC view had settled on the latter, with the result that 57 per cent of petitions referred to subject committees in the first year of the Parliament, but only 17 per cent in the second.

What are the constraints to their influence? The more active gatekeeper role performed by the PPC and its staff (including the ability to filter frivolous claims by serial petitioners), combined with the lack of a mechanism to appeal a decision made by the PPC, has led Carman (2006) to suggest that the process is not as open and transparent as the CSG envisaged. There has also been a range of practical problems in the operation of the petitions system – finding time in subject committees to debate the issues and make recommendations, territorial disputes between the PPC and subject committees when the petition is handed over, a lack of PPC resources to travel and investigate petitions, the time lag between the initiation of a petition and its presentation to decision-makers, the lack of time given to petitioners addressing the PPC (often only three minutes plus questions), and the insufficient level of public knowledge of petitions.

What is the tangible effect of petitions? If our focus is on satisfaction with the process itself, then the evidence is promising. When interviewed, most petitioners report that they are generally happy with process (Carman, 2006), which supports the idea that the petitions process is there to deepen a power-sharing relationship between 'the people' and Parliament and further participative democracy (the problem of serial petitioning notwithstanding) (Arter, 2004). However, if we are looking for examples where petitions have gone on to set the political agenda and then make an identifiable difference to public policy decisions, we may be more disappointed. Certainly, the constraints outlined above suggest that petitions are as likely to reach their final destination as sperm in the fallopian tubes. Lynch and Birrell (2001) give examples of their impact, suggesting that 'reactive' petitions supplemented other forms of pressure on an issue. However, it is notable that the examples given – such as petitions against removing provisions on the 'promotion of homosexuality' in schools (section 28/ 2a) and opposing housing-stock transfer in Glasgow (which fed into Scottish Parliament committee inquiries) – were not successful in reversing policy decisions. In other cases – such as free personal care, Hepatitis C compensation, fuel poverty, the Borders Rail Campaign and policy on telecommunications masts – the petitions may have set the ball rolling for parliamentary consideration (Lynch and Birrell, 2001: 12; the Procedures Committee, 2003, also gives the example of community opposition to the spread of sewerage sludge).

Perhaps the most telling example of the practical public policy effect is Carman's (2006) discussion of building regulations regarding hot-water supplies (the aim of the petition was to ensure the widespread use of thermostatic valves after high profile cases of children being scalded). Carman's interview with PPC convener Michael McMahon suggests that the petition was such a success that he and the Presiding Officer arranged for a document marking the occasion to be framed and displayed in the Scottish Parliament. Yet, this reaction also betrays how unusual it is for a petition to have this effect. Further, Carman's discussion suggests that the petition was one of a number of factors in the final decision. His list of other contenders for most successful petitions reinforces the limitations to the process, with the big winners including the introduction of prayers before parliamentary meetings, the guarantee of debates on certain issues, and several examples where the outcome *coincides* with the aim of the petition. The Procedures Committee itself suggests that we should not expect too much from petitions, since their role was limited from the start. They are most effective as a means to set the agenda; raising issues and hoping that they receive enough attention from decision-makers (indeed, Carman suggests that many petitioners feel successful if their topic reaches this stage).

Interest groups and participation

A much more direct form of participation is through interest groups. The hopes, associated with new politics, for an improved pluralist democracy

Box 11.5   Interest groups: the post-devolution experience

- Devolution caused a profound shift of group focus, with many Scottish groups increasing their policy capacity and UK groups increasing the resource of their Scottish arms.
- Groups have a positive image of the Scottish Parliament and Scottish Government and choose to 'hedge their bets' and influence both.
- Both the Scottish Parliament (MSPs and committees) and the Scottish Government (ministers and civil servants) are much easier to access, with fewer resources required by groups to engage and a greater willingness of decision-makers to consult.
- Groups enjoy regular dialogue with MSPs and civil servants.
- The terms of engagement have changed, from the lobbying and complaining which characterized engagement with the Scottish Office, to substantive debate and engagement on policy issues with the Scottish Government.
- Networks have also developed between groups with similar interests – such as the 'gang of 5' business groups (including the CBI and Chambers of Commerce) – and more common ground has been found between a range of economic and social groups around Scottish Government themes such as social inclusion.

See Keating and Stevenson (2001) and Keating (2005) for further details.

referred to widespread consultation between the Scottish Government and a broader range of groups, with less time spent talking to the 'usual suspects' and more with previously excluded groups. Access for groups would be more frequent and of a better quality than in the past; the consultation process would be more open, perhaps with a clearer link between group effort and the end result. But how do we go about assessing the fulfilment of these aims? The most direct way is to talk to a wide range of interest groups and ask them to assess their experiences since devolution (and, if possible, to compare them with pre-1999 consultations). Box 11.5 reports the key findings of research conducted within the first two years of devolution.

It suggests that the experience of interest groups is broadly (although not completely) in line with the hopes associated with new politics. Groups are generally positive about devolution, feel engaged and listened to, and benefit from their proximity to decision-makers. Therefore, devolution has marked a profound and enduring shift in the fortunes of interest groups trying to influence Scottish policy (similar conclusions are also reported by groups in Wales). Interest groups report better relations than they experienced before devolution, and most suggest that their lobbying experiences are superior to those enjoyed at the UK Government level.

However, there are several arguments which may qualify this rosy picture. The first point (made by Jordan and discussed to an extent in Jordan and

Stevenson, 2000) is that since many of the groups interviewed were associated with the devolution movement, they would be very unlikely to report that devolution did not make a difference (in other words, 'they would say that, wouldn't they?'). The second suggests that these new consultation arrangements may be borne out of necessity rather than choice. The Scottish Government suffers from a relative lack of policy capacity in comparison to the UK Government. The legacy of the Scottish Office is a civil service engaged in policy implementation rather than policy formulation. It lacked capacity following devolution and relied heavily on outside interests for information and advice. As Keating (2005a: 106) suggests, this factor combined with a smaller political arena (with closer personal contacts and easier coordination) explains high levels of participation.

Third, *interest-group* devolution may explain why Scottish groups are so enthusiastic about relationships with government. They are comparing their influence now with their lack of influence before devolution (as relatively neglected regional offices), rather than the influence their *UK counterparts* enjoyed (50% of groups lobbying in Scotland fall into this category – see Keating, 2005a: 65). Similarly, independent groups are comparing their access as Scottish groups in devolved territories with their previous UK experience of competition with groups who had more resources and better access to UK decision-makers (22% are Scottish organizations and a further 19% from a Scottish region; the remaining 9% are UK or international organizations with no Scottish office). Devolution may therefore be as much about reducing competition as opening channels of access. Or, groups may find that an issue that was crowded out by other agendas in the UK may receive greater prominence in Scotland according to its policy conditions. This may affect, for example, farming, timber, fishing and meat industries which make a greater contribution to the Scottish economy (although of course the issue of the Scottish Government's influence in these areas is another matter).

Fourth, as Jordan and Stevenson (2000) suggest, comparisons are often based on a skewed idea of group–government relations in the UK. Yet, the barriers to entry have always been low and since devolution we have seen a profound shift in the use of information technology to manage consultations. Consultation lists are large and groups are generally included if they ask. The process on this scale therefore becomes 'cosmetic'; a 'trawling exercise' with low-level civil-service involvement (Grant, 2000). Maloney *et al.* (1994: 32) distinguished between 'peripheral insider' groups (engaged but not influential in the process) with core or specialist insiders who enjoy more frequent and fruitful contact with government. This is relevant to Scotland where groups report better access but, 'claim that it is still too early to tell whether the consultation process offers them any real influence' (Keating and Stevenson, 2001). In more recent interviews, respondents are still reticent on the link between access and influence, suggesting that it is 'easy to speak to the civil service but not to change things'. Often, groups will also report the higher likelihood that civil servants will act as gatekeepers to ministers, particularly if the issue is no longer on the Scottish Government's agenda.

Fifth, we are rarely comparing like-with-like when we study the top level of government in each country. In Scotland the interest-group population is relatively small, allowing senior ministers and civil servants the ability personally to manage policy communities. In England the terrain is vast and the scope of government is divided into more manageable sub-sectors at lower levels of government (or government agencies). It is at this lower level of government that London-based groups are more likely to express satisfaction with their participation.

Sixth, it is the size of the interest-group population in England which exaggerates the appearance of 'top-down' policy-making which excludes many groups. There are fewer 'winners' and more 'losers' to highlight their exclusion or lack of influence. In Scotland, while groups may feel more included there is still a process of winning and losing. In part, this relates to the irony of capacity: although devolution presents the best opportunity to exchange resources for influence, many groups may not have the capacity to exploit it. Much depends on the status of groups before devolution, with independent groups reporting fewer problems compared to devolved arms of UK organizations with insufficient organizational devolution. Some may have one member of staff with no research capacity. So, for example, the biggest winner is often local government (and its associated professional groups) which is relatively well-resourced and a crucial player in the implementation of policy. Or, there are dominant groups within particular policy areas, such as the Educational Institute for Scotland or the British Medical Association (Box 11.6).

Seventh, in Scotland and the UK there is the same logic to regular consultation with the 'usual suspects'. These groups have resources (expertise, representation, advice) valuable to government. In Scotland there is a growing acknowledgement by groups and government on this point. After an initial flurry of activity, groups have become more selective in their approach to consultation responses, while governments are increasingly aware of the greater need to consult those most affected by, and involved in, the implementation of policy. A good example of this process is when some groups talk about pre-consultation, or even in some cases what might be clumsily called pre-pre-consultation! In other words, some groups are contacted before the consultation goes out to the general public. Others are asked to form working groups to advise the Scottish Government on what the consultation should look like. Therefore the consultation may eventually be wide but by the time the questions are asked of the public, many answers have already been provided.

Finally, interviews with such a large number of groups will throw up a range of responses to the same questions. In particular, many groups report fluctuating fortunes according to the agenda of the Scottish Government at any particular time. For example, many business groups were initially

Box 11.6   Pluralism and the usual suspects

Although most groups may report better links with the Scottish Government, the 'usual suspects' may still be consulted most. We can see this in a range of policy areas. In compulsory education, there is less group competition than we find in England. The Educational Institute for Scotland is by far the biggest union with 58,000 members (its closest 'rival', the Scottish Secondary Teachers' Association has 8,000) and head-teacher organizations do not have the status enjoyed in England. This means that the EIS dominates professional representation in pay negotiations since 'seats at the table' are allocated by size. In health, the British Medical Association and Royal College of Nursing are consulted routinely, while the remainder of the health profession struggles for systematic inclusion (via the Allied Health Professions). In issues relating to local government, although individual professions are represented, COSLA is by far the most consulted. In issues related to business, the 'big 5' (Confederation of British Industry, Institute of Directors, Chambers of Commerce, Scottish Financial Enterprise, Scottish Council for Development and Industry) formed a group which excluded the Federation of Small Businesses. In issues related to the environment, Friends of the Earth is realistic about its influence as long as environmental policy shares a department with agriculture. Further, since the drafting of legislation requires expertise, the Law Society of Scotland and Faculty of Advocates are called upon more than most. Yet, it is still appropriate to describe the Scottish system as pluralistic: (a) because no group dominates one policy area to the exclusion of all others; and (b) this large range of elites competing for governmental attention and public policy resources ensures that no group dominates the policy-process as a whole. Of course, this also suggests that this brand of pluralism is not synonymous with equality of access and power. Rather, it is 'elitism's close cousin' (Moran, 2005: 16).

opposed to devolution and it took them some time to develop a meaningful relationship with the Scottish Government. This was particularly the case for groups representing landowners and seen as the 'old guard' with close links to previous Conservative Governments. In contrast, social groups and trade unions already had a good relationship with government following the election of Labour in 1997. These groups were supportive of devolution and were able to build on relationships immediately. There was also a strong social policy agenda immediately following devolution. This meant that social and voluntary groups were more likely to seek and gain access. Then, from 2003–07, there was a significant shift of focus to the importance of the economy perhaps at the expense of social issues. Labour's punitive focus on crime also had the potential to undermine, or at least detract attention from, the initial focus on social inclusion (for example, homelessness groups worried that the focus on anti-social behaviour undermined the security of housing tenancies). As a result, business groups felt more influential in this second term and some social groups felt marginalized following the shift.

Conclusion

The hopes associated with new politics relate to a number of concepts relevant to the study of democracy, and this chapter shows that the fulfilment of these aims has varied.

Representative democracy – devolution solved the 'democratic deficit' in which the Scottish population voted for one party but got another. There is now a greater sense in Scotland of a link between electoral response and governmental responsiveness (particularly following the election result in 2007 which resulted in minority government rather than a coalition with a larger majority). However, the SCC focus on better forms of democracy may have contributed to a reduced faith in indirect representation.

Microcosmic representation – the main success of devolution has been a significant gain in the representation of women within the Scottish Parliament. There were also some signs of a move away from a career path from local to national government and lower levels of private education than in the UK. However, as a whole, MSPs are just as likely as MPs to be white, middle-aged, middle-class, and university educated with a professional background.

Deliberative democracy – the Scottish Civic Forum was the main plank of attempts to develop new means to determine collective outcomes (by extensive arguments offered by and to participants affected by policy decisions). However, the project struggled to gain popular support and folded after six years following a loss of funding.

Participative democracy – the public petitions process was further developed as a means for a limited form of direct democracy which reflected Scotland's 'collective and community traditions'. It is also held in high regard by MSPs and participants are generally satisfied with their experience. However, there are few examples of petitions which go on to have a direct policy impact. Rather, the aim of petitions is to set the agenda and hope that other organizations respond to the issues.

Pluralist democracy – perhaps the most direct route to decision-makers is by lobbying through an interest group, particularly since there is some evidence that the Scottish Government does not just consult with the 'usual suspects'. Most groups interviewed are satisfied with the consultation process, feel that decision-makers are accessible and that their opinions are listened to. However, the extent to which this results from a different culture rather than necessity or capacity is debatable. There is also mixed evidence regarding the extent to which the Scottish process differs from the UK.

The evidence suggests that the much criticized Westminster style of democracy should not be disregarded as an enduring influence. The architects of devolution emphasized a wide range of new forms of democracy, but from a starting point which is fairly traditional. Perhaps the image conjured up is a journey from London to the Scandinavian or Nordic consensual democracies, but by bus rather than plane. Scotland's democratic processes still rest on the centrality of the Scottish Government to public policy, while the primary role of the Scottish Parliament is to scrutinize government rather than act as a hub for new types of participation. Grander visions of the potential impact of new democratic processes have not been realized.

But what are we to make of this evidence? Mitchell suggests that, 'measured in terms of political power', participatory initiatives associated with the Scottish parliament 'appear more symbolic than effective' (2004: 39). This is difficult to dispute since, overall, the new mechanisms to ensure democracy in Scotland have had a marginal effect. Yet, a marginal effect can also be a significant effect. In other words, given that the power of the 'centre' is strong in almost every country, it would be unfair to hold Scotland up to a higher standard than anywhere else.

Further reading

On democracy in the UK see Weir and Beetham (1988); for arguments in favour of deliberative democracy see Cooke (2000); for a classic work on representative democracy see Schumpeter (1943); for a contemporary discussion of representative democracy in the UK see Judge (1999); and for details of representation in Scotland post-devolution see Bennie *et al.* (2001), Shephard *et al.* (2001) and Keating and Cairney (2006). For defining works on pluralist democracy see Dahl (1961), (1971) and (1989). On participation, the defining UK empirical study is Parry *et al.* (1992). For details on the Scottish Civic Forum and civic democracy see Lindsay (2000, 2002), McTernan (2000), Paterson (2000a) and Scottish Civic Forum (2001). For details on the Petitions Committee see Cavanagh *et al.* (2000), Lynch and Birrell (2001) and Carman (2006).

Online sources

The (now defunct) Scottish Civic Forum Homepage   http://www.civicforum.org.uk/
Convention of Scottish Local Authorities   http://www.cosla.gov.uk
Friends of the Earth Scotland   http://www.foe-scotland.org.uk
Stonewall Scotland   http://www.stonewallvote.org.uk/scotintro.htm
Scottish Council for Development and Industry   http://www.scdi.org.uk
Charter 88 Scotland Events   http://www.activist.org.uk/charter88/scotland/events.html
Scottish Trade Union Congress   http://www.stuc.demon.co.uk
CND Scotland   http://dspace.dial.pipex.com/cndscot
CBI Scotland   http://www.cbi.org.uk/scotland
Scottish Council for Voluntary Organizations   http://www.scvo.org.uk

Chapter 12

Conclusion

Studying Scottish politics

Anyone studying Scottish Politics for the first time could be forgiven for thinking that: (a) devolution began in 1999 and (b) that the cost overruns and delays in building the Scottish Parliament were the most important issue. This is the picture painted by a Scottish media 'discovering' the importance of Scottish political institutions and not liking what it sees. In part, much of this initial discontent can be explained by the period of transition, with the political and administrative classes taking time to adjust to the institutional changes taking place. During this period the new Scottish Parliament was plagued with bad news stories, with politicians struggling to demonstrate the added value of devolution and the spiralling cost of the building (from £40 million to over £430 million when it was officially opened in 2004) itself taking centre-stage. However, devolution has gradually matured to become a settled part of the UK's constitutional landscape. A majority of the Scottish electorate have consistently indicated a preference for a self-governing Scotland in the UK, with the independence option being favoured by only 28–35 per cent of the Scottish population since 1999 (see Table 12.1).

Table 12.1 *Recent trends in Scottish constitutional preferences*

	May 1997 (%)	*Sept 1997 (%)*	*1999 (%)*	*2001 (%)*	*2003 (%)*	*2005 (%)*
Scotland should:						
Be independent, separate from UK and EU or separate from UK but part of EU	28	37	28	27	26	35
Remain part of UK with its own elected Parliament	54	41	58	60	55	44
Remain part of the UK without an elected Parliament	18	17	10	9	13	14

Sources: Scottish Election Study 1997, Scottish Referendum Study 1997, Scottish Social Attitudes Survey various years.

There is, however, little evidence that the Scottish electorate's preference will evolve into independence. There is no sign that devolution has impacted in any significant manner on the Scottish electorate's future constitutional preference.

But how should we study these new political arrangements? This book has suggested that a focus on the broad parameters, institutions and the historical legacy of Scottish politics is a useful starting point, and it has also compared Scottish and UK politics in great detail. The UK remains a useful reference point – particularly due to the inextricable linkages in the union but also the points of departure that exist and have been accentuated since 1999. We have reflected on the expectations engendered by the campaigns for home rule pre-devolution, and this perhaps represents a good case study of the role of idealism in political change. There were some rather naïve expectations that, when set against the contemporary reality of Scottish politics, look hopelessly unrealistic. On the other hand, the ideas associated with new politics set the tone for much of the 'honeymoon period' of Scottish politics and are still referred to in parliamentary debates. We have also attempted to broaden our discussion of Scottish politics by placing it in a wider comparative dimension and assessing the relevance of concepts developed within the political science literature.

Not least of these is the emphasis in the literature that political behaviour often takes place outside the traditional executive, legislature and administrative institutions of government. The story of Scottish politics should not be limited to Scotland's governing institutions. Whilst the decision-making processes which take place within these institutions is important, collective deliberation and political debate takes place at many different levels and in many different contexts. Understanding power relationships within and between these different levels is a key focus for any student of Scottish politics, and a broad understanding of who (or what) influences the agenda of Scottish politics is crucial to an understanding of power in Scotland. As Schattschneider (1960) suggests, politics is about the 'mobilization of bias', or making sure that attention and resources are devoted to one issue and not another. The basic purpose of any organization involved in politics is to bias the political system in its favour. A study of power therefore involves identifying the interests of those engaged in Scottish politics when they present an ideology or principles as the basis for their motivation.

This is true of institutions at all levels such as community pressure groups, local authorities, quangos, political parties, interest groups, the civil service, the UK Government, the EU and global multi-national companies. It is also true of the media in Scotland which can be partisan in its coverage even when purporting to be neutral. The study of politics involves an appreciation of agenda-setting processes and identifying those groups (and issues) which are *excluded* from politics as a result of this mobilization of bias. This is particularly relevant to a form of devolution which highlighted the hitherto exclusion of social groups on the basis of gender, race, class and geography.

Our starting point was an appreciation of the historical context within which Scottish politics takes place. An account of Scottish politics which concentrates exclusively on contemporary political practice would be misleading and inaccurate. It would be like telling the story of British politics without appeal to constitutional conventions, institutional history and historical legacy of the UK State. In other words, the birth of the Scottish Parliament did not follow an 'immaculate conception'.

However, the 'past' does not simply survive – it requires institutions that will reflect and reproduce it. So which aspects of the past have the most relevance today? First, the differences established since the union with England in 1707 still remain in the Scottish legal system, religion, education and local government organization. Second, the responsibilities of the Scottish Parliament were inherited from the administrative devolution arrangements of the past, and these powers developed incrementally following the decision to establish the Scottish Office. The Scottish Office began as a small patchwork of different agencies, but continued to grow in line with the expansion of the UK state in the twentieth century. Devolution as a policy evolved as much from a conservative rather than radical impulse – it was built on, and designed to preserve, the pre-existing landscape of public institutions in Scotland. The non-reserved functions of the Scottish Parliament almost directly mirror the responsibilities of the Scottish Office pre-devolution. Thus, although the devolution process created an increased potential for political and policy diversity, it was built on the foundations of existing structures.

Third, revisiting this period of Scottish politics is important in understanding the growing concern about a democratic deficit despite a system of free and fair elections in the UK. This led to the articulation of alternative sources of democracy: participatory democracy in which the Scottish population would seek to influence decisions made in Scotland directly rather than through a ballot box which seemed so remote; pluralist democracy, in which interest and social groups would seek to counter policies 'unsuitable' for Scotland at all levels of implementation; and deliberative democracy, in which a separate level of debate about the direction of UK policies implemented in Scotland could take place.

Fourth, the pre-devolution experience is valuable because it provides us with evidence about the experience of qualified autonomy. The question of whether Scotland has a political system *now* depends not only on the existence of UK decision-making powers, but the likelihood that these will be *exercised* to undermine decisions taken in Scotland. Constitutionally Westminster could use its powers to dissolve the Scottish Parliament and the UK Government could interfere in policy areas deemed to be completely devolved. However, the Scottish Parliament and Government already enjoy a legitimacy and authority which makes this politically unrealistic.

However, since there is such a wide range of matters in which reserved and devolved issues intersect (including when devolved areas are Europeanized), the issue of UK power in Scottish affairs remains. Yet, the experience of long periods of autonomy caused by neglect, or long periods of low UK interest in Scottish matters (cf Bulpitt, 1983), suggests that UK dominance in entangled responsibilities is by no means inevitable.

Finally, Paterson (1994) has long encouraged us to consider Scotland's relatively small size and the place in the world of independent states of a similar size. This is still relevant to discussions of European influence in which we may be comparing a Hobson's choice between uncertain influence as part of a big player in the EU and a more certain but smaller influence as an independent member.

Is there a Scottish political system now?

The force within Scotland to resist UK assimilation is strongly linked to feelings of Scottishness which have existed for centuries. Indeed, it is this combination of distinctly Scottish interests and the wide range of institutions within which to articulate them, which prompted so much debate about the existence of a Scottish political system.

Kellas' argument contained in four editions of *The Scottish Political System* challenged the conventional wisdom of UK politics by suggesting that the distinctiveness of Scottish politics was such that it merited the label 'political system'. Only this term did, 'justice to the scale and nature of the phenomena found in Scottish politics' (1989: 4). Kellas highlighted factors such as the self-containment of many policy areas in Scotland and the indigenous bureaucratic culture. Scotland's political institutions were distinctive within a union rather than unitary state, and this difference allowed a level of policy autonomy for Scotland to go its own way. Distinct policy communities in areas such as education and health, combined with an enabling funding system, increased the scope for Scottish solutions to Scottish problems. Finally, and perhaps most importantly for current debates, he suggested that the political system would be made complete with the establishment of a separate legislature (1984: 162).

Of course, the counter-argument is that the UK state effectively controlled this level of discretion – the UK Treasury determined the level of funding that Scotland enjoyed and the ultimate decisions resided in the UK Cabinet in London rather than the Scottish Office in Edinburgh. Indeed, the experience of Thatcherism suggests that previously assumed levels of autonomy were often overturned by determined Conservative ministers.

Yet, the story does not end there because a significant literature still challenged the myth of the British unitary state (Mitchell, 1990a, 1996b; Midwinter *et al.*, 1991; McCrone, 1992; Paterson, 1994; Brown *et al.*, 1998). Each highlighted, in different ways, how a sense of Scottishness permeated all of Scotland's key political institutions. For example, to McCrone (1992) the neo-nationalist agenda of Scottish politics in the 1980s and 1990s was not associated with the traditional 'identity garments' of nationalism (language, religion, ethnic culture etc.) but post-material values such as autonomy and accountability. For Keating and Midwinter (1984) and Midwinter *et al.* (1991) while there was no political system, they witnessed a series of complex policy networks, linking Scottish actors to one another and to non-Scottish networks.

Further, and most importantly for current debates, there was agreement in the literature that the Conservative Government's handling of territorial management in the 1980s and 1990s pushed the constitutional issue to the forefront of Scotland's political agenda. In other words, there was not a widespread belief in the literature that a Scottish political system existed. However, there was more agreement that a challenge to the political arrangements negotiated for Scotland would produce a significant political response based on the importance of Scottish national identity. In turn, this response was addressed by devolution (although there is still a sense of 'unfinished business').

But did devolution and the establishment of a separation legislature make the political system as complete as Kellas suggests? In terms of Almond and Coleman's (1960) three categories – of recruitment, articulation and aggregation – outlined in the introduction, the Scottish dimension of each has undoubtedly grown post-devolution. However, in each case the transformation is not complete:

- Although the Scottish Parliament provides a new career path for elected representatives, this competes with paths towards the UK and European Parliaments. Similarly, those choosing a career in public administration in Scotland may work for an institution whose accountability chain runs upward to Edinburgh or London.
- Scotland now enjoys its own 'interest articulation' processes such as voting, while parties now seek to project themselves as the party most concerned with Scotland's national interest. However, the evidence from Scottish and UK elections suggests that most voters do not know (or care) who is responsible for what.
- There has also been a profound shift in 'interest aggregation' processes such as the lobbying by groups to government. Interest groups have increasingly focused their attention on Edinburgh and the nature of post-devolution consultation on policy issues contrasts markedly with the defensive form of lobbying by many during the Conservative years. However, the evidence also suggests that groups maintain links at Scottish, UK and European levels.

In other words, the evidence of this book confirms that there is much more substance to the Scottish political process since devolution. There are undoubtedly a multitude of political interactions taking place in Scotland that did not take place before 1999; however, the irony of multi-level governance caused by the diffusion of power both upwards and downwards is that the term 'political system' has diminishing relevance at this level. Therefore, on the one hand, devolution has undoubtedly enhanced Scottish legislative and governing authority. The 'idea' of Scotland in a broad cultural sense has transformed institutions, with the Scottish Parliament giving physical and democratic expression to this idea; and its existence lends greater legitimacy to the 'authoritative allocation of values' in Scotland (Easton, 1965). Key questions of Scottish politics have been decided increasingly at the Scottish level and the Scottish Government has gradually transformed from a government department applying UK policy, to a government in its own right with its own policy and leadership capacity (Keating 2005a: 23).

On the other hand, 'power devolved is power retained'. Scotland continues to be dependent on **fiscal transfers** from the UK Treasury, while decisions on the major issues of the state such as macro-economic policy, taxation, foreign, defence and national security policy are made elsewhere. The Scottish Parliament is legally subordinate to a UK Parliament in the process of ceding authority to the EU, with the Europeanization of policy and globalisation of economies fostering a level of interdependence that transcends nations and regions. In turn, academic debate has perhaps moved on, from the examination of Scottish autonomy within the UK, to the influence of Scottish political institutions in a wider process of multi-level governance.

Fiscal transfers:
Money transferred
from the UK Treasury
to the Scottish
Parliament.

New politics: aspirations not realized?

Despite the legacies of the past, the key phrase for the architects of devolution was 'new politics' in which a wide range of problems identified in the Westminster system of government would be overcome. A combination of the new Parliament and the proportional electoral system would result in fairer representation, cross party coalition politics, power sharing rather than executive dominance, a strong role for committees and enhanced scrutiny of Scotland's executive branch of government. It is not only representative democracy which would be enhanced. Power-sharing would extend to closer links between state and civil society through parliament, with a focus on the right to petition parliament (participatory democracy), the committee role to ensure that the Government consults widely (pluralist democracy) and a civic forum to introduce a wider range of voices in detailed pre-legislative debates (deliberative democracy). However, as a number of our chapters demonstrate, not all of these aspirations have been realized, which is not surprising given the evidence about the nature of power and politics previously gathered in the political science literature (regarding the role of parties, the primacy of the 'centre', the logic of consultation with the 'usual suspects' and the limits to wider participation) in the UK and beyond.

In the case of political parties, we may reasonably assume that criticisms relate to the worst excesses of partisanship, in which political posturing becomes more important than reasoned debate. However, as Chapter 3 notes, this neglects the vital functions parties perform in Scottish politics. Parties are a key link in the accountability chain between government and citizen, and since devolution each has enjoyed enhanced autonomy to perform this role more effectively.

Scottish parties also became closer to 'the people' in the post-devolution period, although this is heavily qualified by the experience of Labour from 1999–2007. Although Scottish Labour effectively controlled its own destiny, its UK leadership still enjoyed considerable power and this reduced the 'liberating potential of devolution' (Keating, 2005a: 218). Many 'constitutional conservatives' within the UK Labour Party appear to have viewed devolution as an 'event' rather than a process (Bradbury and Mitchell, 2005). Therefore, only since 2007 and the election of the minority SNP Government has the devolution genie been well and truly let out of the bottle.

Devolution has certainly resulted in a more fluid, dynamic and competitive party system, and this has been fuelled by new voting systems combined with the changing behaviour of the Scottish electorate. Scottish voters are increasingly 'non-aligned', with traditional party cleavages such as class and religion decreasing in salience. As Mitchell (2005: 25) argues, Scotland now possesses:

> A peripheral identity combined with a class identity, two of the societal cleavages in electoral politics in Europe in the modern age identified by Lipset and Rokkan (1967), to create an effective political force for political autonomy.

However, this autonomy combined with increased party competition has not yet produced a plethora of new or innovative ideas. The parameters of the Scottish party political agenda have actually narrowed.

This is despite the post-devolution agenda emphasizing the greater democratization of public life in Scotland. The Home-Rule campaigners of the 1990s, encountering the democratic deficit in an era of (perceived) widespread disillusion with politicians and the need to 'sell' devolution, *over*sold the potential of these new forms of democracy. This resulted in unrealistic expectations about the prospect of the diffusion of power from the government to the 'people'.

The evidence on the subject of democratic change is mixed. One of the most immediate successes was the increase in gender-based political representation. However, there was relative inattention to other sources of exclusion such as race, disability and age. In the field of participatory and deliberative democracy the experience of the now disbanded Scottish Civic Forum must be classified as a failure, with low levels of participation and government commitment to the concept. In contrast the public petitions process tends to be held in high regard with individuals indicating satisfaction with their experience. Many have successfully set the agenda, prompting the Government or parliamentary committees to take the issue further. However, few get beyond this stage and the happiest participants are perhaps those with the lowest expectations – of raising an issue and having their 'voice heard'.

Finally, the experience of pluralist democracy is that interest groups have not only shifted their lobbying activity to the devolved institutions, but enjoyed regular dialogue, substantive debate and engagement with MSPs and civil servants. However, there is no conclusive evidence to suggest that the form of pluralist democracy offered by the Scottish Government is superior to that of the UK government. Both recognize the 'logic of consultation' with affected interests, while the closer links between groups and government in Scotland may recognize its relative lack of policy capacity, particularly in the early years when civil servants were adapting to their new roles.

Although the Scottish Parliament has acted as a hub for new forms of democracy, it should be remembered that it is the Government where most key decisions are taken. The Parliament's primary role remains as a scrutinizer of the executive's legislation and policy-making activity. It has enhanced the scrutiny and accountability of the public sector in Scotland (McGarvey 2008: 40). It has also given collective expression to Scottish popular sovereignty and granted legitimacy to the Government though these activities (Mitchell, 2005: 33; Judge, 1993).

However, the evidence suggests that the home-rule campaigners' aspirations of an outward-looking Parliament have only been partially fulfilled; the Parliament is essentially an enhanced version of the Westminster model. The CSG recognized the need for the Government to govern and its plans for committee powers may be seen as an improvement on Parliament's traditional scrutiny role rather than the pursuit of an innovative or new relationship. Indeed, the structure and operation of the Scottish Parliament perhaps reflects what Westminster would look like today if it wasn't saddled with an inheritance of conventions and idiosyncratic procedures. Members have greater legislative power and committees are genuinely powerful and can be pivotal. In comparison to other Western European Parliaments it is a powerful institution.

Yet, its power compared to the Scottish *Government* is much less significant. Although it can legislate, the power of MSPs and committees is undermined by resources constraints, inadequate support, legislative workloads and member turnover (and inexperience). Although committees consider the principles of legislation before examining detailed amendments, there is little evidence to show that this process profoundly affects the final result.

The Scottish Government

The Scottish Government is Scotland's more powerful political institution. It has access to the civil-service machine and the resources necessary to consult with groups and to research, initiate, draft, redraft, monitor and evaluate bills. Minority government is likely to increase the scope for a more assertive Parliament and a government more sensitive to parliamentary demands. However, the opposition parties may lack sufficient resources to monitor what the Scottish Government does *and* provide a well-thought-out alternative.

Therefore, despite the expectation surrounding new forms of democracy, Scotland's political system still has a powerful executive at the centre. However, it is easy to exaggerate its power if we treat it as a coherent organization with a powerful figurehead (for example, the First Minister or the 'core executive') rather than a large and often unwieldy set of organizations with weak central control. We may also exaggerate its role if we focus on the 'most devolved' areas, rather than those in which the Government must negotiate with the UK or follow the EU when formulating policy.

The relatively small size of the Government's responsibilities, geographical scope and Cabinet may suggest that coordination and control from the 'centre' is easier. Although a 'presidential' style of politics may not be achievable in the UK (Bevir and Rhodes, 2006), perhaps it is more likely in Scotland. Yet, a range of factors undermine this assumption. The norm will be coalition or minority government. The governing party will always be reliant on others. Moreover, if the experience of Labour 1999–2007 is indicative, problems of central control will be compounded by internal party in-fighting. There also remains a weak centre, with the First and Finance Ministers lacking the resources held within the UK Cabinet Office and the Treasury. This suggests that most 'day-to-day' power resides within a range of individual departments and their ministers. Further, the First Minster may have no *desire* to centralize, and the early strategy of Alex Salmond reflects a greater desire to cement Scotland's position on the world stage.

A more concrete attempt towards coherence came with the SNP's 2007 creation of a smaller cabinet (to take the lead on efficiency savings) and a finance department with a much more significant capacity to oversee cross-cutting issues. Yet, as in the Labour years, we can see more convincing explanations for 'joined-up government' arrangements in straightforward politics (the position of 'minister for everything' reflects the status of ministers such as Wendy Alexander and John Swinney rather than the logic of organization). It should also be noted that the practice of 'ministers without ministries' was *inherited* from the old Scottish Office days in which there were far fewer ministers.

Central ministerial control may also be qualified by its dependence on the civil service, which is often portrayed similarly as a single actor rather than a collection of departments or individuals. In this case, the civil service was initially described as a force of inertia, reflecting its traditional role as a constant during periods of alternating government, or its inclusion within the unified UK Home civil service. Yet, a more convincing explanation for the role of the civil service comes from its *inability* rather than *unwillingness* to adapt quickly enough to changing political circumstances. Devolution has transformed the executive branch of government in Scotland from a relatively quiet backwater of routine administration and parochial Scottish politics to the focal point for the development, legislation and implementation of policy. A period of learning on the job was therefore necessary. New relationships (with many more ministers and a Scottish Parliament now on its doorstep) and policy capacity (to research and develop rather than just implement) took time to develop. Civil servants also came to rely much more on interest groups, policy experts and local authorities. Therefore, this paints a picture of power diffusion rather than centralization.

Finally, the lack of central control may reflect the sheer complexity of governance arrangements in Scotland today. Public policies in Scotland are implemented by an eclectic mix of different types of institutions, agencies and public bodies. Leading and co-ordinating these new networks of public-service provision is not easy even in a relatively small state. Further, in the case of local government, the Government faces competition over levels of legitimacy granted by elections and local circumstances, while local authorities can also draw on their own levels of finance, professional expertise and close relations with key interest groups. The Scottish Government is 'in charge' of these bodies, but also dependent on their cooperation for policy success. The notion that the Government can simply use its authority to effect change neglects the complex, multi-layered nature of public policy processes.

The Scottish Government may be the biggest player in Scotland, but its power is exaggerated if we overstate its coherence and neglect the amount of dependency on other organizations in the governance process.

The Scottish Government in the wider world

Although the evidence suggests that the Scottish Government is the key player *within Scotland*, this does not mean that it is necessarily the biggest player in *Scottish politics*. A focus on multi-level governance reveals not only interdependence during the implementation of policy, but also in the formulation of policy when devolved areas intersect with reserved and Europeanized aspects of policy. There is no clear-cut division between reserved and devolved powers, while in areas such as environmental and agricultural policy, Europeanization maintains a formal role for the UK (as the Member State) in Scottish affairs.

The experience from 1999–2007 suggests that intergovernmental relations were fairly smooth and based on the rejection of formal types of contact such as the Joint Ministerial Councils. Rather, civil servants maintained informal channels, while Labour ministers shared information and took soundings via the party route. These are positive reasons for a lack of formal contact since the relationship suits both parties, while an increasingly minor UK interest in Scotland may lead to further examples of executive devolution in which national policies are left for Scottish interests to adapt to suit. However, there were also negative reasons. The rejection of regular formal contacts reflected Whitehall's disengagement from devolution, with ministers and civil servants 'forgetting' to consult with Scottish interests on matters which affected them directly. The breakdown in communications leaves the Scottish Government unable to engage in EU negotiations early enough to make a difference and ensure a relatively smooth process of implementation further down the line.

The early experience of the SNP administration is a push towards more formal contacts between civil servants (i.e. operating *as if* the services were separate), more regular formal meetings between UK and devolved ministers, and more direct contacts between the Scottish Government and European institutions, with Salmond keen to press the case for Scotland to 'take the lead' on issues with a particularly Scottish angle (such as fishing quota negotiations). However, this is not a radical break from the past and one need not automatically associate formality with conflict (particularly since the informal route was initially exploited by the SNP to raise issues in public that were normally kept behind closed doors). Indeed, nationalist parties have governed in Quebec, Catalonia and the Basque Country without secession automatically reaching the top of the agenda.

Policy change, convergence and divergence

Taken as a whole, the evidence points to as many good reasons to expect policy convergence as divergence. New politics therefore referred to new political *processes* rather than new *policies*. In 1981 Ross suggested that, 'Scottish administration is distinguished from its English equivalent more by how it does things than by what it does' – and this emphasis has continued for much of the first decade of devolution. The desire for policy divergence may not reflect a desire for policy *change*. As noted, the driver for devolution was, in part, a desire to stay the same, in contrast to the type of policy innovation witnessed during the Thatcher period (and continued under Blair). The social democratic consensus in Scotland may have stifled the type of policy innovation apparent in ideologically competitive environments.

There are also a range of factors for divergence which are heavily qualified. The intergovernmental financial relationship allows spending autonomy but within the context of financial constraints and inherited commitments. Public-sector professionals may have more of a role in Scotland, but in many cases they present part of a UK-wide professional consensus. The SNP may strive for difference but also settle for the appearance of governing competence.

This is not to say that that policy change was not significant following devolution. Rather, we did not witness the type of radical change associated with, say, Central and Eastern European countries making a break from the Soviet Union. A comparison of Scottish and UK legislative and policy divergence since 1999 highlights that the 'break' from the UK was more muted, in reflection of broadly similar attitudes, shared information, policy learning and continued interdependence (furthered by EU integration).

Each example of clear divergence can also be heavily qualified: the smoking ban was followed by England (in the end, suggesting policy *change* rather than divergence); the policy on student fees was limited by a reserved collection system, and free care for older people demonstrated well the 'implementation gap'. Responses to this policy from above (the Treasury) and below (local authorities) undermined the level of funding going directly to older people and towards their care services.

Yet, a longer term analysis may suggest that major policy change results from the day-to-day decision-making processes of those delivering policy. Existing differences or decisions to diverge may have a 'butterfly effect' – these differences multiply since diverging policies throw up different problems which have to be addressed in a different way. Eventually, the frames of reference change profoundly in each country, with contact and policy learning between Scotland and England diminishing because their political systems seem so different that there is little value in exchanging policy experiences. Indeed, the more complex or removed from central control these delivery systems are, then the greater potential for this type of day-to-day divergence. This suggests that a focus on legislation and flagship policies alone may (paradoxically) exaggerate *and* underestimate levels of policy divergence. In either case, a longer time period is required to analyse policy change and a complete picture cannot be painted with reference only to processes taking place at the 'top'.

Nor can it be painted with reference only to contemporary political processes. *The* most important factor in Scottish politics – how Scotland gets its money now and how much it will receive in the future – was determined decades before devolution and remains unscathed to this day. Therefore, the Barnett formula is the best advert for going beyond the analysis of contemporary and visible decision-making in Scottish politics. In essence the yearly transfer of the Scottish block grant from the Treasury (and Scotland's almost exclusive financial dependence on it) is an institutional device that implants the legacy of the previous year's expenditure decisions as the base from which Scottish politics operates year-on-year. The Barnett formula is used to calculate the incremental adjustment to this base. Its continued utilization is reflective of the historical conservatism in the Scottish-UK intergovernmental financial relationship. The maintenance of Barnett appears to demonstrate a level of Scottish power, since its historically determined financial advantage is maintained (with few signs of a 'squeeze') and it enjoys the autonomy to direct its own spend.

It also gives vivid expression to the incremental nature of policy-making. Politicians inherit before they choose (Rose 1991), and Scottish politics takes place in the context of the historical legacy of previous commitments. The policy paths in many areas, whilst not pre-ordained, are pretty restrictive when the weight of expenditure commitments, the well documented tendencies of government bureaucracies to favour existing policies and resist innovation, and interest-group pressure are considered. For the analyst of Scottish politics the focus should therefore be on identifying the economic, social and political factors which help explain the gradual modification of the historical legacy. Scottish politics tends to be an incremental process.

Power and politics in Scotland

Our attempts to pin down the most powerful actors within Scottish Politics bring us full circle, to consider the role of agenda-setting and preference-shaping (see Box 1.1, p. 2). Our experience suggests that power is a shifting phenomenon and its nature is determined by the scope and direction of our analysis. Depending on where we look, power is both diffuse and concentrated, pluralist and elitist, explicit and implicit. Examples include:

- The Scottish Government – our analysis of new forms of democracy and the new role of the Scottish Parliament suggest that power is concentrated within the Government. Yet, ministers rely on the civil service; civil servants rely on interest groups; and both rely on a wide and diffuse range of organizations to organize and deliver policy.
- Scotland and the UK – Scotland is the junior partner and the ultimate decisions on the fate of Scottish politics reside elsewhere. Yet, the day-to-day politics are decided within Scotland, with the UK Government generally taking a back seat in the 'most devolved areas'. It is true that the UK 'elephant in the room' remains. Virtually every major Scottish political institution is dwarfed by its UK equivalent. Compare and contrast the prestige, finance and political resources of the office of the First Minister to that of the Prime Minister, the Scottish Government to the UK Government, the civil service in Edinburgh to that in Whitehall, Scottish Labour Party to the UK Labour Party. Further, each UK equivalent can *potentially* intervene in its Scottish equivalent. However, as Bulpitt notes, 'it is a mistake to equate potential power with actual power' (1983: 29–30) and devolution has undoubtedly enhanced the scope for Scottish policy autonomy.
- Knowledge is power – in the modern environment of disclosure, new information and communication technologies, a wide and varied news

media and freedom of information it has become more difficult for any government to control information flows and manage the political agenda. For example, it is difficult to imagine the Scottish Government following the example of the UK Government not to disseminate a Department of Health and Social Security Report which highlighted inequalities in health care (Black Report, 1980), and there is some evidence to suggest a greater sympathy towards freedom of information. This trend has been accelerated by the SNP (perhaps to a large extent for party political reasons) which was keen in 2007 to highlight the suppression of politically sensitive information by the UK in the past (for example, UK civil service research in the 1970s which highlighted the viability of independence) and the Scottish Government in the present (for example, by publishing the Howat report on public sector reform).

Therefore, any discussion of power and politics in Scotland must acknowledge the structural and institutional context in which politics takes place. Scottish political actors make decisions and choices, responding to external pressures, but with political outcomes not merely dictated by pressures. A key theme of this book has been that Scottish politics today, and the environment which underpins it, reflect the interaction of conscious political choices with unanticipated events and longer-term political, social and economic processes. Events ('dear boy, events') and the reaction to those events may be as useful to explain the developments in Scottish politics as the structures put in place by the architects of devolution.

The constitutional question

Devolution marked a response by the UK state to the prospect of territorial separation which was successful in the short term. At the top of Scotland's agenda, the language of nationalism was replaced by the language of new politics and making devolution work. Yet, the Scottish constitutional debate still remains and, contrary to former Labour Shadow Scottish Secretary, George Robertson's prediction, nationalism has not been killed 'stone dead' by devolution. Indeed, the election of the SNP in 2007 election has reinvigorated a sense of Scottish nationalism and unfinished business. The current devolution settlement no longer appears (in the late John Smith's oft-cited phrase) 'the settled will of the Scottish people'. Instead, the SNP Scottish Government has instigated a 'national conversation' on Scotland's constitutional future (see Box 12.1 and Scottish Executive, 2007d).

A notable feature of the 2007 election campaign was that the terms of the constitutional debate changed. The message from the unionist political parties was no longer the uniform, 'Scotland can't afford independence and it would be a disaster'. Only the Scottish Labour Party carried on with this line, with

Box 12.1   The SNP's 'national conversation'

After its election in 2007, the SNP sought to ignite a public debate on Scotland's constitutional future. The new Government outlined three options (although the SNP is clear on which it prefers):

- Retention of the devolution scheme as set out in the Scotland Act 1998.
- Redesigning devolution by redrawing the boundaries of devolved and reserved powers.
- Independence.

However, the fate of this debate depends to a large extent on two factors. The first is the new pragmatic attitude of the SNP Government, keen to reinforce its image of governing competence by engaging with its new powers and working within both the constraints of a devolution settlement and the need to work with other parties in Parliament. This is reflected in its first legislative programme and its 'first 100 days' commitments which were revised to reflect its minority government status (see Cairney, 2007c, for a full review). The second factor is the stance of the other political parties towards an independence agenda, which has shifted since the 2007 election campaign.

both the Liberal Democrats and Conservatives more willing than previously to acknowledge that Scotland *could* be a vibrant independent nation. The majority of Members of the Scottish Parliament elected at the 2007 Scottish Parliamentary elections stood on manifestoes advocating further devolution (Scottish Executive, 2007d: para 6.2). However, Labour, the Conservatives and the Liberal Democrats have all amended their rhetoric since the election of the SNP. All three are in a sense united by unionism – while they may favour an extension of the Parliament's powers, they are also reluctant to engage in a debate initiated by the SNP and geared towards (in their view) the independence agenda rather than a broader discussion of the success of devolution so far. The parliamentary arithmetic in 2007 was also with these parties in this issue.

Therefore, the 'national conversation' perhaps resembles a hybrid of a green and white paper. In other words, the SNP is clear on its aims, but also open to public debate about how far it can go in the current climate. The long-term aim of independence has perhaps been replaced by the short term obstacle not of persuading the public to vote for independence in a 2010 referendum (its stated preference), but persuading the public to persuade the other parties to hold one!

As political scientists we should perhaps be wary of further conjecture about Scotland's constitutional future. However a few final points which tie in with themes of the book are worth noting.

First, at a practical level the only mechanism for amending the constitution in Scotland is a new Act of the Westminster Parliament (or an amendment to the 1998 Scotland Act). Even if a consensus of Scottish public opinion, political parties, civic institutions, the Parliament and Government all supported the idea of more powers for the Scottish Parliament they will still require the compliance of the Westminster Parliament. Thus if there is to be further constitutional reform (most likely to be in the direction of increasingly levels of autonomy for Scotland) then the mechanics of intergovernmental relations are likely to be utilized. The clearer the direction given by 'the people' (for example, through a referendum) then the greater resources the Scottish Government has in these negotiations.

Second, the springboard for change need not necessarily emerge from Scotland. The Barnett formula and the West Lothian Question continue to appear sporadically on the UK political agenda. To those that raise them –most commonly English MPs and the UK leadership of the Conservative Party – the 'English Question' (see Box 12.2) remains unresolved, with independence for Scotland no longer an option rejected out of hand. This is particularly significant during the premiership of a Scot elected in Scotland.

Plurinational states: States characterized by the presence of more than one national group within the their borders

Third, if independence was to take place it may not be in the 'big bang' manner some of its opponents or advocates envisage. New forms of shared and divided sovereignty are emerging in other **plurinational states** (Keating, 2004a: 331). Enhanced self government is more likely to be a gradual process with fiscal,

---

Box 12.2 The English question

The 'English Question' refers to an examination of England's uncertain place within the Union following devolution. It is rising frequently to the top of the UK agenda as more and more English MPs refer to the one-sided and 'unfair' nature of constitutional and financial issues. Constitutional issues such as the West Lothian question (Box 8.1) remain unresolved and MPs from Scotland, Wales and Northern Ireland continue to vote on matters affecting England alone (without the ability of English MPs to return the favour). The Conservative Party has suggested the creation of an English Grand Committee in the House of Commons to deal with legislation specific to England. However, opponents suggest that few issues are 'England only' (since at the very least they impinge financially on other territories) and point to party-political reasons for this suggestion (since it would effectively give the Conservatives rather than a Labour Government the control over English policy). Financial issues refer to the per capita public expenditure 'advantage' that Scotland enjoys, and the growing perception that English taxpayers are funding more generous policies in Scotland such as the abolition of tuition fees in higher education and free personal care for older people. Although there is no real English equivalent to Scottish nationalism (with cultural expressions of identity reserved mainly to sport), its development could yet play a key role in deciding the future of the UK.

economic, defence, foreign and some domestic policy powers shared over a transition period. The UK constitution has tended to evolve gradually to accommodate change. There is little reason to think that the independence experience would be different.

Fourth, if constitutional independence did take place, Scotland would still be inextricably linked with its geographic neighbours. The physical proximity and economic linkage of Scotland with the rest of the UK would mean inevitable pressures for similarities in social, economic, public expenditure and taxation policies.

A fifth point is that if further devolution or independence is to take place it is likely to require the type of party and civic society cooperation and consensus engendered by the Scottish Constitutional Convention in the 1980s and 1990s. However, one should not mistake consensus on constitutional matters for agreement on what type of policies a more devolved or independent Scotland should pursue. The post-devolution experience has shown that constitutional consensus soon disappears and the 'normal' political environment of partisanship and argument reemerges.

A sixth point is that in other parts of Europe more pluralistic ways of thinking about political authority and self-government are evident. Nationalists in Wales, Catalonia and the Basque country are not necessarily seeking full statehood, but exploring new ways in which nations can now act and be represented. In the modern era what matters is the powers a nation's institutions have and their capacity to project themselves in new supranational and global networks of decision-making. In Europe the German Länder, Spanish autonomous communities, Belgian regions and communities and the devolved bodies of the UK are now directly implementing EU laws and regulations and are increasingly calling for a recognized role within the EU (see Keating, 2004a: 326–30). This reflects what Rosenau (1984) calls **cascading interdependence** in the contemporary global political environment with decision-making taking place in national, state, supra-national and global institutions.

Cascading interdependence: The rapidly changing patterns of institutional interaction in the world which is characterized by vertical interdependent relationships in a fragmented environment.

Final remarks: difference and dependence, continuity and change

An understanding of Scottish politics requires a breadth of knowledge of many different levels of government, the many different stages of the policy-making process and the myriad of institutions beyond government. A key theme of this book has been to emphasize that politics takes place out-with the formal machinery and mechanisms of traditional political institutions. As well as acknowledging the broader governing context, the scope of analysis must incorporate an analysis of public opinion, electoral behaviour, electoral processes and campaigning, extra-parliamentary democratic processes and the policy networks of interest groups linked to the Parliament and Government.

Politics in Scotland is different from UK politics, but many of these institutional differences existed in the past. Multi-layered governance, incremental policy-making, the Barnett formula, Scotland's 32 local authorities, quangos and other institutions of governance all existed in more or less the same forms in 1999 as they exist today. Further, much change has not been of the fundamental revolutionary 'root-and-branch' variety. The significant historical legacy continues to shape the structure, style and practice of Scottish politics. The cumulative impact of devolution and the institutional changes associated with it are significant but are built upon the long established structure of government and politics in Scotland.

Scottish politics pre-devolution was inextricably linked to UK politics and it remains so through various financial and intergovernmental processes. It is difficult to talk of a Scottish political system when its institutions do not have the ability to decide on the overall size of Scottish public expenditure, fiscal powers are so marginal and its permanent bureaucracy remains part of the UK Home civil service. Ultimate legal (though not necessarily political) authority is retained in Westminster and Whitehall. The UK state developed devolution and a new institution – the Scottish Parliament – to regulate home rule demands, ensure its own survival and to ensure the continued viability of the wider UK political system.

The election of the minority SNP administration in May 2007 may *potentially* result in radical political change. The SNP administration behaves more like a Scottish Government and does not appear as subordinate to the UK Government as the Scottish Executive of 1999–2007. There are already signs that the constitutional change agenda is moving to the forefront of Scottish politics again. However, even if Scottish independence were actually to happen in the short to medium term a key theme of this book would still be relevant; understanding how Scotland came to be independent would require an appreciation and understanding of how Scottish politics has evolved in recent decades. The novelty of constitutional change should be tempered with the routine of longer term governance.

Bibliography

Adams, J and P. Robinson (eds) (2002) *Devolution in Practice: Public Policy Differences within the UK* (London: Institute of Public Policy Research).

Agranoff, R. (2004) 'Autonomy, Devolution and Intergovernmental Relations', *Regional and Federal Studies*, 14(1): 26–65.

Allan, A. (1990) *The Myth of Government Information* (London: Library Association).

Almond, G.A. and J.S. Coleman (1960) *The Politics of Developing Areas* (Princeton NJ: Princeton University Press).

Anderson, C.W. (1977) *Statecraft: An Introduction to Political Choice and Judgment* (New York, NY: John Wiley & Sons).

Arbuthnott, J. (2006) *Putting Citizens First: Boundaries Voting and Representation in Scotland – the Arbuthnott Report* http://www.arbuthnottcommission.gov.uk.

Arter, D. (2002) 'On Assessing Strength and Weakness in Parliamentary Committee Systems: Some Preliminary Observations on the New Scottish Parliament', *Journal of Legislative Studies*, 8(2): 93–117.

Arter, D. (2003) *The Scottish Parliament: A Scandinavian Style Assembly?* (London: Frank Cass).

Arter, D. (2004) 'The Scottish Committees and the Goal of a "New Politics": A Verdict on the First Four Years of the Devolved Scottish Parliament', *Journal of Contemporary European Studies*, 12(1): 71–91.

Audit Scotland (2004) *Commissioning Community Services for Older People* (Edinburgh: Audit Scotland).

Bache, I. and G. Bristow (2003) 'Devolution and the Gatekeeping Role of the Core Executive: The Struggle for European Funds', *British Journal of Politics and International Relations*, 5: 405–27.

Bache, I. and M. Flinders (eds) (2004a) *Multilevel Governance* (Oxford: Oxford University Press).

Bache, I. and M. Flinders (2004b) 'Multi-level Governance and the Study of the British State', *Public Policy and Administration*, 19(1): 31–52.

Bachrach, P. and M. Baratz (1962) 'Decisions and Non-decisions', *American Political Science Review*, 57: 641–51.

Bains Report (1973) *The New Local Authority Structures: Study Group on Local Authority Management Structure* (London: HMSO).

Baker D., N. Randall and D. Seawright (2002) 'Celtic Exceptionalism? Scottish and Welsh Parliamentarians' Attitudes to Europe', *Political Quarterly*, 73(2): 211–26.

Ball, R., M. Heafey and E. Fitzgerald (2000) 'Private Finance Initiative – a Good Deal for the Public Purse or a Drain on Future Generations?' *Policy and Politics*, 29(1): 95–108.

Balsom, D and I. McAllister (1979) 'The Scottish and Welsh Devolution Referenda of 1979', *Parliamentary Affairs*, 32(4): 394–409.

Batley, R. and G. Stoker (eds) (1991) *Local Government in Europe: Trends and Developments* (Basingstoke: Palgrave).

Baumgartner, F. and B. Jones (1993) *Agendas and Instability in American Politics* (Chicago: Chicago University Press).

BBC News (10.10.07) 'Clash over Foot-and-Mouth "Cash"' http://news.bbc.co.uk/1/hi/scotland/7037943.stm.

BBC News (20.9.07) 'BBC Chief in Pledge to Scotland' http://news.bbc.co.uk/1/hi/scotland/7004263.stm.

BBC News 22.10.06 'UK "Has Squandered Oil Revenues" http://news.bbc.co.uk/1/hi/business/6070866.stm.

Bell, A. and A. Bowes (2006) *Financial Models of Care in Scotland and the UK* (York: Joseph Rowntree Foundation).

Bell, D. (2001) 'The Barnett Formula' http://www.economics.stir.ac.uk/staff/dnfb1/Barnett%20Formula.pdf.

Bell, D. (2003) 'Care for the Elderly: A Fiscal Timebomb?', Paper presented at ScotEcon conference, June 2003.

Bell, D. and A. Christie (2001) 'Finance – The Barnett Formula: Nobody's Child?' in A. Trench (ed.), *The State of the Nations: The Second Year of Devolution in the UK* (London: The Constitution Unit).

Bell, D. and J. Mitchell (2001) 'Progress Report: Funding a Decentralised System of Governance' http://www.ucl.ac.uk/constitution-unit/research/devolution/project-10.html.

Bennett, M., J. Fairley and M. McAteer (2002) *Devolution in Scotland: The Impact on Local Government* (York: Joseph Rowntree Foundation).

Bennie, L. (2000) 'Small Parties in a Devolved Scotland', in A. Wright (ed.) *Scotland: The Challenge of Devolution* (Aldershot: Ashgate).

Bennie, L. (2002) 'Exploiting New Electoral Opportunities: The Small Parties in Scotland', in G. Hassan and C. Warhurst (eds), *Tomorrow's Scotland* (London: Lawrence & Wishart).

Bennie, L. (2004) *Understanding Political Participation – Green Party Membership in Scotland* (Aldershot: Ashgate).

Bennie, L., J. Brand and J. Mitchell (1995) 'Thatcherism and the Scottish Question', in C. Rallings, D. Broughton, D. Denver and D. Farrell (eds), *British Elections and Parties Yearbook 1995* (London: Frank Cass).

Bennie L., J. Brand and J. Mitchell (1997) *How Scotland Votes* (Manchester: Manchester University Press).

Bennie, L., D. Denver, J. Mitchell and J. Bradbury (2001) 'Harbingers of New Politics? The Characteristics and Attitudes of Candidates in The Scottish Parliamement Elections, 1999', in J. Tonge, L. Bennie, D. Denver and L. Harrison, *British Elections and Parties Review Vol. 11* (London: Frank Cass).

Bevir, M. and R.A.W. Rhodes (1999) 'Studying British Government: Reconstructing the Research Agenda', *British Journal of Politics and International Relations,* 1(2): 215–39.

Black Report (1980) *Inequalities in Health Case* (London: DHSS).

Black, R.W. (1999) 'Holding to Account – the Arrangements for Accountability, Scrutiny and Audit under the New Scottish Parliament', *Institute of Public Sector Accounting Research Policy*, Paper 6, University of Edinburgh.

Bochel, J. and D. Denver (1981) *The Referendum Experience: Scotland 1979* (Aberdeen: Aberdeen University Press).

Bogdanor, V. (1999) *Devolution in the United Kingdom* (Oxford: Oxford University Press).

Bogdanor, V. (2001) *Devolution in the United Kingdom*, paperback ed. (Oxford: Oxford University Press).

Boon, M. and J. Curtice (2003) *Scottish Election Research* (Edinburgh: The Electoral Commission).

Bradbury, J. (2006) 'Territory and Power Revisited: Theorising Territorial Politics in the United Kingdom after Devolution', *Political Studies*, 54: 559–82.

Bradbury, J. and J. Mitchell (2000) 'Devolution, New Politics for Old?' *Parliamentary Affairs*, 54(2): 257–75.

Bradbury, J. and J. Mitchell (2007) 'The Constituency Work of Members of the Scottish Parliament and National Assembly for Wales', *Regional and Federal Studies*, 17(1): 117–45.

Bradley, J. (1995) *Ethnic and Religious Identity in Modern Scotland* (Aldershot: Avebury).

Brand, J. (1978) *The National Movement in Scotland* (Leuven: Routledge & Kegan Paul).

Brand, J., D. McLean and W. Miller (1983) 'The Birth and Death of the Three-Party System: Scotland in the Seventies', *British Journal of Political Science*, 13: 463–8.

Brand, J., J. Mitchell and P. Surridge (1993) 'Identity and Vote. Class and Nationality in Scotland', in P. Norris *et al.* (eds), *British Elections and Parties Yearbook 1993* (London: Harvester Wheatsheaf).

Brand, J., J. Mitchell and P. Surridge (1994a) 'Will Scotland Come to the Aid of the Party?', in A. Heath, R. Jowell and J. Curtice (eds), *Labour's Last Chance?* (Aldershot: Dartmouth).

Brand, J., J. Mitchell and P. Surridge (1994b) 'Social Constituency and Scottish Nationalism', *Political Studies*, 42(4): 616–29.

Bromley, C. and J. Curtice (2003) 'The Lost Voters of Scotland: Devolution Disillusioned or Westminster Weary?', *British Elections and Parties Review*, 13: 66–85.

Bromley, C., J. Curtice, K. Hinds and A. Park (2003) *Devolution – Scottish Answers to Scottish Questions?* (Edinburgh: Edinburgh University Press).

Bromley, C., J. Curtice, K. Hinds and A. Park (eds) (2006) *Has Devolution Delivered?* (Edinburgh: Edinburgh University Press).

Brown, A. (1999) 'Taking Their Place in the New House: Women and the Scottish Parliament', *Scottish Affairs*, 28.

Brown, A. (1999) 'The First Elections in the Scottish Parliament, May 1999', *Representation*, 36(3).

Brown, A. (2000) 'Designing the New Scottish Parliament', *Parliamentary Affairs*, 53(3).

Brown, A. (2001) 'Scotland', *Parliamentary Affairs*, 54(4).

Brown, A., D. McCrone and L. Paterson (1998) *Politics and Society in Scotland* (Basingstoke: Macmillan).

Brown, A., L. Paterson, D. McCrone and P. Surridge (1999) *The Scottish Electorate: the 1997 General Election and Beyond* (Basingstoke: Macmillan).

Brown, C. (2001) *The Death of Christian Britain* (London: Routledge).

Browne, A. (27.10.07) 'Give the Scots Financial Independence – So Long as they Pay for it Themselves', *Daily Mail* http://www.dailymail.co.uk/pages/live/articles/news/news.html?in_article_id=490032&in_page_id=1770.

Bruce, S., T. Glenndinning, M. Paterson and I. Rosie (2004) *Sectarianism in Scotland* (Edinburgh: Edinburgh University Press).

Budge, I. and D. Urwin (1966) *Scottish Political Behaviour: A Case Study in British Homogeneity* (Longmans Green).

Bulmer, M., M. Burch, C. Carter, P. Hogwood and A. Scott (2002) *British Devolution and European Policymaking* (Basingstoke: Palgrave).

Bulmer, S., M. Burch, P. Hogwood, and A. Scott (2006) 'UK Devolution and the European Union: A Tale of Cooperative Asymmetry?', *Publius*, 36(1): 75–93.

Bulpitt, J. (1982) 'Conservatism, Unionism and the Problem of Territorial Management' in P. Madgwick and R. Rose (eds), *The Territorial Dimension in United Kingdom Politics* (Basingstoke: Macmillan).

Bulpitt, J. (1983) *Territory and Power in the United Kingdom* (Manchester: Manchester University Press).

Burns Report (2000) Report of Committee of Inquiry into Hunting with Dogs in England &Wales 9th June 2000 http://www.archive.official-documents. co.uk/document/cm47/4763/4763.htm.

Burrows, N. (2000) 'Relations with the European Union' in G. Hassan and C. Warhurst (eds), *The New Scottish Politics: the First Year of the Scottish Parliament and Beyond* (Edinburgh: The Stationery Office).

Butler, D. and D. Stokes (1974) *Political Change in Britain* (London: Macmillan).

Butler, D., A. Adonis and T. Travers (1994) *Failure in British Government – The Politics of the Poll Tax* (Oxford: Oxford University Press).

Cabinet Office (2003) *Table AB: Permanent Staff By Government Office Region, Responsibility Level And Ethnic Origin, 2003* http://www.civilservice.gov.uk/ management/statistics/publications/xls/report_2003/diversity_tables/table_ ab.xls.

Cabinet Office (2005) *Civil Service Statistics 2005: Location* http://www.civil service.gov.uk/management/statistics/publications/xls/report_2005/table_a.xls.

Cabinet Office (2007) *13 June 2007 – Quarterly public sector employment statistics* http://www.civilservice.gov.uk/management/statistics/employment/index.asp.

Cairney, P. (2002) 'New Public Management and the Thatcher Health Care Legacy: Enough of the Theory, What about the Implementation', *British Journal of Politics and International Relations*, 4(3): 375–98.

Cairney, P. (2006a) 'Venue Shift Following Devolution: When Reserved Meets Devolved in Scotland', *Regional and Federal Studies*, 16(4): 429–45.

Cairney, P. (2006b) 'The Analysis of Scottish Parliament Committees: Beyond Capacity and Structure in Comparing West European Legislatures', *European Journal of Political Research*, 45(2): 181–208.

Cairney, P. (2006c) 'The Scottish Executive', in P. Jones (ed.), Scotland Devolution Monitoring Report January 2006 (London: The Constitution Unit) http://www.ucl.ac. uk/constitution-unit/research/devolution/devo-monitoring-programme.html.

Cairney, P. (2006d) 'Public Policies', in P. Jones (ed.), *Scotland Devolution Monitoring Report September 2006* (London: The Constitution Unit).

Cairney, P. (2007a) 'The Professionalisation of MPs: Refining the Politics-Facilitating Explanation', *Parliamentary Affairs*, 60(2): 213–33.

Cairney, P. (2007b) 'Using Devolution to Set the Agenda? Venue Shift and the Smoking Ban in Scotland', *British Journal of Politics and International Relations*, 9: 73–89.

Cairney, P. (2007c) 'The Scottish Parliament', in P. Jones (ed.), *Scotland Devolution Monitoring Report January 2007* http://www.ucl.ac.uk/constitution-unit/research/devolution/MonReps/Scotland_Jan07.pdf.

Cairney, P. (2007d) 'The Scottish Executive', in P. Jones (ed.), *Scotland Devolution Monitoring Report January 2007* (London: The Constitution Unit) http://www.ucl.ac.uk/constitution-unit/research/devolution/MonReps/Scotland_Jan07.pdf.

Cairney, P. (2007e) 'Public Policies', in P. Jones (ed.), *Scotland Devolution Monitoring Report January 2007* http://www.ucl.ac.uk/constitution-unit/research/devolution/MonReps/Scotland_Jan07.pdf.

Cairney, P. (2007f) 'The Scottish Executive', in P. Jones (ed.), *Scotland Devolution Monitoring Report April 2007* (London: The Constitution Unit).

Cairney, P. (2007g) 'Public Policies', in A. Paun (ed.), *Scotland Devolution Monitoring Report September 2007* (UCL: Constitution Unit) http://www.ucl.ac.uk/constitution-unit/research/devolution/MonReps/Scotland_ Sept07.pdf.

Cairney, P. (2007h) 'The Scottish Executive', in A. Paun (ed.), *Scotland Devolution Monitoring Report September 2007* (London: The Constitution Unit).

Cairney, P. and M. Keating (2004), 'Sewel Motions in the Scottish Parliament', *Scottish Affairs*, 47: 115–34.

Calvert, P. (2002) *Comparative Politics: An Introduction* (New Jersey: Pearson Education).

Cant, B. and E. Kelly 'Scotland's Ethnic Minority Population', *Scottish Affairs*, 12.

Carman, C. (2006) *The Assessment of the Scottish Parliament's Public Petitions System 1999–2006* (Edinburgh: Scottish Parliament) http://www.scottish.parliament.uk/business/committees/petitions/reports-06/pur06-PPS-assessment-01.htm.

Cavanagh, M., N. McGarvey and M. Shephard (2000) 'Closing the Democratic Deficit? The First Year of the Public Petitions Committee of the Scottish Parliament', *Public Policy and Administration*, 15(2): 67–80.

Chapman, J. (2007) 'Scots to Axe Prescriptions – Leaving England to Pick Up the Bill', *Daily Mail* (UK edition) http://www.dailymail.co.uk/pages/live/articles/news/news. html?in_article_id=488944&in_page_id=1770.

Childs, S. (2004) *New Labour's Women MPs: Women Representing Women* (London: Routledge).

Christie, A. and K. Swales (2006) 'The Barnett Allocation Mechanism: Formula plus Influence?', *Centre for Public Policy for Regions Discussion Paper 10*, http://www.cppr.ac.uk/media/media_4293_en.pdf.

Clark, A. (2006) 'Post-Modern Campaigning? Constituency Party Activities in the 2003 Scottish Parliament Elections', *Scottish Affairs,* 55: 87–106.

Clarke, H., D. Sanders, M. Stewart and P.Whiteley (2004) *Political Choice in Britain* (Oxford: Oxford University Press).

Clarke, I. (2000) 'How Scotland Voted in 1999', in A.Wright (ed.), *Scotland: The Challenge of Devolution (*Aldershot: Ashgate).

Clarke, J., A. Cochrane and E. McLaughlin (1994) *Managing Social Policy* (London: Sage).

Coleshill, P., A. Gibson, A. Jaconelli and J. Sheffield (1998) 'The Private Finance Initiative: Private Opportunity at the Public's Cost?', *Scottish Affairs*, 24: 128–42.

Colomer, J.M. (2005) 'It's Parties That Choose Electoral Systems (or, Duverger's Laws Upside Down)', *Political Studies*, 53: 1–21.

Communities Committee (2007) *Legacy Report*, Scottish Parliament Paper 802 http://www.scottish.parliament.uk/business/committees/communities/reports-07/cor07-07.htm.

Consultative Steering Group (1999) *Shaping Scotland's Parliament: Report of the Consultative Steering Group* (Edinburgh: The Stationery Office).

Convery, J. (2000) *The Governance of Scotland: A Saltire Guide* (Edinburgh: The Stationery Office).

Cooke, M. (2000) 'Five Arguments for Deliberative Democracy', *Political Studies*, 48: 947–69.

Cowley, P. (2001) 'Voting in the Scottish Parliament: The First Year', in J. Tonge, L. Bennie, D. Denver and L. Harrison, *British Elections and Parties Review Vol.11* (London: Frank Cass).

Coxall, B. and L. Robins (1999) *Contemporary British Politics* (Basingstoke: Macmillan).

Crewe, I. (1988) 'Partisan Alignment Ten Years On', in H. Berrington (ed.), *Change in British Politics* (London: Frank Cass).

Crick, B. (1964) *In Defence of Politics* (Chicago: University of Chicago Press).

Crick, B. (1993) *In Defence of Politics*, 4th edn (Harmondsworth: Penguin).

Culyer, A. (2001) 'Equity – Some Theory and its Policy Implications', *Journal of Medical Ethics*, 27, 275–83.

Curtice, J. (1999) 'The New Electoral Politics', in G. Hassan and C. Warhurst (eds), *The New Scottish Politics* (The Stationery Office).

Curtice, J. (2002) 'Adding up the Figures: Conclusions from 2001', in M. Spicer (2002) *The Scotsman Guide to Scottish Politics* (Edinburgh: The Scotsman).

Curtice, J. (2004) 'Restoring Confidence and Legitimacy: Devolution and Public Opinion', in A. Trench (ed.) (2004) *Has Devolution Made a Difference? The State of the Nations 2004*, London: The Constitution Unit.

Curtice, J. (2005) 'What Makes Scotland Want Something Different?', in J. Ermisch and R. Wright (eds), *Changing Scotland: Evidence from the British Household Panel Survey* (Bristol: Policy Press).

Curtice, J. and S. Herbert (2005) 'STV in Local Government Elections: Modelling the 2003 Results', SPICE Briefing 05/31 (Edinburgh: Scottish Parliament Information Centre).

Curtice, J., D. McCrone, A. Park and L. Paterson (eds) (2002) *New Scotland, New Society?* (Edinburgh: Polygon).

Curtice, J. and M. Steed (1997) 'The Results Analysed', in D. Butler and D. Kavanagh (eds), *The British General Election of 1997* (Basingstoke: Macmillan).

Dahl, R.A. (1961) *Who Governs? Democracy and Power in an American City* (New Haven: Yale University Press).

Dahl, R.A. (1971) *Polyarchy: Participation and Opposition* (New Haven: Yale University Press).

Dahl, R.A. (1989) *Democracy and its Critics* (New Haven: Yale University Press).

Daily Mail (22.10.07) 'Scots to Axe Prescriptions – Leaving England to Pick Up the Bill' http://www.dailymail.co.uk/pages/live/articles/news/news.html?in_article_id=488944&in_page_id=1770.

Dalton, R. (1996) *Citizen Politics: Public Opinion and Political Parties in Advanced Industrial Democracies* (Chatham, NJ: Chatham House Publishers).

Dardanelli, P. (2005a) 'Democratic Deficit or the Europeanisation of Secession? Explaining the Devolution Referendums in Scotland', *Political Studies*, 53(2): 320–42.

Dardanelli, P. (2005b) *Between Two Unions: Europeanisation and Scottish Devolution* (Manchester: Manchester University Press).

Denters, B. and L.E. Rose (2005) *Comparing Local Governance: Trends and Developments* (Basingstoke: Palgrave).

Denton, M. and M. Flinders (2006) 'Democracy, Devolution and Delegated Governance in Scotland', *Regional and Federal Studies*, 16(1): 63–82.

Denver, D. (1997) 'The 1997 General Election in Scotland: An Analysis of the Results', *Scottish Affairs*, 20.

Denver, D. and I. MacAllister (1999) 'The Scottish Parliamentary Elections 1999: An Analysis of the Results', *Scottish Affairs*, 28: 10–31.

Denver, D. and I. MacAllister (2003) 'Constituency Campaigning in Scotland at the 2001 General Election', *Scottish Affairs*, 42.

Denver, D., J. Mitchell, C. Pattie and H. Bochel (2000) *Scotland Decides: The Devolution Issue and the Scottish Referumdum* (London: Frank Cass).

Denver, D., R. Johns, J. Mitchell, J. and C. Pattie (2007) 'The Holyrood Elections 2007: Explaining the Results', Paper presented to the Elections, Public Opinion and Parties Conference, 7–9 September, University of Bristol, 2007 http://www. scottishelectionstudy.org.

Devine, T. (2006) 'In Bed with an Elephant: Almost 300 Years of Anglo-Scottish Union', *Scottish Affairs*, 57: 1–18.

Devine, T. (ed.) (2000) *Scotland's Shame? Bigotry and Sectarianism in Modern Scotland* (Edinburgh: Mainstream).

Devlin, K. 'Brown Warns SNP over Oil Demand' *The Telegraph* 27.4.07 http://www. telegraph.co.uk/news/main.jhtml?xml=/news/2007/04/26/nsnp26.xml.

Devolution and Resource Accounting and Budgeting, ESRC devolution briefing 23 http://www.devolution.ac.uk/pdfdata/Briefing%2023%20-%20Lapsley.pdf.

Diamond, L.J. and M.F. Plattner (eds) (2006) *Electoral Systems and Democracy* (Baltimore: John Hopkins University Press).

Donnachie, I., C. Harvie and I. S. Wood (eds) (1989) *Forward! Labour Party Politics in Scotland 1888–1988* (Edinburgh: Mainstream).

Downs, A. (1957) *An Economic Theory of Democracy* (New York: Harper & Row).

Dunleavy, P. (1980) *Urban Political Analysis* (Basingstoke: Macmillan).

Dunsire, A. and C. Hood (1989) *Cutback Management in Public Bureaucracies* (Cambridge: Cambridge University Press).

Dyer, M. (1999) 'Representation in a Devolved Scotland', *Representation*, 36(1): 18–28.

Dyer, M. (2001) 'The Evolution of the Centre Right and the State of Scottish Conservatism', *Political Studies*, 49(1): 30–50.

Easton, D. (1953) *The Political System* (New York, NY: Knopf).

Easton, D. (1957) 'An Approach to the Analysis of Political Systems', *World Politics*, 10: 383–400.

Easton, D. (1965) *A Systems Analysis of Political Life* (New York: John Wiley).

Elcock, H. (1989) 'The Changing Management of Local Government', in I. Taylor and G. Popham (eds,) *An Introduction to Public Sector Management* (London: Unwin Hyman).

Elcock, H. and M. Keating (eds) (1998) *Remaking the Union: Devolution and British Politics in the 1990s* (London: Frank Cass).

Elcock, H., G. Jordan, A. Midwinter and G. Boyne (1989) *Budgeting in Local Government* (London: Longman).

Electoral Commission (2003) *Scottish Elections 2003* http://www.electoralcommission.org.uk/files/dms/Scottishelections_11227-8862__E__N__S__W__.pdf.

Enterprise and Culture Committee (2007) *Legacy Report*, Scottish Parliament Paper 814 http://www.scottish.parliament.uk/business/committees/enterprise/reports-07/ecr07-06-vol1.htm.

Entwistle, T, (2006) 'The Distinctiveness of the Welsh Partnership Agenda', *International Journal of Public Sector Management,* 19(3): 228–37.

European and External Relations Committee (2007) *Report on an Inquiry into the Scrutiny of European Legislation* (Edinburgh: Scottish Parliament).

Ezzamel, M., N. Hyndman, A. Johnsen and I. Lapsley (2005) Money Matters: Devolution and Resource Accounting and Budgeting *Devolution Briefing* No. 23 http://www.devolution.ac.uk/pdfdata/Briefing%2023%20-%20Lapsley.pdf.

Fawcett, H. (2003) 'Social Inclusion Policy Making in Scotland', *The Political Quarterly*, 74(4): 439–49.

Fawcett, H. (2004) 'The Making of Social Justice Policy in Scotland', in A. Trench (ed.), *Has Devolution Made a Difference? The State of the Nations 2004* (Exeter: Imprint Academic).

Ferguson, L., P. McGregor, K. Swales and K. Turner (2003) 'The Regional Distribution of Public Expenditures in the UK: An Exposition and Critique of the Barnett Formula' http://www.devolution.ac.uk/pdfdata/Regional_distribution_of%20public_expenditures_in_the_UK.pdf.

Finlay, R.J. (1997) *A Partnership for Good: Scottish Politics and the Union since 1880* (Edinburgh: John Donald).

Finlay, R.J. (2001a) 'Does History Matter? Political Scientists, Welsh and Scottish Devolution', *Twentieth Century British History*, 12(2): 243–50.

Finlay, R.J. (2001b) 'New Britain, New Scotland, New History? The Impact of Devolution on the Development of Scottish Historiography', *Journal of Contemporary History*, 36: 383–94.

Finlay, R.J. (2004) *Modern Scotland 1914–2000* (London: Profile).

Flinders, M. (2004) 'Icebergs and MPs: Delegated Governance and Parliament', *Parliamentary Affairs*, 57(4): 767–84.

Flinders, M. (2007) 'Analysing Reform: The House of Commons, 2001–5', *Political Studies*, 55, 174–200.

Ford, M. and P. Casebow (2002) 'The Civil Service' in G. Hassan and C. Warhurst (eds), *Anatomy of the New Scotland: Power, Influence and Change* (Mainstream: Edinburgh).

Foster, C. and F. Plowden (1996) *The State under Stress* (Buckingham: Open University Press).

Fraser, D. (2007) 'A New Union . . . without England?', *The Herald*, 18.7.07.

Fry, M. (1987) *Patronage and Principle: A Political History of Modern Scotland* (Aberdeen: Aberdeen University Press).

Gallager, M., M. Laver and P. Mair (2006) *Representative Government in Modern Europe*, 4th edn (New York: McGraw Hill).

Gallagher, T. (ed.) (1991) *Nationalism in the Nineties* (Polygon).

Gamble, A. (1990) 'Theories of British Politics', *Political Studies*, 38(3): 404–20.

Garner, R. and R. Kelly (1998) *British Political Parties Today*, 2nd edn (Manchester University Press).

Garside, J. (2002) 'The Scottish Media', in G. Hassan and C. Warhurst (eds), *Anatomy of the New Scotland: Power, Influence and Change* (Mainstream: Edinburgh).

Gay, O. (2003) 'Evolution from Devolution: the Experience at Westminster', in Hazell, R. (ed.) (2003) *The State of the Nations 2003: The Third Year of Devolution in the United Kingdom* (London: The Constitution Unit).

Gibson, J.S. (1985) *The Thistle and the Crown. A History of the Scottish Office* (Edinburgh: HMSO).

Grant, W. (2000) *Pressure Groups, Politics and Democracy in Britain*, 3rd edn (London: Philip Allen).

Gray, L. (2007) 'SNP Gathers Forces to Fight Trident Missile Replacement', *The Scotsman* http://news.scotsman.com/scotland.cfm?id=1686982007.

Gray, L. (26.1.07) 'Study Finds No Benefit in Fiscal Autonomy as McCrone Calls Time on Barnett', *The Scotsman* http://news.scotsman.com/topics.cfm?tid=447&id=134592007.

Gray, L. (6.9.07) 'SNP Unveils Grand Plan – but Critics call it "Policy Lite",' *The Scotsman* http://news.scotsman.com/scotland.cfm?id=1420922007.

Green, J. (2007) 'When Voters and Parties Agree: Valence Issues and Party Competition', *Political Studies*, 55: 629–55.

Green-Pedersen, C. (2007) 'The Growing Importance of Issue Competition: The Changing Nature of Party Competition in Western Europe', *Political Studies*, 55: 607–28.

Greer, S. (2003) 'Policy Divergence: Will it Change Something in Greenock', in R. Hazell (ed.) (2003) *The State of the Nations 2003: The Third Year of Devolution in the United Kingdom* (London: The Constitution Unit).

Greer, S. (2004) *Territorial Politics and Health Policy: UK Health Policy in Comparative Perspective* (Manchester: Manchester University Press).

Greer, S. (2005a) 'The Politics of Health-Policy Divergence', in J. Adams and K. Schmueker (eds), *Devolution in Practice: Public Policy and Differences within the UK* (Newcastle: IPPR).

Greer, S. (2005b), 'Becoming European: Devolution, Europe and Health Policy-Making', in A. Trench (ed.), *The Dynamics of Devolution* (London: The Constitution Unit).

Greer, S. (2005c), *The New EU Health Policy and the NHS Systems* (London: The Nuffield Trust) http://www.nuffieldtrust.org.uk/ecomm/files/090205 EUhealth system. pdf.

Greer, S. (2005d) 'The Territorial Bases of Health Policymaking in the UK after Devolution', *Regional and Federal Studies*, 15(4): 501–18.

Griffith, J.A.G. (1974) *Parliamentary Scrutiny of Government Bills* (London: George Allen and Unwin Ltd).

Hague, R. and M. Harrop (2001) *Comparative Government and Politics* (Basingstoke: Palgrave).

Harvie, C. (1994) *The Rise of Regional Europe* (London: Routledge).

Harvie, C. and P. Jones (2000) *The Road to Home Rule* (Edinburgh: Polygon).

Hassan, G. (1999) *Labour and Scottish Nationalism: A History from Keir Hardie to the Present* (London: Lawrence & Wishart).

Hassan, G. (2002a) 'A Case Study of Scottish Labour: Devolution and the Politics of Multi-Level Governance', *Political Quarterly*, 73(2): 144–57.

Hassan, G. (2002b) 'The Paradoxes of Scottish Labour: Devolution, Change and Conservatism' in G. Hassan and C. Warhurst (eds), *Tomorrow's Scotland* (London: Lawrence & Wishart).

Hassan, G. (ed.) (2004) *The Scottish Labour Party: History, Institutions and Ideas* (London: Lawrence & Wishart).

Hassan, G. and C. Warhurst (2001) 'New Scotland? Policy, Parties and Institutions', *Political Quarterly*, 72(2): 213–26.

Hassan, G. and C. Warhurst (eds) (2002) *Tomorrow's Scotland* (London: Lawrence & Wishart).

Hay, C. (2002) *Political Analysis: A Critical Introduction* (Basingstoke: Palgrave).

Hayes, M.T. (2001) *The Limits of Policy Change: Incrementalism, Worldview, and the Rule of Law* (Washington D.C.: Georgetown University Press).

Hazell, R. (ed.) (2000) *The State and the Nations: The First Year of Devolution in the United Kingdom* (Thorverton: Imprint Academic).

Hazell, R. (ed.) (2003) *The State of the Nations 2003: The Third Year of Devolution in the United Kingdom* (Thorverton: Imprint).

Heald, D. (1983) *Public Expenditure* (Oxford: Martin Robertson).

Heald, D. (2001) 'Decentralization in Some Non-Federal Countries: The Case of the United Kingdom', Québec Commission sur le Déséquilibre Fiscal, International Symposium, Québec City, 13–14 September http://www.devolution.ac.uk/Heald%202.htm.

Heald, D. and McLeod, A. (2002) 'Public Expenditure', in Constitutional Law, 2002, The Laws of Scotland: Stair Memorial Encyclopaedia, Edinburgh, Butterworths, paras 530, 532–36 http://www.abdn.ac.uk/crpf/barnettoriginal.pdf.

Health and Community Care Committee (2000) *Inquiry into the Delivery of Community Care in Scotland* (16th Report) http://www.scottish.parliament.uk/business/committees/historic/health/reports-00/her00-16-01.htm.

Heclo, H. and A. Wildavsky (1974) *The Private Government of Public Money* (Toronto: Macmillan).

Heclo, H. and A. Wildavsky, 2nd edn (1981) *The Private Government of Public Money* (London: Macmillan).

Heggie, G. (2003) 'The Story So Far: The Role Of The Scottish Parliament's European Committee In The UK–EU Policy Cycle', *Scottish Affairs*, No.44.

Henkel, M. (1991) *Government, Evaluation and Change* (London: Jessica Kingsley).

Heywood, A. (2002) *Politics*, 3rd edn (Basingstoke: Palgrave).

Heywood, A. (2007) *Politics*, 4th edn (Basingstoke: Palgrave).

Hill, M. and P. Hupe (2002) *Implementing Public Policy* (London: Sage).

Himsworth, Chris (2004) 'The General Effects of Devolution Upon the Practice of Legislation at Westminster', Appendix 1 to House of Lords Select Committee on the Constitution 15th Report of Session 2003–04 *Devolution: Its Effect on the Practice of Legislation at Westminster* (HL Paper 192) (London: The Stationery Office).

Hindess, B. (1995) *Discourses of Power: from Hobbes to Foucault* (Oxford: Blackwell).

Hjern, B. (1982) 'Implementation Research – the Link Gone Missing', *Journal of Public Policy*, 2(3): 301–8.

Hjern, B. and D. Porter (1981) 'Implementation Structures: A New Unit of Administrative Analysis', *Organizational Studies*, 2: 211–27.

HM Government (1999) *Modernising Government* (London: HMSO).

HM Treasury (2004) 'Funding the Scottish Parliament, National Assembly for Wales And Northern Ireland Assembly Fourth Edition' http://www.hm-treasury. gov.uk/media/CB2/3C/Funding_the_Scottish_Parliament_National_Assembly_ for _Wales(296kb).pdf.

HM Treasury (2005) *Public Expenditure Statistical Analyses 2005* (London: The Stationery Office).

HM Treasury (2006) *Public Expenditure Statistical Analyses 2006* (London: The Stationery Office) http://www.hm-treasury.gov.uk/media/375/5A/cm6811_ comp.pdf.

HM Treasury (2007a) *GDP deflator September 2007* http://www.hm-treasury. gov.uk/economic_data_and_tools/gdp_deflators/data_gdp_guide.cfm.

HM Treasury (2007b) *Public Expenditure Statistical Analyses 2007* (Cm 7091) http://www.hm-treasury.gov.uk/media/E/B/pesa07_complete.pdf.

Hoggett, P. (1996) 'New Modes of Control in the Public Sector', *Public Administration*, 74: 9–32.

Hogwood, B.W. (1987) *From Crisis to Complacency? Shaping Public Policy in Britain* (London: Oxford University Press).

Hogwood, B.W. (1992) *Trends in British Public Policy* (Buckingham: Open University Press).

Hogwood, B.W. (1995) 'The Growth of Quangos' in F.F. Ridley and D. Wilson (eds), *The Quango Debate* (Oxford: Oxford University Press).

Hogwood, B.W. (1999) 'Quangos in Scotland' in G. Hassan (ed.), *A Guide to the Scottish Parliament* (Edinburgh: The Stationery Office).

Hogwood, B.W. and L. Gunn (1984), *Policy Analysis for the Real World* (Oxford, Oxford University Press).

Holliday, I. (2000) 'Is the British State Hollowing Out?', *Political Quarterly*, 167–76.

Holyrood Magazine (19.10.07) 'Independent Mind', http://www.holyrood.com/ content/view/1480/10524/.

Hood, C. (1991) 'A Public Management for All Seasons', *Public Administration*, 69: 3–19.

Hood, C. (1994) *Explaining Economic Policy Reversals* (Buckingham: Open University Press).

Hood, C., C. Scott, O. James, G. Jones and T. Travers (1999) *Regulation Inside Government* (Oxford: Oxford University Press).

Hood, J. and N. McGarvey (2002) 'Managing the Risks of Public–Private Partnerships in Scottish Local Government', *Policy Studies*, 23(1): 21–35.

Hood, J., I. Fraser and N. McGarvey (2006) 'Transparency of Risk and Reward in UK Public–Private Partnerships', *Public Budgeting & Finance*, 26(4): 40–58.

Hooghe, L. and G. Marks (2003a) *Multi-level Governance and European Integration* (Maryland: Rowman and Littlefield).

Hooghe, L. and G. Marks (2003b) 'Unravelling the Central State, but How? Types of Multi-level Governance', *American Political Science Review*, 97(2): 233–43.

Horgan, G. (2004) 'Inter-institutional Relations in the Devolved Great Britain: Quiet Diplomacy', *Regional and Federal Studies*, 14(1): 113–35.

House of Commons Information Service (2006) *Private Members' Bills Procedure* http://www.parliament.uk/documents/upload/l02.pdf.

House of Commons Information Service (2007) *Parliamentary Stages of a Government* Bill http://www.parliament.uk/documents/upload/l01.pdf.

House of Commons Library (2003), *The West Lothian Question*, http://www.parliament.uk/commons/lib/research/notes/snpc-02586.pdf.

House of Commons Library (2005) Concordats and Devolution Guidance Notes http://www.parliament.uk/commons/lib/research/notes/snpc-03767.pdf.

House of Lords Select Committee on the Constitution (2002) *Devolution: Its Effect on the Practice of Legislation at Westminster* (15th Report of Session 2003–04, HL Paper 192). London: The Stationery Office.

Hutchison, I.G.C. (1996) 'Government', in T. Devine and R. Findlay (eds) (1996) *Scotland in the Twentieth Century* (Edinburgh University Press).

Hutchison, I.G.C. (2000) *Scottish Politics in the Twentieth Century* (Basingstoke: Palgrave).

Inglehart, R. (1977) *The Silent Revolution* (Princeton, NJ: Princeton University Press).

Irvine, J., I. Miles and J. Evans (eds) (1989) *Demystifying Social Staistics* (London: Pluto Press).

Irvine, M. (2004) 'Scotland, Labour and the Trade Union Movement: Partners in Change or Uneasy Bedfellows?', in G. Hassan (ed.), *The Scottish Labour Party: History, Institutions and Ideas* (Edinburgh: Edinburgh University Press).

Jenkins-Smith, H.C. and P.A. Sabattier (1993) *Policy Change and Learning: An Advocacy Coalition Approach* (Westview Press).

John, P. (1998) *Analysing Public Policy* (London: Continuum).

Jones, B. and M. Keating (1982) 'The British Labour Party: Centralisation and Devolution' in P. Madgwick and R. Rose, *The Territorial Dimension in United Kingdom Politics* (Basingstoke: Macmillan).

Jones, P. (1999) 'The 1999 Scottish Parliament Elections: From Anti-Tory to Anti-Nationalist Politics', *Scottish Affairs*, 28.

Jordan, A.G. and D. Halpin (2006) 'The Political Costs of Policy Coherence? Constructing a "Rural" Policy for Scotland', *Journal of Public Policy*, 26: 21–41.

Jordan, A.G. and W.A. Maloney (1997) 'Accounting for Subgovernments: Explaining the Persistence of Policy Communities', *Administration and Society*, (29): 557–83.

Jordan, A.G. and L. Stevenson (2000) 'Redemocratizing Scotland. Towards the Politics of Disappointment?', in A. Wright (ed.), *Scotland: the Challenge of Devolution* (Aldershot: Ashgate).

Jordan, A.G. and J.J. Richardson (1987) *British Politics and the Policy Process* (London: Allen & Unwin).

Judge, D. (1993) *The Parliamentary State* (London: Sage).

Judge, D. (1999) *Representation: Theory and Practice in Britain* (London: Routledge).

Judge, D. and D. Earnshaw (2002) 'The European Parliament and the Commission Crisis: A New Assertiveness?', *Governance*, 15(3): 345–72.

Keating, M. (1998) *The New Regionalism in Western Europe: Territorial Restructuring and Political Change* (London: Edward Elgar).

Keating, M. (2001) *Nations Against the State: The New Politics of Nationalism in Quebec, Catalonia and Scotland*, 2nd edn (London: Palgrave).

Keating, M. (2004a) 'The United Kingdom as a Post-Sovereign Polity', in M. O'Neill (eds), *Devolution and British Politics* (Harlow: Pearson).

Keating, M. (2004b) *Plurinational Democracies: Stateless Nations in a Post-Sovereignty Era* (Oxford: Oxford University Press).

Keating, M. (2005a) *The Government of Scotland: Public Policy Making after Devolution* (Edinburgh: Edinburgh University Press).

Keating, M. (2005b) 'Higher Education in Scotland and England after Devolution', *Regional and Federal Studies*, 15(4): 423–35.

Keating, M. and D. Bleiman (1979) *Labour and Scottish Nationalism* (London: Macmillan).

Keating, M. and P. Cairney (2006) 'A New Elite? Politicians and Civil Servants in Scotland after Devolution', *Parliamentary Affairs*, 59(1): 43–57.

Keating, M and A.F. Midwinter (1984) *The Government of Scotland* (Edinburgh: Mainstream).

Keating, M. and L. Stevenson (2001) 'Submission to The Scottish Parliament Procedures Committee Inquiry into CSG Proposals and their Implementation' http://www.scottish.parliament.uk/business/committees/historic/procedures/repo rts-03/prr03-03-01.htm.

Keating, M., L. Stevenson, P. Cairney and K. MacLean (2003) 'Does Devolution Make a Difference? Legislative Output and Policy Divergence in Scotland', *Journal of Legislative Studies*, 9(3): 110–39.

Kellas, J. (1984) *The Scottish Political System*, 3rd edn (Cambridge: Cambridge University Press).

Kellas, J. (1989) *The Scottish Political System*, 4th edn (Cambridge: Cambridge University Press).

Kellas, J. (1991a) 'European Integration and the Regions', *Parliamentary Affairs*, 44(2): 226–39.

Kellas, J. (1991b) 'The Scottish and Welsh Offices as Territorial Managers', *Regional Politics and Policy*, 1: 87–100.

Kellas, J. (1992) 'The Social Origins of Scottish Nationalism', in J. Coakley (ed.), *The Social Origins of Nationalist Movements* (London: Sage).

Kellas, J. (1994) 'The Party in Scotland', in A. Seldon and S. Ball (eds), *Conservative Century* (Oxford University Press).

Kellas, J. and Madgwick (1982) 'Territorial Ministries: the Scottish and Welsh Offices', in P. Madgwick and R. Rose (eds), *The Territorial Dimension in United Kingdom Politics* (London: Macmillan).

Kelso, A. (2007) 'The House of Commons Modernisation Committee: Who Needs It?', *The British Journal of Politics and International Relations*, 9(1), 138–57.

Kemp, A. (1993) *The Hollow Drum: Scotland Since the War* (Edinburgh: Mainstream).

Kendrick, S. and D. McCrone (1989) 'Parties in a Cold Climate. The Conservative Decline in Scotland', *Political Studies*, 37: 589–603.

Kingdon, J. (1999) *Government and Politics in Britain* (Cambridge: Polity).

Kingdon, J.K. (1984) *Agendas, Alternatives and Public Policies* (London: Harper Collins).

Kircheimer, O. (1966) 'The Transformation of the Western European Party Systems', in J. LaPalombara and M. Weiner (eds), *Political Parties and Political Development* (Princeton N.J.: Princeton University Press).

Kirkpatrick, I. and R. Pyper (2001) 'The Early Impact of Devolution on Civil Service Accountability in Scotland', *Public Policy and Administration*, 16(3): 68–84.

Laffin, M. (1986) *Professionalism and Policy: The Role of the Professions in the Central-Local Relationship* (Aldershot: Gower).

Laffin, M. (2005) 'The Politics of Coalition in a Devolved Britain: How the Liberal Democrats Have Shaped Scottish and Welsh Public Policy', Paper Presented to Political Studies Association Conference, Leeds http://www.psa.ac.uk/journals/pdf/5/2005/Laffin.pdf.

Lang, I. (1992) 'Address to the Reinventing Government Conference', Eglinton Management Centre, Edinburgh 7.2.93.

Lang, I. (2001) *Blue Remembered Years* (London: Politico's).

Lasswell, H. (1936) *Politics: Who Gets What, When, How?* (New York: McGraw-Hill).

Leach, R. and J. Percy Smith (2001) *Local Governance in Britain* (Basingstoke: Palgrave.

Leach, R., B. Coxall and L. Robbins (2006) *British Politics* (Basingstoke: Palgrave).

Leach, S., J. Stewart and K. Walsh (1994) *The Changing Organisation and Management of Local Government* (London: Macmillan).

Leftwich, A. (ed.) (1984) *What is Politics?* (Oxford: Basil Blackwell).

Leicester, G. (2000) 'Scotland' in R. Hazell (ed.) (2000), *The State and the Nations: The First Year of Devolution in the UK* (London: The Constitution Unit).

Levitas, R. (1999) *The Inclusive Society? Social Exclusion and New Labour* (Basingstoke: Macmillan).

Lijphart, A. (1999) *Patterns of Democracy: Government Forms and Performance in Thirty Six Countries* (New Haven, Conn: Yale University Press).

Lindblom, C. E. (1979) 'Still Muddling, Not Yet Through', Public *Administration Review*, 39: 517–25.

Lindsay, I. (2000) 'The New Civic Forums', *Political Quarterly*, 71(4): 404–11.

Lindsay, I. (2002) 'Civic Democracy', in G. Hassan and C. Warhurst (eds), *Anatomy of the New Scotland: Power, Influence and Change* (Mainstream: Edinburgh).

Lipset, S.M. and S. Rokkan (eds) (1967) *Party Systems and Voter Alignments: Cross-National Perspectives* (London: Collier-MacMillan).

Lloyd, G. (2000) 'Quasi Government in Scotland – A Challenge for Devolution and the Renewal of Democracy', in A. Wright (ed.), *Scotland: The Challenge of Devolution (*Aldershot: Ashgate).

Lowi, T. (1969) *The End of Liberalism* (New York: W.W. Norton & Company).

Lukes, S. (1974) *Power: A Radical View* (Basingstoke: Macmillan).

Lynch, P. (1998) 'Third Party Politics in a Four Party System: the Liberal Democrats in Scotland', *Scottish Affairs*, 22: 16–32.

Lynch, P. (2001) *Scottish Government and Politics* (Edinburgh: Edinburgh University Press).

Lynch, P. (2002a) 'Partnership, Pluralism and Party Identity: The Liberal Democrats After Devolution' in G. Hassan and C. Warhurst (eds), *Tomorrow's Scotland* (London: Lawrence & Wishart).

Lynch, P. (2002b) *SNP: The History of the Scottish National Party* (Welsh Academic Press).

Lynch, P. (2006) 'Governing Devolution: Understanding the Office of First Ministers in Scotland and Wales', *Parliamentary Affairs,* 59(3): 420–36.

Lynch, P. and S. Birrell (2001) 'Linking Parliament to the People: The Public Petitions Process of the Scottish Parliament', *Scottish Affairs*, 37: 1–14.

MacDonnell, H. (2007) 'Salmond Promises a Bonfire of the Quangoes', *Scotsman*, 29.10.07.

MacMillan, J. (2000) 'Scotland's Shame', in T.M. Devine (ed.), *Bigotry and Sectarianism in Modern Scotland* (Edinburgh: Mainstream).

Macwhirter, I. (2002) 'The New Scottish Political Classes', in G. Hassan and C. Warhurst (2002) *Anatomy of the New Scotland* (Edinburgh: Mainstream).

Mair, P. (ed.) (1990) *The West European Party System* (Oxford University Press).

Maloney, W.A., A.G. Jordan and A.M. McLaughlin (1994) 'Interest Groups and Public Policy: The Insider/ Outsider Model Revisited', *Journal of Public Policy*, 14(1): 17–38.

Marinetto, M. (2003) 'Governing beyond the Centre: A Critique of the Anglo-Governance School', *Political Studies*, 51(3): 592–608.

Marr, A. (1992) *The Battle for Scotland* (Harmondsworth: Penguin).

Marsh, D., D. Richards and M.J. Smith (2001) *Changing Patterns of Governance in the United Kingdom* (Basingstoke: Palgrave).

Marsh, D. and R.A.W. Rhodes (eds) (1992a) *Implementing Thatcherite Policies: Audit of an Era* (Buckingham: Open University Press).

Marsh, D. and R.A.W. Rhodes (eds) (1992b) *Policy Networks in British Government* (Oxford: Clarendon Press).

Marsh, D. and G. Stoker (2002) *Theory and Methods in Political Science*, 2nd edn (Basingstoke: Palgrave).

Mattson, I. and Strøm, K. (2004) 'Committee Effects on Legislation', in H. Döring, and M. Hallerberg (eds), *Patterns of Parliamentary Behaviour* (Aldershot: Ashgate).

Maud, Sir John (Chairman) (1967) *Committee on the Management of Local Government*, Vol 1: Report (London: HMSO).

Mazey, S. and J. Mitchell (1993) 'Europe of the Regions: Territorial Interests and European Integration – the Scottish Experience', in S. Mazey and J. Richardson (eds), *Lobbying in the European Community* (Oxford University Press).

McAllister, I. and R. Rose (1984) *The Nationwide Competition for Votes* (London: Francis Pinter).

McConnell, A. (2004) *Scottish Local Government* (Edinburgh: Edinburgh University Press).

McCrone, D. (1992) *Understanding Scotland: The Sociology of a Stateless Nation* (London: Routledge).

McCrone, D. (2000) 'Scottish Opinion Polls May 1999–June 2000', *Scottish Affairs*, No. 36.

McCrone, D. (2001) 'Opinion Polls in Scotland: June 200–June 2001', *Scottish Affairs*, No. 37.

McCrone, D. (2001) *Understanding Scotland: The Sociology of a Nation*, 2nd ed, (London: Routledge).

McCrone, D. and B. Lewis (1999) 'The 1997 Scottish Referendum Vote', in B. Taylor and K. Thompson, *Scotland and Wales: Nations Again?* (University of Wales Press).

McEwan, N. (2002) 'The Scottish National Party After Devolution: Progress and Prospects' in G. Hassan and C. Warhurst (eds), *Tomorrow's Scotland* (London: Lawrence & Wishart).

McEwan, N. (2005) 'The Territorial Politics of Social Policy Development in Multi-level States', *Regional and Federal Studies*, 15(4): 537–54.

McEwan, N. (2006) *Nationalism and the State: Welfare and Identity in Scotland and Quebec* (Brussels: P.I.E.-Peter Lang).

McGarvey, N. (1998) 'Local Government Expenditure Trends 1946–1994: A Political Economy Macro Level Analysis', *Strathclyde Papers on Government and Politics*, No.111.

McGarvey, N. (2001a) 'New Scottish Politics, New Texts Required', *British Journal of Politics and International Relations*, 3(3): 427–44.

McGarvey, N. (2001b) 'Accountability in Public Administration', *Public Policy and Administration*, 16(2): 17–28.

McGarvey, N. (2002) 'Intergovernmental Relations in Scotland Post Devolution', *Local Government Studies*, 29(3): 29–48.

McGarvey, N. (2005) 'Local Government North and South of the Border', *Public Policy and Administration*, 20: 90–9.

McGarvey, N. (2008) 'Devolution in Scotland: Change and Continuity' in J. Bradbury and J. Mawson (eds), *Devolution, Regionalism and Regional Development: The UK Experience* (London: Taylor Francis).

McGarvey, N. and A.F. Midwinter (1995) 'Reshaping Social Work Authorities in Scotland', *British Journal of Social Work*, 26: 209–21.

McLean, I. (2003) 'Devolution Bites: Devolution has Allowed Social Policy Experiments in Scotland and Wales. But it also has Unintended Effects', *Prospect*, 84: 20–1.

McLean, I. and A. McMillan (2003) 'The Distribution of Public Expenditure across the UK Regions', *Fiscal Studies*, 24(1): 45–71.

McMahon, P. (2002) 'How McLeish Made Up his Policies on the Hoof', *The Scotsman* 26.1.02 http://news.scotsman.com/topics.cfm?tid=190&id=95992002.

McMahon, P. (2005) 'Squeeze on Scottish Budget to Cost 120,000 Jobs', *The Scotsman* 22.3.05 http://thescotsman.scotsman.com/index.cfm?id=305142005.

McPherson, A. and C. Raab (1988) *Governing Education. A Sociology of Policy since 1945* (Edinburgh: Edinburgh University Press).

McTernan, L. (2000) 'Beyond the Blethering Classes: Consulting and Involving Wider Society' in G. Hassan and C. Warhurst (eds), *The New Scottish Politics* (Edinburgh: The Stationery Office).

Midwinter, A.F. (1992) 'The Review of Local Government in Scotland – A Critical Perspective', *Local Government Studies*, 18(2): 44–54.

Midwinter, A.F. (1995) *Local Government in Scotland* (Basingstoke: Macmillan).

Midwinter, A.F. (2004a) 'Financing Devolution in Practice: The Barnett Formula and the Scottish Budget, 1999–2003', *Public Money and Management*, June, 137–44.

Midwinter, A.F. (2004b) 'The Changing Distribution of territorial Public Expenditure in the UK', *Regional and Federal Studies*, 14(4): 499–512.

Midwinter, A.F. (2005) 'Budgetary Scrutiny in the Scottish Parliament: An Adviser's View', *Financial Accountability and Management*, 21(1): 13–32.

Midwinter, A.F. and R. Burnside (2004) *Key Trends in the Scottish Budget (SPICE Briefing 04/16)* http://www.scottish.parliament.uk/business/research/briefings-04/sb04-16.pdf.

Midwinter A., F. M. Keating and J. Mitchell (1991) *Politics and Public Policy in Scotland* (Basingstoke: Macmillan).

Midwinter, A.F. and N. McGarvey (1998) 'The Reorganisation in Scotland – Managing the Transition', in S. Leach (ed.), *Local Government Reorganisation* (Frank Cass: London).

Midwinter, A.F. and N. McGarvey (2001a) 'In Search of the Regulatory State: Evidence from Scotland', *Public Administration*, 79(4): 825–49.

Midwinter, A.F. and N. McGarvey (2001b) 'The New Accountability? Devolution and Expenditure Politics in Scotland', *Public Money and Management*, 21(3): 47–55.

Miller, D. (2000) 'Scotland's Parliament: A Mini-Westminster, or a Model of Democracy?', in A. Wright (ed.), *Scotland: The Challenge of Devolution* (Aldershot: Ashgate).

Miller, W. (1982) 'Variations in Electoral Behaviour in the United Kingdom' in P. Madgwick and R. Rose, *The Territorial Dimension in United Kingdom Politics* (London: Macmillan).

Miller, W. (1981) *The End of British Politics? Scots and English Political Behaviour in the Seventies* (Oxford: Clarendon Press).

Milligan, T. (1999) 'Left at the Polls: the Changing Far Left Vote', *Scottish Affairs*, 29: 139–56.

Mitchell, J. (1990a) *Conservatives and the Union. A Study of Conservative Party Attitudes to Scotland* (Edinburgh: Edinburgh University Press).

Mitchell, J. (1990b) 'Factions, Tendencies and Consensus in the SNP in the 1980s' in A. Brown and R. Parry (eds), *Scottish Government Yearbook 1990* (Edinburgh: Unit for the Study of Government in Scotland).

Mitchell, J. (1996a) *Strategies for Self-Government* (Edinburgh: Polygon).

Mitchell, J. (1996b) 'From Unitary State to Union State: Labour's Changing View of the United Kingdom and its Implications', *Regional Studies*, 30(6): 607–11.

Mitchell, J. (1996c) 'Scotland in the Union, 1945–95: The Changing Nature of the Union State', in T. M. Devine and R. J. Finlay (eds), *Scotland in the 20th Century* (Edinburgh: Edinburgh University Press).

Mitchell, J. (2000) 'New Parliament, New Politics', *Parliamentary Affairs,* 53(3): 605–21.

Mitchell, J. (2001) 'The Study of Scottish Politics Post-Devolution: New Evidence, New Analysis and New Methods?', *West European Politics*, 24(4): 216–23.

Mitchell, J. (2003a) *Governing Scotland* (Basingstoke: Palgrave).

Mitchell, J. (2003b) 'Spectators and Audiences: The Politics of UK Territorial Finance', *Regional and Federal Studies*, 13(4): 7–21.

Mitchell, J. (2003c) 'Third Year, Third First Minister', in R. Hazell (ed.), *The State of the Nations 2003* (London: Imprint).

Mitchell, J. (2004) 'Scotland: Expectations, Policy Types and Devolution', in A. Trench (ed.), *Has Devolution Made a Difference? The State of the Nations 2004* (Exeter: Imprint).

Mitchell, J. (2005) 'Scotland: Devolution IS Not Just for Christmas', in A.Trench (ed.), *The Dynamics of Devolution: The State of the Nations 2005* (Exeter: Imprint Academic).

Mitchell, J. (2006) 'Evolution and Devolution: Citizenship, Institutions and Public Policy', *Publius: The Journal of Federalism*, 36(1):153–68.

Mitchell, J. and D. Bell (2002) 'Funding a Decentralised System of Governance', *Nations and Regions Project 10* (London: UCL) http://www.ucl.ac.uk/constitutionunit/research/devolution/project-10.html.

Mitchell, J. and L. Bennie (1996) 'Thatcherism and the Scottish Question', in *British Elections and Parties Yearbook 1995* (London: Frank Cass).

Mitchell, J. and J. Bradbury (2004) 'Devolution: Comparative Development and Policy Roles', *Parliamentary Affairs*, 57(2): 329–46.

Mitchell, J. and the Scottish Monitoring Team (2001) 'Scotland: Maturing Devolution', in A. Trench (ed.), *The State of the Nations 2001* (Thorverton: Imprint Academic).

Mooney, G. and L. Poole (2004) 'A Land of Milk and Honey? Social Policy in Scotland After Devolution', *Critical Social Policy*, 24(4): 458–83.

Mooney, G. and G. Scott (2004) *Exploring Social Policy in the New Scotland* (Policy Press).

Moore, C. and S. Booth (1989) *Managing Competition – Meso Corporatism, Pluralism and the Negotiated Order in Scotland* (Oxford: Oxford University Press).

Moran M. (2001) 'The Rise of the Regulatory State in Britain', *Parliamentary Affairs*, 54(1): 19–34.

Moran, M. (2005) *Politics and Governance in the UK* (London: Palgrave).

Musgrave, R.A. and A.T. Peacock (1958) *Classics in the Theory of Public Finance* (London).

Nairn, T. (2001) 'Post UKania', *New Left Review*, Jan–Feb.

Newton, K. and M. Brynin (2001) 'The National Press and Party Voting in the UK', *Political Studies*, 49: 265–85.

Newton, K. and T. Karran (1985) *The Politics of Local Expenditure* (London: Macmillan).

Niskanen, W.A (1971) *Bureaucracy and Representative Government* (Chicago: Aldine and Atherton).

Niskanen, W.A (1973) *Bureaucracy: Servant or Master?* (London: Institute of Economic Afairs).

Norton, P. (2005) *Parliament in British Politics* (Basingstoke: Palgrave).

Osborne, D. and T. Gaebler (1992) *Reinventing Government* (Reading MA: Addison Wesley).

Page, A. and A. Batey (2002), 'Scotland's Other Parliament: Westminster Legislation about Devolved Matters in Scotland since Devolution', *Public Law*, Autumn: pp. 501–23.

Page, E. (2006) 'How Policy Is Really Made', Public Management and Policy Association http://personal.lse.ac.uk/Pagee/Papers/PMPA%20Ed%20Page%202006.pdf.

Page, E.C. (2001) *Governing By Numbers* (Oxford: Portland).

Page, E.C. (2003) 'The Civil Servant as Legislator: Law Making in British Administration', *Public Administration*, 81(4): 651–79.

Page, E.C. and V. Wright (eds) (1999) *Bureaucratic Elites in Western European States* (Oxford: Oxford University Press).

Park, A. (2002) 'Scotland's Morals', in J. Curtice, D. McCrone, A. Park and L. Paterson (eds), *New Scotland, New Society?* (Edinburgh: Polygon).

Parry, G., G. Moyser and N. Day (1992) *Political Participation and Democracy in Britain* (Cambridge University Press).

Parry, R. (1986) 'Privatisation and the Tarnishing of the Scottish Public Sector', in D. McCrone (ed.), *The Scottish Government Yearbook 1986* (Edinburgh: Unit for the Study of Government).

Parry, R. (1987) 'The Centralization of the Scottish Office', in R. Rose (ed.), *Ministers and Ministers* (Oxford: Clarendon).

Parry, R. (1993) 'Towards a Democratised Scottish Office?', *Scottish Affairs*, 5.

Parry, R. (1999a) 'The Scottish Civil Service', in G. Hassan (ed.) (1999) *A Guide to the Scottish Parliament* (Edinburgh: The Stationery Office).

Parry, R. (1999b), 'Quangos and the Structure of the Public Sector in Scotland', *Scottish Affairs*, 29: 12–27.

Parry, R. (2001) 'The Role of Central Units in the Scottish Government', *Public Money and Management*, 21(2).

Parry, R. (2002) 'Leadership and the Scottish Governing Classes', in G. Hassan and C. Warhurst (eds), *Tomorrow's Scotland* (London: Lawrence & Wishart).

Parry, R. (2003) 'The Home Civil Service After Devolution', *The Devolution Policy Papers* http://www.devolution.ac.uk/policy_paper_parry.htm.

Parry, R and Jones, A. (2000) 'The Transition from the Scottish Office to the Scottish Government', *Public Policy and Administration*, 15(2): 53–66.

Parsons, W. (1995) *Public Policy* (Aldershot: Edward Elgar).

Paterson Advisory Group (1973) *The New Scottish Local Authorities: Organisation and Management Structures* (Edinburgh: HMSO).

Paterson, I. (2000) 'The Pulpit and the Ballot Box: Catholic Assimilation and the Decline of Church Influence', in T.M. Devine (ed.), *Scotland's Shame? Bigotry and Sectarianism in Modern Scotland* (Edinburgh: Mainstream).

Paterson, L. (1994) *The Autonomy of Modern Scotland* (Edinburgh: Edinburgh University Press).

Paterson, L. (1998) *A Diverse Assembly: The Debate on the Scottish Parliament* (Edinburgh University Press).

Paterson, L. (2000a) 'Civil Society and Democratic Renewal', in S. Baron, J. Field and T. Schuller (eds), *Social Capital: Critical Perspectives* (Oxford: Oxford University Press).

Paterson, L. (2000b) 'Scottish Democracy and Scottish Utopias', RSA Lecture.

Paterson, L. (2003) *Scottish Education in the Twentieth Century* (Edinburgh: Edinburgh University Press).

Paterson, L., A. Brown, J. Curtice, K. Hinds, D. McCrone, A. Park, K. Sproston and P. Surridge (2001) *New Scotland, New Politics?* (Edinburgh: Polygon).

Payne, G. (1987) *Mobility and Change in Modern Society* (Basingstoke: Macmillan).

Payne, T. and C. Skelcher (1997) 'Explaining Less Accountability: The Growth of Local Quangos', *Public Administration*, 75(2): 207–25.

Peacock, A.T. and J. Wiseman (1967) *The Growth of Public Expenditure in the United Kingdom* (London: Allen & Unwin).

Peters, B.G. (1997) 'Can't Row, Shouldn't Steer: What's a Government to Do?', *Public Policy and Administration*, 12(2): 51–61.

Pierre, J. (ed.) (2000) *Debating Governance* (Oxford University Press).

Pierre, J. and B. Guy Peters (2000) *Governance, Politics and the State* (Basingstoke: Macmillan).

Pierre, J. and G. Stoker (2000) 'Towards Multi-Level Governance', in P. Dunleavy *et al.* (eds), *Developments in British Politics 6* (Macmillan).

Political Quarterly (2003) Special Issue – Focus on Scotland, Welfare Reform: Has Devolution Made a Difference?, 74(4).

Pollitt, C. (1995) 'Justification by Works or by Faith? Evaluating The New Public Management', *Evaluation*, 1(2): 133–54.

Pollock, A. (2006) 'The Exorbitant Cost of PFI is now being Cruelly Exposed', *The Guardian*, 26.1.06.

Pottinger, G. (1979) *The Secretaries of State for Scotland 1926–76* (Scottish Academic Press).

Power, M. (1997) *The Audit Society* (Oxford: Oxford University Press).

Pratchett, L. and M. Wingfield (1996) 'Petty Bureaucracy and Wholly-Minded Liberalism? The Changing Ethos of Local Government Officers', *Public Administration*, 74: 639–56.

Pressman, J. and A. Wildavsky (1973) *Implementation* (Berkely: University of California Press).

Procedures Committee (2003) *The Founding Principles Of The Scottish Parliament* http://www.scottish.parliament.uk/business/committees/historic/procedures/reports-03/prr03-03-vol01-04.htm

Pulzer, P. (1975) *Political Representation and Elections in Britain* (London: Allen & Unwin).

Pyper, R. (1999) 'The Civil Service: A Neglected Dimension of Devolution', *Public Money and Management*, 19(2): 45–9.

Pyper, R. (2000) 'The First Minister and the Scottish Government', in G. Hassan and C. Warhurst (eds), *The New Scottish Politics* (Norwich: The Stationery Office).

Reade, E. (1987) *British Town and Country Planning* (Milton Keynes: Open University Press).

Reed. M. (1993) 'Organisations and Modernity: Continuity and Discontinuity in Organization Theory', in J. Hassid and M. Parker (eds), *Post-modernism and Organisations* (London: Sage).

Rhodes, R., P. Carmichael, J. McMillan and A. Massey (2003) *Decentralizing the Civil Service* (Open University Press).

Rhodes, R.A.W (1996) 'The New Governance: Governing without Government', *Political Studies*, 44(4): 652–67.

Rhodes, R.A.W. (1988) *Beyond Westminster and Whitehall* (London: Unwin Hyman).

Rhodes, R.A.W. (1994) 'The Hollowing Out of the State: The Changing Nature of Public Service in Britain', *Political Quarterly*, 138–151.

Rhodes, R.A.W. (1997) *Understanding Governance* (Buckingham: Open University).

Rhodes, R.A.W. (2000) 'The Governance Narrative: Key Findings and Lessons from the ESRC's Whitehall Programme', *Public Administration*, 78(2).

Richards, D. and M. Smith (2002) *Governance and Public Policy in the UK* (Oxford: Oxford University Press).

Richards, D. and M. Smith (2004) 'The "Hybrid State": Labour's Response to the Challenge of Governance', in S. Ludlam and M. Smith (eds), *Governing as New Labour* (London: Palgrave).

Richardson, J.J. and A.G. Jordan (1979) *Governing Under Pressure* (Oxford: Martin Robertson).

Ripley, R. (1985) *Policy Analysis in Political Science* (Nelson-Hall: Chicago Ill).

Roddin, E. (2004) 'Has the Labour Party or the Liberal Democrats Proved More Successful in the Partnership for Scotland Coalition 1999–2003?', *Scottish Affairs*, 48 (Summer), 24–49.

Rokkan, S. and D. Urwin (1983) *Economy, Territory, Identity, Politics of West European Peripheries* (London: Sage).

Rose, R. (1982) *Understanding the United Kingdom: The Territorial Dimension in Government* (London: Longman).

Rose, R. (1986) 'Steering the Ship of State: One Rudder but Two Pairs of Hands', Appendix 15 of HC 92-II (1986) Civil Servants and Ministers: Duties and Responsibilities, Seventh Report from the Treasury and Civil Service Committee, Session 1985–86.

Rose, R. (1991) 'Inheritance Before Choice in Public Policy', *The Journal of Theoretical Politics*, 2(3): 263–91.

Rosenau, J. (1984) 'A Pre-Theory Revisited: World Politics in an Era of Cascading Interdependence', *International Studies Quarterly*, 28.

Rosie, G. (2002) 'Network Scotland: The Power of the Quango State' in G. Hassan and C. Warhurst (eds), *Anatomy of the New Scotland: Power, Influence and Change* (Mainstream: Edinburgh).

Ross, J. (1981) 'The Secretary of State for Scotland and the Scottish Office', *Studies in Public Policy* 87 (Glasgow: University of Strathclyde).

Rush, M. (2005) *How Parliament Works* (Manchester: Manchester University Press).

Russell, M. and J. Bradbury (2007) 'The Constituency Work of Scottish and Welsh MPs: Adjusting to Devolution', *Regional and Federal Studies*, 17(1): 97–116.

Sabatier, P.A. (1993) 'Policy Change Over a Decade or More', in P.A. Sabatier and H.C. Jenkins-Smith (eds) (1993) *Policy Change and Learning: An Advocacy Coalition Approach* (Boulder, CO: Westview Press).

SAC (Scottish Agricultural College) (2002) Conservation Newsletter 62 http://www1.sac.ac.uk/envsci/External/ConsNews/62.htm.

Salmon, T. (2000) 'An Oxymoron: The Scottish Parliament and Foreign Relations?', in A. Wright (ed.), *Scotland: The Challenge of Devolution* (Aldershot: Ashgate).

Saren, J. and J. Brown (2001) 'Government', in J. Mitchell (eds), *Quarterly Monitoring Programme: Scotland* (London: Constitution Unit) http://www.ucl.ac.uk/constitution-unit/monrep/scotland/scotfeb01.pdf.

Saren, J. and J. McCormick (2004) 'The Politics of Scottish Labour's Heartlands', in G. Hassan (ed.), *The Scottish Labour Party: History, Institutions and Ideas* (Edinburgh: Edinburgh University Press).

Sarlvik, B. and I. Crewe (1983) *Decade of Dealignment* (Cambridge: Cambridge University Press).

Schattchsneider, E.E. (1960) *The Semi-Sovereign People* (New York: Holt, Winehart & Winston).

Schlesinger, P. (2000) 'Communicating to a New Polity: the Media and the Parliament', in G. Hassan and C. Warhurst (eds), *The New Scottish Politics: the First Year of the Scottish Parliament and Beyond* (Edinburgh: The Stationery Office).

Schlesinger, P. (2004) 'The New Communications Agenda in Scotland', *Scottish Affairs*, 47: 16–40.

Schlesinger, P., D. Miller and W. Dinan (2001) *Open Scotland? Journalists, Spin Doctors and Lobbyists* (Edinburgh: Polygon).

Schmueker, K. and J. Adams (2005) 'Divergence in Priorities, Perceived Policy Failure and Pressure for Convergence', in K. Schmueker and J. Adams (eds), *Devolution in Practice 2006* (Newcastle: IPPR North).

Schofield, K. and R. Dinwoodie (2007) 'Alexander urges Labour to be Radical', *The Herald*, 17.8.07.

Schumpeter, J.A. (1943) *Capitalism, Socialism and Democracy* (London: Allen & Unwin).

Scottish Branch of the Society of Local Authority Chief Executives (1994) *The New Management Agenda* (Edinburgh: SOLACE).

Scottish Civic Forum (2001) *Building Participation in the New Scotland* (Edinburgh: Scottish Civic Forum).

Scottish Constitutional Convention (1990) *Toward's Scotland's Parliament* (Edinburgh: SCC).

Scottish Constitutional Convention (1995) *Scotland's Parliament: Scotland's Right* (Edinburgh: Convention of Scottish Local Authorities).

Scottish Council Foundation (2002) *Rethinking Representation* www.scottishcouncil foundation.org/pubs_more.php?p=63&go=1.

Scottish Countryside Alliance (2000) Response to the Protection Of Wild Mammals (Scotland) Bill http://www.mediahouse.co.uk/news/items/news_14_full. html#7.%20Implementation%20and%20enforcement%20issues.

Scottish Executive (2000) *Scotland's Budget Documents 2000–01: Budget (Scotland) Bill* (Edinburgh: The Stationery Office) http://www.scotland.gov.uk/library2/ doc12/scbu-00.asp.

Scottish Executive (2001a) *Review of Public Bodies: Discussion Paper* (Edinburgh: Scottish Executive).

Scottish Executive (2001b) *Scottish Social Statistics 2001* (Edinburgh: Scottish Executive).

Scottish Executive (2001c) *Public Bodies: Proposals for Change* (Edinburgh: Scottish Executive).

Scottish Executive (2001e) *Scottish Economic Statistics 2001* (Edinburgh: Scottish Executive).

Scottish Executive (2002a) *Building a Better Scotland: Spending Proposals 2003–2006* (Edinburgh: Scottish Executive).

Scottish Executive (2002b) *Closing the Opportunity Gap: Scottish Budget for 2003–6* (Edinburgh: Scottish Executive).

Scottish Executive (2005) Draft Budget 2006–07 http://www.scottish Government.gov.uk/Publications/2005/09/06112356/24263.

Scottish Executive (2006a) *Government Expenditure and Revenue in Scotland 2004–5* (Edinburgh: Scottish Executive) http://www.scotland.gov.uk/ Resource/Doc/159996/0043602.pdf.

Scottish Executive (2006b) *Transforming Public Services: The Next Phase of Reform* (Edinburgh: Scottish Executive) http://www.scotland.gov.uk/Publications/ 2006/06/15110925/0.

Scottish Executive (2006c) 'Consultation On Protecting Vulnerable Groups: Scottish Vetting And Barring Scheme' http://www.scotland.gov.uk/Resource/Doc/ 92657/0022210.pdf.

Scottish Executive (2007a) *Scotland's Budget Documents 2006–07: Budget (Scotland) (No.3) Bill* (Edinburgh: The Stationery Office) http://www.scottish executive.gov.uk/Publications/2006/01/16161641/2.

Scottish Executive (2007b) *Scottish Local Government Financial Statistics 2005–06* (Edinburgh: The Stationery Office) http://www.scotland.gov.uk/Publications/ 2007/01/09093510/0.

Scottish Executive (2007c) 'Structural Funds 2000–2006' http://www.scotland.gov.uk/Topics/Business-Industry/support/17404/8422.

Scottish Executive (2007d) *Choosing Scotland's Future: A National Conversation* (Edinburgh: Scottish Executive).

Scottish Government (2007) *Scottish Cabinet and Ministers* http://www.scotland.gov.uk/About/14944/Scottish-Cabinet

Scottish Labour & Scottish Liberal Democrats (2003) *A Partnership for a Better Scotland: Partnership Agreement Edinburgh: Scottish Government* http://www.scotland.gov.uk/library5/government/pfbs-00.asp.

Scottish Minister for Parliamentary Business (2002) House of Lords Inquiry http://www.publications.parliament.uk/pa/ld200102/ldselect/ldconst/147/2051511.htm.

Scottish National Party and Scottish Green Party (2007) *Cooperation Agreement* http://www.scottishgreens.org.uk/site/id/5798/title/Green_SNP_Co_operation_Agreement.html.

Scottish Office (1991) *The Structure of Local Government in Scotland: The Case for Change – Principles of the New System* (Edinburgh: HMSO).

Scottish Office (1992) *The Structure of Local Government in Scotland: Shaping the New Councils* (Edinburgh: HMSO).

Scottish Office (1993a) *Scotland and the Union: A Partnership For Good* (Edinburgh: Scottish Office).

Scottish Office (1993b) *The Internal Management of Local Government in Scotland: A Consultation Paper* (Edinburgh: The Scottish Office).

Scottish Office (1998a) *Shaping Scotland's Parliament: Report of the Consultative Steering Group on the Scottish Parliament* (Edinburgh: Scottish Office).

Scottish Office (1998b) *Principles Of The Scottish Parliament's Financial Procedures: Final Report By The Financial Issues Advisory Group* (Edinburgh: The Stationery Office) http://www.scotland.gov.uk/government/devolution/fiag-00.asp.

Scottish Parliament (2001) *Public–Private Partnerships and the Private Finance Initiative: A Review of the Recent Literature* (Edinburgh: SPICE).

Scottish Parliament (2007) *Staff Organisation* http://www.scottish.parliament.uk/corporate/organisation/index.htm.

Scottish Parliament Information Centre SPICE (2000a) 'The Barnett Formula' http://www.scottish.parliament.uk/business/research/pdf_res_notes/rn00-31.pdf.

Scottish Parliament Information Centre SPICE (2000b) *Royal Commission On Long Term Care (Sutherland Report)* (Research Note 00/78) http://www.scottish.parliament.uk/business/research/pdf_res_notes/rn00-78.pdf.

Scottish Parliament Information Centre (SPICE) (2000c) *Quangos, and the Governance of the SQA* RN 00/81 29 September (Edinburgh: Scottish Parliament Information Centre).

Scottish Parliament Information Centre (SPICE) (2001) *Public–Private Partnerships and the Private Finance Initiative: A Review of Recent Literature* (Edinburgh: Scottish Parliament Information Centre).

Scottish Parliament Information Centre SPICE (Scottish Parliament Information Centre) (2007) *Election 2007* http://www.scottish.parliament.uk/business/research/briefings-07/SB07-21.pdf.

Seawright, D. (1999) *An Important Matter of Principle: the Decline of the Scottish Conservative and Unionist Party* (Darmouth: Ashgate).

Seawright, D. (2002) 'The Scottish Conservative and Unionist Party: "The Lesser Spotted Tory"?' in G. Hassan and C. Warhurst (eds), *Tomorrow's Scotland* (London: Lawrence & Wishart).

Settle, M. (29.10.07) 'Cameron Hints that Conservatives will Review Barnett Formula', *The Herald* http://www.theherald.co.uk/politics/news/display.var. 1792069.0.0.php.

Settle, M. (9.7.2007) 'Sewel wants Barnett Formula Ditched' http://www.theherald. co.uk/politics/news/display.var.1528914.0.0.php.

Seyd, B. (2002) *Coalition Government in Britain: Lessons from Overseas* (London: Constitution Unit).

Seyd, B. (2004) *Coalition Governance in Scotland and Wales* (London: Constitution Unit).

Shaw, E. (2003) 'Devolution and Scottish Labour: The Case of Free Personal Care for the Elderly', Paper presented to the Political Studies Association Conference, Leicester http://www.psa.ac.uk/journals/pdf/5/2003/Eric%20Shaw.pdf.

Shephard, M. and P. Cairney (2004) 'Consensual or Dominant Relationships with Parliament? A Comparison of Administrations and Ministers in Scotland', *Public Administration*, 82 (4): 831–55.

Shephard, M. and P. Cairney (2005) 'The Impact of the Scottish Parliament in Amending Government Legislation', *Political Studies*, 53 (2): 303–19.

Shephard, M., N. McGarvey and M. Cavanagh (2001) 'New Scottish Parliament, New Scottish Parliamentarians?', *Journal of Legislative Studies*, 7(2): 79–104.

Shugart, M.S. and M.P. Wattenberg (eds), (2003) *Mixed Member Electoral Systems: The Best of Both Worlds?* (Oxford: Oxford University Press).

Simeon, R. (2003) 'Free Personal Care. Policy Divergence and Social Citizenship', in R. Hazell (ed.), *The State of the Nations 2003* (London: Imprint).

Sky News (28.4.2007) 'Exploring The North South Divide' http://news.sky.com/ skynews/article/0,,30100-1262942,00.html.

Sloat, A. (2000) 'Scotland and Europe: Links Between Edinburgh, London and Brussels', *Scottish Affairs*, 31: 92–110.

Smith, J. (2003) 'An Incremental Odyssey – The Structural Europeanisation of Government Bureaucracy', *Scottish Affairs*, No. 44.

Smith, M. (1994) *Paper Lions. The Scottish Press and National Identity* (Edinburgh: Polygon).

Scottish National Party (2007) 'Scotland Pays her Way – and More' http://www.snp. org/independence/questions/scotlandpaysherway.

SOLACE (1994) *The New Management Agenda* (Edinburgh: SOLACE).

Steel, D. (2001) 'A Dozen Differences of Devolution', Speech to the Oxford Student Union, 4.6.01.

Stewart, J. (2000) *The Nature of British Local Government* (Basingstoke: Macmillan).

Stewart, J. and G. Stoker (1988) *From Local Administration to Community Government* (London: Fabian Society).

Stewart, J. and G. Stoker (1995) *Local Government in the 1990s* (Basingstoke: Macmillan).

Stewart, J. (2003) *Modernising British Local Government* (Basingstoke: Palgrave).

Stirling, T. and R. Smith (2003) 'A Matter of Choice? Policy Divergence in Access to Social Housing Post-devolution', *Housing Studies*, 18(2): 145–58.

Stoker, G. (1998) 'Governance as Theory: Five Propositions', *International Social Science Journal*, No.155.

Stoker, G. (2004) *Transforming Local Governance* (Basingstoke: Palgrave).

Stoker, G. (ed.) (1999) *The New Management of British Local Governance* (Basingstoke: Macmillan).

Stoker, G. (ed.) (2000) *The New Politics of British Local Governance* (Basingstoke: Macmillan).

Stoker, G. and D. Wilson (eds) (2005) *British Local Government into the 21st Century* (Basingstoke: Palgrave).

Stokes, D.E. (1963) 'Spatial Models of Party Competition', *American Political Science Review*, 57(2): 368–77.

Stokes, D.E. (1992) 'Valence Politics', in D. Kavanagh (ed.), *Electoral Politics* (Oxford: Clarendon Press).

Stone, C. (1989) *Regime Politics – Governing Atlanta 1946–88* (Lawrence: University of Kansas Press).

Surridge, P. and D. McCrone (1999) 'The 1997 Scottish Referendum Vote', in B. Taylor and K. Thompson, *Scotland and Wales: Nations Again?* (University of Wales Press).

Sutcliffe, J. (2002) 'Subnational Influence on the Structural Funds: The Highlands and Islands of Scotland', *Regional and Federal Studies*, 12(3) (Autumn): 102–27.

Sutherland, S. (1999) Royal Commission on Long Term Care for the Elderly, *With Respect to Old Age* (London: The Stationery Office) http://www.royal-commission-elderly.gov.uk/.

Taylor, B. (2002) *Scotland's Parliament: Triumph and Disaster* (Edinburgh: Edinburgh University Press).

The Scotsman 30.11.02 'Criticism over Fire Strike Remarks' http://thescotsman.scotsman.com/index.cfm?id=1333232002.

Trench, A. (ed.) (2001) *The State of the Nations: The Second Year of Devolution in the UK* (London: The Constitution Unit).

Trench, A. (ed.) (2004) *Has Devolution Made a Difference? The State of the Nations 2004* (London: The Constitution Unit).

Trench, A. (ed.) (2005) *The Dynamics of Devolution The State of the Nations 2005* (Thoverton: Imprint).

Trench, A. (2004) 'Devolution: The Withering-away of the Joint Ministerial Committee', *Public Law*, 513–17.

Twigger, R. (1998) 'The Barnett Formula' http://www.parliament.uk/commons/lib/research/rp98/rp98-008.pdf.

Unison (2001) *Public Service, Private Finance* (London: Unison).

United Kingdom Government, Scottish Ministers, the Cabinet of the National Assembly for Wales and the Northern Ireland Executive Committee (2001) *Memorandum of Understanding and Supplementary Agreements* http://www.dca.gov.uk/constitution/devolution/pubs/odpm_dev_600629.pdf.

Walker, G. (1996) 'Varieties of Scottish Protestant Identity', in T.M. Devine and R.J. Finlay, *Scotland in the Twentieth Century* (Edinburgh: Edinburgh University Press).

Warner, G. (1988) *The Scottish Tory Party: A History* (London: Weidenfeld and Nicolson).

Watts, R. (2007), 'The United Kingdom as a Federalized or Regionalized Union', in A. Trench (ed.), *Devolution and Power in the United Kingdom* (Manchester: Manchester University Press).

Weir, S. and D. Beetham (1998) *Political Power and Democratic Control in Britain* (London: Routledge).

Wheatley (1969) *Report of the Royal Commission on Local Government in Scotland* (Edinburgh: HMSO).

Wildavsky, A. (1979) *The Art and Craft of Policy Analysis* (London: Macmillan).

Wildavsky, A. (1964) *The Politics of the Budgetary Process* (Boston, Mass: Little Brown).

Wildavsky, A. (1975) *Budgeting: A Comparative Theory of the Budgetary Process* (Boston: Little, Brown).

Winetrobe, B.K. (2001) 'Counter-Devolution? The Sewel Convention on Devolved Legislation at Westminster', *Scottish Law and Practice Quarterly*, pp .286–92.

Winetrobe, B.K. (2003) 'Collective Responsibility in Devolved Scotland', *Public Law* (Spring): 24–31.

Winetrobe, B.K. (2005), 'A Principled Approach to the Sewel Parliamentary Processes', Submission to Procedures Committee Sewel Convention Inquiry', http://www.scottish.parliament.uk/business/committees/procedures/inquiries/sewel/07-winetrobe.htm

Wright, A. (2000) *The Challenge of Devolution* (Aldershot: Ashgate Press).

Index